The Red Sandals:
A Memoir

Jing Li

© Jing Li, 2022
The Red Sandals: A Memoir
Published by Sand Hill Review Press, LLC
All rights reserved

www.sandhillreviewpress.com
1 Baldwin Ave, Ste 304
San Mateo, CA 94401

ISBN: 978-1-949534-25-2 (paperback)
ISBN: 978-1-949534-28-3 (case laminate)
Library of Congress Control Number: 2021910604
Graphics by Backspace Ink
Photos by Jing Li

Names: Li, Jing, 1956-, author.
Title: The red sandals : a memoir / Jing Li.
Description: San Mateo, CA: Sand Hill Review Press, 2022.
Identifiers: LCCN: 2021910604 | ISBN: 978-1-949534-25-2 (paperback) | 978-1-949534-24-5 (ebook) | ISBN: 978-1-949534-28-3 (case laminate)
Subjects: LCSH Li, Jing, 1956- | China--Biography. | Women--China--Biography. | English teachers--China--Biography. | China--Biography. | China--History--Cultural Revolution, 1966-1976. | China--Social life and customs. | BISAC BIOGRAPHY & AUTOBIOGRAPHY / Personal Memoirs | BIOGRAPHY & AUTOBIOGRAPHY / Cultural, Ethnic & Regional / Asian & Asian American | BIOGRAPHY & AUTOBIOGRAPHY / Educators
Classification: LCC CT3710 .L5 2022 | DDC 979.4/004951/0092--DC23

Printed in the United States of America. No part of this book may be used or reproduced in any manner whatsoever without prior written consent of the publisher except in the case of brief quotations embodied in critical articles and reviews.

The Red Sandals is a memoir. It reflects the author's present recollections of experiences over time. Many names and characteristics have been changed to protect the privacy of others. To tell her story, some events have been compressed and some dialogue has been recreated. Writing a memoir is a deeply emotional experience, which has enabled the author to further understand the turmoil of her past in both China and America. All of her characters are hard-working decent people who also have been impacted by the circumstances around them. There is no blame here. If there is blame it exists in the Chinese anti-feminine culture of old, Mao's policies, the compelling need to emigrate to seek a better life, and the pressures of the American system.

—Sand Hill Review Press

This book is dedicated to the special people from both my worlds:

China:

Lao Ye Ye, my blind paternal great grandfather, who babysat me when I was barely one. He made me giggle and laughed with me all day long

Water Li, my quiet and loving paternal grandfather, my morale cheerleader

Ai Ying, my loving "milk mother," who took over nursing me when I was two months old

Jade, my iron-tough paternal grandmother, who toiled in the cornfields on her painful three-inch bound feet to make her only precious son a leisurely city man

Magnolia Zhang, my mother, who passed onto me her brainy genes and fiercely competitive spirit

Bright Light Li, my father, who shaped my lifetime stubborn attitude to refuse to bow down to mediocre authority

Vic, my husband, who played team and supported my solo journey to America by taking care of our small daughter back in China

My dedicated teachers, who recognized my desire to learn, nurtured my ambition to excel, and inspired me on my lifelong journey of my own beloved teaching career:

Mr. Shi, my first grade teacher, a giant in education despite his three-foot-tall body height.

Miss Pan, my beautiful third grade music teacher, who made me a star

Mrs. Fan, my third grade Chinese language teacher, who called on me to read my writings out loud as the model in class

Mrs. Ma, my third grade math teacher, who praised me for having an exceptionally good memory and a fast learner

Mr. Zhu, my high school Chinese language teacher, who fine-tuned my Chinese writing

Mr. Zhang, my high school English teacher, who led me into the wonderland of fascinating English language

America:

Mrs. Barbara & her late husband Dr. Dale Brandt (RIP), my host family from Pendleton, Oregon, who initiated Christmas joy in my heart

Mrs. Eleanor & her late husband Dr. Charles Rosenquist (RIP), my host family from Pendleton, Oregon, whose kindness and wondrous humor brightened my spirit.

Mr. & Ms. ShirleyAnn and Robert Wimberly my Master Teacher from Pendleton, Oregon, who introduced me to the beautiful America I fell in love with

Dr. Edythe Leupp and her late husband Tom Leupp (RIP), my sponsor and professor at Southern Nazaren University, Oklahoma, whose Christian generosity laid the cornerstone to my American journey

Sister Corrine Mohrmann, my guardian parent and director at St. Vincent's Day Home at Oakland, California, who led me to my Christian baptism and my American Dream

Contents

A note to the reader: 15
    Why and How I Wrote My Memoir in English,
    My Second Language

Photo List 21

Part One 25
    Born Unwanted 生不逢時：
    A Peasant Girl at Red Stone Bridge Village —
    Birth to Age Eight

Chapter 1 27
    The Red Sandals
    紅涼鞋

Chapter 2 31
    Red Stone Bridge
    赤石橋

Chapter 3 35
    Lost Dream
    失去的夢

Chapter 4 45
    My First Photo
    一歲照片

Chapter 5 48
    My Milk Mother
    回憶奶媽

Chapter 6 54
　Grandmother
　奶奶

Chapter 7 59
　Grandpa
　爺爺

Chapter 8 63
　Laughter with Lao Ye Ye
　我的老爺爺

Chapter 9 66
　Portrait of a Sore Winner
　不得意的勝利者

Chapter 10 70
　I Will Eventually Swallow It!
　我總要咽下去呢

Chapter 11 73
　My First Watermelon
　西瓜

Chapter 12 77
　A Born Stubborn Dog
　天生一只倔狗

Chapter 13 80
　Tumbleweed in the Desert without Roots
　無根的沙蓬

Chapter 14 82
　Peach, Apple, Grape, and Cherry
　桃，蘋果，葡萄，櫻桃

Chapter 15 88
　*Scrambled Eggs *Stir-fried Tofu
　煎雞蛋 * 炒豆腐

Chapter 16 92
　My First Grade Teacher, Mr. Shi
　我的啟蒙老師

Chapter 17 97
   My First Book
   我的第一本書

Chapter 18 101
   "She used a bamboo stick to write her test! Ha ha!"
   她考試沒筆,用破竹席枝寫

Chapter 19 104
   "You ran home in the rain to get the umbrella?!"
   冒著雨跑回家去取傘?

Chapter 20 106
   My Soap! My Soap!
   肥皂

Chapter 21 110
   Dad Came Back — Down and Under
   爸爸下放回村

Chapter 22 114
   Miracle Scar
   膝蓋上的傷疤

Chapter 23 118
   The Date-Red Horse
   棗紅馬

Part Two 121
Darkness Before Dawn 黎明前的黑暗:
Chinese Cinderella in Taiyuan City's Blue-Collar
Dirt Yard — From Age Eight to Eighteen

Chapter 24 123
   Arriving in Taiyuan City
   來到太原

Chapter 25 131
   My First Day of School in the City
   上學第一天

Chapter 26 138
   Lost on the Way to the Zoo
   去動物園的路上

Chapter 27... 143
   The Frightening Morning
   可怕的早晨

Chapter 28 147
   The Morning My Mother Visited My Hospital Ward
   病房探訪

Chapter 29 151
   Be Chairman Mao's Good Child for Dr. Wong
   做毛主席的好孩子

Chapter 30 157
   My Beautiful Music Teacher, Miss Pan
   美麗的音樂老師潘虹

Chapter 31 161
   Cultural Revolution. No More School
   文化大革命，不能上學了

Chapter 32 169
   Life and Death at Age Ten
   十歲生死關

Chapter 33 173
   A Bad Case of Guilt: Five Hard-Boiled Eggs
   五顆煮雞蛋

Chapter 34 176
   One Brother for Each Parent
   爸媽每人只要一個弟弟

Chapter 35..180
   Bowl in the Yard
   丟在院子裡的碗

Chapter 36 183
   My Mother's Smiling Face on a Dog's Body
   笑臉

Chapter 37 187
Growing Up Early
早熟

Chapter 38 192
My Rooster, My Hero
我的大公雞

Chapter 39 194
Face-saving and Divorces
離婚

Chapter 40 198
Family Picture without My Mother
父子四人合照

Chapter 41 205
Switching Tongues
外語

Chapter 42 209
High School Tuition
十元學費

Chapter 43 212
English 900
英語900句

Chapter 44 218
Dream to Be Free & Different
夢想自由

Chapter 45 224
Out of High School, Out of Future
高中畢業等於失業

Part Three 229
  Phoenix Rising from the Ashes 鳳凰復生:
  Famed English Teacher at Elite No. 5 Secondary
  School – From Age Eighteen to Thirty

Chapter 46 231
  My Childhood Giggling and Laughter Returned
  童年的歡笑聲又回來了

Chapter 47..240
  Trapped by "House Business"
  房事

Chapter 48 249
  Taiyuan Teachers' College
  太原師範

Chapter 49 261
  English Teacher at Elite No. 5 Secondary School
  太原五中英語老師

Chapter 50 268
  Crossing the Forbidden Creek
  悼念爺爺

Chapter 51 272
  Married to Vic – and His Family
  婚嫁

Chapter 52 278
  What If It's a Girl?
  要是女孩兒呢?

Chapter 53..283
  I'm Sorry, It's Not a Boy
  不是男孩

Chapter 54 289
  My Maiden Homecoming
  回娘家

Chapter 55 293
　Propelled
　動力

Chapter 56 299
　Beijing Foreign Language Institute
　北京外國語學院

Chapter 57 309
　Runaway Number One!
　更上一層樓

Chapter 58 313
　At the Friendship Store
　友誼商店

Chapter 59 319
　America, at Last!
　終於見到了夢中的美國

Chapter 60 325
　Pendleton, Oregon
　寧靜恬美的澎德頓市・俄勒岡州

Part Four 335
My Odyssey in America 奮鬥紮根在美國

Chapter 61 337
　Frog at the Bottom of the Well
　井底之蛙

Chapter 62 342
　Hardest Part of a 10,000-Mile Journey Is the First Step
　最艱難第一步

Chapter 63 346
　Coming to Flock in San Francisco
　風雨獨立舊金山

Chapter 64 354
　Family Reunion — Swimming Upstream
　團圓後的艱辛

Chapter 65 359
   Twilight Zone in Amazing America
   美國公立學校哈哈鏡

Chapter 66 367
   Lost Battles and a War
   恰似竹籃打水一場空

Chapter 67 377
   Swan Song
   天鵝悲鳴

Epilogue 391
   後記

Acknowledgements 395

About the Author 399

A note to the reader:

Why and How I Wrote My Memoir in English, My Second Language

THE IDEA OF WRITING my survival life story came to me by accident in 1999.

I was forty-three, a battle-fatigued and unfulfilled public high school teacher in San Francisco. I'd just started having more time for myself as I was finally getting out of my 20-year parental-obligation marriage after years of waiting for my daughter to turn eighteen. So, one weekend I went to the San Francisco Book Fair at Fort Mason looking for some good bargains on used books–much needed "brain food" to nurture my intellectually famished mind.

Wow, it felt like a book paradise!

Wide-eyed amazed, I wandered from table to table full of books in the crowded Book Fair inside the massive high-ceilinged warehouse. I felt like that small starving peasant girl in rags again growing up in China's remote mountains, where I first saw a glass jar of bright colorful bean-sized candies in the one-room general store in my birth village of Red Stone Bridge.

As a small child, I lived through famine, emotional and physical abuse and escaped through school and good grades. But Mao's Cultural Revolution took away my only joy at age ten, when schools were shut down, teachers beaten, publicly humiliated, and many were murdered. Books were burned, banned and denounced as evil. The only printed words in abundant supply was "savior" Mao's revolutionary theory in his *Little Red Book* 紅寶書 on how power came out of the barrel of guns and people's democratic dictatorship against class enemies. We were made to memorize his little red book word by word.

I felt so fortunate to live now in freedom America.

As I passed by a small quiet booth in the vast crowded warehouse, a black-and-white sign caught my eye: "*Writing Salon. We teach you how to write about your life.*" Something came alive in my heart. I wanted to learn to be a writer in English! I needed to feel accomplished writing in my second language. I needed to find my lost sense of self-worth that I had while teaching in the best elite high school back in China, ironically, a totalitarian regime.

I wanted to write about how I had survived famine, abuse, and pestilence. Watery millet soup was my staple baby food as well as the staple for all my family. Cold and heat were the punishment of the seasons and the struggles of peasant life seemed to grind everyone down to smooth rocks. There was no time for affection, only time for cursing and anger and by the time I reached ten I had escaped death several times at hands of my own family. Can I blame them? Their spirits were splintered as well. Love was a luxury we didn't know. And then came Mao's atrocious Cultural Revolution.

What I did not know at the time, until 2007, was that writing had also been my mother's dream. She lost her lifelong dream after her failed secret attempt to abort me with a heavy pinewood washboard. I now realize that her frustration and anger about her truncated life were taken out on me.

"Do you accept someone like me who wasn't born into English?" I asked the lone woman sitting inside the Writing Salon booth, my anxious Chinese-accented voice trailing off into the vast space.

Elegantly dressed, the woman looked very friendly and pleasant. "Why, yes, of course! We welcome anyone who wants to learn." Ms. Jane Underwood's smile was heartwarming. Tears came to my eyes. A great sense of relief comforted my soul—the acceptance and kindness of strangers always made my heart fill with joy.

Like a newborn calf thinks of itself as powerful as a tiger, 初生牛犊不怕虎 in the Chinese proverb, I burst onto the writing scene, my English-crafting skills next to none, my descriptive vocabulary scarce. In my first ambitious attempt to write for Jane Underwood's Writing Salon critique class, I grabbed "decapitated" to describe my grandmother's three-inch bound feet. And I'd just figured out the difference between the look-alike twins, "salon" and "saloon."

Writing my memoir was an uphill battle in the midst of my stressful full-time public high school teaching job. On top of trying to describe everything in English, the hardest part was reliving my painful childhood memories.

Long Live Chairman Mao! I learned my very first English words in middle school. And I'd never had a chance to take any English writing courses for either my bachelor's degree in English from China, or my master's degree in education which I hurriedly earned in America within less than a year, September 26, 1989–May 20,1990.

To improve my English reading speed, I watched *Jeopardy!* and everything else with captions turned on. Vigilantly, I looked out for tricky look-alike triplets, such as, "persecute, prosecute and prostitute." And, I was, still am, self-conscious of being too quick to speak for fear of mixing up the sound-alike twins, such as "anise" and "anus."

To hone my writing techniques, I read books on English writing craft. To fine-tune my storytelling skills, I devoured well-written memoirs and inspiring real-life stories. Two childhood memoirs deeply resonated with me: *Angela's Ashes* by Frank McCourt, and *My Childhood* by Maxim Gorky. Both McCourt and Gorky survived their old-world wretched childhoods. Their lives mirrored my own. Someday could I write what happened to me?

Trying to complete my memoir was like traveling on a long-rope bridge, with no end in sight, hanging over the gulf in between two drastically different languages and cultures. And on that bridge was me, a tiny scurrying ant alone, shouldering a larger-than-life load, tirelessly searching and mediating between the two complex worlds: China, at its ancient declining age of nearly five thousand years; and America, in its robust infancy but already the inspiring leader of the world.

Finally, my perseverance started paying off. In 2007, my 2,500-word essay "My Story as a New American Immigrant" won Second Place in The Jack London Writers Nonfiction Contest from the California Writers Club.

"Did you write in Chinese, Ms. Li?" my American high school students of Mandarin Chinese asked me, wide-eyed in disbelief.

"Do Americans read Chinese?" My smarty-pants answer made the teenagers laugh.

With my newly gained self-confidence, I applied for MFA program at University of San Francisco. I was rejected. Crushed was my hope to learn much-needed writing skills. I would have gratefully paid the $30,000 tuition by refinancing my mortgage.

Well, my peasant grandmother didn't call me a "born-stubborn dog!" for nothing. I was determined, more than ever, to finish writing my memoir. On my own.

I searched and attended many writers' workshops, critique groups, open mic's, conferences and summer writing programs all over the San Francisco Bay Area, and beyond California in Iowa and Wisconsin.

One story at a time, slowly but surely, I kept writing and taking my stories to my critiquing groups for feedback. Most were encouraging, soul-comforting and therapeutic—my vital source of inspiration. It helped me uncover my buried childhood memories. To have my voice heard was healing. My heart was nurtured, my spirits high, and my confidence boosted.

I also learned to distinguish misguided suggestions for my writing from well-meaning people, as I wholeheartedly humbled myself, trusting every American writer as my English language teacher. My wondrous year of 1986-87 in Pendleton, Oregon as an international exchange teacher, had me believe that all Americans were friendly and should be trusted as my friends.

Sadly, from time to time, I'd receive some not-well-intentioned comments that pickaxed open my invisible raw scars from my childhood trauma. These mean-spirited comments would catch me off guard and shock me into distress. Quietly, I'd flee to cocoon myself at home, licking my wounds alone. Soon, I'd pick myself up and continue to search for a new writing group.

I was racing with time.

I didn't want to turn sixty without achieving my authorship goal. Often frustrated with my slow writing speed, I wished I could write faster. Also hindering my progress was reliving my fear-and-tears-filled childhood. Memories overwhelmed me with debilitating heartaches, sending me to curl up on the couch and sob for hours at a time.

At one point, I became tired of struggling with my emotional turmoil. To find an easy way out, I veered off my memoir to write something that came naturally to me and didn't require any emotional entanglement. In a few short months, I completed my 400-page manuscript, *Basic Mental Math for Kids*. For my heart still yearned for teaching. I wanted to teach America's young kids to do math in their heads, to calculate everyday money without using an electronic calculator – a very useful skill for balancing their checkbooks when they grow up. The arithmetic mental math skills I learned before age ten in China were sufficient enough to do my own IRS taxes in paper and pencil, hardly in need of an electronic calculator.

"Oh, that's nice," my writers' world responded in 2014, when I proudly showed my brick-thick Mental Math for Kids manuscript at the Mt. Hermon Christian Writers' Conference. "But we want to read your fantastic memoir!"

But I thought *Basic Mental Math for Kids* was more important work!

Okay, then, it looked like I had no choice but to hang in there and complete my memoir. I got down on my knees, and prayed for God to grant me strength, wisdom, and peace. Miracles started to happen again.

2014 to 2016, I was published in seven anthologies, including the *Magic of Memoir* by SheWritesPress, and the "California Writers Literary Review."

October 2015, "My First Watermelon" won the First Place Award for Nonfiction Contest by the CWC Redwood Branch. And, in 2017, my memoir *The Red Sandals* won the Grand Prize at the San Francisco Writers Conference.

By completing my memoir, I realized how I survived my childhood. Through writing I learned a new way to see myself. I had broken the chain of four generations of unwanted girls in my family—my grandmother, mother, myself, and my daughter. Although we all survived our ancient Chinese female-genocidal culture, we were all left with deep emotional and physical scars.

It's been quite a re-traumatizing experience completing my memoir, especially writing in my second language which I acquired artificially by starting with studying the English sentence structures and grammatical rules in China.

I hope my story will be helpful to readers who, despite their good fortune of being born in America, may have also suffered a harsh childhood, or lived in poverty, or been abused emotionally and physically, or endured a loveless marriage. I know the emotional pain of what it's like to be disrespected not only at home but in the workplace. But through this memoir I also realized that it was my dog-stubborn never-give-up nature that put me back on track—every time!

It is also my hope, dear reader, that you'll find a glimpse of inspiration from my dog-stubborn and never-give-up spirit to pick myself up from right where I was knocked down, start over and keep going to make the best of what is left in this earthly short life.

My kindergarten class. 1960. I'm squatting at front row, fifth from the right.

This photo was taken at my birth village of Red Stone Bridge, 2015, part of my kindergarten class as adults. I'm flanked by my childhood best friends, Love Lily, in black blouse, and Pink Flower, in short sleeves. Everyone in the group has lived in the remote village all their lives, except the tallest man, Jia Cheng Cheng who lives in a nearby town.

Photo List

My kindergarten class. 1960. I'm squatting at front row, fifth from the right. 20

This photo was taken at my birth village of Red Stone Bridge, 2015, part of my kindergarten class as adults. I'm flanked by my childhood best friends, Love Lily, in black blouse, and Pink Flower, in short sleeves. Everyone in the group has lived in the remote village all their lives, except the tallest man, Jia Cheng Cheng who lives in a nearby town. 20

This kerosene oil lamp was the only lighting I lived by before age eight. 34

July, 1957. I was fourteen months old in this hand-colored photo. ..45

My milk mother in her later years, holding her grandson in front of her home. Oh, the memory of these two-leaf wooden doors. I still remember how eager I was to push them open, cross that high threshold and see my milk mother's happy sunshine smiling face, just like the heartwarming smile she had in this photo. 53

This is my paternal grandmother, Jade, and me. 54

1960. Taiyuan City, at the studio of Ding Zhang. 66

Look at the smiles on both mother and son. 69

1964. This family photo was taken at Rising East studio, Taiyuan City. 123

1965. This photo was taken at Red East photography studio, Taiyuan City. 143

My mother and me. I was still wearing the same hair style for my star performance at Children's Palace. Notice the big lump, my "thick-neck disease," in the front of my neck. 160

My mother and me, at Anti-Imperialism studio. 183

The year was 1970. This gloomy family photo was the calm after the storm. 194

This photo was taken in 1971 at the city center of May 1 Square, Taiyuan. 198

July 26, 1973 was the date I noted in this beautiful and very special book that accompanied me on my journey to the fascinating English world. 212

July 1, 1974. Photo of my high school Class 16. 218

June 29, 1979. My English class at Taiyuan Teachers' College, Class 29, with professors and the Party leaders. I'm the first one on the left in the next-to-the-last row. I'm ducking down so I could be the same height as the other girls. 260

Winter 1979. Me. Aged twenty-three. New star teacher at No. 5 Secondary School. 267

1984. I'm standing in front of the Audio and Video building at Beijing Foreign Language Institute. 308

This is my prized suitcase strap. I not only paid a lot for it but humiliation as well, my price for breaking into China's Foreign-Guests-Only "Friendship Store" in 1986. I still have it to this day. Just so you know, my dignity returned. 318

I'm sitting alone on the front lawn of Concordia College in Bronxville, New York. 320

In front of the headquarters of American Field Service (AFS) in New York. The American lady in sunglasses was an AFS volunteer coordinator. This was a thrilling day! 324

Mr. Robert Wimberly, my Master Teacher, and I, at the Pendleton School District office, holding a special Chinese banner of 友誼-Friendship, specially hand-embroidered from No. 5 Secondary School, the top elite college-bound high school in Taiyuan, Shanxi where I taught. 327

My first Christmas with Dr. Dale and Mrs. Barbara Brandt in their home. 328

My Pendleton friends surprised me with a lovely "Monkey Birthday!" So fun! 329

Dr. Rosenquist and the Oregon young trooper – the special prankster for my birthday! 330

Dr. and Mrs. Rosenquist, my 3rd host family, introduced me to America's amazing 31-Flavors ice cream. Ice cream was my daughter's favorite. It became one of my powerful motivations to get my daughter to live in America, even just for the amazing ice cream alone! 331

Oregon's governor Vic Atiheh cooking pancakes at Pendleton's annual rodeo Let'er Buck! Wow, I couldn't believe it that such a down-to-earth nice man was the state's highest official. He was so approachable just like a common folk, so different from the Chinese Communist authoritarian leaders. 334

At my master's graduation with Dr. Edythe Leupp and her (late) husband Tom Leupp 344

Part One

Born Unwanted 生不逢時:

A Peasant Girl at Red Stone Bridge Village — Birth to Age Eight

Chapter 1
The Red Sandals
紅涼鞋

AS A SMALL CHILD growing up with my paternal grandparents in north central China's deep pine forest mountains, I was forever curious about my grandmother's tiny crooked feet. Every time she sat on the small wooden stool facing the sod wall in the corner of our one-room house to soak her feet in the big iron washbasin full of steamy water, I'd rush over to sneak a peek.

My grandmother's three-inch-long bound feet looked like a pair of pale, naked dead birds made out of wheat flour dough. Each big toe stood alone pointing forward while her four small toes were crush-bent underneath her sole. The back of her feet arched up like a smooth round steamed bun with each sole a hollow cleft after the front feet and heel were crunch-pushed toward each other.

"Get out of here, you nosy creature!" Grandmother would yell, panicked by my prying eyes, hurriedly stretching out her big, knobby field hands over her feet. "What's there to look at? Nothing but these two ugly things! Ouch, so hurting . . ." I'd watch her eyes squeeze shut, her toothless mouth gasp, every wrinkle in her sun-browned high-cheek-bones carved in pain.

"Damn my parents!" Grandmother would say between her gasps. "Yes, I dare to speak unfavorable words against my revered father and mother, even though they have passed. Look how they hurt me . . ."

Born in 1912, Grandmother was one of the last generation of victims of the barbaric practice of Chinese foot-binding. For one thousand years, all little girls between ages three and five, rich or poor, had to have their tender little feet maimed into a pair of exquisite three-inch-long flowers shaped like "golden lilies." Chinese men were said to relish as erotic their women's tiny pointed feet, the original flesh-and-blood version of today's Western stilettos.

Grandmother was five years old when, one day, her mother soaked her feet in special fragrant herbal water. As Grandmother screamed in flooding tears of pain, her mother crushed, bent and force-wrapped her feet into two iron-tight pointed stubs with *guo-jiao-bu* 裹腳布, a ten-foot-long strip of black cotton cloth, as her own mother did to hers when she was a child. The cloth was not to be loosened for months at a time, and then, let the rotting pus out before they were wrapped back up, only this time tighter.

"It's for your own good, my daughter," her mother sobbed. "So a good man will want to marry you."

All the while, her father reminded her to behave like a demure lady.

Grandmother's feet felt like they were held over a fire, slowly roasting. The excruciating pain kept her awake all night. She dared not cry out loud, but whimpered and sobbed quietly to herself, always fearing her father's scolding.

"They didn't have to harm me like this." Tears ran down Grandmother's cheeks, as she rubbed her arched-up-like-a-cat's-back deformed feet.

The flesh-rotting, bone-crushing custom was abolished in 1911, one year before Grandmother was born, when the Republic of China overthrew the Manchu Dynasty. The new government would send out special inspectors to the remote mountain villages to catch and punish people who still bound their young daughter's feet.

"Other girls my age in my village were spared by their parents, but no, not that knuckleheaded stubborn father of mine. He insisted on sticking to the despicable old tradition. Every time the inspectors came to the village to catch the illegal foot-binding, he'd carry me up to the attic, hide me under stacks of hay, and tell me not to make a sound. Damn that fool!"

"Why didn't they find me a rich husband instead of this useless weakling peasant grandfather of yours?" Grandmother lifted the front of her faded black cotton shirt to wipe her tears. "Oh, how I suffered working alongside him like a beast in the cornfields."

Grandmother gave birth to eight babies, my father her first-born, during the fourteen-year span (1931-45) of the brutal Japanese invasion of China during WWII. On her painful stubby feet, Grandmother would lead her small children in hushed silence at midnight running for their lives into the deep mountain caves.

Throughout her eighty-six years of life, Grandmother cried tears of pain over her "golden lily" feet.

As her first grandchild born a girl instead of a gold-valued boy, I was a disappointment to Grandmother. My earliest memory is of her eyeing me hard, sideways: "Those tiny slit eyes and that pig snout mouth look just like that bad-omen ugly mother of yours."

But there was one thing Grandmother made me feel good about.

My feet.

"Oh, just look at these darling feet." Grandmother would reach out to caress my child's feet, a look of great envy and rare affection in her now-soft eyes. "They are gorgeous . . . so flat . . . so free to grow. Lucky child, born in good times. Your feet don't have to suffer. Oh, they are meaty big plump feet just like mine. You would have suffered terrible pain just like I did. Girls with skinny, smaller feet didn't suffer as badly."

On the morning of June 1, 1962, International Children's Day, I woke up smiling and giggling, my six-year-old heart leaping for joy. Today was going to be a very special day because Grandmother's promise was to make my dream come true. I was finally allowed to wear the beautiful red sandals my parents sent from the city.

I'd been waiting for this moment like a restless ant on a hot stove. Grandmother had kept my red sandals locked, alongside my beautiful doll, in her scrap bundle inside the big black floor chest. Every time I saw her reach down into the chest for her treasured bundle, I'd hurry over for a glimpse of my red sandals. The bright color was just like the bright red wild berries Grandpa picked for me on his way down the mountains after toiling all day in the commune's cornfields. Like the comforting glow of the fire in our brick stove on a cold winter's day, it warmed my heart.

But Grandmother wouldn't allow me to try the shoes on. She said they were too pretty, too brand-new for my dirty feet. She kept saying that my feet were not big enough. I'd have to wait till the next June 1.

Today was finally the day! My face couldn't stop smiling. I couldn't wait to put the red sandals on and show off to my first-grade classmates. This was the first time I felt good that my parents lived in the faraway-city with my two younger brothers.

I clapped, cheered, and jumped for joy as Grandmother set the sandals in front of me. Sitting down on the wooden floor stool, I kicked off my homemade cloth shoes and carefully placed my feet on top of my old shoes to avoid touching the dusty earthen floor. Gingerly, I began to inch my feet into the cool, smooth and soft-like-rubber but magically see-through red sandals.

Oh, no! Why were my heels still hanging out but the shoes were already full? Well, no matter. I should just push hard. Grandmother had said the shoes were ready for my feet today. They HAD to fit. But as I finally stuffed my heels inside, my big toes were crunched up tight and stiff, butting heads like the thick long stick Grandpa used to prop against the door at night. They were hurting badly.

I couldn't understand it — Grandmother had said this year was the right time when the red sandals would fit. Why did my feet feel too big for them? Today, my first grade class was going to parade through the village to celebrate Children's Day. I had to wear them. I stood up but could only walk unsteadily, like Grandmother on her painful tiny stubby three-inch-long bound feet.

I limped around the floor, hoping and wishing for my red sandals to become bigger. But they didn't. I sucked in the pain and hobbled out to join my classmates. But the pain became worse, and finally unbearable. Halfway through the parade, I took off my red sandals and held them in my hands, walking barefoot on the village's rocky dirt street.

Once home, I quietly handed over my dream red sandals to Grandmother.

"Why?" asked Grandmother simply. "Don't you want to wear them?"

In tears, I shook my head, not knowing what to say, startled that she didn't look surprised.

Sitting down on the stool, I inspected my feet. Blood seeped out quietly from under my big toenails. The right toenail was broken in half vertically with a bulging ridge.

I never saw my beautiful red sandals again.

Chapter 2

Red Stone Bridge

赤石橋

MY BIRTH VILLAGE, Red Stone Bridge, remains forever picturesque in my memory.

Surrounded by majestic mountains of dark green pine forest and lying forty-li (fifteen miles) off the main road through the *Qin* Valley in northern central China's Shanxi Province, it's so obscure that Google Earth doesn't pinpoint it. But for thousands of years, the Red Stone Bridge villagers have lived on, helping China produce the world's largest population of one billion people.

A small clear creek cut through the middle of my childhood village, separating the village into east end and west end, with the main street running from east to west. At the west end of the village, a red stone bridge crossed over another wider and deeper creek that ran to join the South River at the foot of the South Mountain. It was my favorite childhood place to play.

The official entrance to the village was at the east end, where the roaring East River flowed by. The village's primary school 赤石橋完小, the first-through-sixth grades, stood just two houses away up the river. Gray tile-roofed houses of brick, mud and pinewood were perched on the hills surrounded by the mountains.

My grandparents lived at the west end of the village inside the Li family's earthen courtyard. They lived in their east-facing house. The bright warm sun brightened the house in the morning. Across the yard lived my great grandparents, parents of my grandpa, in their west-facing house. The brighter hot sun heated up their house in the afternoon. And the best house inside the Li family courtyard, the south-facing house, lived my grandfather's younger brother and his family. The warm sun brightened the house in the winter. And it was nice and cool in the summer.

My grandparents, the eldest son and daughter-in-law, were supposed to live in the best house in the family courtyard, according to the ancient Chinese filial rule, but my great grandparents apparently favored their younger son over their eldest son, my grandfather. His wife, my grandmother, wasn't happy about this situation. Loud, forceful, explosive-tempered, ambitious, hardworking, bright-brained, illiterate, Grandmother overruled everyone in her quiet, good-natured, timid in-law's family, standing toe to toe with the world on her three-inch bound feet.

In the corner of the yard was the six-feet deep open sewage covered by two huge slabs of flat stone with a half-foot wide slot to squat on. The square courtyard was enclosed by an earthen wall without an actual door but an arched earthen entrance with two huge square rocks placed on each side, like two lions in rich people's courtyard, guarding the gateway. Just a hundred yards away facing the Li family courtyard was the majestic South Mountain, with the roaring South River at its foot.

In between the Li's courtyard and the South Mountain was a well shed, one of the two in Red Stone Bridge. Villagers roped down a wooden bucket into the deep well to reel up water by an iron handle. They then shoulder-poled two thick wooden buckets of water home for drinking, cooking, and hand-and-face washing. To do their laundry, villagers went to either the East River or the South River, where they scrubbed their bed sheets and clothes on a smooth, flat river rock.

The all-year-round deep mountain air was cool and lung-cleansing fresh, especially in the mornings. That's why I'm in deep love with San Francisco's nice, cool and beautiful-like-a-bride's-veil fog.

Life in Red Stone Bridge was simple and primitive.

Each family lived in a one-room house, functioning all-in-one as kitchen, living room, dining room, bedroom and bathroom. Half of the room, from wall to wall, was taken up the family's platform bed called a *kang* 炕, — still an important part of village homes all over northern China. Built from brick and mud, the *kang* stood hip-high and was covered with a thin, thorny, reed-woven mattress made from reeds like bamboo. Attached to one end of the *kang*, next to the door, was a brick cooking stove, whose chimney was a built-in tunnel burrowing underneath the *kang* to keep it heated.

At night, the *kang* was the communal bed for the entire family, lined up like human logs. During the daytime, everyone's cotton-padded quilts were rolled up against the wall to clear off the *kang*'s surface and make it the center of the family's daily social activities. The *kang* became the communal space for family chatting, conversing with visiting relatives, playing chess and cards on rainy and snowy days, birthing, holding wedding ceremonies. It offered a safe space for crawling babies, older kids doing their homework, using their knees as a desk. It was also the platform for women's sewing and mending, the working arena for husbands grinding soaked soybeans to make tofu, the comforting corner for the sick and invalid being nursed, the hospice bed for the frail elderly, and the final three-day resting place for a loved one's coffin.

Up till age eight, I lived on my grandparents' *kang* in their one-room house. Privacy was an unknown concept.

For toiletry needs, each family a six-foot-deep and equally wide giant hole in the ground, covered by two huge slabs of river rocks, and centered by two, 2x4-foot-long pieces of pinewood, forming a half-foot-wide squatting slot. Rain or snow, we went outside to use the open-sewage squatting toilet. A clay chamber pot was brought in for the night and emptied into the outhouse in the morning.

The outhouse manure provided our only source of fertilizer for vegetables and other crops. Hence, organic food! Men dipped a huge ladle, nailed onto the top end of a ten-foot-long stick, into the manure pool, dished out the contents into two big wooden buckets, and shoulder-poled them for miles to fertilize the vegetables.

All year round, the deep cool mountain air drifted by, carrying with it the stench of raw sewage. The odor was especially strong during the summertime. But we were oblivious, sitting in the yard eating out of our soup bowls and slurping our soup of grated corn flour with boiled green beans, zucchini, cabbage, potatoes, or carrots.

I grew up the first eight years of my life at Red Stone Bridge, but my life story didn't begin there.

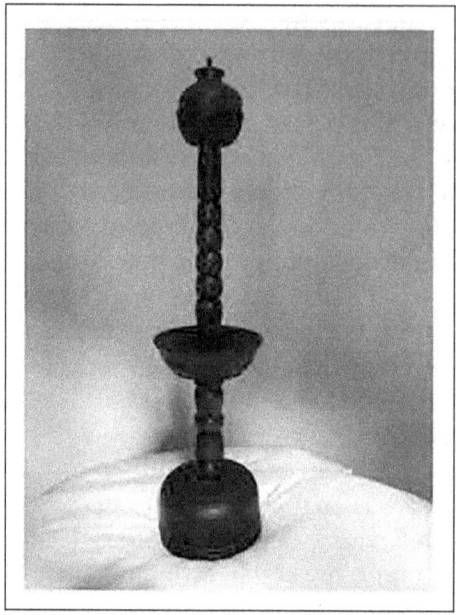

This kerosene oil lamp was the only lighting I lived by before age eight.

Chapter 3

Lost Dream

失去的夢

MY MOTHER, MAGNOLIA, was born in 1935 in the village of 潤崖底 *Beneath the Cliff*, thirty *li* (ten miles) up the Qin Valley from Red Stone Bridge.

Magnolia was four years old when she walked with her mother out of their village into the deep mountain trails. Her mother was weeping, holding Magnolia's toddler brother in her arms. A strange man was walking with them, but never said a word.

It turned out that Magnolia's opium-addicted peasant father had sold his wife and two children to a human trafficker. Fortunately, her paternal grandmother discovered the secret sale in the nick of time and sent her four other strong sons to rescue them. Once home, Magnolia's uncles beat their brother mercilessly and kicked him out of the family home in hopes of teaching him a lesson.

But the next day, Magnolia's twenty-five-year-old father did not return. The family searched the hills beyond their family courtyard. They found her father's body dangling from a tree. He had hanged himself out of shame.

Magnolia's twenty-three-year-old mother was now widowed and blamed for being a "bad omen." Her in-law's family believed she had caused her husband's death. She was disowned and forbidden to take her two small children, Magnolia and her toddler brother.

The ancient Chinese culture dictated that the moment a bride crossed the threshold of her in-law's family home, her own parents lost all their rights to claim her, to speak up for her, or to defend her if she was mistreated. 生是婆家的人，死是婆家的鬼: *A daughter-in-law was her in-laws' family property in life and death.* Even her own children became the sole, legal property of the deceased husband's family. A Chinese wife's duty went beyond being married to her husband. Her first duty was to her father- and mother-in-law, her new parents, who had the right to determine her fate.

"Please let me nurse my baby son, just one last time, please," Magnolia's mother begged.

Magnolia watched her mother sobbing, her tears flowing, her head leaning against her in-law's door, her hair disarrayed all over her face. She saw her mother's breast milk seeping through the front of her shirt, dripping onto the dirt floor. Her grandmother had hidden her little brother inside.

The next morning, Magnolia heard her uncles yelling and cursing outside. Her mother had crept back and hidden behind the bushes outside the Zhang family's courtyard. She was hoping to catch a glimpse of her baby son. But the brothers threw rocks and sticks at her.

"We'll break your legs if we catch you lurking around here again!" They yelled as she ran.

That was the last time four-year-old Magnolia heard her mother's voice until she turned twelve. The orphaned Magnolia and her baby brother now lived with their paternal matriarchal grandmother, who, according to the Chinese culture, commanded the filial duty to be taken care of by her married sons.

When twelve-year-old Magnolia was finally thought old enough, she walked the fifteen *li* on the mountain trails down the valley to visit her mother. But her little brother was never allowed to see his mother. A gold-valued male child was too important to be "contaminated" by his bad-omen mother. The toddler grew up with no memory of her. He was spoiled into a lazy and entitled boy.

A Chinese daughter-in-law, like Magnolia's mother, was a dowry-bought asset to her in-laws. Like a valuable horse, she was to be ridden and bred. The pictographic Chinese language reflected the tradition: The word for "mother" 媽 is composed of two side-by-side radicals: "female 女" + "horse 馬".

After being condemned by her in-laws, Magnolia's mother was charity-gifted to a fifty-year-old hunch backed peasant as his wife. The vibrant twenty-three-year-old, with a beautiful face, who loved to smile and laugh, soon became involved in the biggest and most daring scandal in the entire Qin Mountain region: She had an affair with a twenty-eight-year-old peasant. The two were caught making love deep in the cornfields. Now Magnolia's mother was labeled a "bad omen slut." Her reputation was so damaged that she was later forbidden to attend her daughter Magnolia's wedding. She was thirty-four when she died after screaming for months in pain from a stomach ache.

Magnolia's grandmother sent her to school in the village supported by her uncles' families. A bright child, Magnolia excelled as the all-time top student, one who especially loved writing. But none of her uncles were willing to pay the hefty two-hundred-pound millet tuition to send her beyond their village's first-through-fourth-grade primary school.

Magnolia dreamed of going back to school. "I'll never want to swallow others' charity soup and live with their resentful eyes again," young Magnolia vowed in tears.

For the next two years, she walked fifteen *li* down the valley to take the boarding school's annual entrance examinations. Both times she scored the first place, but each time she was turned away. Someone had to pay for her tuition.

A mere peasant girl, Magnolia was dreaming of the impossible.

Eager to unload her as a burden of another mouth to feed, one of Magnolia's aunts thought of Jade, a cousin, who lived thirty *li* down the valley in Red Stone Bridge village. She had an eighteen-year-old son named Bright Light.

Loud and domineering, Jade and her quiet, good-natured husband, Water, doted on their only surviving son. They toiled from dawn to dusk, saving "between their teeth" to keep him in school. They also made their two younger daughters work beside them in the fields to grow food. For Bright Light, a gold-valued boy, they had great expectations. He was groomed to live a leisurely life as an educated man in the city, far away from the millet fields.

Bright Light's mother had learned firsthand the worthlessness of being a female. The brightest and prettiest girl in her maiden village, Jade loved learning. But her parents bound her feet to attract a husband, and sent her duller brother to school.

When her eighth, and last, child was born, Jade grabbed the tiny ankles of her minute-old newborn daughter and threw her headfirst into the urine pot to drown. "Not another cheap flat piece of female!" Jade cried in shame. "Old Heaven God, why do you punish me like this?"

Water wrapped up his newborn daughter and handed to his wife, Jade. But she turned her head away, refusing to look at the girl. He set the baby in the corner of the kang. Miraculously, the baby came to by herself. She survived to be my aunt Er Gu, eleven years older than me. Unlike her two older siblings, my father and his middle sister, Er Gu grew up a bit slow-brained. Everyone in the family called her "dumb idiot." Her near-drowning in urine had also permanently destroyed her sense of smell. But like a quiet rabbit, Er Gu learned to defend herself by raising her hand to cover her face when her mother hit and slapped her, and by looking down in shame when her father yelled at her in frustration.

Ironically, decades later, this unwanted daughter was the only one who waited faithfully on her mother Jade's death bed, while the other two smart children were hundreds of miles away in the city busy with their own lives.

"Whoever sends me to school, I'll marry their son." Fourteen-year-old Magnolia had sent out her word-of-mouth proposal. It reached Bright Light at Red Stone Bridge. At age eighteen, he was already complaining to his mother, Jade, for not having found him a wife: "All my friends in the village are married but me." He was fascinated with Magnolia's story. A pretty girl with a brain, an all-time Number One student, and one who wanted more education? How refreshing and romantic!

Bright Light wanted to meet Magnolia.

Unlike her naive son, shrewd Jade saw the underlying trouble. "How could we possibly afford to pay for a second tuition? Can't you see your weakling father and I, on my painful three-inch bound feet, are already breaking our backs toiling in the fields just to pay for your school?"

A spoiled son, Bright Light was oblivious to her parents' hardship.

"A daughter-in-law should be the family's helping hands." Jade tried reasoning patiently with her son, the only person for whom she was willing to hold back her explosive temper. "Whoever heard of a peasant wife living as an idling goddess on the backs of her in-laws?"

The son turned a deaf ear to his mother. After all, it was his mother who had taught him the importance of being a gold-valued boy. Jade had told her daughters: "Your brother is the sun, and you two girls are the moon and star — you move around him. His wish is your command."

Bright Light wouldn't even wait for his mother to arrange for the village's go-between woman to handle the matchmaking, a marriage practice since beginning of time. He walked alone the thirty *li* up the valley to meet Magnolia at her village.

Magnolia and Bright Light met at the home of her adoring teacher, Mr. Yang Wen Bing, a revered local figure.

His heart pumping wildly, Bright Light walked into the one-room house. Bashful and nervous, he glanced over to the corner of the room and for the first time laid eyes on his dream girl. Her eyes cast down, Magnolia looked demure, sitting on the small wooden stool. As he entered the room, she glanced up quickly to smile shyly at him.

Teacher Yang jumped up to his feet from sitting on the *kang*. He shook Bright Light's hand, praising him for his desire for the "smartest girl ever."

"Now you two youngsters have met and liked each other," the worldly teacher lost no time hustling along. "Magnolia, why don't you go ahead and leave us men to talk business?"

Smiling demurely, Magnolia stood up quietly and walked to the door, passing in front of Bright Light. He blushed, admiring her tall, slender figure.

"Young man," Teacher Yang assured Bright Light, "you will have a very bright future if you marry this extraordinary girl. What an asset an educated wife is to her husband!"

Half an hour later, an elated Bright Light shook hands with Mr. Yang, pledging his solemn promise: Yes, his parents would send Magnolia back to school right after the wedding.

Years later when I was a teenager, Bright Light, my father, complained: "But I never got a good look at her! I'd never have agreed to marry that ugly bad omen."

Theirs was a lifelong stormy, miserable marriage.

And, Jade, my grandmother, never forgave Teacher Yang for having manipulated her "naive-like-an-idiot" son into the marriage.

During the bloody Cultural Revolution (1966-76), the Red Guards hunted down Mr. Yang, then the principal at Red Stone Bridge's primary school, and beat him to death. His head was split open, his tattered body thrown into the well. "Served the SOB just right!"

my grandmother uttered under her breath, her eyes shining in satisfaction. I was baffled at her hissing vengeance.

In 1950, nineteen-year-old Bright Light wed fifteen-year-old Magnolia.

As fate would have it, a few days before Magnolia's boarding school entrance examination, her mother died. The ancient tradition required her to fulfill her filial duty by staying indoors in mourning for a full month. But she wasn't about to let her dream die. Covered from head to toe in her heavy white mourning gown, Magnolia walked fifteen *li* down the valley to the village of *Shi-hui-wan* to take the test. She must have looked like a scary floating ghost out of a tomb in the classic Chinese stories of haunting spirits.

"What an abnormal creature!" Her mother-in-law, Jade, was beyond disgusted.

Not surprisingly, Magnolia aced the test and was officially accepted into her long-awaited two-year boarding school.

Then Magnolia sensed trouble. Jade had been strangely silent about sending her to school while keeping busy packing for Bright Light's return to his boarding school. Hiding her anxiety, Magnolia lay low, watching in silence for the precise moment.

Lunar New Year Day was a time for harmony. No tears, no quarreling, no breaking any objects in round shapes in order to avoid any bad luck for the coming year. It was also a special face-saving time when well-wishers in the village went around from house to house visiting their relatives' families. Everyone dressed in their once-a-year new clothes, the younger generation paying respect to their elders.

Magnolia refused to get out of bed. She wept and sobbed while the visiting guests crowded the small floor space in the one-room house.

"Oh, my dear child." Red-faced with embarrassment, Jade gritted her teeth, acting innocently. "What's wrong?"

Magnolia howled louder.

"No! You can't leave!" Magnolia cried, leaping up and grabbing Bright Light as he bent down to shoulder-pole the two baskets his mother had packed for him, one sack of millet tuition, his clothes and a bed roll of cotton padded futon. "What about me?" Magnolia yelled. "You and your mother promised to send me back to school if I married you. What happened to your promise?"

Bright Light's mouth fell open but no words came out. He turned to look at his mother, who stood calmly by watching, her three-inch bound feet planted apart, her hands crossing over her apron, her back erect.

"Well, why don't you let go of your husband?" Magnolia's mother-in-law prodded. "You and I can talk about this later."

"No way!" Magnolia protested. "You have to make it clear to me right now. Fulfill your promise or I'm walking out for a divorce."

"Okay, okay," Jade backed down, hiding her seething anger. "Go ahead. Let go of him. We'll send you to school, too." Proud Jade had never cowered from anyone, especially a lowly female beneath her.

Thus, the two women became engaged in a cold war that lasted the rest of their lives.

Magnolia sailed smoothly into her dream life, her horizons now broadened. She'd soon discover a much better man than the one she'd married, her handsome young teacher, Mr. Doo.

Rumors soon spread into the ears of her mother-in-law, Jade and husband, Bright Light.

"Magnolia," her classmates asked her. "Who are you knitting those nice socks for?"

"Oh, for my Teacher Doo." Magnolia blushed, her eyes dreamy. Doing needlework for a man was a romantic gesture of affection from a Chinese maiden.

I remember once my father, Bright Light, blurting out indignantly: "Mr. Doo was a principled man with integrity. He'd never want anything to do with that bad-omen ugly thing!"

Finally, two years of doubled-up sweat and blood were now coming to fruition for Bright Light's toiling parents. Magnolia was graduating from primary school, a brilliant all-time top student. But she wanted more schooling.

"Why don't you go on to the Teachers' Training School? It's a suitable career for a woman, especially with the free tuition, room and board." Jade suggested.

"No, I want to go on to middle and high school. I want to go to college." Magnolia dreamed of becoming a journalist. After graduation, she didn't return to her in-laws' home in Red Stone Bridge but instead went back to Beneath the Cliff, her maiden village. Unbeknownst to her in-laws, Magnolia had already found another way forward with better prospects. The government had just issued a new policy to grant merit-based scholarships to promising offspring of poor peasants.

Magnolia was well qualified academically, except that, alas, she was married! A married Chinese woman had no place in society except under her in-laws' roof birthing and raising children.

But she wasn't to be deterred. With the help of her dead father's brother, Magnolia obtained a truth-concealing reference letter from the mayor of her maiden village: Yes, Magnolia was a poor peasant orphan. She thus sailed smoothly into the secondary school in the ancient town of Ping Yao, the same school from which her husband Bright Light had graduated.

謀事在人,成事在天。 *People plan, but Heaven decides*, so says the Chinese proverb.

Fate awaited to destroy Magnolia's dream.

The principal of her boarding school called Magnolia to his office. "Someone informed us that you're married," he revealed – and promptly revoked her scholarship.

Discouraged but undaunted, Magnolia decided there was only one thing left to do.

On that fateful weekend of October 1 in 1955, Communist China's sixth birthday, Magnolia hitchhiked a 200-*li* ride on an open-top truck to the city of Taiyuan, where her estranged husband worked as a geographical surveyor, measuring mountains and hills.

When Magnolia found him, Bright Light was living in a dorm he shared with three roommates. Housing and everything else was in shambles in the post war-ravaged China after fourteen years of a brutal Japanese invasion (1931-1945), followed by another four years of bloody civil war (1945-49.)

"I want a divorce," Magnolia demanded.

"But the court is closed for the holiday," Bright Light replied, talking Magnolia into staying with him for the three-day weekend. Everyone had gone home for the holiday. They slept in the cook's bed *kang* in the kitchen.

When the weekend was over, they'd struck a deal: Yes, she'd agree to stay married if he promised to pay for her education.

On Monday morning, a happy Bright Light put a smiling Magnolia onto the bus back to her school. He'd given her twenty *yuan*, enough to tide her over for the remaining semester.

But Magnolia's dream wasn't meant to be.

She soon discovered she was pregnant – with me. Magnolia, who was now twenty, had never considered the possibility of getting pregnant. Why should she? No pregnancy had ever occurred during her five-year marriage.

Magnolia was devastated. Still, she was determined to stay in school, at any cost, until she realized her dream of becoming a writer. She searched the campus and found a thick heavy pine washboard in the storage room. She hid it in her dorm room. Whenever no one was around, she'd push it hard and repeatedly against her pregnant belly. She also jumped violently in her P.E. class. The unwanted life inside her had to go.

Divine Intervention. My life couldn't be snuffed out.

In utter despair, Magnolia finally had to give up her dream. She cried her grieving tears alone while walking the ninety-*li* mountain trails by herself back to her maiden village to give birth. But Chinese tradition said it was a bad omen for a married daughter to give birth in her maiden home, even though she had been orphaned.

Magnolia sent a distress message to her mother-in-law at Red Stone Bridge, requesting to be picked up. Still seething mad at her daughter-in-law's desertion of the Li family, Jade didn't respond. Magnolia's uncles ended up having to hire an expensive horse-drawn cart to bring Magnolia back to her in-law's house. She had to give birth at Red Stone Bridge.

I was born there in May, instead of July, my time due for this earthly life, inside my grandparents' small mud hut infested with scurrying shining brown bed bugs and jumping fleas.

The minute my grandmother Jade saw me born a girl, instead of a gold valued boy, she put on a long face, walking around on her three-inch-bound feet doing her chores without saying a word for two days. As her firstborn grandchild, I was supposed to be born a boy. It was the Li family tradition that the firstborn child be a male, like my father, and my grandfather before him.

Jade was now even more convinced that her daughter-in-law Magnolia was a bad omen to the Li family. She blamed Magnolia's now-dead mother for ruining her son Bright Light's wedding day by peeking out from behind the wall of an outhouse by the roadside as Magnolia's wedding procession was passing by. Magnolia's mother, a damaged-goods woman, was forbidden to be anywhere in sight during the wedding. When she was spotted hiding behind the outhouse wall, Jade had become furious: "Why the hell did she have to show her bad-omen face to ruin my Li family's luck! Damn her to hell!"

Magnolia, my mother, never forgave me for being born.

I didn't find out any of that until one day in 2007, when I was fifty-one and had spent two decades living in my beloved new home country, the United States of America. That day, I was working on my memoir with my writing group when a fellow writer asked me a simple question.

"Why did your mother never smile at you when you were growing up?" The question made me think. Because I didn't know the answer.

I decided to get on the phone and call my mother in China. My heart pounding, my temples bursting, I felt intimidated, afraid that she'd refuse to answer me. Growing up, I'd never felt I was good enough to be entitled to receive anything from my mother, including an answer to a personal question like this one.

But, yes! Amazingly, my mother responded. I secretly thanked my almighty ten thousand American dollars she'd recently half sweet-talked and half guilt-tripped me into raising. I had to refinance my San Francisco home mortgage so as to gift the money to her favorite child, the older of my two younger brothers. Now unemployed, overweight, recovering from a serious stroke, my brother was still living in the same blue-collar dirt yard he was born into.

Through the phone line from the other side of the earth, my mother started with an awkward chuckle and a hesitant sigh in response to my question: "Mother, would you please tell me what happened before I was born?"

That's when she told me.

Chapter 4

My First Photo

一歲照片

July, 1957. I was fourteen months old in this hand-colored photo.

THE RED SANDALS: A MEMOIR

THE PHOTO WAS TAKEN at Red Stone Bridge Harvest Fair, which was, and still is, held annually on June 23rd of the lunar calendar.

The arm holding me in place from behind was not my mother's, but Aunt Da Gu's, my father's middle younger sister. My father hadn't met me yet. And he wasn't to until I was four. At this time, I didn't know my mother, either. She'd left me when I was two months old. My father had found her a job in the faraway city of Taiyuan, where she joined him to be away from the harsh life of peasantry.

I learned who my parents were from the 1x2-inch black-and-white photo on the earthen wall in my grandparents' one-room house. The woman with pouty, thick lips, small, silent dark eyes, and an annoyed face was my mother. And the man, his hair combed-up smoothly at front, smiling an awkward toothy smile, was my father.

What was I so earnestly clutching in the photo? It looked like some raggedy toy the photographer used to hold a toddler's attention long enough to snap a picture. I looked live-wired enough to sprint away if the hand hadn't held me in place. From the way I tightly held onto that raggedy photo prop with both hands, I can see I'd already developed my serious attitude toward the world — I wouldn't let any opportunity slip through my fingers once I had the chance.

"Oh, my!" Grandmother would tell me what Red Stone Bridge villagers said about me. "This *nu-zi* 女子, *female child*, is going to grow up looking just like fat-bellied Mrs. Jia: big, tall and strong, with manly broad shoulders, thick arms and bow legs!"

"*Nu-zi*," was my name for the first year of my life, just like many other less-valued female babies in Red Stone Bridge. When Aunt Da Gu came back to visit the village from her postal job in town, she named me Cai Mei 彩梅, *colorful blossom*.

In the 1950's, Communist China's Mao-worshipping had reached a fever pitch. People named their babies to reflect the current political climate dominated by Communist leader Mao Tse-tung. Popular kids' names in that era were *Jian-Guo* 建國 *(founding of the country)*, Ai-Guo 愛國 *(loving the country)*, "Jian-Jun 建軍" *(building the army)*, Ai-Bing 愛兵 *(loving the soldiers)*, Ai-Min 愛民 *(loving the people)* and so on.

My name, Cai Mei (*a colorful blossom*), reflected the political movement in my birth year of 1956, when Mao launched his movement of "Let Hundred Flowers Bloom," 百花齊放.

Look at my little self, a picture of health — my ripe-apple cheeks, my robust little bow legs, my curious raised-high eyebrows and alert small-like-black-beans eyes. Would you have guessed that I had been near the brink of death just two months before this photo was taken?

Chapter 5

My Milk Mother

回憶奶媽

I WAS TWO MONTHS OLD, when my 21-year-old mother was getting ready to upgrade her peasant life. My father had found her a secretary job in the faraway city of Taiyuan. Like a Heaven-sent angel, a twenty-five-year-old peasant woman who also lived in Red Stone Bridge came to my rescue and became my "milk mother." Her newborn baby son had just died and was looking for a baby to nurse.

Ai Ying took me home with her. My parents were to pay her eight yuan ($1.20 in USD) a month, an astronomical fortune for a peasant family. Ai Yin had abundant breast milk. She blessed me in her nurturing bosom for ten precious months, a crucial period of time that set me up with an amazingly strong immune system.

Right before my first birthday, Jade, my grandmother, came to Ai Ying's house unannounced. Forcibly and abruptly she pried me out of Ai Ying's nurturing arms, leaving my milk mother's overflowing breast milk wasted, and her breast in bursting pain.

A mere female grandchild, I didn't deserve the sky-high monthly nursing fee any longer. Extremely thrifty and stingy, Grandmother had it all figured out. I was going to be fed with plain millet soup as my staple baby food, supplemented with some store-bought biscuits. It still only cost a fraction of the eight yuan to Ai Ying.

And, Grandmother was going to make my blind, great grandpa Lao Ye Ye, father of my grandfather, to babysit me during the daytime, while she herself had to toil in the commune's cornfields and cook, clean, wash, sew, feed pigs and chicken.

Grandmother miscalculated. Her plan for me backfired, to her greatest dismay. I, the littlest and the weakest, rioted.

I screamed and cried all day and all night. "Like a wild bucking horse," Grandmother described to me in later years, that I fast-pace crawled all over the *kang*, looking for my milk mother. I'd spit out the millet soup she spoon-forced into my mouth and push away any hands reaching out to console me. I banged my head against the hard mud wall till I knocked myself out. I'd carry on as soon as I came to. Quickly, I was reduced into a silent bundle of teary mess, dying of dehydration and exhaustion in the corner of family's brick and mud bed, *kang*.

"What an untamable wild spirit! A terrible temper!" Grandmother was frustrated to no end. "A born stubborn dog!"

Why didn't my grandmother simply let me die of my "natural causes?" After all, she'd watched one of her own baby daughters die, and thrown another into the urine-filled chamber pot to drown at birth.

Could it be that frighteningly bright-brained Grandmother had eyes on back of her head? Was she already foreseeing my future usefulness as her fighting paw against my mother, her despised daughter-in-law? In their lifelong cold war, the two women smiled to each other's face while stabbing at each other's back.

Whatever caused her change of heart, Grandmother swallowed her pride and went to plead with my milk mother to come back and save my life for another half month. She promised to pay the nursing fee. My ever-loving and forgiving milk mother agreed and brought me back to life. But Grandmother ate her promise. Instead of money, she paid my milk mother a pair of semi-old rain boots. Growing up, I'd hear Grandmother complain under her breath how ungrateful Ai Ying was, not appreciating her "nice and still new rain boots."

My earliest memory of my milk mother was her sunshine smiling face. I remember my longing desire to see her. After outgrowing my blind great Grandpa Lao Ye Ye's confined home, I ventured off as soon as my little legs could carry me. I found myself another happy place to hang out: my milk mother's home down the village's dirt and rock main street.

Walking into her gateless earthen yard, my heart cheered when I saw my milk mother's face looking out through the small glass window. Bursting through the two-leaf wooden doors into her sunshine-filled one-room house, I looked forward to my milk mother showering me with her loving fuss. Resting my elbows on the edge of the *kang* looking up at her, I was elated as she told me how fast I'd grown and what a bright child I was.

I was eager to see my milk mother also because she always had a special treat for me: a precious walnut-sized dried steamed bun. In those famine years, the staple food for all, young or old, was watery millet soup and boiled vegetables three times a day. A bite of dried steamed bun was a pure magic in my child's eyes. My milk mother was a little better off than most of the villagers because her husband was the traveling salesman. He bought supplies for Red Stone Bridge's one-room general store.

To my great annoyance, Grandmother didn't want me to visit my milk mother.

"Cai Mei! Cai Mei! Where are you looking for your death?" Grandmother's dreadful yelling would pierce my ears from outside, irritating to my child's mind and heart. Hurriedly, I'd hide myself in the corner between the *kang* and the floor chest, shutting my eyes, holding on tight to my tiny special treat of dried steamed bun.

Then I'd hear the terrifying sound of Grandmother bursting through the door.

"You little demon!" Grandmother yelled, trudging on her three-inch bound feet charging straight at me. She ignored my milk mother sitting on the *kang* holding her baby. "You cheap, thin eyelids! Don't you have any dignity? Eating others' food and making me lose face! What made you think any outsiders would love you?"

Then Grandmother pried open my hand to snatch away my precious snack and smacked it down on top of the floor chest. I started howling. Whack, whack! Grandmother smacked me hard. I screamed louder, struggling to get out of her big, calloused, gripping hands, my butt pulling back, tug-of-war style.

But I was no match. Grandmother quickly dragged me to the door, where I'd turn to look desperately at my milk mother, my teary eyes begging for her help. How disappointed and helpless I felt to see her pleading only in her soft voice, with a sad smile: "Please, Mrs. Li . . . Why don't you let the child have a bite? It's nothing, just a small piece of snack . . . the child's hungry . . . please . . . don't . . . Mrs. Li . . ."

But Grandmother was deaf to my milk mother's pleading. She would drag me over the foot-high wooden threshold, out the door, and all the way into the dirt and rock street. As she yelled and cursed, I screamed in flooding tears. The old, the small, we'd tangle and struggle all the way home at the west end of the village.

"Never seen a bad-omen creature like this worthless female piece!" Grandmother would yell, tossing me down on the river rock steps leading into the house. Then she'd forget about me and go about her chores.

I wasn't about to give in. Instead, I started sneaking around to see my milk mother. On my way to her home, I'd look around and over my shoulders to make sure Grandmother was nowhere to be seen. But, somehow, she always found out and came after me like a scary, haunting ghost.

When her eldest daughter, my aunt Da Gu, came back home to the village once in a while, Grandmother would send her to hunt me down and drag me out of my milk mother's happiness-filled home. Da Gu didn't yell as loud as Grandmother but had the same sharp tongue with hurting words just like her mother, and her small hands were just as rough.

The mother and daughter finally subdued my small child's "rebellious bones."

I went to see my milk mother less frequently, Grandmother kept saying things like: "Your milk mother doesn't love you. She only loved the boy she once wet-nursed after you. He was from the village of Qing Yang Wan, five *li* away down the valley. But the poor boy was ill-fated and died at age two."

Grandmother's story did make my child's mind wonder sometimes if my milk mother really loved me. But her loving smile always melted my doubt.

Starting at age ten, two years after I was sent to the faraway city of Taiyuan, I'd come back to the village every summer. And every time, I'd visit my milk mother.

I loved hearing my milk mother telling me my baby story.

One day she suddenly couldn't find me. "Oh, dear Old Heaven God," my milk mother said. She became panicked. Did I crawl into the six-foot-deep manure pool toilet around the corner of the house? Down on her hands and knees, she looked into the giant manure pit for signs of life.

Suddenly she heard a roar of laughter. It came from the small side room, where a group of schoolboys lived. They were from the surrounding deeper mountain villages to attend school at Red Stone Bridge. How relieved she was when she found me propped up sitting on top of the small desk in the middle of the *kang*. I was all smiles, babbling happily, enjoying being the center of attention and making my pig-snout faces on prompts from my captivated audience!

"What a little comedian this little child is!" the amused schoolboys exclaimed to my milk mother.

My mother also told me my baby story when I was six months old. She was once passing by Red Stone Bridge, on her way to see her bedridden grandmother in her maiden village Jian Ya Di, 澗崖底, thirty *li* up the valley. My mother decided to drop in at my milk mother's house.

"Heavens!" my mother was dismayed at the sight of me. "How come she looks like that?" I was sitting in the middle of my milk mother's family *kang*. "What happened to my baby I left behind four months ago? Ugh, what an ugly haircut . . . and the rag on her. Look at her puffed up cheeks! So fat they make her tiny eyes disappear altogether!"

My mother said her heart was broken when I pushed her hands away and cried frantically. "Hell with you," my mother told me she muttered. "You don't want me? Fine, I don't care about you, either."

My mother left promptly. She never came back to Red Stone Bridge again until twenty-four years later to make her eloquent speech, that awed the villagers, at my grandfather's funeral.

My milk mother in her later years, holding her grandson in front of her home. Oh, the memory of these two-leaf wooden doors. I still remember how eager I was to push them open, cross that high threshold and see my milk mother's happy sunshine smiling face, just like the heartwarming smile she had in this photo.

Chapter 6
Grandmother
奶奶

This is my paternal grandmother, Jade, and me.

I SMILE EVERY TIME I see this photo. Look at our serious faces mirroring off each other. It reminds me of the couple in Grant Wood's famous painting, American Gothic: she, plump, round-faced, and big, round-eyed, and he, thin-faced, pointed-chinned, and bald-headed.

How old was I in the photo? Three or four? That'd make Grandmother forty-seven or forty-eight. She was born in 1912, forty-four years older than me, in the Year of the Mouse, and I, the Year of the Monkey. Grandmother said that my birth month, April on the lunar calendar, was a bad-omen month for a Monkey. She said it showed in my eyebrows that took after my father: "These eyebrows, too thin, too short, a sign of lonely life."

Looking at my eyes, I can still hear Grandmother's scoffing voice and see her sideswiping me her dirty looks: "Those tiny slit eyes, just like that ugly mother of yours."

How I'd wished my eyes were bigger and pretty like the beautiful doll in a pink satin dress Grandmother kept locked in her big tall chest. She said it was too good for me to play with. Only once in a while I was allowed to hold the doll for a little bit.

Look at my little face, all scrubbed clean, my spit-wet hairband neatly plastered on my forehead. I can still feel Grandmother's rough knobby fingers pressing down hard. I remember my hair wasn't usually this smooth but tangled and matted solid.

"Come back and comb my hair!" I'd frantically cry, holding a small fine-toothed wooden comb, with several teeth missing, chasing after Grandmother and Aunt Er Gu. They were walking out of the yard to work in the commune's cornfields. I dreaded being left alone and locked out the house every day.

My tearful plea always worked on kindhearted Er Gu, who was thrown into the urine pot to drown at birth by her mother, my grandmother. She'd hesitantly turn to look at me, her eyes soft, apologetic.

"Idiot!" Grandmother would stamp her small bound feet, craning her neck to yell at Er Gu. "Just ignore her! Who has time to pamper her? I already tried but her hair is too matted and the comb too small. Let's go already! We don't have all day! Can't you see the sun is already high up in the sky? It's noon time!" Grandmother was good at exaggerating.

Ignoring her mother, Er Gu would walk back to me. She'd take the little comb and try to comb through my matted hair. But quickly she'd sigh, shaking her head and scrambling to join Grandmother, who was waiting on her tiny bound feet and glaring angrily at us.

Panicking, I'd burst out crying, dropping myself down in the middle of the earthen yard and watching helplessly as the two women disappeared. Then I'd roll and flail in the dirt until the bright sun dried my tears and the fluffy cotton-like white clouds slowly floated away with my sadness. The quiet blue sky finally calmed me, as the chirping birds in the blossoming peach tree cheered me up.

In the photo I looked clean and neat. But I wasn't like that most of the time. I remember the back of my hands and feet rough and looking like black leather, with dirt and grime being part of my skin.

Once in a while, I was given a little bit of water to wash my face and hands in a small iron washbasin. "Grandmother, I'm ready!" I'd cry out excitedly, my hands stretched out flat, side by side, snuggly covering the entire bottom of the small washbasin. I'd crane my neck to look up, squatting down on the small crowded brick and dirt floor and waiting for Grandmother to pour water. Drip drop. A few splashes came out of the chipped iron-porcelain drinking jug in her hand. It didn't even cover the back of my hands. "More, please," I'd plead. Drip drop. "More!" I didn't like Grandmother's stinginess. "How much is enough?" Grandmother would burst out yelling, glaring at me. "You think your weakling grandpa can keep up with you, shoulder-poling buckets of water home after toiling all day like a poor beast?"

"What a disgusting looking child!" Aunt Da Gu would yell at me when she came home. "The lice and ticks in your hair could be braided into cloves of garlic!" She was just like her mother, good at exaggerating things. Grabbing me and pulling me over to her, she'd hold me between her legs, forcing me to squat down over the washbasin half full of warm water. Her hands were small and soft-skinned but just as rough and hard as Grandmother's big calloused field hands.

"A filthy pig!" Da Gu would yell into my ears, while scrubbing my face, neck, and ears. "Hold still! You have the nerve to cry? Mother!" She'd turn to yell into the air at Grandmother, who was somewhere in the house working away like a scurrying busy ant, in and out, up and down the wooden ladder to the attic, on her small crooked three-inch-bound feet. "How could you neglect a child into such a disgrace?" Da Gu would pull and yank my head, my ears, my hair this way and that while I struggled and screamed, soapy water stinging my eyes, tears and mucus flowing into one stream and dripping down. I firmly remained Aunt Da Gu's helpless captive until she was well done with me.

Look at Grandmother's thick, knobby-knuckled field hands. I never saw them in gloves. She did all her chores with her bare hands: pulling grass and weeds on the hills for pig feed, gathering dried, prickly twigs in the fields for kindling, prying off dried kernels off the cobs, washing clothes in the icy cold South river, hoeing and raking in the cornfields, tying a donkey to the round stone mill to grind corn, soy beans, barley and millet into flour. The palms of her hands were as rough as a grater.

Grandmother's hands were also too rough for hugging or wiping off my tears but for slapping and smacking her youngest daughter, my teenage aunt Er Gu and me. But they also worked soft magic, too. With a rolling pin, she could roll a bowl-sized corn flour dough into a large piece of paper-thin sheet and cut it with a cleaver, at a flying speed, into fine, pine-needle like noodles. Her sewing and embroidery needlework were the envy of all women at Red Stone Bridge. With no pattern to follow, she could also cut a piece of red paper into a bird, a mouse, a tiger, a blooming peony flower, and Chinese characters of double happiness 喜喜, the only Chinese words she knew. She called herself an "open-eyed blind." Her parents sent only her brother to school. They made her do household chores after binding her feet at age five. All because she was a worthless female.

"Grandmother, would you teach me how to do paper cutting?" I'd plead, fascinated, my mind and hands eager and itchy to learn. I wanted to help decorate our paper-pasted window with my own paper cutting to celebrate the Chinese Lunar New Year.

"Who has time for *you*?" she'd shove me out of her way. "Can't you see I'm busy?"

When Grandmother turned fifty, her hands started shaking badly, all the way to the rest of her eighty-six years of life. She'd cry from the embarrassment of being unable to hold her bowl still, cursing my mother, her despised daughter-in-law, for causing her the disease.

What did my smiling face look like? I can still hear myself giggling and laughing all the time with Great Grandpa Lao Ye Ye, and Grandpa, and with my childhood friends. I remembered laughing so hard that I bent down holding my aching tummy. My happy giggling and laughter always irritated Grandmother, for some strange reason. "You're like an annoying noisy wild bird!" She'd yell. "The whole village can hear you!" I'd just ignore her, carrying on, feeling too good to stop, trying to stay out of the range of her big, smacking hands.

I wish Grandpa had been in the photo with me.

Chapter 7

Grandpa

爺爺

GRANDPA WAS MY morale cheerleader. He saw the opposite in me as Grandmother did.

"My darling Mei Mei, brightest child ever!" Grandpa would smile, his eyes sparkling joy.

"She's nothing but a worthless female piece." Grandmother would frown at me.

"Dian-dian-jiu-xing 點點就醒 — *one slightest hint*, she gets it!" Grandpa would say, beaming and looking at me lovingly.

"She's just nosy. 狗咬一聲就在頭 At the first dog barking, she's leading the pack!"

"Why can't you be like Mei Mei?" Grandpa would scold my aunt Er Gu, his youngest daughter, whom Grandmother threw into the urine pot to drown at birth. "Not even a fraction of Mei Mei's brain!" He was frustrated with Er Gu's slow brain and untidy clumsiness. "It's all your fault," he'd turn to Grandmother, the only time he was brave enough to speak up against her. "You wretched woman. The urine damaged her brain."

"Oh, shush!" Grandmother would snap her face away. "She was just born stupid."

As her parents argued, Er Gu sat quietly, her head hung low. But no one ever noticed the special trait she had but neither of her two smarter siblings did: a trusting and soft heart.

"Dumb idiot!" I'd follow everyone's example and yell at Aunt Er Gu. And I'd even throw rocks at her when I was mad, usually after Grandmother roughed me up. But Grandpa was still amused by my childish bullying tantrum. "He-He-He . . ." Grandpa would chuckle. His darling granddaughter Mei Mei could do no wrong.

Grandpa and I were like two peas in the pod. He'd chuckle. I'd giggle. And making my pig-snout faces and cracking jokes could keep Grandpa entertained and forget all his worries.

I was happiest when Grandpa walked into the yard from toiling all day. His face would brighten up. My best memory was when he opened his hand showing me the most amazing magic: a couple of bright red wild berries! Overjoyed, I'd jump up and down. They were not only lifesaving food, but exquisite art in my child's eyes. The prettiest red color I'd ever seen. Grandpa had saved them all day for me in his pocket. Bright berry red remains my favorite color.

How I loved the times when Grandpa didn't disappear into the commune's cornfields behind the massive South Mountain all day. I'd follow him around watching him do his chores: bunching together and stacking up the ears of corn around the thick wooden pole in front of the house and carrying them up to the attic when dried; sharpening his sickle on the flat stone; ax-splitting firewood.

I enjoyed watching Grandpa making tofu on the *kang*. First, he'd grind a bucket of soybeans, soaked soft in the basin overnight, with a miniature stone-milling grinder. Then he'd light up the fire with twigs in the brick stove. The finely ground soybean milk was boiled in the cast iron caldron. As the liquid came to boiling, he'd sprinkle half bottle of a special conditioning liquid, 鹵水, to make soybean liquid condense into solid. Then he'd dish out the now-soft solid mixture into a big wicker-woven basket sitting over a three-feet-tall clay storage jar to let drain into solid tofu. And finally he'd cut the tofu into 4 x 4 inch squares, ready to be stir-fried to celebrate the special Lunar New Year or the August 15th Moon Festival.

Grandpa was a rare and fine scholar among the Red Stone Bridge villagers. His parents lived thriftily and saved diligently to send him to school. He had actually graduated from the village's primary school of the sixth grade. He could have stayed in the city, making a leisurely living as an accountant, with health insurance, salary, guaranteed pension and privileged social status after his service in the army. But Grandmother had made him come back home to Red Stone Bridge to fulfill his filial duty taking care of his aging parents.

It happened right before the Communist government locked down China's countryside, 85 percent of the nation's population. No peasants were allowed to move to live in any town or city. They were forced to forever remain peasants to send their harvest of grains for the city dwellers to live on but receive no health insurance or even a penny from the government. And their children and grandchildren for generations to come would also forever be peasants. A massive second-class was thus created. They toiled until one day they dropped dead in the fields or couldn't get out of bed.

Grandpa could've been a fine artist, too. For he knew how to draw luscious bright red peony flowers, lovely green trees, singing birds, majestic mountains and flowing rivers as if they were real and alive. He could brush-write handsome and finest looking Chinese calligraphy. Every year, in celebrating the Lunar New Year, he'd write calligraphy characters on red scrolls and paste them on our house door frames.

I was Grandpa's best helper, grinding the ink stick in the palm-sized round stone ink tray for him to dip his brush in. He praised me for being very careful and never spilling a drop of ink. After writing each character, Grandpa would patiently show me how to read it. Many villagers would ask Grandpa to write on their red scrolls. He was always happy to oblige, and never charged anyone a penny. Grandmother complained about his "useless" kindness.

At break time after a whirling-wind of chores, Grandpa would sit on the floor stool, his back against the tall black floor chest facing the door, his eyes half closed, his mind far away. I'd been waiting for this precious do-nothing moment to have some fun. Like a happy chirpy bird, I climbed on Grandpa's back, craning my neck to make my "piggy snout" faces at him to make him smile and chuckle and call his mind back from far away. I giggled while my heart sang. Grandpa stood up to give me a piggyback ride, strolling back and forth on our small brick and dirt floor, humming in rhythm to his self-made happy tune:

"Chin-chin ye-chin-chin; chin-chin-ye-chin ye-chin-chin . . ."

I giggled louder while Grandpa chuckled heartily. Our happiness always made Grandmother irritated. "Get down!" she'd yell. "Worthless female piece! What makes you think you're so special to be pampered like that?" But it felt so good gluing my face on Grandpa's back. I loved his scents on his coarse, black cotton cloth shirt collar, a mixture of his sweat, pine needles and cones, warm sunshine and earth from the deep mountains and open fields.

"You hear me?" Grandmother yelled louder at me. "Look at you, big and heavy like a donkey! You want to break your weakling grandfather's back so we all starve to death? Do you see any other male in this house to bring in food to keep us fed and alive?"

I ignored Grandmother and pressed my face harder into Grandpa's back, holding on as tight as I could. Her claw-like hands jerked me off his back and in a flash, I crashed down to the thorny reed-woven mat covering our brick and mud *kang*.

I'm sorry, my child, Grandpa's sad eyes said to me. He then sat back down on his small wooden floor stool, his back against the big, black floor chest, his eyes closed halfway, and his mind faraway . . .

Chapter 8

Laughter with Lao Ye Ye

我的老爺爺

LAO YE YE WAS my great grandfather, father of my grandpa. Like father, like son, both of them were quiet men of few words, very good-natured. And both of them were frequent targets for the big bully men in charge of the village.

Lao Ye Ye toiled in the cornfields all his life until he lost his eyesight. He lived with his senile wife, my great grandmother, in the west facing house, across from my grandparents' east-facing house, in the Li's square courtyard with a peach tree. Great grandmother was a simple-minded and good-natured woman. She'd burst out giggling nonstop whenever she heard someone farting. No matter how much Lao Ye Ye scolded her, she couldn't stop giggling and laughing.

Confined indoors all day, Lao Ye Ye babysat me. He was another Heaven-sent gift to me after my milk mother. For lack of basic nutrients in my hungry little tummy, he made it up by nurturing my spirit with his loving heart. His home was much needed peace and tranquility, away from my grandmother's nagging and yelling.

My earliest happy memory was giggling and laughing all day with Lao Ye Ye. His family bed *kang* was my romper room. My playground was his yellow earthen yard, where Lao Ye Ye carried me on his back, strolling and humming, just like his son, my loving grandpa, did me. We played together there in the warm golden sun.

Lao Ye Ye laughed a lot. When he laughed, his long, white beard shook up and down, his droopy eyelids half covering his cloudy gray, blind eyeballs. He made me laugh hard when he tickled me under my arms, on my tummy, and in the middle of my feet.

"*Ds ds guo guo, ds ds guo guo!*" my agitated grandmother would yell from across the courtyard. "The oldest, the youngest, you two have no dignity! What's there to be happy about?"

Grandmother was like a dried corn cob, scraping hard.

I loved the game Lao Ye Ye and I played every day. It went like this:

"Cai Mei, time to take Lao Ye Ye to the main street," Great Grandpa would say.

"OK, Lao Ye Ye." I'd fetch and put his shoes under his dangling, waiting feet wearing his homemade cloth socks. Then I'd bring over his walking cane from behind the carved pinewood door by the three-feet-tall water storage clay jar.

"Lao Ye Ye, let's go!" My right hand would pick up his left hand. Together we'd stride across the foot-high pinewood threshold. And out we'd go into the bright earthen yard under the clear blue sky and bright warm golden sunshine.

I'd giggle secretly while leading my blind great grandpa Lao Ye Ye. Plotting my naughty plan, I was up to no good. Holding my excitement and giggling under my breath, I'd tiptoe, leading my blind great grandfather Lao Ye Ye straight to the dead corner of the courtyard enclosed by a tall wall of river rocks. Then I'd let go of his hand.

"OK, Lao Ye Ye. Here you are, the main street. Go ahead, walk on yourself," I'd cover my mouth, giggling secretly.

"Really, this is the main street?" Lao Ye Ye raised his cane, poking in front of him.

"Yeah, go ahead. Go on walking a few more steps, you'll be right there, the main street!" I'd bend down, laughing quietly.

"Oh, you rascal, Mei Mei," Lao Ye Ye would say endearingly. "This is not the main street." His walking cane would touch the stone wall. How I'd then burst into loud laughter, jumping up and down, and clapping my hands, until my tummy hurt.

"Oh, you little rascal. You tricked Lao Ye Ye! Get over here, let me see how you tricked your Lao Ye Ye." He'd open his arms, standing in place, waiting for me to jump into his arms to get my rewarding hug. Together we'd giggle and laugh some more.

The next day, and the next, and the next day after that, we'd play our favorite game of "Taking Lao Ye Ye to the main street" over and over, again and again.

I eventually ventured out of Lao Ye Ye's loving, confined care to play outside on my own in the wilderness all over the village.

One day while playing outside in the street around the corner from our courtyard, I heard people crying. It sounded odd because they weren't children's crying voices. I ran back home. The crying was coming from inside Lao Ye Ye's house. I rushed in and saw him lying under his cotton padded quilt, face up in the middle of the *kang*, his eyes closed, his face as white as his long beard quietly resting under his chin.

Lao Ye Ye's three sons, Grandpa and his two old-men brothers, were kneeling alongside his body. All three of them had their heads bowed. So, it was they who were crying out loud! Their tears were flowing down their faces, their running noses dripping onto Lao Ye Ye's quilt covering him. I'd never seen Grandpa crying. Why was Grandpa crying like a child?

"Lao Ye Ye," I shook his feet in white socks under the quilt that covered him. But Lao Ye Ye didn't hear me. He wasn't moving and wouldn't wake up.

Sad and confused, I ran outside into the yard, wanting somebody to tell me what was going on. Grandmother was rushing over across the yard, holding in her arms a large *bo-qi* a wicker-woven container shaped like a giant shovel with three sides up.

"Grandmother, what's going on? What happened to Lao Ye Ye?" I tugged at her sleeve.

"Get out of my way!" Grandmother yelled at me, jerking her sleeve free. She was in a bad mood. Like always. "What do you think happened, dumb idiot? Out of my way!" Grandmother glared at me, trudging away into the south-facing house, home of Grandpa's brother.

The quiet courtyard was getting crowded, as more and more adult villagers arrived. They rushed and bustled around me, too busy to notice a small girl. Everyone was busy, except me. I was too young to know they were preparing for Lao Ye Ye's funeral. And no one ever explained to me what happened to my beloved Lao Ye Ye.

Chapter 9

Portrait of a Sore Winner

不得意的勝利者

1960. Taiyuan City, at the studio of Ding Zhang.

I WAS FOUR. My grandparents took me to visit my parents living in Taiyuan City for the first time. In this family photo, I sat centered on the tall stool wearing my new clothes: my pretty blue and pink floral pants, new socks and shoes, handmade from scratch by Grandmother. I was wearing my special red velvet hat. Grandpa sat on my right side, Grandmother on the left. Standing at the back were my parents: my mother, twenty-five, my father, twenty-nine.

Sitting in Grandmother's lap was Nimble, my younger brother. He was two-and-one-half years old. He was also born two months premature like me. But unlike me, he remained a sickly child, and much smaller for his age.

Not yet in this family photo was Cricket, my youngest brother. He wouldn't be born until three years later, in 1963.

Notice my grandmother's small bound feet. They looked almost the same size as my toddler brother's cotton-padded loafers.

Growing up looking at this photo on the earthen wall of my grandparents' one-room house, I never thought of anything unusual. That is, until now, over four decades later, when I'm living in America.

My mother's gloomy face remained the same. But my father's face looked different in the photo. Gone was his usual half-toothy, awkward and shy smile. Even Grandpa looked stressed, too.

Notice how annoyed my little face looked. My "pig snout mouth" was sticking out. My right hand was nervously pinching at my beautiful floral pant leg above my right knee. Something unpleasant must've happened right before this photo was taken. But, what?

I searched my memory but recalled nothing about that moment, although I *did* have a vivid memory of a lot of things during that visit in my parents' small, one-room apartment: my mother's silent eyes and gloomy face that frightened me, and her smiling face and loving eyes for my brother Nimble while holding him in her arms.

I also remembered wondering why Grandmother didn't get mad at me or smack me as she did back home in the village. Forceful and harsh grandmother no more, only a calm and mild grandmother. She talked to me patiently, half-heartedly, when once trying to stop me from eating out of a bowl of stir-fried cabbages. My mother had just bought it from her factory's cafeteria.

"My darling child," Grandmother said to me demurely, instead of harshly. "Mei Mei, sweetie, please stop eating now. It's for everyone to share at the meal time." But she showed no sign of smacking me, so I ignored her, too hungry to even mind my mother's silent eyes.

I was too young to understand that China was at the peak of its disastrous manmade famine. That small dish of stir-fried vegetables was the only dinner for the entire family, the six of us. To make matters worse, I burst out a cheer holding up my chopsticks: "Look, I found a meat!"

"Well, good for you!" My mother's sarcastic tone was wasted on my four-year-old blissful ignorance.

I also remembered crying one night at bedtime, which caused my father to yell at me. The fiery, itchy, tiny, wiggly worms were crawling in and out of my bottom again. Holding my rear end up in the air, I begged Grandmother to pick them out for me. That was how it was done back home in the village. But strangely, Grandmother wouldn't help me. She kept pushing me down: "Behave yourself! There aren't any worms."

So many things I remembered vividly, except the moment frozen in this family photo.

I had to find out. I called my father in China. It was 2007.

"Dad, why was I looking so unhappy in the photo?"

"Why else?" my father was quick to answer, as if he remembered it from yesterday. "Always your stubbornness. You insisted sitting on that special centerpiece tall stool. But we planned for your brother Nimble to sit on it. You know, he's the boy, our Li family's roots. You're only a girl, not supposed to be centered. We wanted you to sit on the side in your grandmother's lap. But, no, you just wouldn't listen to reason, kicking and screaming, wanting the stool for yourself. After we peeled you away from the stool, we couldn't drag you off the floor. You caused such a disturbance. It was embarrassing. The studio staff finally lost their patience. So we had to quit fighting you and let you have your way. Always stubborn like that. Always wanted your way . . ."

I smiled, as my father told the story. Good for my rebellious little self!

Picture Perfect!

The photo below was a "makeup" so my brother Nimble could be properly "centered."

Look at the smiles on both mother and son.

What does it feel like being loved by your own mother? I'm still as wide-eyed clueless today as when I was four.

Chapter 10

I Will Eventually Swallow It!

我總要咽下去呢

GRANDPA HAD AN all-time favorite story to tell about me.

A horse had died in the village. Its meat was divided among the villagers. Grandpa brought home his portion, a palm-sized piece of horse meat. Grandmother cut it into bite-sized pieces. She sizzled it in the small, black cast-iron wok with a few drip-drops of vegetable oil she kept hidden in a black jar under the floor chest.

The smell of meat cooking made my mouth water. I couldn't wait to taste it. But to my great disappointment, Grandmother moved the wok to the back of the brick stove and promptly covered it with its wooden lid.

"No eating right now. That's for later!" Grandmother eyed me hard sideways.

I planned my move. She didn't call me a "born-stubborn dog" for nothing. As soon as her back was turned, I grabbed the chopsticks, at a flying speed, and snatched the biggest piece of horse meat. In a flash, it was in my mouth. It was burning hot but too delicious for me to care.

"Spit it out!" Grandmother yelled. "It's too big for your mouth! You'll choke to death!"

"He-He-He! . . ." Grandpa chuckled, looking greatly amused, sitting on his floor stool.

"No!" I jerked my head away as Grandmother tried to pry open my mouth. "Watch me! I will eventually swallow it!"

Swallow it, I did, my cheeks bulging, my neck stretching like a juvenile rooster.

Grandpa cheered me on. Grandmother tossed me her dirty looks.

"I will swallow it eventually!" Grandpa would chuckle heartily, telling the story for years to come.

I still remember my childhood "snacks" during those famine years.

"Grandmother, I'm hungry." I'd come back home from playing outside, begging.

"Hungry, hungry, all you know is eat!" Grandmother would yell, glaring at me. "What made you think I have anything for you? Do you think your weakly grandfather can bring extra food home like those Communist cadre leaders in power?"

But I knew there was always something Grandmother squirreled away somewhere in the house. Everyone in Red Stone Bridge knew that. Other villagers broke their pennies in half; Grandmother broke hers in four. She always managed to put away something for rainy days, no matter how little there was to begin with.

When many villagers' chimneys remained smokeless because there was not a single grain of millet left to make a bowl of soup, Grandmother always had something hot being boiled in our big, cast-iron wok. Even just some hot water when things got really bad. She made our food last by adding extra water or by grinding the shells of grain into the flour.

As I cried and begged, Grandmother would sometimes give in. Taking off her tiny pointed shoes, she climbed up to the *kang* and knee-walked to the corner. Standing up, she'd reach into a bamboo basket hanging on a big iron hook dangling from the corner of the pinewood ceiling. As my eyes fixed on her hand, a small dried steamed bun appeared, left over from the Chinese New Year's feast, with green dots of mold on it. Sitting back down, Grandmother cracked the rock-hard steamed bun over the pinewood edge of the *kang*. The shining silky thread was stretching out between the two broken pieces like a spider's web.

"Eat slowly," Grandmother would say, handing me the walnut-sized piece. I nibbled on my precious snack. The dots of green mold didn't bother me. It was part of the delicious. And for the rest of my life, I couldn't bring myself to waste a single grain of food. And sometimes I still can't resist the urge to lick my plate clean when no one is around!

But a tiny piece of dried steamed bun from New Year's leftovers wasn't always there. And when I cried from hunger, Grandmother would open the top of shining black floor chest to take out her treasured bundle of scraps: odds and ends of cut-out cloth from her sewing. Tucked among them was some dried herbal licorice, 甜草根, sweet grass roots, a special traditional healing medicine for coughs. Grandpa had dug them out in the deep mountain trails.

Grandmother carefully broke off an inch or two.

"Chew it slowly. Don't eat it up all at once." Grandmother held it up high out of my reach and made me promise.

Amazing how I survived and grew up to be 5'7" tall. With my brain intact!

Chapter 11

My First Watermelon

西瓜

ONE BRIGHT SUNNY DAY, I was playing with my little girlfriend Love Lily by the clear-water creek that divided the village into the west end and east end. We were making mud cakes and singing at the top of our voices the village kids' mud-cake song: "ba-er ba-er da huo shao . . . san gen nian nian da huo shao . . ." We were having great fun churning out mud cakes just like the adult villagers did their mud-oven-baked bread in the annual harvest fair.

"Love Lily! Love Lily! Come over here!" Love Lily's grandmother was waving her hand, standing a few feet away. Why didn't she just walk over here? My child's mind wondered.

"No, I don't want to. We are making our mud cakes!" Love Lily yelled back.

"Come on, sweetie! Come home with Grandma." Love Lily's grandmother hurried over to take her hand. Her face round, suntanned dark brown with chiseled wrinkles, Love Lily's grandmother was the Communist leader in charge of the village women. Her voice could be heard from all over Red Stone Bridge. Her nice white teeth looked like two rows of white corn on the cob. Her salt-and-pepper hair was in a bun at the back of her head, just like my grandmother.

"I've got a treat for you, a water-melon!" She bent down to whisper into Love Lily's ear.

"Yay!" I jumped up in joy because I overheard the magic word "watermelon" in her whisper. Tossing down my mud cakes, I jumped up and followed Love Lily and her grandmother. It was too exciting. I had never tasted a watermelon before.

"Oh, no, no, no! You're not coming with us." Love Lily's grandmother turned around to grab hold of my shoulders, turning me back to face our mud cake direction. "*You* are going to your own grandmother's home. *We* to ours." She took Love Lily's hand and walked swiftly away from me.

But the word "watermelon" was too delicious to let go. I trailed behind them. No fun for me at home with my own grandmother. She had nothing for me to eat, but yelled at me all the time.

"Turn around and go back to tell your grandmother they are selling watermelons in the store. She'll buy you one." Love Lily's grandmother's loud voice was cheerful. But I didn't feel the hope. My grandmother never liked to buy me anything. She'd yell, telling me I was nothing but a worthless burden to my weakling grandpa.

"Go on home, child, quit following us. Go home and tell your grandmother to buy you a watermelon before they are sold out. Hurry up. They are very sweet watermelons. Have you tasted a watermelon before? No? Oh, my, they are delicious! Hurry, go on home." Love Lily's grandmother kept trying to convince me, walking briskly ahead of me. Her house was around the corner from my grandparents' at the west end of the village.

I didn't miss a step, following them all the way to their doorstep. I pushed and squeezed myself in before she could close the door on me. Love Lily cheerfully climbed up to their *kang*. I saw a pretty, green-striped watermelon sat in the middle! Her grandmother rushed over to cover it with her apron and pushed it into the far corner against the wall.

"You really ought to go home now," she said to me, urgently. I settled myself on the small wooden stool by the *kang*. "I heard your grandmother already bought you a watermelon. Hurry home!" At her words, my heart skipped a beat, but my mind hesitated telling my heart it was too good to be true. My butt remained firmly glued on the floor stool. My eyes were fixed at the bulge under the cover of the wrinkled gray apron in the far corner of the *kang*. Love Lily started thumping her butt up and down, her eyes shifting from me to her grandmother, then to the hidden watermelon under the apron.

"Listen to me, child. For real I saw your grandmother bought you a watermelon." Love Lily's grandmother now sounded more convincing. "She's waiting for you to get home and eat it. Hurry before they eat it all up!"

But I knew that no one else was home but Grandmother. Grandpa left the house every day at the first rooster's crow to work in the faraway cornfields on the other side of the South Mountain, and Er Gu was in school. Who are "they" that are eating Grandmother's watermelon? I just couldn't picture in my mind an image of a watermelon sitting in the middle of my own grandmother's *kang* waiting for me.

I kept my eyes fixed on that fascinating watermelon under the apron – this one was real.

Giving up trying to convince me, Love Lily's grandmother climbed up to the corner of *kang* to take the apron off the watermelon and twirled it back to the edge. She then lifted up the big pinewood cutting board from the floor behind the door and laid it flat on the *kang*. Setting the watermelon on the cutting board, she drew the cleaver from the slot between the *kang* and the floor chest. Raising her arms high with the cleaver, she aimed. Swish! The watermelon was split right in half.

Wow! How pretty the inside was, red dotted with many tiny black seeds. A cool, fresh and sweet smell rushed into my nose. It smelled even sweeter than Grandmother's pumpkins. I watched as Love Lily's grandmother carefully and gingerly sliced the whole watermelon into small, thin, triangular pieces. The cutting board was now a puddle of red juice. Love Lily's grandmother bent down to put her mouth onto the cutting board. Whoosh! She sucked the juice right into her mouth.

"Mmm . . ." My mouth watered.

Are they going to start eating it now? I waited anxiously. But to my great disappointment, Love Lily's grandmother suddenly turned around to quickly grab hold of my hands and pulled me up from the floor stool.

"That's enough. Come on, you're going home."

I tried hard to resist, my butt pulling back, my usual tug-of-war style as I did with my own grandmother. But I was no match for her. The old woman was just as tough and strong, dragging me to the door. With a firm push, I was out. She quickly closed the door and latched it from inside. My shirt corner was caught in between the two-leaf doors.

"Open the door! My shirt!" I cried.

"Keep pulling hard. You'll get it out," Love Lily's grandmother called out from inside. Struggling myself free, I ran all the way home, feeling half sad and half hopeful.

"Grandmother, I want to eat watermelon, too!"

"Say what?" Grandmother yelled back. She sounded surprised. "What nonsense are you talking about now?" She didn't look up, sitting on the wooden threshold of the house, picking out small rocks and stones from the soybeans in a big *bo-qi* on her lap.

"But Love Lily's grandmother said you bought me a watermelon!"

"What watermelon?" she yelled, "Who in the world can afford to eat a watermelon but a ruling Communist cadre like her?"

"But they are selling watermelon down at the store. Love Lily's grandmother bought one for her. She said you bought one for me, too." I whimpered, realizing there was no watermelon.

"What? Who said that! What made you think I can afford to buy *you* a watermelon?"

I dropped myself down onto the wooden threshold, quietly wiping my tears on the back of my hands, picturing my friend Love Lily sitting on her grandmother's cozy, warm *kang*, eating piece after piece of that beautiful watermelon. I wished her grandmother were mine. I wished her mouth were mine so I could find out what that gorgeous watermelon tasted like.

"I just can't stand people like Love Lily's grandmother," my grandmother said in a lowered voice, talking to herself. "Making up stories like that to make my granddaughter cry. So you're generous? Why didn't you let my child have a taste of your watermelon? Such an insincere person. Always calling her granddaughter sweetie this and sweetie that! All lip service! I despise phony people like that. I'm a straightforward person, honest with a sincere heart. I don't know how to use fluffy words I don't mean. I just don't believe you really love your granddaughter that much."

Grandmother's words that day, for years to come, had me believe that love was not about expressions in soft tones, affectionate words or encouraging smiles; and that true love was all about harsh words, yelling, and restraining from material rewarding; and that true love was diamond-in-the-rough, sharp-edged, with your loving heart hidden behind your gloom and anger.

Chapter 12

A Born Stubborn Dog

天生一只倔狗

"A BORN STUBBORN DOG!" Grandmother's yelling still rings in my ears today.

Raised, the first eight years of my life, by my illiterate but brilliantly bright and exceptionally strong, peasant grandmother, I was in constant will-power battles with her.

Until I was born, Grandmother had no rivalry in her iron-fisted Li household. My good-natured grandfather was henpecked into total obedience. And my aunt Er Gu, was a scared rabbit in front of both her parents, my grandparents.

I remember crying a lot in the dark evenings, when the flickering kerosene oil lamp made spooky dancing shadows on the earthen walls, while hot steam was twirling out of the cast-iron wok where millet soup was boiled.

"Shut up!" Grandmother would glare at me, feeding twigs into the stove. "If you don't close your trap right now, I'm going to drop a piece of burning ember into it!"

I didn't feel like stopping. It felt good screaming out my grief.

"Are you going to stop or not?" Grandmother picked up the foot-long iron chopsticks.

Was she really going to do it?

Grandmother swiftly dug the iron chopsticks into the stove and picked out a burning ember. Holding it over the stove, she turned to look at me: "Shut up or I'm dropping it in."

I turned up my volume.

"You little demon! Come, open wide, let me drop it right in there!"

I could feel the heat under my nose. Reluctantly, I closed my mouth, muffling my sobbing.

"Waah!" I burst out with vengeance once the burning ember had been safely removed from under my nose.

"Oh, you little devil!" Grandmother reached for the iron chopsticks again. Out came another piece of burning ember, bigger and brighter, closer to my mouth, more intense heat.

"Stop howling or I'm dropping it in!"

I snap-shut my mouth, stuffing my boiling anger inside.

"You stubborn dog! What an abnormal spirit! Just like that bad omen mother of yours!"

Sometimes my non-stop crying took place in the middle of the night. And the more Grandmother yelled and spanked me, the louder I'd get. She'd suddenly throw off my cotton-padded quilt and drag me stark naked off the *kang*. Everyone slept naked at night. Clothes were too precious for tear and wear in mere sleep. Shivering with cold, I was dragged across the brick and dirt floor all the way to the door, screaming at the top of my lungs.

"You little demon, I'm going to throw you out to feed the wolf," she threatened.

"Why don't you talk to the child nicely?" Grandpa mumbled his protest, peeking out from under his quilt. The sole bread earner of the family, Grandpa had the honor of sleeping in the best section of the *kang*, the warmest spot by the windowsill, where the chimney tunneled through underneath the cooking stove. "You don't have to be that rough with the child."

"Talk?" Grandmother turned to roar and glare at Grandpa. "Have you ever seen a born stubborn dog like this useless female piece?"

Grandpa immediately became quiet.

"You damned stubborn dog," Grandmother gripped my head in her big hands and pressed it sideways to the wooden door. "Listen! Hear the wolf howling at the door outside? It's waiting to eat you alive! Stop crying or I'm opening the door and toss you into its bloody mouth."

"Don't open the door, please!" I panicked, stamping my bare feet on the cold dirt floor, my naked body shivering in fear of being eaten alive by the big, bad wolf.

Grandmother released her grip on me. I shot back onto the *kang*, into my quilt.

"Grandmother, please make me a golden red flower shirt." I came home from school with a new desire. The prettiest girl, Cherry Blossom, in my class was wearing one. Her big, bright eyes and long eyelashes made her beautiful. She even looked lovely when she cried.

"Oh, you cheap thin eyelids." Grandmother was irritated. "Always want what others have. What made you think you're special like Cherry Blossom? Her dad makes money working in the village's only store. Her mother loves her. How about you? Your weakling grandfather is nothing but a useless peasant."

I trailed Grandmother when she went to the store.

"Grandmother, look!" I called out excitedly, pointing to the high shelf against the wall on the left side of the room. A roll of luscious red and bright golden flowery cloth stood out among the rest. She turned her head briefly in the direction of the cloth and walked to the door.

"No! . . ." I grabbed the back of Grandmother's shirt trying to pull her back. She was out of the store in no-time, dragging me behind. I burst out crying, dropping myself into the middle of the dirt street in front of the store, flailing and kicking. Grandmother ignored me.

I jumped up to grab a fistful of dirt and rocks and threw them at Grandmother's back. She turned to toss me a dirty look but walked on. My second fistful landed on her shoulders. Hobbling on her stubby feet, Grandmother turned around and came at me. Whack, whack! Her big, rough hands smacked me. I struggled with her, screaming and rolling in the dirt. She gave up and walked away. I jumped up and threw another fistful at her. She was too far away to be hit.

"What a feisty spirit this mere female child is!" A toothless old man grinned in cheer. He'd been watching while sunbathing against the store wall. A woman walked by, holding her small boy's hand, looking at me curiously.

Desperate, I dropped myself back down to the rocky dirt ground and cried even louder, only to watch helplessly as Grandmother slowly trudged out of sight.

Chapter 13

Tumbleweed in the Desert without Roots

無根的沙蓬

THE WORLD OUTSIDE GRANDMOTHER'S HOUSE always fascinated my child's mind. I couldn't wait to get away from her and play in the wilderness, on the hills, in the clear water of a small creek by the South Mountain, or hang out in neighbor's homes. Anywhere was better than home with Grandmother. As soon as I scraped the last grain of millet off my bowl, I'd take off running.

Under the bright golden sunshine and the clear blue sky, I was an unbridled free spirit, safe from Grandmother's yelling and nagging and her resentful dirty looks. A blissfully happy child, I was oblivious to the poverty all around me, singing and running around, my hair uncombed and matted, my face unwashed, black grime growing into the skin on the back of my hands and feet, and my sleeves stiff and shining from wiping my runny nose.

I'd pick and split the ends of a hollow stem (shaped like an American plastic drinking straw), then put it in my mouth to make the continuous popping sounds as I sang. The split ends of the stem would "pop," curl and finally "bloom" into a "flower." *Bao, bao, bao hua hua*; 爆,爆,爆花花; – pop, pop, flower popping; *bao ha yi duo hao hua hua!* 爆下一朵好花花! – out popped a pretty flower! My small child's mind and heart became peaceful and contended when I was alone, being nurtured by the fresh cool mountain breeze, warm sunshine, and clear blue sky. I could freely laugh out loud as much as my heart desired, racing myself all over the hills.

Occasionally a green jeep or an open-top, dark truck would drive through the village. I was so fascinated with the magic flying machine that I couldn't tear my eyes off it. How did its wheels turn so fast, but the wooden and iron wheels on the village's ox-pulled cart so slow? As the vehicle flashed by, I'd jump up from crunching down by the dirt roadside and chase after it in the clouds of dust. I loved the fragrant smell of gasoline. There was nothing exotic like it in Red Stone Bridge!

As the darkness blanketed the sky, I'd wander off into someone else's home instead of going home for dinner like other kids.

Sitting myself down quietly on their small floor stool, I'd watch the neighbor's family sitting on their *kang*, around their kerosene lamp. They made delicious slurping sound from eating out of their millet soup bowls. I was amazed how they talked to each other in a quiet tone. It gave me a strange, peaceful feeling. I forgot my own hungry stomach. Their tones were soft, their voices low, the peace and quiet was lulling. I wished Grandmother weren't so loud, yelling and nagging at everyone all the time: Grandpa, Er Gu and me. Why couldn't Grandmother be like these neighboring people?

Suddenly, Grandmother's yelling came from outside in the street. I pretended not to hear.

"Isn't your grandmother calling you?" one of them would say to me.

I kept quiet, sitting unmoved, until the neighbors' third and fourth urging me to go home to my grandmother. I'd reluctantly get up and walk out their door.

"Where did you go looking for your death?" Grandmother shouted louder and angrier the closer she came. Hands crossed over her apron, her tiny bound feet planted apart, she screamed, "You wild demon! Where have you been? You think I have time to wait on you? What are you? Tumbleweeds without roots? Don't you see other people eating their dinner? Who do you expect to feed you? Don't you have a roof over your head?"

Trailing behind Grandmother, I'd carefully stay out of the range of her bony hard striking hands.

Chapter 14

Peach, Apple, Grape, and Cherry

桃,蘋果,葡萄,櫻桃

IT WAS DRIZZLING. On days like this, lunch time took place indoors. Their chopsticks and clay bowls in hand, the villagers walked into their neighbors' houses for socializing. Seating themselves on a low floor pinewood stool or at the edge of the *kang*, they talked about everything going on in the village – marriages and engagements, weather and crops, family feuding, and so on, eating their boiled vegetables with a few precious pieces of grated cornmeal. Lunch was the major delicious meal of the day, mouths smacking, tongues slurping and chopsticks stirring up all that mouth-watering smell and taste of vinegar, chopped fresh green onions, salt, and red chili pepper.

Today's visitor in my grandparents' house was a teenage girl named Gai Mei, the second daughter of Grandpa Shui Min who lived around the corner.

As soon as the girl finished eating and stood up to leave, I sprang up from seating on the kang and knee-walked to the windowsill to see her off. "Just like a nosy dog!" Grandmother would toss me her dirty looks. Pressing my nose against the small glass panel, I looked out into the courtyard, where our peach tree grew by the earthen gate.

"Grandmother," I called out in distress, watching the teenage girl bending down to pick up a peach off the muddy ground. Swiftly she put the precious peach into her pant pocket and quickly disappeared out of the earthen gate, out of my sight.

"Why didn't she give it back to us? That's our peach!" I cried at the great loss.

"What can I do if she didn't?" Grandmother grumbled. How disappointing! Why didn't she act like her usual self, quarreling and yelling and fighting back for what was our Li family's? Grandmother didn't even let me eat a peach, but she let an outsider take one?

Our peach tree was lovely. When it bloomed, the pretty pink petals covered the earthen ground. I loved stringing them up with needle and thread to make them into a long string. And how fascinating it was when tiny buds magically appeared pushing up and away the blossom. Soon around the green leaves, there'd be clusters of tiny green peaches. Then they'd grow into big, delicious, and crispy green peaches with red tips.

Grandmother guarded the ripened peaches closely. Sometimes, she'd pick out a small and scarred one and let me eat it. What did Grandmother do with a tree full of delicious ripe peaches? I didn't know and neither did Grandpa. I never saw Aunt Er Gu, or even Grandmother herself, eat one. She must have sold them secretly to the neighbors and strangers passing through the village.

The commune leaders forbade villagers to sell any of their own food. Private sales were evil capitalism. It made socialism look bad. It was punishable by law with fines, confiscation, even prison time if caught selling anything from one's private home. Grandmother must have been pretty sneaky.

There was an apple tree in neighbor Gai Mei's family courtyard. It was much bigger and taller than my grandparents' peach tree. I was amazed by the beautiful sight of clusters of red apples growing on the treetops. Standing outside by their black-doored gate, I'd gaze up with longing. What did a red apple taste like? Were they as sweet and crispy as my grandparents' peaches?

One day, wandering into the village's one-room general store, I saw my chance. A basketful of apples sat on the floor behind the counter. They weren't as bright red as the neighbor's apples, but just as alluring. I ran all the way home, my mind racing and wondering how to ask Grandmother for money to buy an apple. I already knew the answer would be "No!"

"Grandmother, would you buy me an apple? They have them in the store." I asked anyway. "Buy you what? Who do you think you are, wanting to eat an apple? You cheap, thin eyelid, is there anything that you don't want? Where do you think I should get money to pamper you? Do you see me pee or shit money? What else do you fancy to eat? Ginseng? And you want me to climb up the sky to pick down the moon for you, too? You worthless cheap female piece, nothing but a burden of mouth to feed." Grandmother yelled at me in one breath.

As always, I plotted.

I waited one day when my grandparents took their after-lunch nap on the *kang*. Da Gu, who was home from her post office job, was washing the bowls and chopsticks at the outside mud stove by the door. Cooking took place outside during the summertime.

"Da Gu, here's the dish brush for you." I made sure she didn't walk in to disrupt my plan.

"Oh, what a thoughtful, darling child!" Sharp-minded Da Gu didn't suspect me. Yes!

Quietly and gingerly, I opened the small drawer where Grandmother kept her odds and ends. A twenty-fen paper note ($0.03 USD!) Quickly, I put it inside my pant pocket, not realizing it was equal to Grandpa's two long days of earning with his backbreaking toiling in the commune's cornfields.

I raced down to the general store, then halted at the door. What if the salesman found out that I stole money from home? I'd never bought anything on my own. What should I say? I decided to come back later in the day after dark when nobody was around.

"What do you want, kid?" asked the salesman, the only person in the store.

I didn't know how to ask.

"Does your grandmother know you are here?"

Resting my chin on my hands on the counter, I fixed my eyes on the basket of apples.

"You want to buy an apple?"

I nodded eagerly.

"How much money do you have?"

I opened my palm, showing him the twenty-cent paper note.

"That's all? Fine, here you are." He picked out the smallest and greenest apple on top of the pile and placed it in front of me.

I wanted a big red one. My mind protested.

"Go on home now." The man ignored the words on my mind. "Can't you see it's all dark? Are you sure you didn't steal your grandmother's money?" he said as he put my wrinkled bill in his money box.

I grabbed the small green apple off and rushed out, stuffing it in my pant pocket, just like the teenage neighbor girl hid our peach in hers. Nervous, I looked around. The street was deserted. Not a soul was outside nearby on the village's rocky dirt street. A gust of cold wind was twirling up dust into the air. My mind raced. When should I start eating the precious apple that was finally mine? I couldn't wait to taste it! I had to eat it before I reached home, I decided. Now or never.

Crossing over the clear-water creek, I looked around again. I was still all alone in the cold, empty street. All villagers were home now, sitting on their *kangs* around their small flickering kerosene lamps and slurping millet out of their steamy hot soup bowls.

Slowly, I took the small green apple out of my pocket. Eagerly I bit into it. Yugh! It was hard, bitter, and sour, and hurting my teeth! It was not crispy sweet like a peach. I lost my desire for it. Looking around, I quickly tossed the evidence of my theft into the creek, wishing it to flow away by tomorrow morning.

No one ever found out. That was the end of my fascination with apples.

For years to come, I never liked apples. Only after living in my beloved food paradise America did I finally fall in love with sweetest Fuji apples, the only kind that doesn't have a slightest tart taste.

One bright morning, I came home from playing outside, hungry as usual. My spirit sank when I was greeted by the silent, rectangular iron padlock on the two-leafed house door. Like all the villagers, Grandmother always locked her house door when she was away working in the commune's cornfields.

I pushed the two-leafed doors ajar to peek inside. I couldn't believe what I saw: a bowl of purple-green grapes was sitting on top of the big, tall, black floor chest. Where did they come from? What was the special occasion? But I knew they were not for me.

My stomach growled louder. How I wanted to have a taste of those precious grapes.

I pushed the two-leafed doors as wide as I could, until the opening between the foot-high wooden threshold and bottom edge of the two-leafed doors was the size of a small bowl. Dropping myself down to the dirt ground, face down, bottom up, I thrust in my feet first, then wiggled in my legs over the foot-high wooden threshold, then my butt, then my stomach and back, then my shoulders, finally my head, all in now! I was elated with a rush of happiness. I was now actually inside the locked house. My very first time. I felt strange but safe. The door was locked from outside but I was in! I rushed over to step on the small floor stool to climb up to the top of the chest, where the bowl of beautiful grapes sat awaiting.

How many grapes should I eat without being discovered by Grandmother? Gingerly I picked off one on the side. Mmmm . . . It was so sweet and cool. It felt so good in my mouth. But as soon as it touched down inside my happy stomach, a panic rose. I could almost feel Grandmother's big, calloused hands smacking me hard.

Swiftly I climbed back down to the floor.

Oh, no! My head suddenly became too big to go through the open gap I'd just crawled through. I tried sticking my feet out first. But only my legs and butt went through. My shoulders and head were stuck inside, my stomach flattened in between, and my face cheek-to-cheek on the dirt ground.

Stuck and panicking, I kicked and screamed.

"Oh, my darling child," a gentle, kind voice finally said from above me. It was Er Ye, Grandpa's brother. He lived in the south-facing house next to my grandparents' east-facing house inside the Li family's courtyard. "It's okay, don't be afraid." Er Ye was as quiet and soft-voiced like his brother, my grandpa. "Don't worry, child. Hold still, I'll get you out." He grabbed hold of the left leaf of the door and started twisting and turning to finally unhinge it, lifting the whole door out of its socket.

Er Ye picked me up and set me down on the dirt ground in the warm sunshine. He turned to put the door back in its socket. My body was freed, but my mind was still in shock. I couldn't calm myself down. Sitting in the middle of the earthen yard, I cried my tears of guilt and fear.

"Why are you still crying?" Er Ye turned around and looked at me, smiling.

Are you going to tell my grandmother about me breaking in to steal the grapes? I meant to ask him but my mouth didn't know how to bring out the words.

"Stop crying, my child, it's all right." Er Ye patted my head and went away to go about his chores.

Later that day, I tensed up when overhearing Er Ye telling Grandmother about me being stuck under the locked door. Oddly, to my great relief, Grandmother only shot me a silent, dirty look. She didn't hit me. Nor did she mention anything about the special bowl of grapes, which had now disappeared. I knew better than to ask.

Sweet grapes have remained my lifelong favorite.

Another day, I was running wildly around the village with a bunch of kids.

"Let's get into the old lady's yard," one boy called out. "She has a cherry tree!" We all cheered. I'd never seen what a cherry looked like. Everyone's stomach was growling but no one had any source of food. The old lady always stayed inside. She was known in the village to be too old and too sick to show her face outside her black wooden gate.

I was the last one to climb and jump over the wall.

It was really a cherry tree in the middle of the yard! And the cherries were bright golden and pink. They were much smaller than apples.

"Who is it?" the shaky voice of an old woman called out from inside the house.

"Run!" the bigger kids disappeared in a flash.

"What are you doing in here?" an old, frail lady in a black shirt and black pants, with a black wrap on her head suddenly appeared at the door. I froze, across from her at the gate. Her tiny, pointed bound feet – even smaller than Grandmother's – looked tidy in white socks and black shoes, her thin wrinkled face as white as paper. It reminded me of the dead woman's face I once saw, as her tearful son was putting a dark blue satin gown on her stiff body.

My feet glued to the ground, I was too frightened to move.

"You shouldn't have come into my yard without permission." The old lady's voice was surprisingly kind. It shocked me, because it was strangely pleasant. I had expected her to curse and yell like my grandmother.

"Go on home, child. Please don't come here anymore. Go out through the gate."

My shaky legs nudged me backwards toward the gate, my eyes fixed on the old lady's thin, white face and her black clothes.

Never again did I ever go near that kind old lady's two-leafed black gate. My curiosity to find out what a cherry tasted like disappeared altogether. The kindness of the scary looking but soft-voiced old lady permanently cured my desire to steal.

My childhood dream to find out what a cherry tasted like was finally realized two decades later in the 1980's when the government leader Deng Xiao Ping allowed China's peasants to plant, grow and sell their foods freely, as socialism had collapsed China's economy.

Chapter 15

*Scrambled Eggs *Stir-fried Tofu

煎雞蛋 * 炒豆腐

COMING HOME ONE LATE evening from playing outside, I expected the usual bowl of millet soup for dinner. But instead, I smelled delicious stir-fry in the air. Was my nose playing tricks on me? It wasn't the Lunar New Year, or the Mid-Autumn Moon Festival.

I dashed inside the house to investigate.

I couldn't believe my eyes. Grandmother was really cooking stir-fry with the small, cast-iron wok. A plate full of sunshine golden scrambled eggs was already set aside in the corner of the brick stove. How delicious the whole room smelled. No wonder Grandmother didn't go outside to yell for me to come home for dinner as usual.

Everything inside the one-room east-facing house was different tonight. It wasn't completely dark yet, but the kerosene lamp was already lit. And Grandmother wasn't alone. Two people were sitting side by side on the *kang*. A good-looking young man and a woman. Both were dressed clean and neat. They looked important. Their legs folded, their hands in their laps, they were quietly stealing looks at each other out of the corners of their smiling eyes.

The man was a stranger. He had long legs and smiling eyes. His nose was thin, his black hair shining and neatly combed up. I knew the woman. She was Aunt Da Gu, my father's middle younger sister.

I was too young to understand that it was a special event of meet-your-parents engagement dinner.

It was strange Grandmother acted as if she didn't notice me when I pushed the door open and rushed in. She didn't look up or yell "Close the door!" Instead, she was busy on her stubby three-inch-bound feet, waiting on the two people sitting on the *kang*.

Standing in the middle of the floor, I felt excited by the contagious air of festivity. My mouth watered while my eyes fixed on the two steamy hot dishes of scrambled eggs and tofu Grandmother now placed in front of the two guests.

How odd Grandmother still hadn't said a word to me. Neither had Aunt Da Gu, who'd never skipped telling me that my eyes were too tiny ugly whenever she came back to the village. And, Grandmother walked around me, as if I were invisible, shuffling on her unsteady miniature feet as she placed two pairs of chopsticks, two spoons by the dishes, and ladled out two bowls of millet soup and set them in front of the shy, happy couple.

"Please, eat while it's hot." Grandmother used her nicest voice, the one she saved for Chinese New Year's Day or whenever there were visitors or guests in the house.

Why was nobody seeing me? Da Gu and her man didn't look my way. They were busy smiling at each other. But why not Grandmother? Can't she see me standing right here in front of her in the middle of the floor? Any other day, she'd have hollered and shoved me out of her way.

My stomach growled loudly.

What's happening? Maybe I didn't stand close enough to Grandmother. I stepped up closer, craning my neck to look up at her face: "Grandmother, why are you cooking the special food tonight?" But strangely, she glided right away from me, as if I were part of the air.

"Please," Grandmother kept saying to Da Gu and her man. "Don't wait. Please eat up."

I glued myself standing to the edge of *kang*, my elbows on its wooden border, watching the two special people picking up their chopsticks and sending into their mouths piece after piece of the golden scramble eggs and quivering, tender tofu cubes. My mouth swallowed.

Something suddenly sank my heart. The special food was not for me! I ran outside into the yard, only to stop at the arched earthen gate. Where should I go? It was dark outside. Silent shadows were everywhere. My friends Love Lily and Pink Flower had long gone home to their families. Nobody to play with. Grandpa and Er Gu were nowhere to be seen.

Nearby out of the dark quietness came a donkey's faint, gasping cry. And the three brown horses around the corner by Mrs. Jia's house were neighing. The horses were nice to me and never kicked me. I passed by them every day and they let me stand close to them. They'd blink their long eye-lashed eyes, their legs gently digging the dirt heap they stood on. They'd nod or gently neigh every time I walked away, as if saying good-bye to me. Did they know now I was all alone by myself outside, having no home to go to, just like them?

Scraping my back against the earthen wall, I sat myself down on the square rock to the left of the earthen gate. The South Mountain sat quietly across from me, now in its silent and majestic shadows. At its foot was the South River roaring and rushing along toward the east end of the village. Are they crying sad tears, too?

"What are you doing out here in the dark all by yourself?" a voice asked. I wiped off my tears but was too upset to talk. I knew whose voice it was from — Uncle Lin Huo, nephew of Grandpa. His father was Grandpa's brother, who freed me the other day when I was stuck under my grandmother's locked door after trying to steal a bite of her special grapes. Lin Huo's mother died long ago. She'd screamed for many days while lying on their *kang*. Her stomach hurt, but the family had no money to send her to the hospital in the town of Guo Dao 郭道, forty-*li* away.

"Isn't it dinnertime for you?" Uncle Lin Huo sounded annoyingly cheerful. He was on his way to the well shed shoulder-poling two big, thick wooden buckets. It was one hundred yards between the South Mountain and our gate.

"Cai Mei!" Grandmother's yelling finally came after a long time. "Where are you? Dinnertime! Come back inside!" She sounded like nothing had ever happened, which made me more upset. I wanted her to come out and see that I was sad and angry because of the way she'd ignored me! But she didn't.

The darkness started to frighten me. My hungry stomach wanted me to get up from the cold rock to go inside for food and light. But my hurt heart and stubborn mind kept me sit still.

"You little demon! Come back inside right now!" Grandmother kept yelling out from inside the house.

I stayed silent.

"You still here?" Uncle Lin Huo was on his third trip shoulder-poling buckets of water. His steps were in brisk rhythm to his squeaky wooden shoulder pole, his two heavy buckets of water up and down at both ends. "Why are you ignoring your grandmother? What's wrong?"

I was in no mood to talk to him.

"Auntie!" Uncle Lin Huo snitched, calling out to Grandmother as he walked into the yard. "Cai Mei's sitting right here by the gate!"

Now I hated Uncle Lin Huo, too.

"Fine, you stubborn dog!" yelled Grandmother. "Just go ahead, don't you come back. I'm latching up the door so the big bad wolf from the South Mountain cave can come eat you alive!"

I sprang up and ran into the yard, terrified, feeling defeated, still with a lingering hope that the delicious scrambled eggs and tofu dishes were sitting by the kerosene oil lamp in the middle of the *kang* waiting for me.

The only thing waiting for me was a lone bowl of watery millet soup.

"Now hurry up and eat your dinner!"

"But I want to eat stir-fried tofu and scrambled eggs, too!" I whimpered in tears.

"Say what?! Where in the world do you suppose I get them for you?" Strangely, Grandmother didn't sound very mad, looking at me sideways.

Staring into my millet soup bowl, I could still smell the golden scrambled eggs and the stir-fried tofu cubes sprinkled with green onions that had been served earlier. My chopsticks lazily stirred the lukewarm millet soup in front of me and along with my tears, I managed to swallow the mess down my tight throat.

Chapter 16

My First Grade Teacher, Mr. Shi

我的啟蒙老師

FROM HEAD TO TOE, Mr. Shi stood three feet tall. He became my first-grade teacher because no full-body-sized Red Stone Bridge villagers could do mental math or write handsome Chinese calligraphy like he did.

After Lao Ye Ye, my blind great grandpa, died, I lost my daytime refuge for shelter, fun, giggling, and laughter.

Trudging on her stubby three-inch bound feet, Grandmother took me to Red Stone Bridge's primary school by the roaring East River. "No, my granddaughter isn't too young to start school," she argued loudly with the principal, Mr. Yang Wen Bing. Grandmother still held grudges against Mr. Yang, who was my mother's favorite teacher and the go-between to make my parents' marriage happen.

I became a first grader at age five in Mr. Shi's class.

A dwarf in physical size, Mr. Shi has always stood out as a giant among all my teachers across half the earth from China to America. He not only taught me how to read, write, and do math in my head, Mr. Shi instilled in me a lifelong joy of learning and planted the seeds of my self-confidence.

Most of us first graders in Mr. Shi's class were in rags, our stomachs constantly growling, our hands and feet black with grime, and our unwashed hair covered with lice. Many of us were as tall as our teacher. Some older kids were even taller. Mr. Shi stood the same height as the miniature blackboard on the earthen wall by the pinewood carved windows pasted with off-white soft paper. But we all respected and feared our teacher just the same. In his hands he held the ruling symbol of authority — *jiao-bian*, the teaching whip. The thin, smooth, round wooden stick was the same length as Mr. Shi's entire body height.

一日之師,終身父母 yi-ri-zhi-shi, zhong-shen-fu-mu: *Once thousand-year-old Chinese proverb, you should treat them with the respect and gratitude as you do your own parents.*

Mr. Shi was our supreme ruler inside our first-grade classroom. I was dismayed to see my teacher teased by the village men outside the school. Every day when Mr. Shi walked down the street during breakfast time or lunch break, crowds of village men would make fun of him. Sitting themselves on the stone slabs in front of their houses, or against the back walls of the houses that lined up the village's main rocky dirt street, they'd yell at him, competing with one another.

"Hey, Teacher Shi, hurry up! You're late for class!" They'd burst out laughing.

"Mind you, I got it. Plenty of time, plenty of time!" Mr. Shi laughed back, flashing his bright toothy smile. His chubby legs were almost the same length as his feet, shuffling hurriedly in tiny steps. His thick, heavy, square body tilted to the left, then tilted to the right. His pale long-fingered hands, almost the same length as his short arms, flapped back and forth, back and forth.

Despite China's ancient history boasting the value it placed on education, some Chinese sayings have been unflattering to school teachers: 家有五斗糧,不當孩子王 jia-you-wu-dou-liang, bu-dang-hai-zi-wang: *As long as I've got five bushels of grain to keep me from starving, I wouldn't want to become the king of school children.*

The teaching-and-learning arena inside our first-grade classroom was on the platform *kang*, which, like all other *kangs*, was covered with a thin, rough, reed-woven mattress. The *kang*'s height came to an adult's hip level, but reached the top of Mr. Shi's head. He needed us to help him climb up to the platform so he could teach us.

"All right, kids, come on, lift me up," Mr. Shi would call out to us cheerfully, panting, as soon as he walked into the classroom for the first period of the day. His smile brightened up the bare, earthen-walled classroom and lifted our spirits. At his command, we all rushed up to compete for the honor of helping our teacher. Some grabbed his tiny soft arms; some got hold of his short, chubby legs; still others pushed him from behind. 1, 2, 3! We lifted Mr. Shi's heavy thick-squared body up to the edge of the *kang* till he half-crawled and half-scooted himself all the way to the blackboard by the window in the corner of the room.

Holding his teaching whip, Mr. Shi automatically had invested in him the ancient power of a revered teacher to rule over us, his obedient subjects. He executed swift and equal justice for all offenders. The offenses included: not having remembered the lessons well, not being smart enough to answer his questions correctly, or looking away instead of looking at him or the blackboard, or whispering and chuckling with one's neighbors. The most severe offense was coming to class without homework, usually committed by naughty boys. He'd pick out a bigger boy or two and have them hold the guilty one face down and bottom up. Then Mr. Shi would raise his tiny arm and strike his enormous *jiao-bian* on the child's bottom flesh under his raggedy pants. As Mr. Shi whipped, the offender would cry out his promise to never, ever do it again.

Half a century later in 2015, I went back to China to visit my birth village, where I got together with several of my first-grade classmates. We talked about our teacher, Mr. Shi, our memory still fresh and vivid. And the guys merrily told about Mr. Shi's fearsome *jiao-bian*, and how they tried to outsmart him.

"I would mill around the thick, wooden pole in the center of the room that held up the ceiling. Mr. Shi chased me with his *jiao-bian*. But all his stick hit was not my butt, but the wooden pole! Ha-ha-ha," laughed Jia Cheng Cheng heartily.

"I'd cry out the loudest as soon as his *jiao-bian* landed on my butt, making it sound like I was dying of pain. So Mr. Shi would go soft on me." Wei Zhan Lu beamed proudly about his tricks.

But, yes, what a dedicated and efficient teacher Mr. Shi had been. We all agreed.

I can still see my beloved teacher standing beside the miniature blackboard introducing us to math. Ringing in my ears was a chorus of our crispy loud voices, repeating after our teacher.

"*Jia hao hao*," Mr. Shi read out loud, pointing at the plus sign, making it a fun rhyme by repeating "*hao*," the sign, twice.

"*Jia hao hao!*" we shouted in unison, sitting properly with our feet tucked under our folded legs, our backs straight, hands in our laps.

"*Jian hao hao*," we yelled out the minus sign earnestly, our eyes fixed on the blackboard.

"*Deng hao hao*," we shouted out the equal sign ever so enthusiastically.

"*Jia hao hao . . . Jian hao hao . . . Deng hao hao . . .* ha-ha-ha . . ." How those upper-grade boys teased and laughed at us during recess for our "baby" way of learning math signs like a nursery rhyme.

In the first year of my schooling, Mr. Shi taught us to write calligraphy, count and memorize numbers, and use a smart way to do math in our heads with double-digit addition and subtraction. He praised me in front of the class for remembering all my lessons well. The positive reinforcement was powerful. It shaped my own lifelong teaching career, with passion and compassion for kids of all ages, in both China and America. The smart mental math skills Mr. Shi taught me were firmly imprinted in my small child's brain. Today, I still do my American 1040 taxes in pencil and paper, hardly in need of an electronic calculator.

Mr. Shi built up my self-confidence in school like my grandfather did at home.

Every morning before class, the dusty earthen floor in our classroom needed to be sprinkled with water and swept with a broom. It was a chore for all of us girls, who took turns taking care of our duty. But one morning, Mr. Shi was hard to please. Two girls in a row couldn't do a good enough job. He said the first girl was heavy-handed and splashed too much water out of the washbasin, muddying the floor. And he criticized the second girl for sprinkling too little water in tiny drops, not enough to dampen the dry dust.

"Li Cai Mei, come over. You do it," Mr. Shi called my name. Having noticed the mistakes made by the first two girls, I tried to do the job in a medium way, using my fingers, not the whole hand as the first girl did, or not just the fingertips as the second girl did. I flicked the water out of the washbasin as carefully and evenly as I could while the whole class watched.

Then I looked up nervously at Mr. Shi.

How elated I felt that my teacher's annoyed face had broken into a broad smile.

"Very good!" Mr. Shi loudly praised me. "Did you all see how perfectly Li Cai Mei did that? Go on, finish up." He then nodded at me, entrusting me with sprinkling the entire floor. With my grateful heart jumping in joy, I tried to lock my smile inside my mouth, for girls were not supposed to smile broadly, but be modest and humble at all times.

A couple of years after I was sent away at age eight to live in the faraway city of Taiyuan as a household servant to my parents and two younger brothers, I went back to visit the village in the summer. One day while walking with several other girls, I ran into Mr. Shi. We were giggling and laughing and chatting happily when I spotted Mr. Shi in the distance. I felt embarrassed upon seeing my dwarf teacher walking up to me. I didn't know what to say to him.

Mr. Shi looked smaller than I remembered. In my memory, his short, chubby body was a strong, thick square, but now frail and thin. My face burning, my head hung low, I tried to walk by, pretending not to see him.

"Isn't this Li Cai Mei?" Mr. Shi called out cheerfully, stopping in front of me. "Hey, Cai Mei, you little rascal! How come you don't talk to me? Huh? Don't you remember me, your first-grade teacher? Is that what becoming a city girl does to you, forget your good old teacher? O, you little rascal you. How are you?" Mr. Shi was still the same with his heartwarming smile, looking up at me.

"I . . . am . . . fine," I mumbled, feeling ashamed of myself.

"It's so good to see you. Take care of yourself, okay?" said Mr. Shi ever so cheerfully, his eyes soft, his voice forgiving. He walked on, his long-fingered hands flapping back and forth, back and forth, his frail body tilting to the left, tilting to the right, just the way I remembered.

A few more summers went by. Grandmother told me that Mr. Shi had moved to the city of Taiyuan. "He stands in the streets begging for money and food. People were curious about him, tossing him money. He makes quite a bit every day. His nephew carries him on his back from place to place like a freak show."

A couple of more summers later, Grandmother told me Mr. Shi had died.

"Oh, no. What happened?" My heart sank.

"What else? He was just a crippled dwarf to begin with. He became too sick to stand in the street begging anymore. So he was carried home to die," Grandmother said matter-of-factly.

Tears welled up in my eyes. Afraid Grandmother would ridicule me for being such a sentimental silly idiot "like your mushy-hearted grandfather," I hurriedly stepped outside into the earthen yard to sit on the front steps of flat river rocks. Muffling my voice in my sleeves, I cried, feeling relieved that Grandmother didn't interfere by asking me why I was shedding tears over a mere dwarf.

Rest in Peace, Teacher Shi.

Chapter 17

My First Book

我的第一本書

I FIRST SAW a brand-new book when I was a first grader.

We first graders were lined up and quietly stood at attention on the earthen floor of our classroom. Today was a very important day. Every one of us was getting a new textbook! They were sitting right in front of us, on a worn-out, small, black pinewood desk with chipped paint.

A ray of bright sunshine drifted through the small, checkered pinewood window above the door. It lit up our classroom, shining on the bare mud walls, and came to rest on the big stack of crispy, brand-new, thin paperback textbooks. The pages were so clean and white they looked like new snow. I could smell the fresh ink in the air. I had never seen a brand-new book before, let alone so many of them at once! The only book at home was Grandpa's small notebook. It was all greasy and stained. He'd sit on the *kang* using the window sill as his desk writing with his fountain pen recording in details what he did for each day's work in the fields.

I looked around, expecting to see my classmates' happiness and excitement. But to my surprise, I saw none on those unwashed little faces with their runny noses. Why didn't they look excited at this very special moment? How could they not feel anything when looking at these beautiful, brand-new textbooks? Had they ever seen so many new books before? Of course not! We were all from poor peasant families. The only paper we had was a special piece of calligraphy paper we brought to school from home. With our own *mao-bi,* a brush made with wolf hair, we carefully wrote Chinese calligraphy characters on it. There was no room for mistakes. We made maximum use of our only paper for the day by writing in tiny calligraphy words between the lines of big calligraphy characters, like the tiny soy bean sprouts in between each of the corn rows in the fields.

And the only other kind of paper we saw at home was three pieces of long strips of red paper scrolls. But the scrolls were not even to be touched, let alone used. With big calligraphy characters of classic poems written on them, they were pasted on the door frames. And, they were to stay there throughout the year starting with the Lunar New Year's Eve.

That was all the paper I knew for the first eight years of my life. For toiletry, we used dried hemp sticks with their skin peeled off for making ropes or thin threads to stitch the thick sole of cloth shoes, or dried "silk beard" off the corncobs, or just dried, scraping-rough corncobs.

Facing the fascinating new textbooks, I couldn't stop smiling. But why weren't the other kids smiling? Couldn't their noses smell the brand-new pages? Didn't it remind them of the cool breeze of precious, juicy watermelon slices sitting on the wooden cutting board on a hot summer day? Didn't it also remind them of the cool, mountain springwater their dads, brothers, or grandpas reeled out of the well with a wooden bucket? Didn't they feel like it was the early morning New Year's Day when we were finally allowed to put on our new shirts, pants, and shoes after waiting the whole year? Why were they still dull-eyed and flat-faced?

Why was I the only one with a happy rabbit thumping in my heart?

You're such an abnormal creature! Grandmother's voice jumped into my ears. But my face just couldn't stop smiling. "He-He-He!" I suddenly heard a giggling slipping out of my mouth. Hurriedly, I smacked my hands over my mouth, my left hand on top of my right. Glancing out of the corners of my eyes, I was relieved that no one was stirred by my burst of happiness.

My heart drumming in joy, my hands over my mouth, I let my eyes smile and laugh quietly. The crispy new textbooks in front of me were as alluring as the delicious potstickers our family made sitting in a circle on the *kang* on Lunar New Year's Eve. I could hear the snow-white pages saying hello to me. My hands couldn't wait to touch them.

The teacher started roll calling. I stepped forward to get my precious copy of the brand-new textbook. I touched, admired, caressed, and smiled at it for a long time.

After school, I ran all the way home, holding my new book to my heart.

"Grandmother, please help me wrap my book!" I dashed into the earthen yard, out of breath, after running all the way home from the east end of the village.

"What now?" Grandmother yelled out, irritated as always, dragging her painful tiny bound feet out of the storage shed in the corner of the yard by the open toilet. She was holding an armful of pine twigs. It was time to start the stove and boil millet soup dinner.

"My teacher said we have to cover our new textbook."

"Who has the time for you? Isn't it enough you just spent a fortune on that book?"

"But I don't know how to do a book cover. My teacher said we have to do it tonight," I whimpered, panicking. I had never seen how a book was wrapped.

"Don't you my-teacher me. What made you think I know how?"

"But I got to have my new book covered!" My child's mind didn't connect with Grandmother's illiteracy. Grandmother walked into the house and came out with a half bowl of golden millet grain. Sitting herself down on the foot-high wooden threshold, she started picking out the little, fat, wiggly worms while waiting for water in the wok to boil.

I quietly wiped my tears on the back of my hand.

Uncle Lin Huo walked into the yard. He was Grandpa's nephew, son of Grandpa's brother. They lived in the sunny side south-facing house in the Li's courtyard. Lin Huo didn't do well in school. He had repeated the first grade several times. The villagers laughed at him for being dumb. Grandmother especially didn't think much of him, or his family. His mother was Grandmother's sister-in-law. Grandmother had often quarreled with her.

"Uncle Lin Huo, do you know how to wrap a book? Would you help me, please?" I asked Lin Huo in tears, holding out my brand-new textbook. He was my only hope.

"Oh, sure. I'll help you, sweetie." The teenager's kindness melted away my tears. I smiled, feeling elated. "Does your grandmother have some old newspapers?"

"Grandmother, do you have any old newspapers?"

"Where do you suppose I got any fancy newspapers? Don't you know I'm zheng-yan-xia 睁眼瞎 *open-eyed-blind*?" she snapped, but didn't look up, concentrating on picking worms out of the millet grains.

I turned to look at Lin Huo.

"It's okay, Cai Mei," he said, softly. "Don't worry. I think I've got some old newspapers." He dashed inside his south-facing house and came out with a wrinkled newspaper and a pair of scissors. The paper was from his older brother, a driver in a big city.

"Here, let me show you," Uncle Lin Huo's smile was comforting. His eyes were kind, the same light color as Grandpa's eyes.

"See, you fold the newspaper in half, press and crease a center line, put the book inside the newspaper along the center line to measure, and make sure you leave even margins on all sides." Step by step, this motherless teenager, who was ridiculed for not being smart, showed me how to wrap my very first book in life.

I smiled at Uncle Lin Huo, in grateful tears.

Chapter 18

"She used a bamboo stick to write her test! Ha ha!"

她考試沒筆, 用破竹席枝寫

THE BIG IRON BELL on top of the pole in the schoolyard struck, announcing the end of the early morning class. Time to go home for breakfast. I followed the crowd of kids out into the village's rocky dirt main street. There was a big crowd around the corner. They were mostly men and children. Women had no time to come outside and check things out; they were home cooking breakfast for their families. Men had just come back for breakfast bringing empty stomachs after hours of work in the cornfields.

I saw a long, wide sheet of white paper hanging high up on the side wall of the corner classroom facing the street. The crowd was looking up and reading it. I went closer and saw schoolkids' names written in neat Chinese calligraphy in vertical rows from left to right. Above each name, there was a number. I saw my name, Li Cai Mei 李彩梅 under the number 1. Nobody had told me that it was an ancient tradition that schools displayed kids' grades at the end of each semester in public for all to see.

"Wow, Number One is a girl! Whose family does she belong to?" a tall man in the crowd called out.

"I know! That's her!" A boy in my class jumped out, pointing at me. I hated that annoying smirk. "Her parents live in Taiyuan City. She lives with her grandparents. The old man's house is at the west end of the village."

I broke off running, away from the crowd, but too late not to get an earful of what I was dreaded to hear: "Her stingy grandmother gave her no pencil. She used a stick to write her test! Ha, ha!"

On that final examination day, as my teacher wrote the test questions on the blackboard for us to copy down, I suddenly realized, panicking, that I had no pencil to write with. Nobody ever had a spare pencil. It cost a fortune. Each of us used the same pencil until it became too short to hold in our fingers. Then we'd tie the stub to a stick and finished using it till we wrote the last stroke. I don't remember why I didn't have a pencil on that most important test day. Grandmother always yelled at me if I asked her for anything.

The classroom was quiet, except for kids' sniffling noises. I squirmed, sitting on the *kang* at my little black lacquered desk. Everybody buried their heads, busy writing their test except me.

My teacher looked up, annoyed by my quiet sobbing.

"What made you think you can count on anybody here to solve the important problem for you? Stop crying. Go home, beg your Grandmother. You miss this test you'll have to repeat the grade next year."

Holding back my tears, I scrambled out from behind my small desk and climbed down from the *kang*. Putting my shoes back on, I scampered out of the classroom and raced down the main street toward the west end of the village, but knowing with a sick feeling that no one was home.

Grandpa toiled in the commune's cornfields every day from the first rooster's crow till the darkness blanketed the sky. And Grandmother, on her pair of painful, three-inch stubby bound feet, was also called to work many days of the year alongside able-bodied younger men and women. She only came home a little earlier than Grandpa to cook lunch and dinner.

Out of breath, I saw what I feared. The rectangular iron padlock was hooked onto the iron rings attached to the two-leafed doors. I dropped myself onto the dirt ground and started howling like a lost wolf cub, hoping somebody, anybody to hear me and come to my rescue.

No one came. I was all alone, crying into the vast blue sky and warm bright sunshine. The three brown horses were quietly neighing standing by the half-worn-out earthen wall around the corner. No other voices, adults or kids, but my own crying echoed from the silent South Mountain and the South River at its foot, as if telling me to rush back to my class. Wiping my tears, I picked myself up to race back toward school.

The classroom was still quiet. Everyone was writing away. When my teacher ignored my reappearance at the door, I quietly scampered back up to the platform *kang* and sat properly cross-legged at the black square desk I'd brought from home. It was my father's desk when he was attending Red Stone Bridge's primary school. All the kids had to bring their own desks to school. Those who didn't have a desk at home sat by the sod windowsill and used it as their writing desk, or just used their folded knees.

Anxious, I looked around, from the bare walls to the dusty earthen floor, hoping to find something, anything, to help me to write my test. I perked up when my eyes came to the *kang*'s thorny mattress, braided in dried strips of reed. Quickly lifting up the corner close to where I sat, I broke off a piece of splint, the length of a match. Then I motioned to the girl sitting beside me, wanting to dip into her small ink bottle. I was overjoyed when she nudged it close to me: "Make sure your grandmother pays me back later." Gratefully, I dipped the tiny stick into her ink bottle.

But, alas, the bamboo stick didn't store ink on its tip like a fountain pen would.

Suddenly a pencil stub was tossed onto my desk next to my hand. I couldn't believe my good fortune! I looked up and saw my teacher's back walking away. I grabbed the lifesaving pencil stub and finished my test on time before the bell rang.

"Ha, ha! She used a stick to write her test!" How the naughty boys laughed their stupid heads off, pointing at me during recess time. I felt like crying. My feet glued to the playground, I didn't know where to run to hide myself, forgetting all about I was Number One student.

Chapter 19

"You ran home in the rain to get the umbrella?!"

冒著雨跑回家去取傘?

MY SMALL CHILD'S SENSE of logic was overestimated by my adoring grandpa, a simple man of few words.

Thunder and lightning suddenly broke out when we were in our classroom.

"How are we going to get home in the pouring rain?" we were all worried.

"I've got a good idea," Lan Zi, the biggest girl, called out, her eyes shining with excitement. Older and taller than all of us, she'd failed the first grade several times. We smaller girls thought she was the wisest of us all. We were also afraid of her because she liked shoving us around. "Why don't we run home to get the umbrella and come back? That way, we'll have an umbrella to use when school is over! Isn't it a great idea, girls?" She huddled us around her.

We all agreed.

"Who's got an umbrella at home?" Lan Zi looked at us one by one.

"I don't."

"I don't, either."

"We've only got a straw hat for raining days at home."

"Nah, a straw hat is no fun. Somebody's got to have an umbrella at home." Lan Zi turned her eyes on me. My grandparents were the envy of Red Stone Bridge villagers because their son and daughter-in-law, my parents, lived and worked in the city earning wages.

We did have an umbrella at home, but Grandmother never let me touch it. Only Grandpa could use it on rainy days. Afraid of her, I told

Lan Zi that my grandpa had a big, oil-cloth umbrella. And it was in pretty red color.

"Really?" Lan Zi's eyes lit up. "Let's go fetch it!" We all cheered and followed her.

Maybe Grandmother would be generous today when many of us asked her, I wished.

We rushed out into the pouring rain, five or six of us small girls, following the big girl, splashing our way through the mud puddles on the main street. Our homemade cloth shoes quickly became soaked, squishing water out. We ran all the way from the east end of the village to the west end.

Out of breath, dripping wet from head to toe, we finally burst into my grandparents' home, giggling and laughing.

Grandpa was alone, sitting on the *kang*, his back against the windowsill. Grandmother was somewhere up in the attic, busy with her chores. She never sat idling around, doing nothing.

"What happened?" Grandpa pop-opened his eyes from his quiet daydreaming as usual.

"We are home to get the umbrella!" I reported excitedly, proud of Lan Zi's smart idea.

"What?" Grandpa looked in disbelief. "How *stupid* are you! You ran all the way home bareheaded in the pouring rain to get the umbrella?!" Grandpa was so mad I froze with fear. He had never been so upset with me.

But why not? I argued inside my head. It was raining. We needed an umbrella.

Grandpa was still scolding at us when the sun suddenly came out. The thunder storm over, we turned around and walked back to school, in silence, our shoes squishing wet.

Grandpa was upset for a long time. "You ran home through the storm to get the umbrella?" I never mustered up enough courage to ask him what I did wrong to make him angry.

My quiet, good-natured grandfather wasn't able to articulate and explain to my small child's genuinely confused mind something so obvious from an adult's perspective.

This childhood incident helped shape me into a better understanding teacher. I make sure to always explain clearly the whys and hows to a confused child.

Chapter 20

My Soap! My Soap!

肥皂

"GRANDMOTHER, I WANT TO do laundry in the South River," I announced, rushing in the door excitedly, several girls from my second-grade class at my heels.

"What now?" Grandmother was sitting on the *kang* sewing and stitching a half-inch-thick sole she'd made from tiny scraps of worn rags. "What do you know about washing? You're talking nonsense." She looked harshly at the girls crowding the floor. She didn't like it a bit when I brought any friends home.

Earlier that day the girls had asked me if I wanted to wash some clothes with them at the East River. I was elated. Yes! It was my first time. But I'd asked them if we could go to the South River instead, across from my grandparents' house. They said okay and accompanied me home to ask for my grandmother's permission. We chatted, giggling and laughing like a bunch of wild sparrows.

Now Grandmother was saying no. Not knowing what to do, my friends became quiet.

"But I saw how people scrub their clothes on the flat river rocks at the South River," I pointed out, trying to save face. "I can wash your shirt, Grandmother. Look! It's dirty."

"Are you sure?" Grandmother hesitated, looking down at her blue shirt. Its front had turned grey. She wore it every day cooking, doing household chores, and working in the fields.

"Okay, then. Here is the soap." Grandmother took off her shirt, scooted over to the corner of the *kang* and found a tiny, thin piece of soap, the size of a copper coin, all dried up, chipped and curled at the edges.

"No, I want a new soap!" I refused to touch that pathetic-looking tiny thing. The villagers always teased me that I had a stingy grandmother. I wanted to look good in front of my friends.

"Why? It doesn't take much to wash just a shirt." Grandmother protested.

"But I want new soap."

"Always a stubborn dog!" Grandmother gave up. I smiled as she got off the *kang* to open the big, black deep chest. Out came in her hand a brand-new, 4x8-inch thick block of "pig soap" made from pork fat, color of pale millet. She cracked it hard on the wooden edge of the *kang* and broke rectangular bar right into two 4x4-inch squares.

"Be careful with it now. I'll take your life if you lose it!" Grandmother handed me a half.

"Promise." I sniffed the waxy smell of the brand-new soap, all smiles.

"Silly spirit," Grandmother lightly scolded me, and went back to her sewing.

I stuck out my tongue to make a face, wrapping the precious half bar of soap in her shirt, feeling rich.

"Grandmother Li, we'll help Cai Mei look after your soap," my friends chimed in.

Together we skipped happily all the way down to the South River at the foot of the majestic South Mountain.

It was a peaceful sunny afternoon. The water in the South River was so clear we could see the pebbles at the bottom. Everyone started looking for a flat rock at the riverbank as a wash-board. Spreading our laundry over it, we squatted down and started scrubbing.

I was surprised how big, heavy, and slippery the brand-new half bar of soap became after it was wet. At my very first try of rubbing the soap onto Grandmother's shirt, it slipped right out of my hand into the flowing river. Panicking, I reached down and grabbed it back up. But to my horror, at the second try of scrubbing it against the shirt, the soap slipped out of my hand again! And this time it was immediately carried away by the stream.

"My Soap! My soap!" I jumped up screaming, watching helplessly as it danced its away down the stream, scraping by over the pebbles and rocks at the bottom of the clear water river.

"Somebody, please help me!" I stamped my feet.

My friends all looked up, startled.

"Please help me get my soap back!" I begged the girl to my left.

"No, I don't want to go into the water. It's too deep," she said. The others all quietly looked at one another.

Then I saw a man walking my way up the river. I knew the tall man. He lived with his old parents just a few houses down from my grandparents'. Carrying a hoe on his shoulder, he was about to cross the river on the stepping stones. My soap was floating by where he stood.

"Please, Uncle, help me! See that soap coming your way? Catch it for me, please! It's right by your feet! See it? Please grab it! Grab my soap for me!" I was hysterical and delighted to see hope.

"Nay, I can't catch that," the neighbor man gave me a devil-may-care grin. I was stunned. He took a look down into the river at his feet, a menacing grin on his face, watching my soap flowing right past his feet. I couldn't believe it. He could've easily bent down to grab my soap for me! He was so tall the water wouldn't have even reached his knees. I couldn't understand it. Why wouldn't he help me? I had seen his parents smiling and waving hello to my grandmother.

"Well, it's gone now. Nothing I can do about it," the man looked amused, cackling. "Your grandmother's got money. You'll just have to ask her to buy you another bar of soap. You know you're going to get it from that stingy grandmother of yours." He strolled away toward the village, whistling merrily, his hoe on his shoulder.

I collapsed on the riverbank, tears of helplessness, devastated.

It never occurred to my small child's mind that this man's parents were probably among a number of villagers who resented Grandmother for refusing to lend them money. They all envied my grandparents of their son and daughter-in-law, my parents, working and living a in the city with rationed food that peasants were denied. But they never heard Grandmother, only at home, complain under her breath that her son and daughter-in-law never sent her a penny.

"What am I going to do now?" I was frightened at the thought of facing Grandmother. Her shirt, now wet and spread out on the flat river rock waiting for scrubbing. But I had no more soap to make it clean. Frantically, I started rubbing it against the flat-rock washboard, hoping it would get clean without soap.

The sun was setting. Time for me to face my punishment. The girls suggested that I sneak in and hung my grandmother's shirt on the shrubs by the gate and come back outside to play.

"Maybe by then your grandmother will forget about her soap," they all comforted me.

"Is that you, Cai Mei?" Grandmother called out. I froze. "Why aren't you coming inside?" She sounded suspicious. "Where is my soap? What are you up to? You evil demon offspring! Did you lose my soap? You really lost my whole new bar of soap? Bring it back to me right this minute. Or I'm going to skin you alive!"

"Run!" My friends whispered, peeking in from outside the earthen gate.

Tossing Grandmother's wet shirt onto the thorny shrub, I took off running, just as she trudged out of the house on her stubby, three-inch bound feet.

When it was too dark to stay outside by myself, I knew I had to come back to face Grandmother. When I did, I braced myself, taking in her brain-splitting yelling, feeling too guilty to cry when she slapped me. But no matter how hard she hit, she couldn't make me tell her what had happened to her precious, brand new bar of soap.

I learned as a child that I couldn't count on anyone for help.

Chapter 21

Dad Came Back — Down and Under

爸爸下放回村

AT AGE SIX, I saw my father for the second time.

One day my father just showed up at Red Stone Bridge, alone. It wasn't a visit. He started living with the four of us in the one-room house — my grandparents (his parents), my aunt Er Gu (his youngest sister), and me. No one said anything about his sudden appearance.

And hell broke loose.

None of Grandmother's yelling and smacking prepared me for the sheer terror of my father. He yelled at me angrily. I never knew where to sit or stand or how not to get in his way. He shoved, hit, and slapped me when I didn't know why. He forbade me to go outside and play, even when my best friends Love Lily and Pink Flower poked their heads in, calling me at the arched earthen gate.

"Stay!" he roared, as I jumped up excitedly.

"Sit!" he hissed, pointing to the small pinewood floor stool.

He covered the window with sheets and sat on the *kang* all day. He didn't even go outside to pee in the outhouse at the corner of our courtyard. He made me fetch the heavy clay night chamber pot from outside into the house. "Bring it over, closer!" he'd order, glaring down at me. Trembling in fear, I'd stretch my arm out, holding the urine pot.

"I said bring it closer, dumb idiot!"

Whack! His hand landed smacking the top of my head, lightning fast, his body leaping forward, his legs folded, sitting in the middle of the *kang*. "What the hell are those tears for?" He'd snatch the urine pot out of my hand, turn to face the wall and pee into it. Wiping my quiet tears on the back of my hands, I'd stand still, waiting for him to finish.

"Spill a drop, I'll kill you." My father handed back to me the urine pot, now heavy filled with his warm urine. I held it with both hands, my arms shaking. Gingerly and slowly, I tried hard to keep balance, walking toward the door, across the foot-high wooden threshold, into the earthen yard, finally to the outhouse. Carefully, I'd tilt the urine pot and empty it through the half-foot-wide squatting slot into the six-foot-deep manhole pool of urine and feces.

Ever since my father had come back to the village, everyone in the house had disappeared. Even Grandmother. She hardly stayed home anymore during the day, as she used to, cooking, sifting small, fat worms out of corn flour, picking pebbles and rocks out of red beans, grinding dried whole corn into flour at the stone mill. But now, she'd started joining Grandpa and Er Gu toiling in the cornfields every day.

I used to dread being with Grandmother inside the house. Now I longed for her to be home. I even missed her ear-piercing yelling. It was much better than my father's violent attacks. As tough and rough as she was, Grandmother now acted like a scampering mouse.

"Heavens," good-natured Grandpa finally broke his silence. "I can't take it anymore. What kind of life is this?" His hemorrhoids started bleeding because his beloved only son, my father, started mixing *ge-jian*, the pink-colored, pepper-corn-sized wild berries that caused constipation, into corn flour to make food last.

"It was awful to put up with your dad," Grandmother confessed to me years later. She rarely complained about her precious son, her center of the universe, who could do no wrong.

After Mao's Great Leap Forward movement failed in 1959, forty-five million Chinese peasants died from starvation after no more grass or tree leaves or tree bark was left to eat. And the city dwellers, fifteen percent of China's population could no longer be sustained by the rationed food. As the result, the government started "cleansing" the cities by dispersing people into the countryside to become peasants, who received no rationed food or medical care or any help at all.

Three kinds of people in China's cities were to be flushed out to the countryside. They were 1) "enemies of the people" for speaking against the Communist Party; 2) "bad elements" for being former landlords and well-to-do peasants; and 3) ordinary people with no anti-Party criminal background but were considered mediocre, weak, or sickly.

My father, a blue-collar geological surveyor worker, was categorized as one of the mediocre, the weak and sickly. He lost his salaried city job, his city residential "*hu-kou*" for rationed food, and his wife and toddler son. His wife, my mother, on the other hand, not only wasn't being cleansed out of the city, but promoted due to her outstanding job performance as the head secretary to the president of the Heavy Machinery Factory.

The humiliation and shame were more than my father could bear. He'd since bitterly found out, as a pampered only surviving son, that life was a series of disappointments, and the world didn't revolve around him, as his doting mother had made him believe.

On the eve of his scheduled "send-down" to his ancestors' Red Stone Bridge to become a peasant, my father decided to end his life. He wandered into Taiyuan City's Ying Ze Park and stood in front of the lake for hours in the ear-cutting cold wind.

"Your father was a coward," my mother once laughed, when I was a teenager. "He chickened out from jumping into the lake to take his own life. He said he was afraid the water was too cold, and he wouldn't stand it once he jumped in! Ha-Ha!"

My mother wished my father had taken after his mother's manly strength and resolute, her brilliant brain, articulation, and extreme capability; or his father's quiet good-naturedness, easy-going personality, soft, generous heart, and his thoughtfulness and kindness. But instead, my father took after all his parents' shortcomings and weaknesses: He had his mother's selfish stinginess, narrow-mindedness, unforgiving spirit, and her explosive temper, as well as his father's weak physical features, his timidity, and his paying too much attention to details like a woman.

Defeated in shame and anger, my father went back to square one: in the bottom pit of Chinese society as a peasant, his origin of birth, after all his peasant parents had starved themselves and toiled to keep him in school grooming him to live a leisurely city life.

Like a madman, my father took out his rage behind closed doors.

Grandmother couldn't take it anymore. Although illiterate with a pair of three-inch bound feet, she was brilliant-brained and quick-witted. She hatched a plan to rescue her beloved son by asking for help from her cousin, whose husband was the powerful Number One leader in Shanxi Province's largest coal-mining company in Taiyuan.

"Please help us," Grandmother dictated to Grandpa writing the pleading letter. "Our son is tormenting us. He's out of his mind making our life hell."

Her cousin's husband, Mr. Cui, agreed to do the special favor for his kinfolks. On one condition. My father had to obtain a reference letter from the mayor of Red Stone Bridge that said: Yes, Comrade Li, Bright Light, had been a model peasant after faithfully answering the Party's call to be sent down to the countryside; And that he had diligently earned 200 working points in the cornfields alongside the proletarian leading class of peasants; And that he had correct political thoughts and was red-hearted loyal to Chairman Mao by actively participating in the village's political meetings and events.

Alas! My father had never worked a single day in the cornfields. Since back to the village, he'd earned zero points. He'd been too ashamed to show his face to the villagers. But that didn't deter my grandmother. Trudging on her three-inch-bound feet, she went to plead with the village mayor, and successfully talked him into providing a truth-concealing reference letter.

My father was thus secretly ushered into the city through the backdoor. Now he was an accountant, regaining his *hu-kou* for rationed food and medical care, and reunited with his wife and toddler son. Elated at his homecoming, he at first didn't mind riding on his bike commuting four hours a day to and from work. But my mother refused to use her connections to move his job into her work unit, the Heavy Machinery Factory. Their marriage became stormier than ever. She complained about his stringiness for pinching his pennies. He accused her spending half of her monthly salary on her no-good lazy SOB brother, his wife and their "ugly offspring" back in her maiden village. And this was all on top of her presumed infidelity.

As suddenly as he appeared in my life, my father disappeared.

On the day he left the village, my child's heart cheered. I watched him climb into the one-horse wooden cart heading out of the village.

I was too young to foresee what catastrophe I would soon be facing under my father's reign of terror again. And this time the sheer terror was to last throughout my growing up years, from ages eight to eighteen. Even worse, it was to be joined by my mother's silent eyes and mysteriously angry face.

The darkest age loomed in the faraway city of Taiyuan, waiting for me to turn age eight.

Chapter 22

Miracle Scar

膝蓋上的傷疤

AT AGE SEVEN, I escaped death once again.

"Wake up!" Grandmother's yelling burst into the one-room house. She always started her day early when it was still dark, not even faint light coming to our soft-paper pasted window.

A rush of cold mountain breeze filled my nose as Grandmother burst in the door. Something was wrong with my leg, a very sharp throbbing pain on my right kneecap. Quietly I wished that the pain wasn't real so I wouldn't get in trouble with Grandmother.

"Get up already!" Grandmother yelled again.

"Grandmother, my leg's hurting," I whimpered.

"Your leg hurts? Whose legs are not hurting?" She was bending over the brick stove blowing into the stove to make the kindling burn.

"What happened?" she turned to frown at me, realizing something wasn't right. "Let me see." She flung off my quilt. "Old Heaven God! It's really swollen." She frowned, gingerly pressing on my kneecap, her thick fingers cold and rough. "How did this happen? What am I supposed to do? So busy I don't have time to breathe."

What was going to happen to me? I was frightened.

Grandmother told me to stay in bed. After breakfast when Grandpa and Aunt Er Gu had gone back to work in the cornfields, she went to Dr. Zhang's home around the corner. He was the only doctor in Red Stone Bridge.

"Oh, boy, it looks pretty bad. How long has it been like this?" Dr. Zhang's eyes were soft and kind.

"You'd think I should know. This dumb child acted like a mute idiot. I didn't know anything about it until this morning. Why in the world didn't you say something?! Don't you have a mouth?"

I felt embarrassed by Grandmother's scolding in front of the doctor. I also didn't know how to answer her question. I *did* have a mouth but I just never had the habit of telling her anything about me.

The pain in my kneecap had started many days before. Every day after school, several girls and I would walk to the fields with our bamboo baskets, laughing and giggling in the warm autumn afternoon sun. We were scavenging for leftover soybean stems in the after-harvested fields to help out our families. Every extra scrap of food counted. I tried very hard to fill my basket to the brim. I loved the feeling of being useful and giving Grandmother a reason not to yell at me. Not yelling at me was Grandmother's way of expressing her approval of me.

One day, I found myself having trouble walking fast enough to keep up with my friends. I was quickly left behind in the fields, alone. After dark, I still hadn't picked up enough soybean stems to fill my basket to the top.

"Why only half full?" Grandmother sounded disappointed.

For the next few days, the pain in my right kneecap became worse. I kept bringing home fewer and fewer soybean stems. "Why so little? Were you wasting time playing?"

On that last afternoon, I'd limped behind the other girls in the fields and helplessly watched them far ahead of me. By the time it had become too dark to see, there were only a few soybean stems in my basket, barely enough to cover the bottom. Panicking, I hurriedly went over to the edges of the fields and gathered some "ghost" bean stems, which looked like soybean stems but with empty shells. I knew Grandmother would be angry with me. But at least my basket had looked full for now. The pain was getting worse. I didn't care anymore and limped home alone in the darkness.

"Why so late?" Grandmother yelled down from the attic. Good, she couldn't see me. Relieved, I quickly shoved the basket in between the two big thick tall clay water-storage jars behind the door and climbed up to the *kang* to lie down. My leg hurt badly, my head dizzy.

"Why, these are all ghost beans!" Half asleep, I heard Grandmother talking to herself in a low voice, surprised that she didn't sound mad.

"Why didn't you tell me your leg was hurting?" Grandmother glared at me, as Dr. Zhang stood quietly by.

"Well," Dr. Zhang turned to Grandmother. "Looks like there's nothing I can do. Take her to the hospital in Guo Dao."

Guo Dao was a big town, forty *li* (fifteen miles) away. It took a good half day on a horse-cart ride to get there. Grandmother didn't say anything about taking me to the Guo Dao hospital. I stayed home. For days, I lay in bed dazed and in pain. The swelling on my right kneecap kept growing, now twice the size of my kneecap, puffed up and shiny in odd pink-and-orange color.

Grandpa sat quietly on the small wooden floor stool, looking at me, his eyes sad. He sighed a lot but had nothing of his own to say because he had to listen to everything Grandmother said. And Aunt, Er Gu, too, cried quietly, staring at me and wiping tears on the back of her hand.

Was I dying? Why did Grandpa and Aunt Er Gu look at me like that?

One day, while drifting in and out of sleep, I heard hushed voices over me, but I was too sick to open my eyes. One voice was Grandmother's, the other was that of our neighbor man Shui Min. Tall and broad-shouldered, with square-jaws and wrinkles chiseled into his sun-beaten brown face, Shui Min was the same age as my grandparents. I called him Grandpa Shui Min.

Grandmother admired Shui Min more than she did Grandpa. She'd yell at Grandpa for being a useless weakling man, saying that being his wife was humiliating. "Why couldn't he be like Shui Min, strong and resolute like a manly man?" she'd nag. When Shui Ming and his wife came to chat, slurping out of their meal bowls during breakfast or lunch times, Grandmother would often ask Shui Min for his advice on many things.

"Slice it open to let out the pus" the manly neighbor sounded resolute. "See the swelling? Poison blood in there. Get it out. Fast."

"Slice it open with what?" Grandmother said. "My scissors are dull, and my cleaver is not sharp."

"Why, don't you have a fine porcelain bowl? Break it. You need the clean, sharp edge."

"Well, does it have to be a fine porcelain bowl? Would an old clay bowl do?" Grandmother was still uncertain.

"Boy, you're a hard-core stingy woman, aren't you? Don't be this time. Sacrifice one of your fine porcelain bowls. It might save her life."

Grandmother had three fine porcelain bowls. They were smooth and white like hard-boiled eggs, each one decorated with a painted cluster of purple grapes. We only used them two times a year, for the Lunar New Year and Mid-August Moon Festival. They were forever associated with delicious handmade wheat flour pasta with stir-fried tofu and thinly sliced pork pieces.

"What if she cries and struggles?" Grandmother sounded lost.

"That's easy. One of us holds her down. Are you scared of doing it? Okay, I'll do the slicing. It'll be over before she cries out."

Oh, no! They were talking about me!

Horror gripped me. I couldn't move or make a sound. I wanted to cry and shout, *No!* But no sound came out of my mouth. I wanted to beg them not to cut open my already painful kneecap. I knew from my past illness how strong Grandmother could be when she held me down. She'd pinch my nose shut, pouring a bowl of bitter herbal medicine down my throat.

I started shaking under my cotton padded quilt, stained with tiny spots of blood from crushed lice and fleas.

I begged quietly for Lao Tian Ye, the Old Heaven God, to spare me. The voices grew dim and I slept.

The next morning when I awoke, I didn't feel any pain in my kneecap, but some strange weight hanging down on my knee. I flung open my cotton quilt to investigate. The huge swollen glaze was gone. In its place was a gigantic blister, like a balloon filled with water. I could see dark blood inside, swishing from side to side. I touched the skin but didn't feel anything. It felt like I was touching the bag of fresh liquid tofu Grandpa made. I had no fever.

"Grandmother!" I called out.

She came over, looked at my knee and her eyebrows raised in surprise. She quickly brought over her scissors and cut into my ballooned-up skin. Whoosh! Out poured the bloody, gooey pus. It filled her crockery bowl.

My recovery was swift and painless. The wound dried up, but the flesh never grew back on the left side of my kneecap where a deep gouge formed into an eye-shaped scar, mimicking one of Picasso's paintings. I've always wondered if Grandmother's relief that morning meant she was glad to see me alive or if she was simply pleased that one of her precious porcelain bowls didn't have to be sacrificed to save me.

Chapter 23

The Date-Red Horse

棗紅馬

塞翁失馬,焉知禍福? *sai-wong-shi-ma, yan-zhi-huo-fu* The ancient Chinese folklore told of the story about a wise old man, named Sai Wong, who famously said to his neighbors that one never knew if it meant good fortune or disaster when his prized horse was lost.

Grandmother told me a story about our family's precious horse.

Our Li family had a beautiful date-red horse. Tall and strong, it was in its prime. But one day the precious horse just dropped dead, with no illnesses or injury. It died not long before my birth, when Mao's violent "land reform" movement divided Chinese villagers into four classes, based on how much land, property, and livestock they owned: the landlords, the well-to-do peasants, the middle peasants, and the poor peasants.

The first two classes, the landlords and the well-to-do peasants, were denounced as the enemies of the people. It didn't matter how they'd acquired their land ownership: by family inheritance or through hard work and by pinching their pennies. They were subjected to public beatings and executions. And everything they owned, including their wives and daughters, were confiscated and redistributed to the "proletarian" poor class, many of whom were actually too lazy and unwilling to work. Their children and grandchildren were also guilty by birth. They were stripped of their rights to school or any promotion in life and were forever condemned as social outcasts to be the lowest of the low and poorest of the poor.

The mysterious sudden death of my grandparents' beautiful date-red horse must have been a Heaven-sent gift. It was so timely that it spared our Li family the ill fate of being labeled the enemy of the people for simply owning a horse. Instead, my grandparents were classified as mere "middle class peasants," subjected to no persecution. That precious horse's passing thus also saved the future for my father, who could freely go to school and get an education, and, therefore, it saved my future as well.

"Old Heavens!" Grandmother would whisper in a trembling voice. "The former landlord Su Lin Ze would shake like tree leaves in the violent winter storm, when he was called to the class-enemy denunciation meetings for public beatings and humiliation. Poor man, he was the most hardworking and thrifty in the village, pinching his pennies the tightest. He worked the fields alongside his hired hands and ate the same coarse food and wore the same type of raggedy clothes."

I remembered Mr. Su Lin Ze well. He was a quiet old man in black rags. He walked like a quiet shadow, his shoulders hunched up to hide his neck, his eyes on the ground. Mao's Land Reform movement threw him and his family out of their red-brick houses inside their grand, two stone-lion-guarded courtyard. They were jammed into their old small, dark tool shed as their big houses were confiscated and redistributed to three communist leaders' families.

As a small child, I'd once explored my way into the small, dark shed across from the stone-lion-guarded courtyard with tall, red brick houses inside. The former landlord lady, the wife of Su Lin Ze, was sitting alone on their *kang*. I'd never seen her outside before. An old woman in black from head to toe, she sat the same way Grandmother did: her back straight, her legs folded, her small bound feet tucked under her legs.

Something struck me about the old lady's face. It was a face of peace and calm. Her skin was smooth, plump, and pale from never seeing the sun. It gave me a great sense of comfort. I secretly wished my grandmother would make me feel as peaceful as this "evil landlord's wife."

Soon after Su Lin Ze and his wife were categorized as the enemy of the people, their son, Zi Quan, was expelled from his city job and branded as a "thief." Someone had stolen his handkerchief and planted it at a money-theft scene in the company he worked. He was now a dirt-poor peasant, toiling in the fields alongside his condemned father and grandfather for many years to come.

It fascinated me what a happy man Zi Quan was. Opposite to his scared-like-a-rabbit father, Zi Quan always wore a smiling face, humming a happy tune and cracking jokes, even when he was dragged onto the stage to be publicly humiliated and beaten alongside his father, while masses of peasants shouted slogans at them: "Down with the exploiting evil landlords!"

My grandparents' beautiful date-red horse was surely a Heaven-sent special spirit watching over me. I was to dream of a date-red horse three times: at the ages of twenty-one, twenty-seven and twenty-nine. And each time, I was to make a giant leap up the ladder in life and finally fly out of ashes, like the revived phoenix.

But for now, I was only seven going on eight years old, at my remote, deep mountain birth village of Red Stone Bridge. I had yet to first live through ten more years of the darkest age in my young life in the city of Taiyuan after I turned eight.

End of Part One

Part Two

Darkness Before Dawn 黎明前的黑暗:

Chinese Cinderella in Taiyuan City's Blue-Collar Dirt Yard — From Age Eight to Eighteen

Chapter 24

Arriving in Taiyuan City

來到太原

1964. This family photo was taken at Rising East studio, Taiyuan City.

STANDING AT THE BACK are my parents: my father, thirty-three; and my mother, twenty-nine. Seated in the center is my grandfather, fifty-three. In his lap sits my one-year-old brother Cricket. I'm standing to the left of Grandpa, wearing my brand-new gray-and-lavender-checkered jacket my mother made for me. I would wear this jacket for the next seven years. On Grandpa's other side, stands Nimble, my middle brother, six years old.

Notice my smiling face. A sharp contrast to my mother's angry-looking face. She'd look the same throughout my growing up years. My mother never smiled at me.

Grandpa looked sad, almost on the verge of tears. He and I were to be parted for the first time. Three days after dropping me off at my parents', he went back to Red Stone Bridge alone.

In the photo, I'm smiling. Not because I was happy, but I've just discovered something fascinating. Oh, look! How did Nimble's face get into the mirror in front of us while he's standing on the same side with me? I'd never seen a mirror reflection. And, just as I'd tilted my head to investigate, the cameraman froze my seemingly worry-free smile into this photo.

That morning at breakfast, Grandmother told me I was leaving Red Stone Bridge.

"Your grandpa is taking you to live in Taiyuan today," she said, sounding strangely calm. I turned to look at Grandpa. He and I were sitting on floor stools snuggly side-by-side, our backs against the floor chest across from the door, slurping our millet soup.

No wonder Grandpa was extra quiet today, absently chewing his food, his eyes looking lost in a faraway place.

"It's your mother's turn to love you," Grandmother said. She was sitting on the edge of *kang,* in charge of the ladle, dishing out the steamy hot millet soup into everyone's bowl from the big cast-iron wok.

"Taiyuan is a nice big city," added Grandmother in her soft voice. "It has better schools than this poor nothing-village." She'd even prepared the rare goodies for my trip: several dried sweet Moon Cakes, leftovers from last year's August Moon Festival, and hard-boiled eggs, and my ninety-five cents good-luck money from the Lunar New Year.

It wasn't until decades later that I finally realized the real reason behind my being sent away.

Grandmother had to make her Chinese version of *Sophie's Choice.*

She had to choose over her two grandchildren, me, her granddaughter, or Wu Qin, her grandson. He was Grandmother's maternal grandchild. Having two small grandchildren was too much of a burden for Grandpa, who wasn't in political power or great physical strength to earn enough food to feed us all.

Grandmother chose my boy cousin Wu Qin.

She would have kept me in the village, if I had been a useful babysitter to Wu Qin, who was one and a half years old when his milk mother first dropped him off at my grandparents' doorstep. His parents, my aunt Da Gu and her husband, were too busy working in the city of Chang

Zhi to take care of him, just like mine. But, alas, I was too much of a wild spirit, at age six, resenting having my little boy cousin tagging along. As soon as Grandmother was out of sight, gone to work in the commune's cornfields or do her chores, I'd push the toddler away and run off with my friends and wouldn't come home until after dark. No matter how much she yelled at me, or how hard she smacked me, Grandmother couldn't bend me.

Grandmother had Grandpa write to my parents, their son and daughter-in-law, in Taiyuan, offering me as a good household helping hand and dependable babysitter to my two younger brothers. My mother was overworked, full-time head secretary to the president of her company while taking care of two little boys by herself. My father had long quit coming home every day, riding his bike two hours each way. He now only came home on weekends, Sundays.

Like an eaglet pushed out of its nest to survive on its own, the twisted fate of Divine Intervention uprooted me from my remote mountain village and thrust me into an unknown world.

After breakfast, Grandpa lifted me up into the village's one-horse-drawn pinewood cart, cushioned with straw. Grandmother waved us off, her hands crossing over her worn gray apron, her small bound feet planted apart to keep her steady.

Grandpa and I rode for a good half day on the horse cart for forty *li*. We arrived at the town of Guo Dao at noon and stayed overnight in the Horse-Cart Inn, sleeping in our clothes alongside a dozen other travelers: men, women, and children. The *kang* was packed, people stacked together side by side, like logs. The next morning, we rose in the dark, waiting with the crowd for our ride to Taiyuan: on a livestock open-top truck, standing-room only. Now everyone was packed in like vertical pine-tree logs. I was tightly pressed into the front corner next to the tall gasoline barrel. My eyes were leveled at the cracks on the splintered pinewood boards that fenced the truck.

"Please, folks, don't push! My small granddaughter is here!" Grandpa pleaded with the crowd, stretching out his arms to shield me. The gasoline barrel leaked and splashed gasoline out through the small lid on top and all over my clothes. The truck violently swayed on the narrow mountain trails, people sliding and crashing in all directions. My stomach was turning.

I used to love the smell of gasoline. When I played on the village's roadside, I'd chase after a jeep or truck in the roaring cloud of dust that occasionally flew down the main dirt street just to smell the exotic fuel. But now it made me sick. The trees, bushes, and mountain hills flashed by and blurred my eyes and dizzied my head. The millet soup I had for breakfast rushed out of my mouth like sour water.

Finally, the truck stopped for a break. Someone took pity on me and gave Grandpa some medicine for my motion sickness.

"Sweetie, look at the goodies." Grandpa cheered, two tiny white pills sitting in his calloused palm. "Come, swallow it so you won't feel sick anymore."

Squatting by the roadside among the crowds, I felt dizzy, my body limp like noodles, my stomach rushing in waves up to my throat. How could I swallow the pills without water? But I was too sick to talk. I frowned and elbowed away Grandpa's hand, only to make him chuckle. He was amused. Only with Grandpa did I dare to let out my true feelings.

"Oh, darling baby, won't you take it, please? You'll feel better."

"No! I don't want to!"

"He-he-he . . . Ah, little person, big temper." Grandpa teasingly scraped my nose tip.

"What a spoiled child!" a man squatting by called out. "Needs a good whacking lesson!"

"Awww, . . . just look at this cute little piggy snout," Grandpa ignored the nosy, mean stranger. "It's sticking out like a handle to hold a vegetable oil bottle!"

By the time we reached Taiyuan City, I had poured my stomach inside and out while being squished and slammed around throughout the violent 400-*li* (150 miles) all-day ride.

"So you're here," my parents said to Grandpa and me when we arrived. I peeked from behind Grandpa. I remembered my father and his terror from two years before in the village. I also recognized my mother's same annoyed-looking face from the 1x2-inch, black-and-white photo hanging on the wall at home in the village.

"Why, are you shy?" My father asked. "This is your home now."

"You shouldn't be uselessly shy," my mother said, her eyes silent. "You're the oldest and will have to help me take care of your two younger brothers."

"Are you hungry?" My mother turned to Grandpa.

"Yes, I'm hungry," I said. My stomach was growling.

"Old Heaven God," my mother turned to frown at me. "Listen to your country bumpkin *tu-hua*, backward dialect! People are going to laugh at you."

But I didn't know any other way to talk.

My mother paraded me around the big dirt yard, the crowded residence for hundreds of blue-collar workers at the Heavy Machinery Factory, where my mother worked as the prestigious head secretary to the president. People called her the "pen."

My mother greeted people, chatted and asked if they could spare some of their rationed coupons for detergent.

"She has lice in her hair," my mother explained, looking at me with a disgusted frown. "The backward, deep mountain villagers never wash their hair. And look here," my mother pulled down my front collar to expose a fist-sized lump protruding in the middle of my neck. "Look at her 'thick-neck disease'. The village's water lacks iodine. Now I have to buy expensive seaweeds to cure her disease." But she never bought any just for me. They were too expensive. We only got to eat a little bit of seaweed in soups once a year for Lunar New Year's and Mid-Autumn Festival. Miraculously, my "thick-neck disease," which I understood much later was called a goiter, slowly disappeared over the years. By the time I turned eighteen, it was completely gone without any medical treatment.

My mother assigned me my daily chores: First thing in the morning, I was to take out the two night-chamber urine pots, a small flat one, and a tall spittoon shaped with a narrow neck and wide opening. They stacked on top of each other. I was to empty them into the open sewer outhouse at the far corner of the dirt yard. Then fetch the breakfast of porridge and small, dark steamed buns on the other side of the wall at the factory cafeteria. After we all ate, I was to wash the pots, bowls and chopsticks before going to school. After school, I was to babysit my brother, Cricket, boiling the bottle of milk for him, while keeping an eye on Nimble the troublemaker, then I was to dust and tidy up the one-room apartment.

My mother had a happy sunshine face when she looked at Cricket, cooing her baby-lamb nursery rhyme to him:

小羊兒乖乖 *My darling little lamb,* 把門開開 *Please open the door.* 媽媽回來, 給你吃口奶奶。*My bosom for you.*

Mother also smiled approvingly at my brother Nimble no matter how naughty he was or what bad things he did. He once climbed up to the rooftop of the three-story building from outside. Frantically, my mother begged a young man for help. He climbed up and carefully carried Nimble under one arm while climbing down with his other arm. The huge crowd cheered. Hugging Nimble in happy tears, my mother never scolded him. Another time, he was caught stealing five *yuan* ($0.50USD = one third of a beginning blue collar worker's monthly earning) from her best friend's purse. Instead of punishing him, my mother got mad at her friend. She slammed the money into her friend's hand, and never apologized. And Nimble's first-grade teacher was a frequent visitor to our apartment, complaining tearfully to my mother, about how he disrupted her class by clowning around whenever her back was turned. My mother always promised to punish him, but never did.

For some reason my mother wouldn't smile at me and always frowned at me sideways, as if I'd done something wrong to upset her. I never understood but was too scared to ask her questions, I did my chores carefully and diligently. But she still said I had a wolf-like cold heart, just like my despicable dead-man-walking father. But he, in turn, would yell at me to get out of his face, for he didn't want to see a carbon copy of his bad-omen, slut wife.

Sundays were the most dreadful when my father came home. After pedaling on his bicycle for two hours from his out-of-town job, he was always in a bad mood, irritated, and yelling at both Nimble and me. I couldn't stay out of his way or do anything right to please him. When I went to play outside with my friends, he'd yell for me to come back inside, insisting that I do my homework. Even after I showed him my finished homework, he'd order me to do it all over again. But how? And why? He'd then yell that I was lying, even threatening to beat me.

Occasionally, there was a light-hearted moment when my father was in a good mood. He'd start making fun of his chaotic life: "I ride my bike for two hours and come home covered with dust and sweat. I was tired, thirsty and wanted to have a drink of water. But the thermos bottle is empty. I want to boil some water, but the stove is dead. I want to build a fire by splitting some wood, but I can't find the ax. I call for Nimble to bring me the ax, but Nimble is nowhere to be found!" My father would then smile pleasingly at my mother, only to meet her silent eyes staring back at him.

One night my mother suddenly started yelling at me.

"Can't you see Cricket's soiled pants soaked in the washbasin?" she glared at me, her eyebrows knotted in fury. "They've been sitting in there for days! Who do you wait for to wash them for you? Why do I have to ask you?"

I was shocked and felt bad about myself. But she didn't tell me I was supposed to wash those pants. I hadn't learned how to do laundry. But I was too afraid to speak up.

"What are you standing there for? Take it out and wash them now."

I looked at the clock on the wall. It said 8:30 pm. It was pitch-black outside. I was always scared of the dark. Cricket and Nimble were already in bed. Frightened by my mother's death stare, I squatted down to lift the washbasin full of dark gray water with Cricket's soiled pants in it. It was dead heavy. I could only carry it with my back bent.

"Please open the door for me?" I pleaded.

"Put it down and open it yourself." My mother didn't look up, sitting in the chair knitting.

A gust of cold howling wind smashed on my face. It blew dust up into the air. There was no light in the yard. I was alone in the vast dirt yard, where rows and rows of one-room shacks were now dark shadows. My legs were shaking in fear, my heart racing, my face hurting from the smashing dust flying around in the cold air. Holding the heavy washbasin with Cricket's soiled pants, I inched forward, my back bent, toward the thin, iron-pipe water faucet sticking out three-feet-tall in the middle of the dirt ground. It was the only water faucet shared by hundreds of families. During the daytime, a crowd was always waiting to get water, but now it was all quiet and deserted in the darkness.

How do I wash the soiled pants? Placing the washbasin under the water faucet, I tilted the washbasin to let the dirty water run out into the hole in the ground and turned on the water. The soiled pants were stiff and heavy. I tried but couldn't lift them up.

Another gust of howling wind swirled up the dust and smashed in my face. A sharp grain of dirt got into my right eye. I tried to rub it out, but it was hurting too much. I cried out and stumbled back into the apartment.

"What is it now?" My mother sounded annoyed.

"Sand . . . in my eye . . . wind blew . . ." I sobbed, my hand covering my eye.

"Oh, you're so useless! I only asked you to do a little washing, now you just have to make it more trouble for me? Let me see. Take your hand off your eye! . . . No, I can't see anything in your eye. Get in bed now!" My mother's face was as frighteningly dark as the pitch-black world outside.

I learned to feel guilty.

Chapter 25

My First Day of School in the City

上學第一天

SUNDAY MORNING.

My mother told me to stand on the family bed and try on the new, blue cotton pants she had just sewed for me on her foot-pedaled sewing machine.

"Oh, my! Let us have a good look!" Two middle-aged women, short and chubby, rushed in at each other's heels, like two happy, chirpy birds. They stood in front of the bed, looking up at me, smiling and chatting away, their eyes bright and shining, their hands crossed over their aprons. They filled the crowded floor in our small, one-room apartment like two bundles of warming sunshine.

"Is this really your daughter, Magnolia?" one called out.

"We are next-door neighbors, and you never told us about her?" the other chimed in.

"Yeah, we never heard you had an eight-year-old daughter!"

"Oh, just look how lovely she is!"

"Oh, Magnolia, you are so blessed with such an adorable daughter!"

I blushed, smiling secretly. No one had ever told me I was pretty. To the Chinese standard, only big, double-eyelid eyes were considered to be beautiful. I glanced over at my mother. She was hunched over at the sewing machine, silent, only a faint smile at the corners of her mouth. The two cheerful ladies chatted their way out the door.

"You're going to school today," my mother said to me the next day. "I'll find somebody for you to follow." She also said that I needed a new name for school. From now on my new name would be "Jing" 靜, meaning "serenity, quiet, silence and still." I didn't know it yet, until four decades later, how badly my mother needed the feeling of peace at the sight of me. Every second of my existence was a painful reminder to her that I was the sole reason for the death of her lifelong dream.

My mother stood in front of the open door and eyed the crowd of noisy kids running around in the dirt yard. All of them were carrying schoolbags across their shoulders. And they all talked in the city dialect that was so different from my village dialect.

"Xiao Qiang! Come here!" my mother called over to a boy about my height with short cropped hair. "This is Li Jing. Let her follow you to school, okay? She is also a third grader like you. But you're the year of lamb, and she, monkey. So you're one year older than her. I want you to be like her big brother, all right? This is her first day of school in the city. She's very shy and only talks the village dialect. Keep an eye on her, okay?"

"Okay, come along!" the boy cocked his head at me, dashing away.

"Go follow him," my mother gave me a push. "Don't just stand here."

Terrified, I scrambled after the boy, fixing my eyes on the back of his head, now several kids ahead of me. The dusty yard was like a maze, with rows and rows of one-room shacks packed closely to each other like many matchboxes lined up and glued together. In my village, every family had its own house inside their own courtyard.

I found myself entering a beautiful world very different from my mother's dirt yard, where tall weeds sprouting all over its corners. It turned out that the Heavy Machinery Factory of blue-collar workers, my mother's work unit, couldn't afford a school for its hundreds of workers' offspring. So it paid to send its ghetto yard kids across the street to the school of the white-collar company, named Team 182, a secret code for government project. As I concentrated on chasing after the back of Xiao Qiang's head, I didn't realize I was running out of my dirt yard, onto the asphalt paved street, and into the well-to-do land of Team 182's pebbled walkway.

A magnificent tall building appeared. It was as tall as the majestic South Mountain in my village. I'd never seen such a big building with so many windows stacked on top of one another. And instead of the soft, thin paper covering my village's windows, these windows were all covered with shining glass. Even the walkway was beautifully curved smooth surface, not covered with loose dirt and rocks but embedded with tiny, colorful pebbles, just like the pebble stones in my village's clear-water creek, where I played barefoot, building dams out of sand. How did these cute river pebbles get into the hard-surfaced ground?

Where was Xiao Qiang? I panicked. Which head of cropped hair was his? All the boys had the same cropped short haircut! Did he enter this building? I stopped in front of it, crowds of noisy kids pushing all around me. Hesitantly, I decided to follow the crowd inside.

It took a moment for my eyes to get used to the dimness inside. What a vast world! I'd never seen an enclosed place that held so many people. The ceilings were high. There were so many doors on both sides of the walls. But which one of these doors did Xiao Qiang go in? I felt like crying, standing still as a sea of kids bumped and pushed around me.

Wait! Was that Xiao Qiang disappearing into the last door on the left-hand corner? I ran after him, but halted at the wide-open door. I peeked inside the room. It looked so different from my village school's classroom. There was no half-room-sized platform *kang* with many small, legless square desks we brought from home. This spacious city classroom had a large open floor filled from wall to wall with rows and rows of long-legged, chest-high desks. It was a very bright room with a high ceiling. Sunshine was pouring through two big tall glass windows. Dozens of kids were already inside, walking around, sitting at their desks, standing by the windows looking out, or chatting with each other. They all looked comfortable with one another. No one looked panicking or lost like me.

I felt intimidated. Which one of the desks should I be sitting at if I went in? Which one of these boys was Xiao Qiang? He was my only link to this strange world, but I'd already forgotten what his face looked like! I stepped away from the classroom door, backed myself into the hallway, and glued my back to the wall. I felt like crying.

"Hey! What are you looking at?" a boy's voice yelled in my direction. I blinked my tears away. Across from me, two boys were kneeling in the corner of the hallway, playing marble games. One of them had looked up to yell at me.

Oh, no, please. I wasn't looking at you. I'm just lost. I silently begged the two boys with my eyes, my mother's voice in my ears: "Everybody is going to laugh at your backwards country bumpkin dialect."

"Ha! Look! She is crying!"
"Wah! Wah!"

Ringggg! . . . A loud bell suddenly pierced through the bustling hallway. The noisy crowds vanished into the classrooms on both sides of the walls. I was alone in the vast, empty hallway.

"What are you doing standing there? Go to your class!" A man with a loud voice was walking toward me. My back against the wall, I was too scared to look up, my eyes fixed on the tips of my cloth shoes Grandmother had made for me.

"What grade are you in?" The booming voice was now towering over me.

Shaking my head, I sobbed.

"What's the matter?" The big voice softened. It only encouraged my tears.

"Okay, go to the principal's office now." His big hand reached out to grab my arm.

I froze. In my village school, only bad kids got sent to the principal's room for a session of whacking. But the man kept his firm grip at my elbow and walked me down the hallway.

"Here," The man stopped at a half-open door. "Go on inside. Mrs. Principal, here is a student to see you." He nudged my body through the open door and disappeared into the silent hallway.

"Come here," a woman's voice called from across the room.

My back glued onto the door frame, I was terrified to move.

"What's your name? Why are you crying? Come over here. I'm the principal."

"Hey, I am talking to you. Do you hear me? Look at me and get over here." The woman now lost her patience. I peeked up and saw a plump woman, short hair cropped at her ear lobes, sitting behind a long, wooden desk. Behind her was a tall glass window.

"Okay, who *are* you? Where is your mother? Do you know how to talk?" The principal got up from behind her desk and walked over.

I broke into loud sobbing, my mother's voice warning me that people were going to laugh at my embarrassing country bumpkin dialect.

"Talk to me. Who are you? Where are you from?" The principal bent down to talk to me.

"Okay, okay. Go home and get your mother to come see me." The principal stood up and walked back to her desk.

Home? My mother? I didn't know where my home was or how to find my mother. I couldn't find my way back home because I forgot how I got here.

"Did you hear me? I said turn around and go home and get your mother. Why are you still standing there?" The principal walked back to where I was standing. Putting both her hands on my shoulders, she turned my stiff body around and nudged me out into the empty hallway. "Gee, I've never seen a strange student like this!" The principal closed door.

The silence in the hallway was eerie. Which one of these many doors could lead me outside? My head felt like thick porridge. I couldn't think clearly. Inching forward, I was too frightened to cry, looking nervously to my left and to my right. Finally, a wide gap in the hallway appeared on my right side, with a few steps leading down to a closed door. I gingerly pushed the door. To my relief, it opened to the bright sunshine!

Looking around, I remembered nothing familiar. Did I walk through this pretty garden-like yard? Were these gently swaying willow trees here this morning? I didn't remember the big, round, cement circle, with colorful blooming flowers growing inside, in front of another mountain-high building with the curved pebble walkways leading to the tall, black iron gate. Did I pass through it? It was closed now. Only a small iron door on the side was open. Would I be allowed to pass through?

There was no one around. An old man was walking this way. He went out through the small iron gate to the paved streets on the outside. No one stopped him. I followed him through the gate, relieved that no one questioned me.

Outside the iron gate, a long, smooth black-paved street spread out to both left and right. Which way should I turn? Tears of panic welled back up. Were these big, tall trees lined up the street this morning? Oh, look! There was another iron gate across the street! Was it here this morning? I learned later that was the gate of the Heavy Machinery Factory, where my mother worked.

I walked a few steps hesitantly to my left, then turned back to walk to the right. Which direction should I go? My eyes felt sore in the bright sunlight. Something inside told me to turn to the left. I kept walking until I saw an open yard with two earthen mounds at the entrance. Did I run through it after Xiao Qiang this morning? The rows and rows of the matchbox buildings looked familiar, but

I didn't remember the earthen mound gateway. I decided to go into the yard.

I had to find my mother for the principal. But behind which one of these hundreds of doors did she live? I decided to peek into every closed door. One by one. Row after row. Finally I caught sight of a fuzzy image of a woman who vaguely looked like my mother. Her back turned toward me. She was standing by the bed dressing a baby who looked like my brother. A washbasin sat on the brick-and-dirt floor. I blinked my tears away to look through the crack on the green-painted wooden door, waiting for her to turn her face. She finally did. Yes, it was my mother! I pushed the door open, standing against it, letting out a flood of tears.

"Why in the world are you back already?" My mother's eyebrows knotted up. "Why are you crying? What's the matter? Stop crying! Tell me what happened."

"Principal . . . wants . . . to . . . see . . . you," I sobbed my words out.

"What? What did you do? Why do I need to see the principal? What do you mean you couldn't find your classroom? Didn't I tell you to follow Xiao Qiang? Oh, you're so useless! How can I go see the principal when I'm so busy?"

My tears stopped. I felt bad. I was useless.

I walked behind my mother in silence back to the school.

"Mrs. Principal, I'm sorry," my mother apologized with a humble smile. "I couldn't bring my daughter earlier this morning because I was busy with my baby boy. I'm sorry for all the trouble my daughter has caused you. She grew up in a remote mountain village with her grandparents. This is her first time in the city. She only talks the peasant dialect. Please forgive her."

The principal smiled generously, saying that all city schools, especially her school in the privileged Team 182, were more advanced than backward village schools. She said she was going to give me a test to prove it. She turned to write some math problems on a small blackboard on thin wooden legs by her desk.

"Now tell me the correct answers," the principal looked at me. Right away I knew the answers. I'd learned them in my village school. But I was too embarrassed to open my mouth to speak. I didn't know the city dialect. I glanced up at my mother, who looked at me with a scolding smile.

"Well," the principal nodded with an I-told-you-so smile. "The village school is indeed backwards. Your daughter is one entire year behind. I'm now going to place her in the second grade, not the third."

As a lifelong classroom teacher myself, I learned from my traumatized childhood experience that there are eager-to-speak words behind a child's closed mouth, their question-marked eyes, their shy quietness, and their nervous smile. A compassionate teacher gets down to the child's eye level, smiles, and finds out the right question to ask.

Chapter 26

Lost on the Way to the Zoo

去動物園的路上

IT WAS A SUNDAY MORNING.
"Yay, we're going to the zoo!" Nimble and Cricket cheered.
"What's zoo?" I asked.
"Ha-ha!" laughed Nimble, echoed by Cricket, pointing at me. "*Shan-han* 山漢, *country bumpkin!* She doesn't know what a zoo is! Animals live there!"
I regretted having asked. I hated it when they thought I was dumb because I was born and grew up in my "backward" village. I'd actually kind of guessed it myself. The three pictographic Chinese words for "zoo" 動物園 mean "animal garden."
"I want to go to the zoo, too." I turned to my father.
"*You* want to go, too?" My father looked surprised, more disappointed.
"Yes, I do."
"We only have one bicycle."
"But I've never seen a zoo before."
"Don't you give me that attitude with a dead-looking face like your ugly mother!" my father glared at me. "Why can't you just reason with a pleasant-looking face? I think you should stay home. No? All right then, let's go."
Yes! I was elated. But once we were out of the dirt yard and onto the smooth asphalt main street, my father stopped to look at the three of us, then back at his bike.
"Cricket, come and sit on the front bar." He lifted him up to sit down in front. "Nimble, climb up." He pointed to the back rack of the bicycle. "Now," he looked at me. "What am I going to do with *you*?"
My father was only used to having two kids, not three. I showed no intention of giving up.

"One bicycle, three kids. What am I supposed to do!" My father was annoyed. He started walking with my two brothers sitting on the bike. I trailed behind them. "The zoo is on the other side of the city. It's too far to walk." He stopped again, as if talking to himself, looking at me.

I wouldn't budge.

"Okay, if you have to tag along, go take the bus then." He reached inside his left breast pocket on his white, short-sleeved shirt, his left hand holding onto the handlebar.

I became quietly worried. I had never taken a bus before. Walking to school with a group of girls cross the street from our yard was the only adventure I'd had so far. But I kept quiet because I didn't want to miss the opportunity.

"Here are four cents, half-price ticket. Get off at the zoo and wait for us at the entrance."

"But I'm too tall for half price."

Even back in the village, I was already too tall to pay half price to get into the Chinese Opera show in the schoolyard at Red Stone Bridge's annual harvest fair. How could my father not know that a half-price was only for a child under three feet tall? And I was eight years old, and always taller than most kids my age. My mother was right when she called him a "stingy iron rooster" — he wouldn't contribute a single feather for anyone to make a duster.

"You're still a child. So you pay half price."

How embarrassingly cheap my father was! But my determination to see the zoo made me open my hand to accept his four pennies. Better than nothing.

"Here comes the bus. Go get on it. Go on!"

"This is f-o-u-r cents." The plump woman ticket collector stared at my pennies, her eyes digging hard into mine. "The ticket is eight cents minimum. Where is the rest of the money?"

"I . . . I don't . . . have . . . it. That's all . . . my father gave me," I stammered in shame.

"I would've kicked you off if the bus hadn't started. Where are you going?"

"I . . . to . . . the zoo . . ."

"The zoo?" Her voice raised to a high pitch. "That's clear across the city! You should pay double of eight cents! What kind of cheap father you've got?" She shoved the ticket into my hand, tossing up her chin to motion me to the back of the bus.

It was a long ride. Endlessly long.

"Excuse me, . . . please . . . Is it . . . zoo yet?" I had finally scraped up enough courage and walked up to the front of the bus where the woman ticket collector sat at the high-chaired booth.

"What? The zoo? We've long passed it. Didn't you hear my calling?"

"Master Driver," she turned to the driver of the bus. "Could you stop to let this kid off? Go on, get off now. Just walk back a few stops, and you'll see the zoo. What a dumb child!"

Which way was "back"? Standing on the smooth, paved sidewalk stretching endlessly in all directions, I didn't know where I was, or which way to turn. Anxious, I felt like crying.

A kind-looking old man was passing by me.

"Where is the zoo, Old Grandpa?" I asked.

"The zoo? Oh, see that small gate? That's the back door to the zoo."

No one was guarding the small, rusted iron gate. I wandered in and found myself coming to a pond of greenish water, where a circle of willow trees stood swaying gracefully.

Exhausted, I sat down at the earthen bank.

The sun was burning my hatless head. I was thirsty, wondering if I could scoop up some of it to drink. Then I saw a couple of heads bobbing up and down in the water, their black hair silhouetted against the green water. I blinked to look harder, but they disappeared. I wanted to wait for them to pop back so I could ask where to find the front door of the zoo.

I waited and waited.

"Hey! Go away!" a boy's voice hissed from behind a willow tree. I turned to see a pair of eyes and the top of a black haired head. He couldn't be talking to me because I knew no one.

"Hey! Go away!" the voice hissed again. This time half a face appeared from behind the tree, and a tip of his bare shoulder. I didn't know what to make of it.

"Go away!" A small rock landed where I was sitting. The boy's bare arm was throwing rocks at me. "Go away! Don't look at us. You're sitting right by our clothes!" There were two boys' voices.

Oh, no, they were talking to me! I scrambled up and ran as fast as I could. It finally dawned on me that the two boys were swimming in the pond without their clothes on. How embarrassing! I ran. Nonstop. Somehow, I ran out of the zoo, entirely missing the front gate.

I walked and walked, growing tired and thirsty, panic and frustration boiling inside me. My mouth was dry, my lips cracked and bleeding.

I found myself walking in an open field. No more crowds of people or tall buildings around but an endless field of dark, leafy green cabbages. They were young, perky cabbages, as Grandpa grew back in my village. And the familiar smell of the manure fertilizer reminded me of Grandpa shoulder-poling two big, wooden buckets full of what he had dished out of our outhouse to pour onto the roots of his cabbages. I missed Grandpa.

An old woman wearing a coarse, black shirt and pants and a wide-brimmed straw hat, was watering the cabbages. She dished water out of a bucket, one ladle at a time.

"Hello, Lady Grandmother." Tears of relief came into my eyes.

"Oh, hello, there! What are you doing here all alone? Where are you from?"

"I'm lost on my way to the zoo. Do you know where is *Er-Ying-Pan*?" I could only remember the name of the section of the city, where my parents lived.

"From the zoo? My goodness, poor child! You've circled the whole Taiyuan City!"

"Can you give me some water to drink, please?" My eyes fixed on her water ladle.

"Oh, no, you can't drink this water. It's not boiled. For watering the cabbages only, too dirty to drink. Worms will grow inside your stomach."

"That's okay. Please let me drink some." I was dying of thirst. The water looked nice and clear to me. I couldn't care less about the worms. My stomach always had worms anyway.

Back in Red Stone Bridge, I had tiny, thin itchy worms crawling in and out of my bottom. Now in the city, worms inside my stomach had gotten much bigger and longer. They were longer than brown earthworms after the rain. My school gave out pink, pagoda-shaped pills of "stomach worm killing" medicine. They were crumbling sweet and tasted like candies. We chewed them before swallowing. I'd watch the dead, pale, foot-long worms coming out of me while I squatted over the open manhole. They were twisted like a thick rope.

"Are you sure?" The old lady hesitated, handing me a ladleful. I gulped it down. It was nice and cool, and felt good. I thanked the kind lady with a grateful smile. Then she pointed out the direction to *Er-Ying-Pan*.

After more endless walking, I finally saw a street traffic light in the distance.

Was that my father at the intersection circling around on his bicycle?

It was! He saw me, too, and pedaled toward me.

"Where have you been?" my father yelled, dismounting from his bike. "I told you to wait for me at the zoo. Why didn't you listen? Took you all day? Do you know what time is it now? Six o'clock in the evening! Worried me sick! Come on, we need to go tell the police that you're found." He told me to climb onto the backseat of his bicycle.

As I walked in, my mother glanced up from cooking at the brick stove by the door. She didn't say a word. Her eyes silent. Her face angry. My heart sank. I felt guilty. Not only did I miss my precious first chance to see the zoo, I also ruined everyone else's Sunday weekend — my brothers didn't get to visit the zoo, either.

"Everybody thought you were lost forever!" Little Beauty, my second-grade classmate, exclaimed to me at school. Our mothers were best friends. She and her mother and younger sister lived at the other end of the same row as our one-room shack. Her father was convicted as "counter revolutionary bad element" because he'd criticized the leader of his work unit. He'd long been sent away to a hard-labor camp for "thought reform." Her mother was forced to divorce him.

"The police loudspeaker at the *Da-Ying-Pan* intersection was broadcasting your name all day Sunday." Little Beauty said, fascination reflecting in her pretty, double-eyelid, big eyes.

That's how I lost my sense of direction.

Chapter 27

The Frightening Morning

可怕的早晨

1965. This photo was taken at Red East photography studio, Taiyuan City.

I NEVER LIKED this photo.

I still remember that uncomfortable moment.

"Stand closer to your mother," the camera man had called out, his head under the black cloth cover with the camera box on tripod. I knew he was talking to me, for I'd left a gap in between my mother and me. Getting physically close to my mother was like snuggling up to a burning red hot iron furnace. I hesitantly nudged a little bit over. "No, closer like this!" the camera man dashed over to push me over to my mother.

Look at my stressed-out face, apprehension, confusion. And look at my "thick-neck disease," the lump looked as if a steamed bun was hidden underneath. And, how I hated my ugly haircut. My father had ordered me to sit in the chair and mercilessly chopped my hair all the way above my ear lobes. "Why the tears?" he scolded me. "Nothing wrong with short hair. It's easy to keep it clean and saves some rationed detergent to wash it."

Notice my anxiety – a sharp contrast to my brother Nimble's worry-free, happy grin.

Soon after this photo, disaster struck. A life and death ordeal for me at age nine.

My body started falling apart. I couldn't walk straight. Before landing on the ground, each of my feet had to kick the other ankle bruised and bloody. Then my hands started feeling weak. And my heart went out of order, racing one minute, then slowing down to faint the next. I felt no energy to go outside and play with my friends. After doing my chores, all I wanted to do was to slump down on the small floor stool, my back against the foot of my family's wooden bed.

Strangely, my father started trying to make me go outside and play. But as soon as he hustled me out, I'd sit right down on a pile of loose coal, with no more desire to join my friends, but content to watch them running wild and playing my favorite game, "木頭人," *tag-and-freeze!*

One frightening morning, everything got worse.

My mother woke us up and started dressing Cricket. Nimble and I put on our clothes.

"What's taking you so long?" my mother turned to frown at me. My hands felt so weak they were shaking. My fingers couldn't button my shirt. I tried hard to focus, clenching my hands tight, but the buttons refused to go through the buttonholes.

"What's going on?" My mother was getting angrier. "You're not waiting for me to help *you*, are you? You're supposed to help me, not be a burden. Can't you see the urine pots still sit on the floor? Who do you hope to empty them for you? Hurry up! Nimble's already down on the floor. Take care of it before he topples it over."

"I can't button my shirt," I whimpered, wiping my tears.

"Why on earth are you tearing the brand-new shirt like that? How ungrateful can you be? I just made that for you." My mother grabbed hold of my arm and yanked me over to her. "There's nothing wrong with the buttonholes. You're making me late for work!"

On my way walking to school, I looked down and suddenly noticed, in horror, that one side of my shirt was hanging down longer than the other side. Oh, no what have I done to ruin my brand-new shirt? My mother's going to be really angry with me. I panicked, frantically stretching the shorter side to make it match the longer side.

"Eww, gross!" cried out Little Beauty, my classmate. "Look at the blood on your ankles!"

I shrugged. Nothing new. My ankles had been in a blood-caked mess for a while.

That morning in class, I couldn't write with my hand anymore. It wouldn't listen to my mind. My pencil slid all the way across the paper down to the bottom in my exercise book. No matter how hard I tried to hold it steady, making my hand a fist – it'd slide right down, straight across the paper. Putting my pencil down, I wept, in fear and shame for my failure.

"What's the matter?" Mrs. Yuan walked over to my seat.

"My hand won't write."

"It's your hand again?" Mrs. Yuan's voice softened. I was grateful for my teacher's kind tone. "Didn't your mother take you to see a doctor? I called her two weeks ago about your hand trouble. She didn't say anything?"

I shook my head, startled that my mother knew about it.

"What kind of mother is she?" My teacher sounded upset.

Oh, no, Teacher. Please don't call my mother, my eyes begged her. *I'll be in more trouble if you call her.*

"Tell your mother she needs to take you to see a doctor."

I nodded. That night, I was secretly relieved when my mother didn't mention anything about my teacher or my hands.

"Did you take her to see a doctor?" My father came home on Sunday, asking my mother.

"How am I supposed to do that, busy working and taking care of Nimble and Cricket? It's your job. Your mother brought her up. You take care of her."

My father told me to climb onto the back of his bicycle and pedaled me to the People's Hospital.

Chapter 28

The Morning My Mother Visited My Hospital Ward

病房探訪

OH, I MUST BE DREAMING. I turned my head to the bright window on the right side of my hospital bed. The morning sun was coming in to rest on the clean, white bedsheet. So calm and peaceful. What a difference it was from last night's roaring thunder and slashing rain. I felt so good my toes wiggled in delight. Yawning contentedly, I stretched my arms under the futon.

I'd been very happy here, safely away from my parents and brothers. I enjoyed this spacious, clean hospital ward all to myself. Back home there was no bright sunshine coming through the grime-smudged small window in our crowded one-room apartment. Worse, there was no peace or quiet at home, but my mother's silent eyes, and angry face, my father's violent temper and irritated yelling, and Nimble and Cricket's constant picking on me.

Suddenly, out of the corner of my eye, I caught sight of what I dreaded most: my mother.

Oh, no, I wasn't dreaming at all. It really was my mother walking through the door! I scrambled to sit up in the middle of the bed, folding my legs and locking my fingers in my lap.

"Let me see, did you really cry?" My mother's face smiled, but her almond-shaped small eyes were silent and hard. A group of doctors and nurses followed behind her. They came to stand around my bed, all smiling at me, their kind eyes saying: "Look what a nice surprise we've got for you: Your mommy's here!"

Oh, no! I cried inside. My mother didn't like it when I bothered her. Now I was in trouble, for she had to take the bus and travel to the hospital. Sitting in the middle of my bed, I wrung my fingers nervously, bracing myself for a scolding.

My happiness had started on the day my father carried me on the back of his bike to People's Hospital. Lifting me off his bike, he carried me in his arms, rushing into the big, tall building with people everywhere inside. The hallway looked even longer, the ceiling higher, and the floor smoother, actually shining, than my school. There was a strange smell from the "germ-killing spray" just like the clinic office in my mother's work unit.

This was the first time I'd seen the inside of a hospital, but I was too weak to feel the excitement about this brand-new place. Carrying me in his arms, my father rushed in and out, from one room to another. I felt so uncomfortable and awkward in his arms, I'd never been so close to him. I wanted to jump down to the floor, but had no energy.

In the next room, my father placed me on the flat surface attached to a big square machine. It made clicking and buzzing noises. "Lie still," he told me. My heart was being measured. Then he took me to see Doctor Liu, who sat behind a big desk wearing a white robe and dark-rimmed glasses.

"Your daughter has serious heart problems," Dr. Liu had told my father. "She won't live past twenty-five years of age."

I saw my father's mouth drop open but no words coming out, a look of shock in his eyes. Dr. Liu then told him some long medical terms to explain my heart disease: "feng-shi-wu-dao-zheng 風濕舞蹈症, *involuntary dancing syndrome*; er-jian-ban-xia-zhai 二間半狹窄, *two and a half valves narrow*."

"This child needs quiet and peaceful rest and immediate medical treatment." Dr. Liu continued. "She shouldn't go through any emotional distress or strenuous physical labor. She'll die sooner, before age twenty-five, if she tries to give birth."

Immediately, a sickly woman's face appeared in my head, our second floor neighbor with a severe heart disease. Short and all bones and skin, she looked pale. Her eyes were sunken, and her cheeks sucked-in. Her doctor had warned her against giving birth to a second child. But she'd wanted a baby girl she ignored the doctor's warning. She died while giving birth to a baby girl. Now her widowed husband, a tall and quiet man, struggled to take care of their two kids alone.

"How long does she have to stay in the hospital?" my father asked Dr. Liu.

"At least a month."

My father gulped, his Adam's apple moving up and down.

"How much will it cost me?"

"About 200 *yuan* ($30 USD.)"

"200 yuan?! I only make 60 yuan a month."

"Well, you can keep her home and bring her to the hospital for shots and checkups."

"Oh, no! I only come home on Sundays. There's no peace and quiet at home. My two little boys jump up and down in our family bed all the time."

Then, after thinking for a long time, my father finally spoke. "Okay, Dr. Liu, I will sacrifice 200 *yuan* to keep her in the hospital."

That was the last time I would see my father for a month. My only visitors would be the nice white-robed doctors, and sweet nurses who came in and out with their feather-light steps. They all smiled at me when they talked to me. I loved it and enjoyed every minute of every day. They made me feel special. Two times a day, one of the nurses would bring me my medicines and feel my pulse. They were so gentle even their needles didn't hurt.

The nurses had made me feel beautiful, too. They combed and braided my hair. Every afternoon I had an uninterrupted nap, sleeping till my heart's content. Then one nurse would take me for a walk in the pretty garden full of beautiful flowers, trees, and pretty green plants under the graceful, and swaying willow trees. It was like living in a beautiful picture. The hospital's pebbled walkways were even prettier than my school, a day-and-night difference from my parents' crowded dirt yard with wild, tall weeds sprouting in the corners, mud, dirt and garbage everywhere, and yelling and shouting all day long.

After my daily stroll in the garden, there was always a special treat waiting for me — a yummy hard-boiled egg, browned in tasty soy sauce, sitting in a small, porcelain bowl on my bedside table. At home I wasn't special enough to eat an egg. They were rationed and expensive. My mother saved them for my two brothers. She said they were younger and needed nutrition.

Now, to my horror, I saw that my mother had just followed me to my peace-and-quiet hospital.

"Let me see, did you really cry? Don't you tell me you really cried over some rain last night?" My mother came to stand by my bedside. Her face smiled, but her eyes were still silent. In front of the nice doctors and nurses, she talked differently, using her soft-and-nice voice as if she were talking to my brothers. I shivered in fear. My mother stood over me, her black leather handbag hanging on her left forearm by her shining, stainless-steel watch.

Please, mother, my eyes frantically pleaded with her. *It wasn't me that wanted to bother you. I didn't know the nice nurse was going to call you after she saw me crying alone last night. I was only scared by the terrible thunder and flashing lightning.*

The night before, the frightening thunder and lightning had awakened me. The clock on the wall above the door said 10:30. Now too scared to go back to sleep, I sat up in the middle of my bed. All kinds of scary shadows were dancing on the curtainless glass window with slashing rain. I tried to tell myself that the shadows were only from the wildly swaying willow trees outside on the sidewalk by the streetlamp, but darkness had always frightened me. Holding my breath, I'd hoped to hear footsteps in the hallway from one of the loving nurses. But nothing.

"Oh, you poor sweetie." A soft voice spoke from behind me. Her steps had been so light I didn't hear her. Closing the door gently behind her, the loving nurse gathered me in her arms, whispering in my ears: "Please don't cry. Everything's going to be all right." Her gentle voice and loving touch was so comforting, they melted my fears as she tucked me in.

"Oh, you useless thing," my mother scolded me in a pleasant tone. "Haven't you ever seen a storm before? What's there to cry about? You know I'm busy at home taking care of your brothers and don't have time to come here, right?"

I nodded obediently. *I'm sorry, Mother.*

"No more fussing over nothing, okay?" My mother then turned to the doctors and nurses. "I'm very sorry that my daughter has caused you so much trouble. Please excuse me, I have to get home now to attend my baby boys." She smiled and nodded politely at them, walking out of my hospital ward. I saw pity in the eyes of the wonderful doctors and nurses when they followed my mother out of my ward.

I hope these loving doctors and nurses still liked me, I thought sadly to myself. I wished that they hadn't discovered my dark shame that I wasn't good enough for my mother to love me.

Chapter 29

Be Chairman Mao's Good Child for Dr. Wong

做毛主席的好孩子

I WAS SITTING UP in my hospital bed alone when the door opened. It was a middle-aged man of slight build, his eyes hidden behind his dark-rimmed glasses. After a quick looking around my room, he whirled inside.

Was he one of the doctors in my room when my mother came to the hospital to scold me for crying over the storm? I quietly wondered.

"I'm Dr. Wong," the man said, closing the door, both his hands carefully and noiselessly turning the doorknob. "Don't worry." Dr. Wong walked toward my bed, his steps light as a cat. "Dr. Liu sent me to see how you're doing." He bent down and patted my face affectionately. "I'd like to keep company to a nice girl like you. What a pretty smile you have." He won my heart over right away.

"Oh, no, no, no. Don't get up." He grabbed the chair by the window and set it by my bedside. Sitting himself down, he put his elbows on the edge of my bed and started telling me funny stories and cracked jokes. I giggled and laughed.

Dr. Wong came to visit me every evening about eight o'clock, after the nurses made their last round. He sometimes put me on his lap in the chair or sat on the edge of my bed.

One evening, Dr. Wong pulled out of his doctor-gown pocket a biggest, shiniest book I'd ever seen. "It's called a magazine," he corrected me. I was fascinated by the thick, slippery cover, so different from the thin, fragile pages of my school textbooks and exercise books. He sat me on his lap. The magazine cover showed two men face to face smiling at each other and shaking hands. Chairman Mao, and Premier Khrushchev. Dr. Wong guided my finger along the title.

"What a good reader you are!" Dr. Wong smiled, hugging me. "The smartest second grader ever!" He made me feel good about myself. My parents never praised me, even I brought home straight A's with my teachers' praises.

"Do you want to be Chairman Mao's good child?" Dr. Wong held my chin up and guided my face away from the magazine to look up at him.

"Yes, of course I do," I nodded eagerly. Every child was taught to love Chairman Mao, the savior of the Chinese people. Every kindergartener knew the song by heart:

Heaven is vast, and the earth grand,
But the Communist Party's love for us is the greatest;
Your father's love is great, and your mother's love deep,
But they are nothing compared to Chairman Mao's immense love for us.

"Are you sure you can be loyal to Chairman Mao?" Dr. Wong's eyes now serious.

"Of course, I can!" I felt hurt that he doubted me, just like my father.

"Oh, that's *very* good!" The doctor broke into smile, looking satisfied. He patted my head lovingly. I smiled back with pride. My heart felt good when I was approved and trusted.

The next evening Dr. Wong whirled into my ward in quiet dancing steps. He swiftly and noiselessly closed the door behind him, not making even a clicking sound. "I have a special plan for you today, Li Jing. I'm going to give you a very special treatment to cure your heart disease. But it has to be a secret." He sounded really serious.

Why did it have to be a secret since he was a doctor? I thought to myself but was too respectful to ask. Never question an authority figure, we were taught in school.

"Don't worry. It's not going to hurt you. And you'll like it because it's good for your heart. Remember you promised to be Chairman Mao's good child? You have to keep it a secret."

I solemnly nodded.

I wanted to be a Chairman Mao's good child for Dr. Wong.

"Great. Now lie down, face up, on top of the bed cover. Very good! You make a very good child to Chairman Mao." Dr. Wong climbed onto my bed. Suddenly he dropped his whole body flat on top of mine. He was deadly heavy. I couldn't breathe.

How can this be good for my heart? But I didn't ask, in fear of breaking my promise.

"This is good for you. Don't move," Dr. Wong's voice suddenly became cold. He started sliding his body up and down on top of mine.

What strange behavior! Wasn't he afraid of wrinkling his clothes? His nose was spraying thick, hot air in my face. I really didn't like this special treatment! I held my breath and shut my eyes, hoping the dreadful treatment would be over.

"Open your mouth," Dr. Wong ordered, his voice frightening. His thick tongue suddenly forced itself into my mouth. It felt like a cold, hard, smelly, rubber eraser. It made me gag. He was crushing my chest, too. Using both my hands, I tried to hold his chest up to keep from crushing mine, struggling to turn my head sideways to breathe. I pushed with all my might. To my relief, Dr. Wong suddenly rolled off me and jumped up to the floor. I gasped for air.

"There, the treatment isn't bad, is it?" His soft voice now back, Dr. Wong looked at me with a nice smile. "Remember you promised? Tell no one." He tucked me in and left.

I was secretly happy when Dr. Wong didn't come back the next evening. Or the next few evenings. I really didn't like his special treatment for my heart disease.

Then he was back again, one mid-afternoon, much earlier than his usual eight pm visit.

"Child of Chairman Mao, I need to give you another special treatment. Remember you promised? You will not tell this secret treatment to anybody, not your mom, or your dad, especially not the other doctors or nurses, understand?" Dr. Wong waited for me to nod. My heart gripped tight. "Good girl. Your heart needs this special treatment because it's really good for you." He smiled, patting my cheek lovingly.

He told me to lie down, the same way, on top of the bed sheet. I squeezed my eyes shut, bracing myself, hoping the secret treatment wouldn't be too crushing and suffocating. But no sooner had Dr. Wong crashed his heavy body on top of mine than a loud and fast knocking and banging came on the door.

"Open the door! Open the door!" The shadows of people's heads appeared in the milky, fuzzy glass window on the door. My heart skipped a happy beat. Yes! No more secret treatment.

"Sit up, quick," Dr. Wong whispered in a harsh voice, rolling off me, quickly jumping to the floor, his hands swiftly brushing his hair.

"Remember your promise?" he hissed, pointing at me, walking to the door.

"Open the door! Open the door right now!" The banging became louder and more urgent.

"Okay, okay. Coming!" Dr. Wong called out cheerfully, reaching to turn the dead-bolt.

"What are you doing here? Why is the door locked in the broad daylight?" A plump, middle-aged woman doctor burst in, shot stern questions at Dr. Wong, glancing over at me sitting up in the middle of my bed.

"Hey, hey, hey! How did the door get locked?" Dr. Wong's face was all pleasing smiles. Why was he acting like a little guilty boy caught doing something wrong? His hands kept fidgeting on the dead bolt latch on the door. "Strange . . . How did it lock itself?" Dr. Wong exclaimed, as if to himself, his eyebrows raised high in exaggeration.

What did Dr. Wong do to be talked down to like that?

"I, I, . . . I was just teaching this lonely, little girl to read." Dr. Wong tried to laugh but his voice sounded dry. "You know, her parents are never here, and she doesn't have any visitors. I wanted to help her. Wasn't I reading with you, Li Jing?" Dr. Wong turned to call out to me across the room, his dark-rimmed glasses reflecting thick, white light from the window.

I felt my head nod like a puppet. I was numb.

"You need to report to the president's office, now." The woman doctor's stern voice snapped Dr. Wong's head back to her. "He is waiting for you. We've been looking for you. Quit playing games. We know what you're up to. Better tell the truth." Her voice reminded me of my school principal scolding her tearful, whimpering third-grader daughter in front of my second-grade class. The principal mother was making an example of her daughter, pinching and twisting her daughter's plump cheek like it was a piece of flour dough with no feelings.

"The president looking for me? But why? I wasn't hiding. Okay, fine. Bye-bye, Li Jing. Remember, you're Chairman Mao's good child!" Dr. Wong craned his neck over the crowd of heads and shoulders of other doctors. He waved at me before scampering out the door, his head down, his shoulders hunched.

"Now, child, please don't be scared. You can tell us what he did to you," the woman doctor said as she came to sit by me on my bed, her voice soft now. The other doctors in their white gowns were all looking at me, smiling their assurance. Although her manner was now comforting, her smiling eyes kind, I couldn't bring myself to tell her about Dr. Wong's secret treatment plan to cure my heart disease. My mind raced, my mouth like a wax-sealed Chinese herbal medicine bottle.

I had promised Dr. Wong never to tell, my head kept telling my heart.

"Sweetie, don't be afraid. Did Dr. Wong hurt you?" The nice woman doctor was persistent. "What did he do to you?" All the other doctors' eyes were on me. But I just couldn't bring myself to open my mouth to tell the woman doctor about Dr. Wong's chest-crushing and suffocating secret treatment. The doctors looked at one another. They waited, and waited, finally, they filed out of my room, leaving Dr. Wong's secret buried deep inside me.

Nobody else ever asked me about what Dr. Wong did to me. And I never saw him again.

But something very unpleasant happened.

My father started spending every night in my ward for the remainder of my forty-day hospitalization. After working all day, he'd bike two hours back to the city. Sweat rolling off his dust-covered face, he looked exhausted, irritated, and more short-tempered than ever. Crashing into the small folding canvas chair in the corner of my ward, my father put his feet on the floor, his hands on the narrow wooden armrests, and he shot me a hard look. "You're killing me." I watched him close his eyes and fall asleep.

I felt like a mouse being caged with a cat.

"Everybody thought you're going to die of your heart disease!" Little Beauty, my classmate, exclaimed, when I went back to school. "But you came back healthy, fair skinned and plump!" All the girls in my class were fascinated with the new hairstyle the nice nurses braided for me: a high-strung ponytail split in two, with a pretty pink ribbon tied on top. The girls copied it into a new fashion.

My parents started telling the neighbors that my near-fatal heart disease was caused by a bad cold and not enough sleep because our only family bed was crowded and noisy with my brothers. *You're lying!* I'd cry out inside, but fear kept me quiet.

"Told you not to scare your sister!" My father would slap and kick Nimble, when he caught him jumping out of the dark hallway to scare me. "Dr. Liu said her heart should not beat fast."

What's the difference between the two kinds of fast beating heart? I wondered.

My heart beat faster when I was running around playing catching games with other kids. I was the happiest and excited. How could that be bad for me? But my father would yell for me to stop running and made me stay inside. "Do you want to kill your stupid self?" But when he slapped and kicked and yelled at me, my heart beat faster, too. I was afraid, angry, and sad. It had to be bad for my heart! Why didn't he stop doing that? And my mother's silent eyes and angry face made my heart beat fast, too. But my father never said a word about it.

"Get up!" one day my mother yelled at me. "It's seven o'clock. You're so lazy. The neighbor girl Lotus gets up at 4:30 every morning to light the stove, empty the urine pots, and carry her baby brother on her back, and cooks for her family. But look at you, still sleeping. When can I count on you to be good and diligent like that?"

"Lotus' got a stepmother, but I don't!" I blurted out, irritated.

How could my mother compare me to her? The girl was several years older than me. She was fourteen. Everyone knew she was dumb, not only short and fat, but ugly, too. Her face was meaty, and her short neck in her shoulders, her small eyes hidden under her puffy eyelids, her lips shapelessly fat. And she mumbled instead of talking in clear words.

"What did you say?" My mother turned around to glare at me.

"I said I don't have a stepmother like Lotus." I thought she hadn't heard me.

"You say it again, I'll kick your brains out!" My mother charged at me.

I froze, my heart pounding.

Fear of my parents had paralyzed my ability to speak up.

Chapter 30

My Beautiful Music Teacher, Miss Pan

美麗的音樂老師潘虹

MY THIRD GRADE YEAR was the best, leaving me with a lifetime of fond memories.

Miss Pan Hong, my beautiful music teacher, made me a star.

"Li Jing," Miss Pan called my name in class one day.

I tensed up. Oh, I wasn't doing anything wrong but paying attention to my beautiful teacher, admiring her double-eyelid big eyes with long eyelashes. She reminded me of my childhood doll that Grandmother kept locked in her black chest. She was fair-skinned, her face as smooth as boiled egg-whites painted with peach blossom color, her mouth a plump red cherry, her white teeth even, and her smile pretty. Miss Pan's singing voice sounded like a silver bell. She walked gracefully in her high heels, her flowing dress a swaying willow tree. She looked just like the Chinese fairy-tale lady, *Chang-E* 嫦娥, who by mistake took some secret potion, flew to the moon, lived there with a jade rabbit under an evergreen tree.

"Li Jing," Ms. Pan called me again. I timidly peeked up, wondering why. "Come on, Li Jing, get out of your seat and come over here. Why are you acting like a wooden doll?"

I hurriedly got out of my seat to stand by my teacher, facing the class.

"I'm selecting a few girls for the singing and dancing performance to represent our Team 182 Elementary School," Miss Pan announced to the forty pairs of bright eyes and eager faces. "We will perform in the prestigious Children's Palace for Taiyuan city's VIP leaders."

My heart cheered. Before I came to live in the city, I was also on my village school's singing and dancing team performing on stage for the Dragon Festival. I could still smell the fragrant pink powder on my cheeks and see the pretty red ribbon in my hair. A paper-and-stick hoe on my shoulder, I played one of the children sitting in the bright moon light listening to Mama telling about her poor, sad life in the "old China" before the 1949 Communist liberation.

Now my city teacher, beautiful Miss Pan, had picked me again for the dancing team! And, she made me the leading dancer! There were many third-grade girls who had good looking, big eyes, and prestigious intellectual parents. But out of all the fancy city girls, my teacher picked me, born and raised in the backward, deep mountain village, with small eyes, and "thick-neck disease."

I was grateful and treasured every minute at rehearsal times.

The play was called *One Sunday Morning*: A schoolgirl was on her way to the park for her Communist Youth league activity, when she ran into an old countryside lady who was lost. The old lady was carrying a heavy bamboo basket, walking on her tiny, painful, three-inch bound feet with a cane. She had forgotten where her city relatives lived. The girl helped the old lady, carrying the old lady's heavy basket, and finally found her relatives, who lavished the girl with praise for her good deeds.

I loved playing the lone star. I perfected every dance move Miss Pan taught me. Eight girls fanned out dancing behind me. A popular fourth-grade girl helped sing on the backstage microphone.

But a disaster happened the day before our big performance. My mother did something out of the blue that angered my teacher: She cut my long hair short.

"What happened to your pretty long hair?" Miss Pan gasped at the sight of me.

It frightened me to see my teacher get so upset.

"Why did your mother do that? Didn't she know tomorrow is your big day?"

"She did."

"But why did she cut your pretty long hair short and ugly?"

I shook my head, in tears. I didn't know why.

"Tell your mother to fix your hair pretty!"

I couldn't stop crying when I got home.

"What's the matter?" My mother looked at me sideways, out of the corners of her silent eyes. "So what your hair is short? Your teacher needs to stop fussing over nothing."

My mother salvaged my hair into two buns, one behind each ear. She pulled my hair so hard and tight my scalp hurt.

Our *One Sunday Morning* play was a great success. It won a storm of applause from the packed auditorium. I became a celebrity.

"Look, that's the girl in the show! She's even prettier in person!" I couldn't believe the compliments I heard when I ran into a group of girls in the street. They surrounded me, telling me how they loved the way I sang and danced.

At home, my mother said nothing. She didn't ask me about my big show. But she did do something unusual that puzzled me. She took me to the city's photo studio to have our picture taken together. And, unlike in real life, she even smiled in the photo.

Still, I wished my beautiful teacher Miss Pan was in my mother's place.

I couldn't wait to be picked again next year in my fourth grade.

But my dream was never to come true.

The very next year, before I started my fourth grade, Chairman Mao's Cultural Revolution broke out. Across China, from elementary school to college, all schools were shut down. All students older than fifth graders became Red Guards. They burned books, beat, humiliated, tortured, even killed many teachers.

I was too young to participate, but old enough to remember the scenes of bloody horror.

Soon I heard bad news about my beautiful teacher Miss Pan Hong from some older kids. She was beaten and tortured, accused of being too beautiful, too elegant. The Red Guards shaved off half of her long hair and forced her to shovel manure into a bucket and carry it on her back.

That was the last I heard of my beautiful teacher Miss Pan. She was twenty-four years old.

My mother and me. I was still wearing the same hair style for my star performance at Children's Palace. Notice the big lump, my "thick-neck disease," in the front of my neck.

Chapter 31

Cultural Revolution. No More School

文化大革命,不能上學了

IT WAS A LATE NIGHT, the summer of 1966.

Nimble and I were banging on the closed door to our one-room apartment.

"Ma, open the door!" Nimble yelled.

"Ma, open the door!" I joined in.

But no sound came from behind the thin, narrow wooden door, and there were no signs of people stirring behind the neighbors' darkened windows to the left or right of us.

The moon was bright. Stars were blinking sleepily high above in the midnight sky. A whiff of raw sewage drifting in the air from the outhouse at the corner of the yard.

Grandpa was standing by quietly waiting. He looked tired. I had blisters on my soles.

The three of us had just returned from Red Stone Bridge after walking two days on the mountain trails and riding on the packed train on the third day from the town of Ping Yao. While Nimble and I had walked empty-handed, Grandpa had shoulder-poled two heavy wicker baskets of gifts for my parents: barley flour and golden millet, the specialty of Qin Yuan county.

After we'd arrived in Taiyuan, there was no bus running at late hours. We'd walked the fifteen bus stops in the dead of the night. Now we couldn't wake up my parents.

My brother Nimble and I had spent a fun summer at Red Stone Bridge. The freedom! No chores. No fears. No stress as we ran happily all over the hills and in the fields.

This was the first time Nimble had seen my birth village. Everyone was curious about him, a city boy. Look how cute his deep-set eyes were, they'd exclaimed, like two black beans! And they laughed about his visible hair on his arms, a rare sight for mostly body-hair-free Chinese people. "Here comes the hairy monkey," everyone would tease him, for he was nimble like a monkey, too. He could run up the ladder to our great-grandmother's attic from inside and climb back down the windows from outside! Our great grandmother was hard of hearing, outlived my beloved great grandpa Lao Ye Ye for many years. Nimble taunted her mercilessly. He'd sneak up behind her, yank at her shirt, and then run away before she could turn around. "A monkey bandit!" great grandmother would yell.

I loved coming back to Red Stone Bridge.

Grandpa was loving, as always. And Grandmother surprised me by changing for the better – one hundred and eighty degrees. She didn't yell at me anymore but used her nice voice. She even let me eat a fresh carrot one day after Grandpa shoulder-poled two basketfuls home. "Of course, my dear child, have one." I immediately became grateful to her. She'd even made me my favorite barley flour pancakes. Grandmother's harsh image started fading away in the first eight years of my life in the village. The memory didn't come back to me until decades later when I started writing my memoir.

I also didn't find out until decades later that Grandmother had cried tears all over the village telling neighbors that her despised daughter-in-law, my mother, was abusing both me and her "good-natured" son, my father.

I remember wondering about my milk mother's tear-streaked face when I went to visit her at her home that summer, her tearful eyes with love and pity. Why was she looking at me like that, feeling sorry for me? She must be crying for her recently passed-way small daughter.

The only thing that had irritated me during that good summer back in the village was when Grandmother went out of her way to have conversations with me. She'd interrogate me when no one was around.

"Look at you," she'd exclaim. "sitting there lifeless like a dumb pumpkin. What happened? Remember how you were running around giggling and laughing like the loudest wild birds? Did the heart disease make you dumb and quiet like your Aunt Er Gu? How come you had a heart disease? You were as strong, and healthy as a wild horse when living in the village. Why all of a sudden you got heart disease only after a short few months of living in the city?

"Who was abusing you? Who beat you? Your mother beat you, right? Come on, you can tell Grandmother the truth."

"No, it wasn't my mother. It was my father. He beat me." I didn't like her pressure.

"Nonsense. I don't believe you. You're lying because you're scared of your mother, I knew it. Are you too scared of your mother to tell me the truth?"

"No, my father beat me." I insisted on the truth. I also wanted to tell her that my mother was hurting me, too, not by physical beating, but by her silent eyes, angry face, knotted eyebrows, and cold, heart-piercing words. But I didn't know how to word the invisible hurt in my heart.

"Stop lying about your dad!" Grandmother's face turned into anger, glaring at me, hissing in a low voice. "He buys you food, clothes, everything! What does that bad-omen mother of yours buy for you? She spends all her salary on her no-good lazy brother and his ugly kids."

I realized, reluctantly, what Grandmother said was true: my father was taking care of the family financially, but my mind and heart couldn't help but resent the way she had completely ignored how I was also hurt by my violent father. The more she demanded my unconditional respect, love, and gratitude to my father, the more defiant I became. It became our lifelong head-butting power struggle.

September 1, 1966, the first day of school, was drawing near. I was eager to get back to the city, not because I missed my dreadful parents, but wanted to see my wonderful teachers.

My math teacher, Mrs. Ma, praised me for my photographic memory. I was always the quickest to give the correct answers during her mental-math drill. My Chinese language teacher, Mrs. Fan, read my writings aloud in class as models. I was the class monitor for being the all-time best student. And, oh, how I couldn't wait for Miss Pan to pick me again for the school's dancing team in the new school year to perform at the city's prestigious Children's Palace.

But for some strange reason, Grandmother kept brushing me off, saying that there was no reason to be in a hurry to get back to the city, and that we should just relax and enjoy staying in the village for a little longer. No! I stamped my feet, demanding that she had Grandpa take Nimble and me back to the city on time before September 1.

Grandmother finally gave in. "Always like a born-stubborn dog," she said in her soft voice, tossing me only a mild, scolding look. I'd completely forgotten the harsh image of Grandmother altogether.

We got up at dawn on the day Grandpa took Nimble and me back to the city. Grandmother made us a special going-away meal: fried tofu and handmade pasta of luxurious all-wheat flour. She even prepared precious hard-boiled eggs her hens had laid. We rode the first half day, of forty *li*, on the village's one-horse-drawn pinewood cart to the town of Guo Dao, where we stayed overnight in the Horse-Cart Inn, sleeping in our clothes on the *kang* with a dozen other travelers, just like the first time when Grandpa dropped me off at Taiyuan.

The next morning, we got up early and went out to wait for the bus with a crowd of passengers. We waited and waited till the sun was high up in the sky. But no bus came. Some passersby told us that Chairman Mao's Cultural Revolution had just started in Beijing and all the other big cities. All bus service had been cancelled.

"Why don't we turn around and go back home?" Grandpa asked me. No way. I insisted that he find a way to take us back to the city. Whatever it took. Nothing was making me late for school.

That was why we had walked two whole days, hundreds of *li* on the deep mountain trails, to the town of Ping Yao to catch the train.

But now, after our hard, three-day journey, we couldn't wake up my parents.

"Who is it? What are you looking for?" a man's voice finally called out from inside.

Huh? A stranger's voice!?

"Ma, we're back!" Nimble cried out excitedly.

A middle-aged man poked his head out of the half-open door. I couldn't quite make out his face in the dark. But he was definitely not my father. We were stunned, speechless.

"Who are you looking for?"

"We are looking for our parents and brother Cricket. They live here. We live here."

"Oh, you are Secretary Zhang's kids," he said respectfully, his voice nicer now. "Your family has moved. Your mother has been assigned to an upgraded two-room apartment, much bigger than this one small room. Remember the three-story-high office building by the entrance of the yard? It's a residential building now. Your parents are on the second floor, the second room on the left, the middle entrance."

Grandpa shoulder-poled the two heavy wicker baskets. The three of us walked across the dirty yard to our new home. The moonlight seemed to have dimmed along with our spirits.

"Why are you back?" My father flung the door open, looking irritated, surprised. "Didn't I tell you to wait for my letter?" He turned to scold Grandpa, his good-natured father.

"Well, your mother did tell the kids to wait," Grandpa was apologetic, his voice low and soft. "But Cai Mei insisted we leave. She was worried about missing school."

My father turned to glare at me. My heart shuddered. Grandmother didn't say anything about waiting for any letter! Besides, what was so wrong with not wanting to miss school? But I kept quiet, not daring to speak out.

"Always you and your stupid stubborn head! You never listen! Look what you did, rushed back for nothing. All schools are shut down now. No one knows when they'll be open. Chairman Mao's Cultural Revolution has started."

Our "upgraded" new home had two bare-walled rooms in the three-story-high, old brick office building on the other side wall of the Heavy Machinery Factory. There were dozens of one or two-roomed units on each floor for the hundreds of blue collar workers and their families.

The walls were brushed with lime powder. The only furnishing was a radiator against the wall under the window. In cold winters, we pressed our hands on it for heat, but it usually was lukewarm. We could see our breath. We wore the same thick, cotton-padded coats and pants inside as we did outside.

Like every other family, my father built a coal-burning cooking stove with brick and mud by the door in the outer room of our two rooms.

"Stop opening the door!" my father would yell, irritated that we had to go out to the hallway to use the toilets. "The draft is killing the fire!" He'd bark like a watch dog attending to the weak-flamed stove. Coal was rationed. To make it last, the stove was fed "coal cakes" mixed with mud we dug and carted back from the hills outside the city.

During spring, autumn and summertime, every family cooked outside in the hallway. Each family built their own makeshift brick-and-mud stove at their door. The hallway became so crowded, only one person at a time could pass through in between stoves on both sides of the hallway. And every family stored their piles of loose coal and mud at the foot of their stove.

The hallway was endlessly long. It was pitch black dark like a long underground tunnel. Each family hung a small 15-watt light bulb above its stove. Electricity was expensive, just like food and water. We only turned the light on when cooking.

Three times a day at cooking time, dozens of open-ended chimneys would freely pour out choking black, white and yellow smoke into the hallway, depending on what was being burned inside each stove. The smoke was so thick we could barely see in front of noses.

Amazing that I escaped unscathed, breathing into my lungs, from ages ten to eighteen, that raw, thick coal burning smoke on the daily basis.

The only good thing about our "upgraded" living was that we didn't have to go outside and fetch water with a washbasin or a kettle. And instead of one single water faucet sticking out three-foot-high in the middle of the dirt ground shared by hundreds, we now had one washroom with two water faucets down the hallway on each of the three floors.

The washroom was divided by a wall with a doorless entrance. The inner room had a window. The three squatting toilet stalls were for both men and women. The outer room had no window or lighting. It was always dark. The floor was slippery and thick with grime. Against one side of the wall two water faucets jutted out over a long, half-foot shallow, coarse cement sink. Most of the time, water trickled out of the faucets as well as the flushing toilets. Often times there was no water at all. The three squatting flushing toilet bowls were permanently piled up with foot-high solid human waste. This was my everyday normal life for ten years.

"You're so little, already cooking for your family?" a young woman worker exclaimed when she saw me washing vegetables over the sink one day. "How old are you? Eleven only?" She shook her head in amazement and disbelief. But I couldn't feel her excitement. It was what my parents expected of me.

Gone was the peace, fun, and joy of learning in school. I now was a miserable fulltime servant for my family.

The Cultural Revolution was getting bloody. Workers in my mother's factory were divided into two factions. Each side pledged their undying loyalty to Chairman Mao, while declaring the other side anti-Mao. Soon violence broke out. My mother warned me not to go outside and to keep my brothers inside, too. There were no books in our apartment or anywhere else and toys were unheard of in our blue-collar dirt yard.

Life became a series of blood-splashing horrors.

Through the grime-smudged, small glass window inside our second floor apartment, I watched the world turning mad.

A burly man was beating a slender, pretty-faced woman. He grabbed her arm and swung her around, his fist pounding on her back. She struggled, trying to get away, her long hair flying in the air. His violent pounding on her back sounded like a hammer hitting asphalt concrete. She was crying and screaming, tears and sweat all over her face.

"Beat the slut! Teach her a lesson!" The man's thick-armed wife with a meaty face jumped on her short fat legs, cheering her husband on. Then she joined his beating of the now-battered, pretty-faced woman, but came too close and was smacked in the face by her victim.

"You see that? You see that? You let the slut hit me?" the fat wife's wide mouth cried like a loudspeaker, her plump carrot fingers pointing. "Hit her harder! Hit harder!" The pretty-faced woman collapsed to the ground. The fat wife rushed up and kicked and spat on her.

One tall, rough-looking man dragged his next-door neighbor out into the dirt yard and pummeled him. Then the thug man's wife came out, carrying a big tin kettle of steaming hot boiling water. She poured the boiling water on the fallen man, whose head now looked like a smashed-open watermelon.

Every day truckloads of badly beaten men were paraded through the streets. Their hair had been violently chopped into patches, their faces bruised and swollen. One old man's right eyeball hung out of his eye socket, mucus dripping from it. All of the men's heads were weighed down by a six-foot tall iron cylinder hat, and on their necks huge wooden boards hung by thin iron wires that pulled down and dug into their flesh. Their names were written in big calligraphy characters on the wooden board and crossed out in red – the Chinese symbol of a death sentence for condemned criminals.

These tortured men had been denounced as enemies of the people, their crimes listed above their names: the capitalist roaders, the counter revolutionaries, the anti-Communists, the evil former landlords, the rich peasants, the former nationalist soldiers, the murderers, the rapists, and the thieves. They were being driven to the outskirts of the city to be executed. Their families were billed for twenty Chinese cents ($0.03 USD) for each bullet shot into back of their heads.

One day I was heating up milk for Cricket on my family's brick-and-mud coal-burning stove in the smoke-filled hallway. A neighbor man walked by. He stopped and said to me, smirking, "Did you know your mother was interrogated on the auditorium stage last night? Her arms were held up by two men. They tried to push her head down but – oh, man – she was so stubborn and kept fighting and shouting slogans, *Long Live Chairman Mao!*"

The man's story shocked me and made me sick to my stomach. My mother was born in to a dirt-poor peasant family, orphaned at age four, and grew up loyal to Mao. Why would they humiliate and brutalize *her*?

The bloody horror of madness went on for ten long years. It didn't end until 1976 with Mao's peaceful death.

Chapter 32

Life and Death at Age Ten

十歲生死關

THAT DREADFUL DAY started with no warning.

Nimble, Cricket and I ate our millet-soup breakfast. I carried the aluminum kettle down the smoke-filled hallway to fetch water from the grimy communal washroom to wash our bowls and chopsticks in the cooking pot. Then the three of us went outside to join a bunch of happy screaming kids who were running wild in the yard.

"Let's get out of here and cross the street," a few older kids called out. Everyone yelled hooray. We poured out of our dusty dirt yard onto the asphalt-paved street, where the traffic was mostly made up of bicycles, occasional buses, trucks and jeeps.

Halfway across the street, I heard kids calling my name.

"Li Jing! Li Jing! Over here! Your brother Cricket! He got hit by a jeep!"

I froze. What? Fear gripped me. A few feet away to my right side in the middle of the street, a crowd gathered around a jeep, two men in People's Liberation Army uniforms squatting down and looking at something on the ground. I rushed over and pushed through the crowd.

Cricket was lying on the ground, facing up, his head against the jeep's front tire, his arms and legs spread out, his eyes closed, his face gray, scraped, and covered with dirt and gravel.

Suddenly, the sky twirled above my head. The ground swayed beneath my feet. Everything changed into a strange, silent, slow motion.

I saw my mother running out of the Heavy Machinery Factory. Two women were running alongside her, each woman holding one of her arms. Her knees suddenly buckled, her legs gave out as if they were noodles. She fell down on her knees. The two women pulled her back up by her arms. She continued stumble-running toward the place where Cricket lay motionless.

"Ma . . ." I walked toward my mother, trembling with fear, hoping my tears of sorrow and remorse would soften her heart. I had neglected my duty to hold Cricket's hand crossing the street. My mother's dazed eyes scared me. She looked through me as if I were invisible, her eyes fixed straight ahead in the direction of the jeep.

The crowd followed the two uniformed men as one of them carried Cricket's limp body walking into our two-room apartment on the second floor. They laid him down on the single wooden bed in the outer room. They told my mother that she was welcome to bring Cricket to their army hospital anytime, but it looked like he had a brain concussion. And that, the best cure was to let his brain rest, free of any motion if he traveled to the hospital. My mother nodded numbly – with a forced, polite smile – and sent the men out the door.

"Ma, should I start the stove and boil some water?" I asked, shaking inside out, guilt-ridden. But my mother ignored me. She walked past me to tend to Cricket, her face turned away from me. Racking my brain trying to think of ways to help, I took out the urine pot from under the bed, placed it close to Cricket, and stood aside at attention, my head bowed, my eyes cast down, waiting to serve. But my mother kept her silence, ignoring me. It frightened me more.

How hard was my father going to beat me because I hurt his favorite child?

My mother had once told me how my father acted like an excited child waiting for Cricket to be born: "Wow, I can't believe it. I've created a human, my own flesh and blood."

"He's already created one," I'd said to my mother, meaning my brother Nimble.

"He's already created two," she'd corrected.

Who's the other one? I then caught myself before blurting out: *Oh, it was me.*

As my mother's silent face pounded terror into my heart, my brain raced. I thought of running away. But where could I go on foot? I hadn't yet learned how to ride my family's bicycle, yet. Nor did I have eight cents for the bus fare. And I knew I'd have to face worse consequences if I were captured. I pictured my father dragging me by my hair, kicking and pummeling me until I was dead.

My heart hung in my throat all day, bracing for punishment.

Finally, my father burst in the door, his face ashen, his eyes wild, searching around the room. He dashed over to Cricket's bedside and collapsed to his knees, sobbing. I'd never seen him cry before.

"Ask her." My mother broke her silence, her eyes a cold light.

Standing in the corner of the room, I trembled.

Like a crazed man, my father slowly turned to look at me, his eyes burning with rage. Jumping up to his feet, he charged at me, slapping and kicking. I covered my head with my hands and crumpled to the floor, too frightened to feel the pain, too guilty to cry.

"You just wait," my father roared, out of breath. "If Cricket dies, I promise to come back and finish you off, blow by blow, just . . . like . . . this." He kicked and slapped me one more round to the rhythm of his words. "Get out of my sight, you dumb idiot." He walked back to Cricket to gently touch his favorite son's forehead, stroking his hair, cooing his name, his voice soft.

"Why are you still standing there like a dead tree stump?" My father turned to glare at me. "Waiting for your death? I said I will finish you off later, idiot. Go make yourself useful."

Out of the corner of my eye, I saw my mother sitting in the wooden chair by the bed where Cricket lay, a faint sneer at the corners of her chiseled lips. She'd been watching my father beat me.

"*Old Heaven God*," I pleaded, muffling my cry in bed under my cotton-padded quilt that night, my head and body aching from my father's beating. *What's it like to die? How painful is it going to be when my father beats me to death tomorrow if Cricket dies? Old Heaven God, I'm not afraid to die but I'm scared of pain. Dr. Liu said I won't live past twenty-five anyway. Please, Old Heaven God, make it quick so I can skip the pain. Or, would you let Cricket live so I don't have to die?*

Cricket lay in a coma, but he didn't die the next day. My father shot me his threatening looks, reminding me of my death sentence if death should claim his favorite son.

For the next three days I kept pleading to Old Heaven God to spare my brother Cricket, who lay motionless, his face now swollen purple and black, puffed up like a steamed bun that'd been accidentally dropped into the burning-coal ashes. I did my chores, my heart gripped in fear, trying to stay out of the range of my father's striking hands and kicking feet.

I thought of the truckloads of the condemned-to-die criminals, the counter-revolutionary "bad element" prisoners I'd seen paraded through the streets in the open-top livestock truck before being driven to the execution site to be shot. Their arms were tightly bound behind their backs. Their heads were pressed down or forced back up to face the sky, the executioners' fingers gauging into their eyes. Were they scared, too, like me?

A miracle happened. On the fourth day, Cricket started wiggling his toes. His eyes opened. He moved his head. He smiled at my father and mother when they baby-cooed his name.

"I'll spare your worthless life for now," my father declared, glaring at me.

And the miracle continued: Cricket's brain wasn't affected. Years later he successfully competed to attend one of China's top universities. But my parents never forgave me.

"You nearly killed him!" they'd remind me for years to come.

Fast forward twenty-five years to 1991. I received a baby picture of my brother Cricket's newborn son. My father sent it to me at my studio apartment on Polk Street, in San Francisco.

"Look what a bright and handsome boy he is!" my father marveled in his letter. "He's our Li family's best pride and joy grandchild!"

"Here's the photo of your precious grandson back to you," I wrote, returning the picture. "Cricket's son is your third grandchild, the second grandson. But you act like this is your very first grandchild. I'm sorry but I don't have a big or special enough place to keep this photo."

"Well," my father modestly scolded me, writing back. "Don't you think you're being unreasonable?"

I ignored him.

I phoned to tell this story to my Oklahoma college friend Cindy, who used to be an optometrist back in China but now majored in nursing. "Oh, my goodness!" Cindy was dismayed. "You're so harsh."

Cindy knew nothing about my traumatized childhood.

Still, I couldn't help but feeling a wicked satisfaction in my unforgiving heart.

Chapter 33

A Bad Case of Guilt: Five Hard-Boiled Eggs

五顆煮雞蛋

AFTER THE FIRST FEW YEARS of bloody chaos during Mao's Cultural Revolution, China's schools finally reopened. But it was never the same. Grades no longer counted. Chairman Mao said that knowledge was dangerous, and academic learning made young people stupid.

But one thing stayed the same: my daily go-home-for-lunch time from school. That day, my stomach was growling as I ran upstairs two steps at a time into the smoke-filled dark hallway, only to see no cooking pot sitting on our stove. The padlock was on our door.

Across from our apartment in the crowded hallway stood Da Hu's mom at her family door, stir-frying vegetables on her stove. The sizzling smell of garlic made my stomach growl even louder.

"Do you know where my mother is, Auntie?" I whimpered to the neighbor woman.

"Oh, here you are, Cai Mei." The neighbor smiled, turning to look at me over her shoulder. "Your mother asked me to tell you she is having an all-day meeting today downtown and won't be home till late tonight."

"What? Again?" I burst out yelling. "She has all-day meetings every day! Why do I have to mother my brothers for her?"

"*Ai-ya*," Da Hu's mother exclaimed, stopping her stir-frying and looking me up and down in amazement, chopsticks in her hand. "I didn't know quiet Cai Mei has such a temper!" She handed me the key to our apartment. I kept yelling, feeling good letting out my bottled-up anger and resentment. I never dared to lose my temper in front of my parents.

"Oh, I almost forgot," Da Hu's mother called out before I slammed the door. "Your mother said she left you kids something special to eat."

Wait, what? Really? My mother left something special for me, too? I perked up, my heart giving a happy click, my eyes searching the room. Ah, I saw it. Sitting on the windowsill, out of place, was the dented yellow porcelain mug with chipped edge. I dashed over.

Y-e-s! It was an amazing sight. The old yellow mug was full of hard-boiled eggs soaking in water. I yelped in delight. So many precious boiled eggs altogether. Every three months, each family was given a coupon to buy one *jin* (1.1 pound) of eggs if the stores had them.

Wow, my mother was really generous today. I was too hungry to wonder "why," too young to know that it was one of her ways to cover up her affairs behind my father's back.

I couldn't stop smiling, looking at the precious hard-boiled eggs. I hovered over the dented yellow mug and started counting the eggs bobbing up and down in the water.

Five eggs. Not six. But there were three of us.

I counted again, wishing I was mistaken, hoping to see six eggs.

But still only five.

I instantly understood what my mother expected of me. Her silent eyes planted permanent fear in my heart. I divided the five eggs the prescribed way: two eggs for each of my two brothers, and one for me. Then I went outside to find my brothers playing in the yard and brought them back inside for the special lunch.

I savored every bite of my delicious egg, eating it s-l-o-w-l-y to make it last as long as my brothers' eggs so I didn't have to watch them eating. How I loved the smooth, subtle flavor of the egg white, so nice and cool on my tongue with its delicate, chewy texture. Nothing in the world tasted better. When I grew up and became rich, I wanted to eat as many hard-boiled eggs at one time as my stomach could hold!

As soon as my precious egg had gone down into my stomach, a heavy sense of guilt hit me. I felt ashamed of myself for resenting my mother's absence and throwing a tantrum. How ungrateful I'd been. I had misjudged my mother's kindness and generosity. And worse, I did it in front of the neighbor woman. Desperately, I hoped the neighbor wouldn't tell my mother. But I had a sick feeling that she *would* tell: she'd looked so shocked and taken aback to discover my temper. I wanted to beg her not to tell on me, but too embarrassed about what I'd done and didn't know how to express my thoughts.

I decided to make it up by doing my chores extra carefully after school that day: sweeping the floor, dusting the desk, and made both rooms neat and tidy.

When my mother finally came home late that night, she looked pleased, even a faint smile at the corners of her mouth as she inspected my chores. And her favorite children, my brothers Nimble and Cricket, were happy, safe, and not whining about me.

But I wasn't going to be spared after all. The next day I sensed something terrible was going to happen. My mother's eyes were extra hard, her face a brewing dark storm.

"Okay, darlings," my mother smiled, hugging and kissing Nimble and Cricket. "Go outside and play now."

Bam! My mother slammed the door. Her happy face now twisted into a frightening mask. I shuddered, burying my head into eating out of my bowl at the table, my throat too tight to swallow. A dead silence filled the room. My mother sat down away from me on the floor stool against the wall. Glancing out of the corner of my eye, I saw her glaring hard at me, her long, graceful, willow-leaf-shaped eyebrows tightly knotted.

"You ungrateful evil creature. Despicable wolf's heart and dog's lungs!" she finally broke the silence, cursing. Suddenly, she sprang up to charge at me. Crack! Her stylish black leather high heels kicked me hard on the bony front of my right leg.

I cried out, gasping. The pain was excruciating. Crouching down and doubling over in my chair, I muffled my crying, holding my leg, as my mother stood over me.

"How dare you?" she hissed. "You despicable heartless wolf! Who the hell do you think you are to interfere with *my* whereabouts? What made you think I have to ask for *your* permission to leave home? I wasted that precious egg on your ungrateful cold heart!"

I sat frozen, fixing my tearing eyes on my mother's shining, black leather high heels, terrified that she'd kick me again. My heart back dropped into place when she sat back down on the stool.

Eating out of her bowl, my mother kept her death-glare on me. For a long time.

Chapter 34

One Brother for Each Parent

爸媽每人只要一個弟弟

UNDER THE DIM LIGHT of the 15-watt naked bulb hanging from the ceiling inside our bare-walled apartment, I watched the horror unfolding. My parents were fighting, violently. With a sickening thud, my mother's head hit the cement floor by the brick-and-mud cooking stove. My father came crashing down after her. They wrestled – yelling, cursing, and panting.

Only a few minutes ago, our family was enjoying a rare moment of peace and quiet. Both my parents were in an unusually mellow mood, chatting like the loving couple next door. My mother had a smile at the corners of her mouth as my father fondly looked at her. Standing together by the cooking stove, they were making grated-corn-flour-dough soup with boiled cabbage.

Then my father accused my mother of being careless and wasteful by feeding the stove with too much coal. It all exploded.

"Stingy money slave," she yelled, elbowing him hard in his side. "Do it yourself."

"How dare you." He grabbed her arm.

"Who's afraid of you?" She jerked his hand away.

"You really think I am stuck with you?" he taunted.

"No? Why has your mother been begging me not to get a divorce?" she sneered.

"I *will* divorce you, bad-omen slut," he came back at her.

"Just fine with me, you bastard. Divorce." She stamped her foot.

"I'll be son of a turtle if I don't go through with it this time." He puffed out his chest.

"I want Nimble." My mother called out the name of her favorite child.

"I want Cricket." My father yelled out the name of their mutually favorite son.

I held my breath, waiting to hear *my* name called. Which one of my parents was going to call out "Cai Mei"? I was neither of their favorite. Quietly, I waited.

Neither parent called out my name. They went right back to fighting.

I wasn't wanted! I burst out crying and ran out the door, down the hallway to the only comforting arms I knew, a few doors away, from loving Auntie Yu Xin.

Auntie Yu Xin was the first kindness I'd discovered in the big, cold, dry and dusty city of Taiyuan.

I was eight. One day I ran into my first social problem: Phoenix, my second-grade classmate, had stood me up. We'd made a plan to meet each other at the public bathhouse at Da Ying Pan for our once-a-year bath. I'd waited and waited but she never showed up. Three years older than me, Phoenix liked to play mind games. Her beautiful big eyes smiled sweetly, but she'd say words her heart didn't mean. It puzzled me.

I went to my mother's office but was surprised to see she wasn't alone. I halted at the door, glued my back against the wall, too shy to go in.

"Why, come in," my mother called out after spotting me. "Don't be so useless. It's just your Auntie Yu Xin, the typist clerk." We children called our adult neighbors aunties or uncles to show respect.

I nudged my way in, my back scraping the open door.

"Aw, what a darling girl!" Auntie Yu Xin looked up and smiled at me. She looked younger than my mother. Her eyes were so pretty they looked like the crescent moon, her teeth even and white. I wished my mother would smile at me like that.

Sitting behind a small, square, wooden desk across from my mother's long rectangular desk, Auntie Yu Xin was typing. Click, click, click. The typewriter tapped a pleasant rhythm. I was fascinated by how she moved the handle of the typewriter to pick up a Chinese character like a long-necked crane, and tapped it down onto the paper wrapped on the cylinder.

"What do you want?" My mother looked up from behind her desk, a pen in her hand.

"Phonex didn't keep her promise." I blurted out in tears. "She told me to wait for her but she never showed up."

"Why are you yelling at me?" My mother's response shocked me. "I didn't tell Phoenix not to show up."

I hadn't realized I was yelling. I certainly hadn't meant to make my mother mad. Immediately, I became ashamed of myself. Not only did I not have my questions answered, but I'd made my mother angry with me. And I was greatly embarrassed being yelled at in front of the nice lady Auntie Yu Xin. To my delight, Auntie Yu Xin was quietly smiling at me, her beautiful eyes in sympathy. I wished Auntie Yu Xin were my mother.

Now, hysterical, I burst into Auntie Yu Xin's one-room apartment, where she lived with her engineer husband and their two small boys. "Auntie Yu Xin, Auntie Yu Xin! My parents are fighting. They knocked each other down to the floor. They said they'll be divorced. My mother said she wanted Nimble. My father said he wanted Cricket. But neither of them said my name. How come, Auntie Yu Xin? How come they didn't call my name? Where am I going to live after they divorce?" I blurted it all out in one breath, sobbing uncontrollably.

"Oh, sweetie, there, there." Auntie Yu Xin gathered me into her arms, hugging me. Her husband, tall and strong, rushed out to go and break up my parents' fight.

"Oh, now, now, sweetie, everything is going to be all right." Auntie Yu Xin cupped my face in her comforting hands, looking lovingly into my eyes. "Precious child, don't you mind them. I'm sure you are wanted by both of them. . . . It's just that . . . you're the only girl . . . Your parents didn't want to fight over you, you see? . . . I'm sure they are just being considerate and polite to each other . . . because . . . you see, . . . they can't split you in half, right? I'm sure both of them wanted you. . . . Well, just in case they don't, your Auntie Yu Xin would *love* to have you . . . Who wouldn't want to have a good daughter like you? You know I always wanted a girl . . . It's a blessing to have a pretty and smart daughter like you. I wish I had your mom's luck. But I've only got two boys! . . . And . . . you know, your brothers aren't as fortunate as you are because your grandparents love you more, right? That's why they raised you! See? . . . They will take you back if your parents are divorced. So, you see . . . you don't have to worry about a thing, . . . for you'll have more places to go than both your brothers! See how lucky you are? Okay, sweetie? Please, no need to be sad. And trust me, your Auntie Yu Xin is telling you the truth, right?"

I stopped crying, taking to heart every word of the lifesaving white lie from this precious kindhearted woman.

Auntie Yu Xin was another God-sent angel, just like my milk mother. She saved me from being destroyed psychologically. I would have been, if this loving, caring, kind lady hadn't made me believe that I was loved.

Later that night, I was awakened by a pair of hands caressing my face. No one in my family had ever touched me like that. Cautiously, I opened my eyes a little bit. It was my mother. She was lying next to me, her head on my pillow, nose to nose and face to face with me. My body tensed up.

"You poor thing," my mother said, caressing my face. "Must've been scared."

Mother, you're mistaken. It's only me. Cricket is over there sleeping in the corner. I wanted to point out to my mother about her mistake. But strangely, I couldn't bring myself to do it. I was relishing that special moment when my mother's hands were touching my face. I felt loved as I'd never felt before. I wanted her mistake to go on. This must be how good my brothers felt being loved by our mother.

For the longest time, I wondered why my mother mistook me for my brother Cricket.

Or, did she?

Chapter 35

Bowl in the Yard

丟在院子裡的碗

IT WAS DINNERTIME on a hot summer evening.

I went outside holding my bowl of grated cornmeal with boiled potatoes. The bluecollar dirt yard was full of men (except my father), women, and children, all chatting and laughing as they ate out of their bowls. Everyone was sitting either on a small floor stool brought from home or on stacks of bricks around piles of loose coal used as people's cooking fuel. It was a merry time of the day, just like lunchtime at Red Stone Bridge.

After finishing my meal, I went back upstairs to put my bowl and chopsticks into the cooking pot to be soaked for washing later. Then I rushed back outside to steal a few more moments of fun chatting with my friends.

"Cai Mei!" my father yelled, glaring at me, as I walked in the door. He was standing at the cooking stove. "Where is your bowl? Did you leave it outside and forget to bring it back?"

"No, I brought mine back in," I answered, blood rushing to my face. I hated being accused all the time. "I put it right inside the soaking water in the cooking pot."

"But look here, dumb idiot. One, two, three, four." His finger jabbed at the bowls, making them click against each other. "Are you blind? It's not five."

"I don't know." I caught myself too late, forgetting my father forbade me to answer his questions with "I don't know."

"You don't know, you don't know. What *do* you know, dumb idiot knucklehead?"

Fearing he'd attack me if I said one more word, I became silent.

"Don't just stand there like the dead elm tree stump you are. Go outside and find it."

"But I brought mine back in . . ."

"You'll never admit your wrongdoing, will you?"

"Could it be my mother? She was eating outside, too."

"It wasn't her. I already asked."

"How about my brothers?"

"I don't think so. It had to be you."

"But I brought mine back. It's the one with the chipped edge. That one right there!"

"Shut up, go find it."

Now I really wanted to pour a kettle full of boiling water on his evil head.

"How dare you glare at me like that?" My father raised his hands. I shot out of the door into the hallway, letting out an anguished cry like an injured animal.

I stopped at the entrance to the building. Shadows and darkness and silence in the yard. No more noisy children running around playing. No more chatting adults smacking their lips deliciously as they ate out of their bowls. The lone light pole by the earthen-mound gate cast a faint yellow circle on the dirt ground. Not a single soul around. Only me. Alone.

The air was sticky hot. Swarms of mosquitoes came buzzing and dancing around me, feasting on my face, neck, ears, arms, and legs. The faint lighting from inside the building cast my lonely shadow from behind into a long, slanted shadow, my only company.

What am I supposed to do now? Why did my father force me to come outside to look for my bowl, which was already inside? What was the point of looking when I knew it wasn't outside? I thought of running away. But where could I go in the darkness with not a penny on me?

Frightened by the darkness, I looked around for a place to hide. The door to the building entrance on the left was propped up open against the wall by two bricks. I slid behind it, my back scraping the rough brick wall, my tears flowing down freely. My legs became numb, my eyes sore. I squatted down to bury my face into my arms over my knees.

Old Heaven God, please tell the demons lurking in the dark to leave me alone.

"S-i-s-t-e-r, where - are - you?" Nimble's voice drifted into my ears. My eyes popped open. I must have dozed off. I held my breath and stayed still.

"Come home, Sister!" My brother's annoying voice was getting closer.

"Ha! Found you." Nimble suddenly flung aside the door to expose me. It angered me. Licking my salty lips, I kept my face buried in my arms.

"Sister, Dad wants you to come back home." My brother poked at my arm.

I ignored him.

"Dad said the bowl has been found. Mom forgot to bring hers back inside."

I became angrier. *Told you so!*

"You are not coming back? I'm going to tell." He skipped away.

My face, neck, and ears were throbbing, hot and itchy from mosquito bites.

"Mom and Dad said if you don't come back inside, we're going to lock you outside tonight." Nimble was back with the message.

My pride stopped my panic. I wanted my father to apologize to me! I silently protested and didn't move.

"I'm going to tell."

More footsteps came.

"She's right here behind the door," called out Nimble, the disgusting snitch.

"What the hell are you doing down here, waiting for your death?" my father roared over me. He had the nerve to sound like nothing had happened.

What do you have to say about the bowl? I yelled inside but fear silenced my voice.

"Get up this second. Don't make me kick your brains out!"

Fear made me stand up on my numb legs. I silently followed my father and brother inside, my heart crying out for justice. My father never apologized to me that night. Nor did he ever for the rest of his eighty-six years of life.

Growing up, and all my life, I've been obsessed with getting an apology when I was wronged. Often times, unwittingly, and unwisely, at all costs.

Chapter 36

My Mother's Smiling Face on a Dog's Body

笑臉

My mother and me, at Anti-Imperialism studio.

1969. I WAS THIRTEEN, holding a copy of Chairman Mao's Little Red Book the camera man had thrust into my hand: "Hold it close to your heart." It was a required standard pose for photograph. The Cultural Revolution for savior-Mao-worshipping was at its fever pitch.

The vertical lines scripted on the right in calligraphy were written by Mao's hand-picked successor Lin Biao (he and his family were soon to die in their crashed airplane after his plot to overthrow Mao was discovered): *Read Chairman Mao's books, listen to Chairman Mao's words, and follow Chairman Mao's directions.*

I didn't know why this photo was taken. It was on the day my mother had her hair cut at a barber's shop. I remembered it because of a middle-aged man's mysterious smiling face. He was sitting at the door in a chair. As my mother and I were on our way out, he looked up from behind his newspaper, fixed his eyes on me, and smiled, as if he knew or liked something about me. I blushed, feeling uncomfortable and embarrassed.

My mother's demure-looking face in the photo reminded me of my secret horror.

One day, I wandered alone into the Heavy Machinery Factory, on the other side of the wall at our dirt yard. It was the only place where I could find some printed words to read and satisfy my malnourished brain. Our learning in school was all about memorizing every brand-new instruction from Chairman Mao about how to carry on with the Cultural Revolution.

The front yard of the factory's main administration building was deserted. No one saw me walk up to the large bulletin board, hundreds of posters containing words and images that screamed condemnation in big calligraphy brush strokes: Down with the evil capitalist running dog so-and-so! So-and-so was having shameful extramarital affairs and down with him! Exposed: So-and-so had evil landlord family background! All the names were crossed out in the condemning red color.

Then something caught my eye. It took away my breath, like a hammer to my chest. A cartoon poster on the bulletin board showed my mother's face on the body of a dog! Her face wore a charming smile, her willow-leaf-shaped eyebrows arched up high, her eyes shaped like a dreamy crescent. And her dog's body was wearing a sleek black dress, a white pearl necklace was around its neck.

Comparing a person to a dog was the worst degrading humiliation in Chinese culture.

To describe how a person never changes their personality, Americans say: a leopard doesn't change his spots, but Chinese say: 狗改不了吃屎 gou-gai-bu-liao-chi-shi: *a dog will never stop eating shit*.

"The Rabid Dog, Magnolia Zhang!" The poster title condemned my mother's name.

I was dumbfounded, my temple throbbing, my face burning. I had a bewildered feeling I couldn't describe. I felt dizzy and nauseated. But I couldn't tear my eyes off my mother's charming, smiling face on a dog's body wearing a black dress and white pearl necklace.

All my life, I'd longed for my mother's smiling face. But not like this! It was creepy.

My mother had made a lot of enemies. Like anywhere else in China, the Heavy Machinery Factory was divided into two violent factions, with each side claiming their undying loyalty to Chairman Mao while trying to kill the other. My mother's side was short in numbers. Faithfully following Chairman Mao's order to overthrow all the top leaders in every factory, school, and village, she had turned into a ferocious fighter against her former boss, Mr. Zhao, the president of the factory. Her rival faction also denounced Mr. Zhao, but their members were secretly sympathetic to the fallen president. But my mother's rage and hate for him, unlike her enemy's, was genuine.

And the hatred among adults spewed into their offspring.

"Look at the huge, ugly camel among the sheep!" a skinny short boy in my class one day yelled at me when we lined up in P.E. class. His father was a die-hard faction enemy of my mother's. "Shame! You should go kill yourself!"

"Hey," a girl walked up to me, sneering in my face. "I heard your mother and father had another fight. Is it true?"

It was humiliating that my parents were the only ones among the thousands of blue-collar dirt-yard dwellers who quarreled and fought for divorce. The heavy burden of immense shame was unbearable. Only a harmonious family was supreme and desired in Chinese culture.

"Ha, ha! I heard your father beat you with a shovel and you fought back, is that right?"

But the kids' bullying and insults all paled in comparison to the moment when I discovered the humiliating cartoon of my mother's smiling face on a dog's body.

I wanted to cry but found myself muted, voiceless.

Like a cornered animal, I suddenly lashed out and reached up to rip the poster off the bulletin board. I tore it into pieces and tossed them on the ground. My heart pounding in vengeance and fear, I briskly walked out of the ghostly empty factory yard, the degrading image firmly iron-pressed into my mind.

Had I been discovered, anyone from the mob of my mother's enemy faction would've been entitled to beat me half to death and dump my tattered body at my mother's feet.

I never told a soul about my secret horror.

Chapter 37

Growing Up Early

早熟

NIMBLE AND I were walking behind our father, who was pulling a six-foot-long, thick-handled pinewood cart, we'd borrowed from my mother's factory. We were on our way to downtown to buy rationed loose coal for our cooking stove.

"Where is the rope?" My father suddenly turned to glare at me over his shoulder.

"What rope?" I was baffled.

The wooden cart was flat-bedded with two sides built up one-foot high, and the front and back ends open. Two sheets of aluminum were used to enclose both the front and back ends to keep the loose coal chunks from falling off. But I never thought of a rope to keep the aluminum sheets in place.

"Dumb idiot, you forgot the rope!" my father halted, yelling at me. "How the hell are we going to keep the loose coal on the cart without a rope?"

Since when was it my responsibility to make sure a rope was on the cart? But I was too scared to speak up. My father became angrier as he yelled. Suddenly he dropped the handles of the cart to charge at me, his feet flying up to kick me.

I dodged and ran back home to get the rope as my father went on yelling.

And that was the day I became an adult.

From that day forward, I automatically assumed my duty and responsibility was to take care of everything and everyone. I learned to think and plan ahead. When riding my family's bicycle to buy rationed corn flour or pulling the six-foot long heavy, thick handle-barred wooden cart walking miles to buy frozen cabbages, I'd always double-check to see if I'd had brought a bag or a rope.

My father told me to always lock the bicycle as soon as I dismounted and parked it outside in the dirt yard. "I'll take your life if the bicycle gets stolen," he warned me. I took his warning seriously to heart. It became so firmly imprinted in my head that everything I did was rote and mechanical.

"Where is the key to the bicycle?" Nimble, my brother, asked me one evening, after I carried bicycle upstairs from outside after dark, part of my duty and chores.

"I don't know. I don't have it."

"But the bike is locked."

"Dumb idiot! Where's the key to the bicycle? Why is it locked now that it's safely inside?" my father yelled out from the outer room.

"How would I know? I didn't lock it after I moved it upstairs inside." I was indignant.

"It has to be you!" My father charged into the inner room, glaring at me.

"I know I didn't lock it! You don't believe me, and you never do, but I believe myself!"

"Quit talking back to me, knucklehead, check your pocket!" My father ordered me.

"I'll prove you wrong!" I reached into my right pocket. My hand froze in it. It was the key!! My face betrayed me right away. I wanted to vanish into the dusty cement floor.

"Ha Ha!" my pesty brother Nimble pointed at me and mimicked. "I believe myself! . . . ha ha ha . . ."

"You dead face Dumb idiot," my father yelled at me.

I learned to blame myself whenever things went wrong, and automatically felt guilty when something *did* go wrong. I'd go all out to correct the situation.

One day I was overjoyed when my father brought home a brand-new flashlight for my brother Nimble and me to share. This was the first time, at age thirteen, I'd ever laid my hands on a flashlight. I loved its shining metal shell. It felt so smooth, nice and cool in my hands.

The precious flashlight was not just a luxury but also an emotional comfort. It brought me a rare feeling of joy in my fear-and chaos-filled young life.

"Make sure nothing happens to it," my father had told my brother and me. Of course, we'd take good care of it, we promised. I couldn't imagine myself being so irresponsible as to let something bad happen to the expensive flashlight.

Now my brother and I no longer had to walk in the pitch-black darkness to the outhouse in the far corner of our dirt yard. Because there was always hardly any water trickling out, our second-floor indoor toilets were piled up with solid human waste, so high we couldn't squat down without touching it. How very nice we now had *our own* flashlight to guide our steps onto the squatting cement slot over the six-foot-deep pool of raw manure.

That night before we went to bed, Nimble and I walked to the outhouse. We kept each other company, using the flashlight to light our way. The men's room was on the other half side of the outhouse, and I told Nimble to wait for me when he was done.

I turned off the flashlight to save the battery and, after squatting down, tucked the precious flashlight between my stomach and thigh for safekeeping.

Then the worst happened. Standing up, I forgot all about the flashlight. It rolled right off and fell down the urine-and-feces slope into the six-foot-deep manure pool at the back of the outhouse! The horror made my heart stop.

I cried out, my death sentence by my father! I started pleading with my brother.

"Nimble, what should I do? Dad's going to beat me to death if I go back tonight without the flashlight. Please tell me what to do? Help me! Go down there and get it back!"

"I don't want to go down into the pool of the urine and feces . . ."

"Okay, I'm going down." I didn't hesitate, too gripped by terror to worry about the filth. It never occurred to me that I could drown in that six-foot-deep pool of raw sewage.

As I looked down into the open-sewer pool, the moonlight was reflecting on the flashlight's aluminum case. I saw it wedged into the pool's side slope, not in the middle. Hope!

I told my brother to take off his belt, a thick cloth strip.

I tied one end to my wrist, told Nimble to hold the other end steady, inching down the slope, my toes clutching tight, my legs shaking. The stench was lung-piercing, but no matter. My feet clutched onto a few bricks that were sticking out from the side of the slope, slippery but helpful. Slowly, I bent down. Slowly I stretched out my shaky arm. Oh, yes, my hand touched it! Gingerly I grabbed the flashlight. Slowly I turned around to inch my way back up – one small, slippery step at a time – while guided by Nimble's belt. Finally, I was out, trembling with happiness, relief.

I couldn't take the flashlight home until it looked as good and new. So, I rolled the flashlight in the dirt. I pulled out the foot-tall grass to rub off the dirt and the sticky stink. After that, I wiped it clean with the corner of my shirt.

"Don't ever say a word to Dad," I told my brother.

He kept his word. My father never found out.

Sometimes I couldn't keep things hidden.

My mother found out something had happened to me before I even knew it. One early morning she yelled for me to wake up, agitated as usual. "Get the hell out of bed already! Why do I have to remind you every morning? Why can't you just take up the chores on your own?" Rubbing my eyes open, I found my mother standing over me.

"You damn dead face!" my mother gasped, her eyes fixed on my cotton-padded futon cushion. "Look at the mess you made!"

Fear gripped me. What have I done that's made her so angry? Then I saw it. A fresh blot of bright red blood was soaking through the inch-thick, cotton-padded futon. What's happened to me? Did I do that? Was I bleeding? But why? What was wrong with me? Blood rushed up to my burning neck and face. Panicking, I looked down and touched my underwear. It was soaking wet with blood.

In horror, I looked up at my mother's angry face, her eyes glaring in silent fury, her eyebrows tightly knotted. My questions stuck in my throat. My mind flashed back to the bloody urine I sometimes saw in the night chamber when I took it out to empty it.

I seemed to understand it now. My mother had bled into it at night. Now, me, too?!

"Put these in between your underwear," my mother handed me some folded "straw paper" 草紙, *coarse paper*. So that's why she bought the special straw paper every month! "Don't ever mess up the cotton padded bedding again!" She tossed me her silent, dirty looks.

I slept on top of that bloodstain on my cotton-padded futon for the rest of the year. We only washed our bedding once a year. To begin the yearly process, we had to pull out every stitch of our cotton-padded bedding to separate the sheets and padded cotton. Then we scrubbed the bedding in a washbasin, fetching from the communal washroom down the hallway one heavy basin full of water at a time, rinsed it, line-dried it outside in the dirt yard and sewed the pieces back together in the evening. There was no spare bedding to be had.

Chapter 38

My Rooster, My Hero

我的大公雞

I FINALLY, FOR ONCE, experienced what it was like when someone in my family had my back when I least expected it.

He was my pet rooster, my hero.

One day my father had brought home three little fluffy chicks in a cardboard box. One chick was for each of us. Excited, my brothers and I hovered over the little, furry, chirping things in a shoe-sized straw-paper box. We'd never had any pets, man-made or alive.

"I want this one!" Cricket called out first, pointing to the lively off-white chick, the cutest one. Oh, no, he picked the one I liked. I was quietly disappointed.

"This one is mine!" Nimble announced his choice, the bright yellow one.

That's my second choice! I cried inside.

"Ha, ha, the leftover one is yours!" My brothers called out, pointing to the little runt, ruffled, clumsy.

Nimble and I built a brick-and-mud chicken coop in the yard by our pile of loose coal. All three of our chickens lived in it.

My brothers' chicks turned out to be both hens. But my little, clumsy one grew up to be a big, tall, strong, beautiful rooster, with a majestic bright red, quivering, thick crown. His long, smooth feathers were luscious red and shining black. He walked like a proud peacock. I loved sitting by the chicken coop, watching my rooster parading and strolling around our blue-collar dirt yard.

One day, when I was watching my rooster strolling around in the yard, my mother walked by. And what happened next had me shivering in ecstasy.

As my mother passed by, my rooster suddenly jumped up and attacked her, pecking on her back, pulling her shirt. I was stunned, filled with a secret joy. It felt so good to finally have someone in my corner fighting for me. My precious rooster had to be Heaven-sent!

My mother was startled. As she turned around, my rooster jumped up to attack her again, snatching her front shirt, flying up to get at her face. His ring of beautiful neck feathers in a fury of puff, he kept jumping up to attack the woman who regretted giving birth to me and hated my very existence. Yes!

"You turtle-egg bastard!" my mother screamed, outraged. "How dare you!" She picked up bricks and rocks and threw them at her attacker to force him to flee. Her face pale and fear-stricken, my mother looked as if she'd run into an evil ghost spirit.

The next day, my mother took Nimble to our chicken coop. They chased and caught my rooster. They wrung and broke his neck. Then my mother cooked my rooster for dinner, a sneer at the corner of her mouth.

With a lump in my throat, I watched my mother and both brothers smacking their mouths happily eating my rooster.

My brave rooster. He had my back as a fierce fighter. I was a coward, unable to save his life. And he died for me.

Chapter 39

Face-saving and Divorces

離婚

The year was 1970. This gloomy family photo was the calm after the storm.

NOTICE THAT I AM the only one smiling. But my smile had nothing to do with my heart being happy. I'm smiling because I'd discovered a way to enhance my looks while visiting Red Stone Bridge in the summer.

Hiding myself for hours at a time in the quiet attic of my grandparents' house that summer, I'd intensely studied my thirteen-year-old face in a small, hand-held mirror. As I looked at myself, I'd held alongside my face a picture of China's legendary folksinger *Liu San Jie* 劉三姐. I was delighted to discover that my facial features had a lot in common with the famous star. Both our faces fit the classic Chinese standard for maiden beauty: a goose-egg-shaped oval face, pointed melon-seed chin, slim thin nose, plump cherry mouth, and flying moth eyebrows. And when I imitated the singer's smile, the shape of my mouth looked especially nice and pleasant just like hers. But my spirits always dimmed when I looked above my cheekbones and below my eyebrows and noticed my small eyes. I lacked a pair of beautiful, almond-shaped, double-eyelid, larger eyes, like those of *Liu San Jie* – a perfect Chinese beauty.

That's when I decided to emphasize my strength: my smile. Look at my smile in the photo. It was two worlds apart from Grandmother's grief-stricken face. She looks much older than her fifty-eight years of age.

Grandmother was in the city on a special mission.

My mother had again run away from home. She'd been staying with Cricket in one of her factory's small dorm room, which they shared with four young women. Then one day, my father went after her. She wasn't in. He rummaged through her cardboard box storage under her bed and discovered his carved-jade name seal she had stolen. He couldn't believe his luck! A carved personal seal was as good as someone's signature. My mother was able to use it to claim my father's monthly salary. He finally found her in the factory yard, where they got into a tugging argument, and he punched her in the mouth in front of a lot of people.

My mother vowed to get a divorce. But my grandmother had firmly put her three-inch bound feet down: "Over my dead body you'll get a divorce!" She deeply believed in Confucius's teaching that a woman without a male heir was a walking shame. She dictated Grandpa to write the letter: "No one is taking away my two grandsons to carry some other man's name."

"*Ai-ya*, Old Heavens have mercy." Red Stone Bridge villagers shook their heads sympathetically at my grandparents before they'd left. "All three of your children are going through divorce."

Grandpa sighed quietly. Grandmother lamented in anguish. "Shame, shame! I can't show my face to the world . . ."

Grandmother's turmoil of shame only involved her son, however, not her daughters.

When her eldest daughter, my aunt Da Gu, had gotten divorced, Grandmother couldn't have cared less and didn't say a word about it. But she'd interfered with the divorce of my aunt Er Gu, her youngest daughter, by forcing her to leave her cheating husband, even after he quickly regretted his unfaithfulness and begged to come back. My male-offspring-crazed grandmother had her own hidden agenda: She was eyeing their nine-year-old son, wanting to raise him as her own.

"You stole my son!" Aunt Er Gu cried, yelling at her mother, realizing she'd been duped. "And you turned my son against me, and he doesn't mind me anymore!"

"Dumb idiot!" Grandmother hissed at Aunt Er Gu. "How can you say such horrible things about your own mother? I did you a favor to get rid of your unfaithful SOB husband."

Grandmother, however, didn't think her cheating daughter-in-law, my mother, should be the grounds for her son's divorce. Her reason: "The original nest is always better for kids."

So, as soon as she'd arrived in Taiyuan, Grandmother trudged on her tiny bound feet to my mother's work unit. She appealed to the factory leader, who ordered my mother to come home to work it out.

Look at my demure smile in the photo, you'd never guess how humiliated and deeply traumatized my fourteen-year-old mind and heart had been on that dreadful day when my mother came home. Our two-room apartment was crowded with gawking neighbors: men, women, and children. It was like a circus freak show.

Swallowing her pride, Grandmother begged her despised daughter-in-law to please not divorce her precious only son for the sake of the three children. My mother responded by ranting that my father was a stingy, heartless, and cold-blooded scrooge. Then she said the only way to stop her from a divorce was for her husband to give her more money.

"Okay, my child," Grandmother consented. "As long as you don't divorce him, he'll agree to work it out with you."

My father frowned, sitting on the edge of the bed, fury in his eyes at his mother.

"Good, tell him to give me every penny of his ¥60 *yuan* monthly salary," my mother sneered, savoring her victory as she looked around the room at the gawking spectators. She'd hit my father where it hurt. My father was an infamous penny-pincher. Money was always the major reason for their fighting, besides my mother's infidelity. For years, my father had been outraged about my mother sneaking around spending her salary on her "lazy, no good" brother, his wife, and their five "damned ugly kids" back in the village. My mother had assumed her responsibility for mothering her brother ever since he was an orphaned toddler. When he was a teenager, she'd found him a city job as a day laborer but he'd complained: "Why should I dig ditches in the rain and you sit warm and dry in your office?" So, he quit. My mother had been sending him money ever since.

"Go to hell!" My father yelled, glaring at my mother.

"Oh, come on, please be reasonable, my child," Grandmother glared at my father and turned to plead with my mother. "You've got to let your husband keep some for himself. He has to buy his own food and clothes since his work unit is far away and he can only come home once a week. How about you get ¥30 *yuan*, and he keeps the other ¥30?"

"No! ¥40 *yuan* a month or divorce!" my mother bargained like a dentist with his patient strapped in the chair.

The crowd burst out laughing, greatly amused.

I was dying of embarrassment.

"Okay, okay, 40 *yuan* it is." Grandmother hurriedly agreed, gritting her teeth.

"How am I supposed to live with that?" my father protested.

"Oh, be quiet," Grandmother hushed him.

"Divorce that ugly, bad omen slut might not be a bad thing!" my father yelled.

My mother smirked at him. She'd won. So did my grandmother, who got to keep the Li family's roots: her two male grandchildren, my two brothers. A Chinese marriage is about extension of the family tree by having male offspring.

As for me, I wished my parents were divorced. Whenever they made up, my father's hands were quicker to hit and his feet swifter to kick me, as if he was trying to please my mother.

If my parents got divorced, at least I could get some sympathy and comforting words from the neighbors for having an abusive stepparent, just like my Aunt Er Gu's three small kids, who had to live with a loud, violent, and abusive stepfather.

On the other hand, no matter how miserable we were in our personal and family lives, we had the government's assurance that we always had our savior Chairman Mao's love.

Just look at the shining pin on everyone's chest in this photo. The entire People's Republic of China had reached a fever pitch of worshipping Mao, Chinese people's imminent god. Every kid in my school had a handkerchief full of pins of Chairman Mao's sacred head. We competed with each other to see who got the most pins, the best, biggest, and shiniest collections.

Chapter 40
Family Picture without My Mother
父子四人合照

This photo was taken in 1971 at the city center of May 1 Square, Taiyuan.

A FAMILY PICTURE with my mother missing. She must've either run away again for a short period of time without taking Cricket with her or refused to be in the photo with my father, her sworn enemy. For whatever reason, my father must have wanted to seize the treasured, rare moment when his favorite child, Cricket, was around.

In the background of this photo, Chairman Mao's portrait hangs at the center of the stadium, from which the provincial government officials inspected the annual October 1st National Day parade celebrating the 1949 Communist take-over. On top of the stadium, written in calligraphy, is the government's slogan: *Long Live Chairman Mao*. On both sides, written in vertical lines, is one of Mao's quotations in his own handwritten calligraphy – a quotation every kindergartener was taught to memorize and repeat by heart. Half a century later today, I can still rattle it off: *Marxism and Leninism are the core guidance to our revolution; and Mao Zedong's Thoughts are the foundation of our revolutionary theory:* 領導我們事業的核心力量是馬克思主義，指導我們思想的理論基礎是毛澤東思想。

In the background at far right, on top of the four-story building, are large-scale characters: *Wishing Chairman Mao Ten Thousand Years of Longevity!* 敬祝毛主席萬壽無疆。

Standing in front of me in the photo is Cricket, wearing his Little Red Guard armband on his left sleeve. Every elementary school kid was supposed to be a Little Red Guard, unless their parents were of classified enemy class and condemned as anti-Mao enemies of the people.

Next to Cricket stands Nimble. His pants were all worn-out and his right shoe looks ready to fall apart. Even Cricket, the favorite child of both our parents, is wearing tattered shoes.

I'm tucked in behind my brothers.

Notice that I'm wearing the same jacket my mother had made for me seven years before as a gift when I first came to live in the city at age eight. As my body grew, my mother modified it, cutting out the original collar, extending the sleeves, and lengthening the bottom by adding a foot-long blue cloth to match the replaced dark blue collar. And if you look hard, you can also see my pant legs, now so short they were almost up to my calves.

Like grains, vegetables, coal for cooking fuel, and tissue paper for female monthly menstrual periods, the cloth we used to make our clothes was also rationed. Once a year for the lunar Chinese New Year, each person per family was given a rationed coupon ticket to buy cloth to make new clothes. Communist China's wonderful Socialist idea of equality dictated that every person got the same amount of cloth, no matter how tall or how short they were.

I was always taller than most kids my age and felt awkward about it. In the photo, I'm a full head taller than Nimble, who was only fifteen months younger than me.

"Nothing good comes from being tall but a waste of two extra feet of rationed cotton cloth," was a popular saying that ridiculed tall people.

Chairman Mao's Cultural Revolution had paralyzed China's economy. Factory workers had stopped producing, and peasants hardly grew any grains. The government's radio broadcast told people how long a piece of clothing should last: 新三年，舊三年，縫縫補補又三年 — *Wear it new the first three years, wear it old the next three years; Patch it up and stitch it up to make it last another three years.*

Look at my "bread-loafer" shoes. My grandmother handmade them from scratch. They were cotton-padded for cold winters and kept my feet warm when I walked fifteen bus stops in the ear-cutting icy cold wind, gloveless and hatless, pulling a six-foot-long wooden cart on the slippery icy road to the vegetable store to stand in line for hours to buy rationed frozen cabbages.

One day I became ashamed of my padded shoes when a popular girl in school burst out laughing after she spotted them. Pointing at my feet, she waved and called her friends over to take a look. My face burning, I felt so humiliated that I wanted to vanish into the ground.

In the photograph, both Nimble and I look stressed because of our father's presence. In his standard dress code like all men in China, he looked mild, even good-natured, as he always did in all of his photos. No one could know his frightening, merciless slapping hands and kicking feet.

To this day, I still can't forgive myself for lacking the courage to stand up and stop my father's brutal beating of Nimble one day when he caught him stealing loose change from his pocket. Like a crazed man, my father pummeled hard on Nimble, slapping and kicking his skinny little body. I watched in horror, frozen in place, my heart pounding, my eardrums bursting as each of his loud beatings landing on Nimble's face and body. Forever imprinted in my memory are Nimble's frightened eyes. He looked as scared as a skinny rooster in the grip of a violent monster's hands. His face, neck, and behind his ears remained black and blue for many days.

Fear of my father turned me into a perfectionist. I became my own worst critic. It also reinforced my lifelong defiance toward inept, unjust and abusive authority figures.

I learned to be precise when cooking and measuring our scarce rations of corn, sorghum and wheat flours. One day, I cooked an extra half bowl of my handmade macaroni lunch. My father glared and yelled at me for being stupid and careless. And the next day, I was so nervous that I overcorrected myself by cooking half a bowl too short. "Stupid dumb idiot, you can never do anything right, can you?" My father's hand came smacking down hard on me.

One day I hid myself in the feces-piled, communal squatting toilet stall to quietly cry my tears after my father beat me with the rolling pin. It was the only privacy I could find. The bruises and welts on my arms and legs hurt just as much as the humiliation.

"Where the hell did you sneak away to?" my father wanted to know. He'd noticed my patterns of slipping away after each of his beatings. He then forbade me to walk away from him. I learned to hold my tears and grief until bedtime, when I could cover my head under my cotton-padded quilt and cry in silence.

Another day, my father kicked me so hard I cried out and ran into the inner room. "How dare you scream as I hardly hurt you!" he yelled, chasing after and cornering me against the wall, where he began repeatedly hitting me in my head with the broomstick. "Stop!" I begged, covering my face with both of my hands. But he couldn't stop. He'd been turned into a crazed madman by his failing marriage and his demotion at his job. As I begged, my father's beating rained down harder on me until I finally pushed my way out the door and ran outside into the yard, where crowds of men and women were idling around chatting among themselves, and children were running around playing. The crowds turned their heads to watch me screaming.

"I'll show you never to run out like that to embarrass me!" my father yelled, running into the dirt yard. This was the first time he came running after me during broad daylight in the open. As he started after me, I took off running out of the yard into the asphalt-paved street.

"You've got nowhere to run!" my father yelled from behind me. He was now on his bicycle chasing me! The crowds jeered and followed us out into the street. Collectively, they cheered. Desperate, I dash-jumped across the three-foot-wide ditch that separated the asphalt street from the dirt sidewalk, just as my father's front wheel touched my heels. I surprised myself by my quick wit, greatly relieved when he promptly turned his bike around to ride back into the yard.

One sweltering hot summer day, my father yelled at me from the outer room: "Get over here!" He looked outraged, pointing to a bowl of leftover soup sitting on top of the wooden container that stored our grain and flour. "Look, dumb idiot, the soup is bubbling and gone sour! Didn't I tell you not to cover the leftover soup on hot days?"

"I didn't cover the bowl," I refused to apologize. His striking hands and kicking feet came down on me like lightning. "You're digging your own early grave!" my father roared, as he beat me. "You stubborn idiot! One of these days you'll make me beat you to death! You never admit your wrong doings!"

How I wished my father were educated and intelligent enough to know that any bowl of soup would go bad overnight sitting out at room temperature on a hot summer day, with or without a lid on. Refrigeration didn't reach China's masses until twenty years later in the 1990's.

Unlike my extremely capable mother, my father was average in intelligence and capability. He was frustrated with life after growing up a pampered son, his parents' center of universe. As an adult, reality had hit him hard: the world didn't revolve around him.

And every time our mother ran away from home, taking his favorite son Cricket with her, my brother Nimble and I would become our father's targets for venting his rage. He once forced us to write a letter to her as he dictated it: "Mother, aren't you ashamed of your slutty self? At the ripe old age of thirty-six, and married with three kids, you shamelessly deserted your husband and children to room in the dorm with a bunch of eighteen-year-olds. $18+18 = 36$."

"Go grab your mother's bedding and clothes and make her come home," my father ordered me one day. "I'm leaving now. It's her turn to come back and take care of you and Nimble."

I didn't want to bring my mother back. I didn't miss her but was too afraid to say no to him. I loved the peace and quiet without either one of my hellish parents. It was a lot easier for me to cook just for Nimble and myself.

My father stayed gone for two days. I dragged my feet till the morning of the third day to finally build up my nerve. I went to the factory's dorm building and pushed my way into my mother's room on the second floor. When she saw who it was, my mother tried to slam the door to shut me out but I wedged my foot in the doorway to jam it open.

"You need to come home," I told my mother. "My father is gone."

My mother told me to get the hell lost. I grabbed her futon quilt off the bed and ran. She chased me all the way back to our apartment. Then grabbing the shovel by the stove, she beat me with it until my anger overcame my fear. Letting out a desperate cry, I wrestled the shovel away from her and held it high above my head, ready to smack it down on her head. She backed away.

"Go sleep with your lover *Hu Zong Yuan!*" I yelled. The crowd of neighbors who'd gathered at our apartment door gasped, snickering and chuckling, hands over their mouths. As a daughter, I'd just committed an unforgivable sin: exposing the skeleton in the family closet by telling my mother's shameful, adulterous open secret. The five-thousand-year-old Chinese tradition ruled that children be unconditionally obedient to their parents.

My mother lunged at me, slapping, scratching and pinching me.

"Please, Magnolia," our loving neighbor Auntie Yu Xin – who'd been watching – pulled my mother off me and sat her down. "Why don't you just come back home? Look at your poor two children, Nimble and Cai Mei. They need you, especially Cai Mei has had a bad heart disease."

"What heart disease?" my mother burst out yelling. "She's just fine, she pushes the 100 *jin* (one *jin* equals 1.1 pounds) bicycle up and down the second floor all by herself every day. No pity for her!"

Oh, Mother, what was my choice? I cried inside. But I couldn't get my words out.

My father had told me to guard the bicycle with my life. If something happened to it, he said he'd beat me to death. He said it cost him over two hundred yuan, four times of his monthly paycheck. He would take my life if I didn't carry it upstairs before dark so it wouldn't be stolen.

Mother, you yourself refused to touch or learn how to ride the bicycle, but now you made it sound easy for me to push/wheel the

100-pound Flying-Pigeon bicycle up to the second floor every evening. Did you know how deadly heavy it felt? More than twice my twelve-year-old skinny body. It was made in real iron and steel, for carrying people, sacks of grains, huge bundles of vegetables, and baskets of coal and dirt.

"Either the bicycle or your life," my father warned me.

I had to carry the bicycle upstairs every day before dark. *Mother, you never saw how my skinny arms and legs shook every time I carried it.* I remember my hot face, my throbbing temples, and how my thin fingers clutch-held the vertical bar while trying with all my might to keep the back wheel moving up to the next stair, the one after that, and the next. My weak heart would pound out of my throat. Sometimes I would lose my footing half-way up the stairs then roll all the way back down to the cement dirt floor with the 100-pound bicycle on top of me. Mother never saw how frightened I was, not for my hurt body, but for the bicycle I had been entrusted to secure. I'd pick myself up and immediately inspect it for damage before I could cry out in pain. No one ever came to help me. Not once. Not our neighbors, my mother or my father, or even her favorite child, my brother, Nimble, who was only fifteen months younger than me.

Oh, Mother, look at my hands. Did you ever notice how embarrassed I felt about my right hand? It's sadly much bigger than my left!

I wanted to tell my mother all this, but I couldn't get my words out. Only my teary eyes talked to my mother while she huffed and puffed, cursing and glaring at me.

Suddenly, my father walked in, pushing through the gawking crowd that had spilled into the hallway. "What's going on?" He asked, looking innocent.

"See?" My mother jumped up to her feet. "I knew it! The despicable father and daughter were playing their evil tricks to get me back. I knew she was lying!"

Throwing open the clothes chest, my mother grabbed an armful of her clothes and stormed out.

Chapter 41

Switching Tongues

外語

MY FATHER BROUGHT HOME a surprise gift for Nimble and me: a shortwave transistor radio! It was expensive: thirteen *yuan* ($2 USD) out of my father's monthly salary of sixty *yuan*. It was the first electronic modern device we'd ever laid our hands on.

My brother grinned. I squeaked with joy.

Nimble and I worked out a time-sharing schedule for listening to the radio. We had our individual listening times scheduled down to the minute. No invading each other's time, we agreed. One day I saw Nimble wasting his prearranged time playing outside. When he suddenly came back in and caught me red-handed listening to the radio, my face burning in embarrassment, and I quickly surrendered the radio to him.

Then something fascinating happened one day as I turned the radio dial. A woman's voice came on speaking in a rapid, alien tongue. What was that? There were actually people who talked like that? Who were they? Where were they? I was curious and wanted to find out.

Learning to speak new languages had made me feel accomplished since age eight when I switched from my deep mountain village dialect to Taiyuan city dialect while simultaneously mastering the official standard Mandarin Chinese. There's a vast difference between hundreds of the regional Chinese dialects, each of which could sound as differently as Spanish from English!

Now I dreamed of learning how to switch tongues to that unknown foreign language. But I wasn't allowed to attend middle school, yet. The Cultural Revolution had messed up China's school system after shutting down schools. By 1969, three age-groups of elementary school students of my generation had been stuck in their primary schools, as no secondary school was ready to admit any new students.

Finally, in 1970, kids from my elementary school were force-fed into the neighborhood secondary school, which had more than 2,000 students. We newcomers were inserted in the middle of the semester and not entitled to textbooks. I was frustrated that I'd missed all the important basic beginning lessons in my English class, such as the twenty-six alphabetical letters.

Without a textbook, I couldn't understand what the English teacher was teaching. A middle-aged woman with her hair cut above her ear lobes, a Cultural Revolution style. She parked herself in front of the blackboard and read from her small, thin English textbook in a monotone: "reh wording class, reh ling ling class." Then she'd pause, waiting for us to repeat after her. I was eager to learn but had no idea how to move, switch and manipulate my tongue to speak the strange English sounds the teacher wasn't explaining!

And to make matters worse, I couldn't see clearly sitting in my assigned seat at the last row in the back of the classroom because I was the tallest girl. No one knew my secret shame that I was nearsighted "with two dumb blind holes," as my parents ridiculed me. And, the bowl-thick chimney that snaked through above us from the coal burning iron stove in the middle of the classroom were blocking me. I had to crane my neck to dodge the chimney and squint my eyes to bring into focus the fuzzy image of the teacher.

Everything else I experienced in the new school frustrated me.

I hated the mandatory mid-morning physical exercises time when seas of teenage students poured out of their classrooms to line up and stand at attention in the vast school yard. A loudspeaker perched on top of the three-story main teaching-learning building screamed out rhythmic orders, as all two thousand of us were expected to move our bodies and limbs in synchrony. One, two, three, four, stretch your arms! Five, six, seven, eight, thrust your chest! . . . Bend your left leg . . . Now your right . . . Turn sideways . . . Punch your fist forward . . . Now sideways . . . Bend down to touch your right foot with your left hand. . . . your left foot with your right hand . . . Jump up and down clapping your hands above your head. Repeat . . .

I felt greatly embarrassed as I moved through the whole routine.

And the gossip I heard was worse.

"Who's the new girl? Look how long her neck is sticking out her old fashioned high-collar shirt!" Some girls were talking about me as they giggled and laughed behind me. They'd already noticed my embarrassingly long neck! Back at my elementary school, one girl constantly made fun of my long neck, calling me a "rooster neck." How I hated that.

To cover my long neck, I wore my mother's old blue shirt. It was a pre-Cultural Revolution style: old-fashioned with a high collar. But I could still see how extra-long my neck was when I saw my own shadows at sunset in the school yard. We lined up there after school to practice marching like groups of solders. It was our mandatory military training. With a wooden rifle on our shoulders, we marched in lockstep to the barking orders, just like the People's Liberation Army soldiers, yelling in unison: "Down with the Imperialist America, the Paper Tiger!" Chairman Mao had told us to be prepared for the upcoming war with the Imperialist Running Dog of America.

My frustration with mandatory exercise and military training was less severe compared to my problems in my English class. I still couldn't understand anything the teacher said. Most of the time, I ducked down behind the student in front of me, trying to avoid the teacher calling on me to stand up and repeat after her. It took forever for the bell to ring.

Gone was my longtime confidence in my elementary school years as the all-time highest achiever, my teachers' favorite, and the monitor of my class.

The monitor of my English class took it as her responsibility to help tutor us newcomers and "slow" learners. I was not *"slow"*! But I was glad when the girl explained what the teacher had been saying when she read aloud from the textbook. It was an English translation of Mao's quotation: *"The working class is the leading class."* I'd been hearing the words wrong: "reh wording class, reh ling ling class."

But how did each of these wiggly English letters compare to the square Chinese pictographic characters? I had to understand for my mind to learn.

"Oh, just memorize the whole thing altogether," the sixteen-year-old monitor smiled confidently. That didn't satisfy my inquisitive brain. I remained confused. But I did learn my twenty-six English alphabetical letters from my teen classmate:

"B" — She covered her mouth and giggled. I was embarrassed, too. It almost sounded like "vagina" in derogatory everyday Chinese.

"P" — We both burst out laughing. It sounded exactly like the word "fart" in Chinese!

For the final examination, I tried to cheat, but the teacher came to stand right by my desk, her arms crossed over her chest, as if determined to catch me. She must've spotted me tapping on the shoulders of the student in front of me and whispering. Embarrassed and ashamed, I quickly gave up and turned in my almost-blank test paper and left the classroom.

I failed my English class.

I was secretly happy that grades didn't count anymore. All students were automatically moved up to the next level, regardless of how little we learned.

Chapter 42

High School Tuition

十元學費

JANUARY 1972. I started my high school year.

It was a dreadful day. All students had to pay their high-school tuition. Worried and anxious, I followed the long line of students moving toward the Dean's two-leafed window that was open to the outside sidewalk on the three-story building's first floor. Everyone standing in line was holding money in their hands. Except me.

What should I say to the Dean? That I had no money to pay for my high school? It's ridiculous even hoping to get any sympathy from the school authority, I kept telling myself. Whoever heard of a student being allowed to start school without paying tuition?

I'd never have thought of coming empty-handed to try my luck, shamelessly hoping for a charity, if not for the encouragement of Mr. Zhang, my high-school English teacher.

I'd told Mr. Zhang that I had no money to purchase the English textbook when he was collecting money in class. He asked me why. I had to reveal my secret about my chaotic family life. My mother hadn't been home for months, and my father had just a surgery on his skull. And since he was sick and couldn't answer Chairman Mao's call for all office workers to be "sent down" and toil alongside the peasants, his salary of sixty *yuan* had been cut in half to thirty *yuan* as his punishment.

Would the Dean be as kind and caring as my English teacher?

I'd already registered as a problem in the Dean's eyes during my middle-school year.

My father had refused to let me go with my class and toil in the cornfields alongside peasants in a village thirty *li* away. Chairman Mao had made schools "open door." All students were required to get out of their classrooms for at least six months a year to learn practical skills from the leading proletariat classes of peasants and manual-labor workers.

My father said that I'd be dead after marching two days on the dirt roads in the scorching sun carrying a bedroll on my back, not to mention toiling every day in the cornfields. He told me to tell the Dean what Dr. Liu had warned after my forty-day hospitalization for heart disease at age nine: You must never to do any strenuous physical labor.

"Well," the Dean looked at me sideways. "You're not nine years old anymore and look just fine. If your father insists, why don't you find yourself a school that doesn't have to follow Chairman Mao's open-door policy?"

"Which school doesn't do it?" I was too simple-minded to detect the Dean's sarcastic tone, and got his long, hard stare.

Here I was now, needed to ask the Dean for yet another favor: free tuition.

Nervously, I approached the open window. Sitting behind his desk, the Dean looked at me from above his glasses on the tip of his nose.

"Mr. Dean, my family doesn't have any money to pay for school," I stammered in a low voice, desperately hoping other students behind me couldn't hear me.

"You again?" the Dean remarked, raising his eyebrows. "No, can't do. You just have to turn around and go home to ask your family for the ten *yuan*. You can't go to school without paying."

Red-faced with shame, I ran out of the school's iron gate and all the way to the bus stop.

Grandmother was alone inside our two-room apartment, which felt like a deserted place – dusty, gray, and cold.

"Grandmother, I need ten *yuan*. The Dean won't let me start high school without paying. Give me the money now!" I yelled in frustration.

"Who the hell do you think you're yelling at?" Grandmother shot back. I was shocked.

"I need ten *yuan* for school tuition! Give it to me now!" I took all my frustration out on the only person available for me.

"What made you think I have the money? Why are you asking *me*? I didn't give birth to you! Go ask the one that did!" Grandmother's sharp tongue was like a stabbing knife.

"Give me the money now!"

"You coward! You fight me like a tiger, but you become a coward in front of her!" I hated when Grandmother had found my weak spot. I didn't want to admit that I was indeed afraid of my mother.

"You give me the money, now!" I began crying, tears of desperation.

"What made you think you can just intimidate people to get what you want?" Grandmother yelled, but her hand was reaching to lift the front of her shirt. She had a secret pocket sewed inside her inner shirt. With her badly shaking hands, Grandmother pulled out a wrinkled old handkerchief. Wrapped in it were a few small bills.

"You make sure to pay me back, you little demon!" Grandmother picked out the ten-*yuan* note and handed it to me, along with her dirty looks.

I broke into a smile, wiping away my tears, and ran out the door.

"Now, that's more like it," the Dean said with a satisfied nod when he saw the money in my hand. "Not that hard, was it?"

Chapter 43

English 900

英語900句

July 26, 1973 was the date I noted in this beautiful and very special book that accompanied me on my journey to the fascinating English world.

AFTER MY AMBITION to learn the exotic alien tongue of English fizzled out in my one and a half semester long middle-school, my high-school English teacher, Mr. Zhang Qin, salvaged my desire. He enlightened me and successfully re-ignited my enthusiasm, which eventually led to my accidental discovery of this very important book in my life.

Some students in my class laughed at Mr. Zhang behind his back for his easy blushing, his feminine fair-skin, and his slim figure. But I respected him greatly and was grateful to him for his guidance.

Mr. Zhang noticed my eagerness to learn. His acknowledgement of me motivated me to learn. I quickly became his steady, number-one student, earning the highest grades. I was always the first to memorize, word for word, everything Mr. Zhang taught in class: Communist anthem *The Internationale*; the story of the sixteen-year-old Communist martyr *Liu Hu Lan*. I aced all my English tests.

I was hungry to learn, wishing there were more than just our thin English textbook, a compilation of the Chinese translation of Mao-worshipping slogans and revolutionary theory.

One day after school, I took the bus to downtown. Walking by and looking into the store windows was my favorite pastime. The delicious cooked food: the thin-sliced pork of all parts, steamed rice, and buns. My mouth watered while my stomach growled. But they were all too expensive and out of my reach. Besides money, they also required food coupons. Regardless, I still enjoyed looking at the delectable dishes on display; it felt good to know that delicious things existed out there. And it stimulated my desire to grow up and become somebody so I, too, could eat delicious food whenever I wished.

On that day — July 26, 1973 — walking down the sidewalk, I found myself looking up at a store I hadn't seen before. 外文書店 *Foreign Language Book Store*, said the shining metal sign on the door. What a rare sight! It must have something to do with the American president Nixon's visit to China. And unbelievably, there was no hard-faced guard at the door to keep out the nobodies like me. Looking around, I cautiously walked through the door. No one stopped me!

An amazing sight greeted me inside. I'd never seen so many books before. The room was full of tall shelves filled with books. They were lined up all around the room against the walls behind the counters. There was also a small back room, where books of foreign languages were piled up on the floor. I was even allowed to poke my head in to take a look.

How nice and quiet it was inside this special bookstore. There were no crowds elbowing and shoving their way around as in regular stores. And the sales clerks leisurely stood behind the counters.

A bright, sky-blue shining book caught my eye. Such a pretty blue! A breath of fresh air. *English 900.* It read. My heart swelled in joy. I could read the title!

"Comrade," I anxiously addressed the woman clerk behind the counter. "Can I take a look at the blue book?"

It felt so good in my hands. The shining cover was so smooth like silk and satin on the new bride's futon cover, and so cool, like the surface of a mirror. Its pages were white like clean, new snow. And, oh, how delicate its pages were, thin, yet durable, nothing like my coarse, fragile-paged Chinese schoolbooks. And it smelled exotic, too. So different and refreshing. I felt special holding such a rare beautiful book. It came directly from a publisher in the faraway land of England: the MacMillan Company, London, Ltd.

Trembling with joy, I tried to remain serious-faced. I had to be careful not to show my delight and excitement. People could detect my happiness and accuse me of being *chong-yang-mei-wai* 崇洋媚外: *admiring foreign things from across the ocean*. Admiring the Western World meant betraying to our Chinese pride and dignity.

"How much is it?" I asked, feeling sure that the price was too sky-rocket high for me to pay, then relieved to hear: ¥3.50 *yuan* (= $0.35 USD!) It was expensive but within my means, three-and-a-half months of my allowance. My father gave me one *yuan* a month. And I always saved most of it.

I'd learned to pinch my pennies like my extremely thrifty grandmother. I never used any luxury item, such as lotion on my face or hands. I washed my hair with detergent or just plain baking soda, whatever I could find at home. My only big expense was buying a roll of special straw paper for my "monthly pass." And once in a while I indulged myself by buying a small roll of white nylon sewing thread for crocheting. I also knit sweaters, scarfs, gloves, and socks for my family, not for fun, but as part of my daily chores.

I paid the 3.50 *yuan*. The beautiful book was mine now! I could hear my heart pounding. I felt rich. Carefully I put it in my worn-out canvas schoolbag of grass-green, a fashion color like the uniform of prestigious soldiers, who Chairman Mao said were one of China's three leading classes. The left strap had broken off, and I'd fastened it with a safety pin. My mother still wouldn't buy me a new one, even after I went to complain to her boss, an army officer. China had been taken over by the army after the violence between the factions was getting out of hand. Now my mother hated me more for telling on her.

My mind started racing. What should I do to hide my beautiful book from my father?

My parents had forbidden me to read ever since I was found to be near-sighted in my fifth grade. They yelled at me that my near-sightedness was caused by my reckless reading. And buying a pair of 200-*yuan* glasses was absolutely out of the question. Both of them would yell at me every time they caught me sneaking around reading.

"Why the hell are you so stubborn insisting on doing your dumb reading? You just ruined your stupid face with a pair of blind holes!" My brother Nimble would laugh, echoing my parents: "two blind holes."

My brain was too hungry to stop reading. I'd read anything I could lay my hands on, which wasn't much in our blue-collar dirt yard: usually some old, greasy, wrinkled newspapers that'd wrapped food scraps I came across here and there.

I'd borrowed and read two books thoroughly many times: two novels about Communist revolutionaries that were politically safe. One was about a selfless People's Liberation Army soldier, *Ou Yang Hai*, 歐陽海; the other was about an oppressed young peasant man, *San Beir*, 三輩兒 *escaping and joining the Communist Red Army*.

One day a neighbor boy gave me an old book with no front or back cover. My father saw me reading it and snatched it out of my hands. Its first page told of two Japanese Imperialist Army officers in China during World War II having a killing contest of Chinese prisoners. They were competing to see who could slice off the prisoners' heads faster and cleaner. "Where the hell did you get this?" My father was outraged. He ordered me to get rid of the book immediately.

My brain was so malnourished for something to read that I even committed theft once.

Another day my next-door neighbor and friend *Ya Ping* and I were visiting our neighbor's family across the hallway. I was elated to spot a story book sitting on their bed. I couldn't believe my luck. And it was even a detective story! I'd never read a detective story. Quickly scanning the back cover, I found out it was about a people's enemy fugitive, an ex-landlord eluding his capture by the Communists. He hid himself in the six-foot-deep cave underneath his wife's brick and mud bed *kang* and only came out at night to sleep with his slutty wife. When he was finally caught two years later, he looked like a pale ghost and was executed swiftly. I couldn't put the book down.

"Please, Auntie," I begged the mistress of the family. "Can I please read your book?"

"No way, can't do." The woman was firm. Good books were too precious to go around.

But I wouldn't, couldn't forget the book and promptly plotted to steal it. I asked my friend Ya Ping to distract the Mrs. and then swiped the book under my shirt and went straight back to our apartment. But just as I started reading the first page, the Mrs. marched in. Only my frantic, tearful apology softened her heart enough not to report my crime to my parents for punishment.

Now as I held my own exotic, beautiful blue book, *English 900*, I planned to keep it safely hidden away from my father, so he wouldn't destroy my dream to learn English. I didn't even plan to show it to my favorite English teacher, Mr. Zhang.

Fortunately, no one was home. My mother and Cricket were still gone. Nimble was staying in the school dorm with the performing team rehearsing for the show of 智取威虎山, *Taking the Tiger Mountain*, in which he played a Nationalist army guard. It was one of China's eight standard revolutionary model operas, orchestrated by Mao's wife, 江青 *Jiang Qing*, China's only type of entertainment for the entire ten years of the Cultural Revolution.

My only private space in my family's bare-walled, two-room apartment was under my pillow. Sitting on my wooden bed under the 15-Watt naked light bulb hanging down on a thin wire from the ceiling, I wiped my hands vigorously on my clothes before gingerly turning the fine, delicate pages of my precious *English 900*. I couldn't wait to "decode" each of the 900 sentences, armed with my grand knowledge of the twenty-six English alphabetical letters.

Hello.
How are you?
How do you do?
My name is Smith, what's your name?

These sentences sounded so human, nothing like Mao's revolutionary teaching by shouting slogans to never forget the class struggles. "Kill class enemies mercilessly and ruthlessly – and as coldly as icy cold winter," Mao proclaimed.

And every chance I got, after doing my chores, I'd take out my beautiful *English 900*, first to gaze at it, and admire it and then carefully open it and read it.

Until one day I almost lost my precious book when my father snuck up on me.

"How dumb and stupid can you be, spending a fortune on a useless damn book?" he yelled, glaring at me, snatching it out of my hands.

How did he guess correctly that I owned the book? "No, it's not . . . mine." I surprised myself with enough courage to lie so smoothly to his face. I was risking a beating. He always frightened me into telling him the truth, even though he never believed me anyway. I hated him for that.

"I borrowed it from my friend," I heard myself lying calmly, bracing myself to fight him to the death if he decided to destroy my beloved book.

To my great relief, my father thumbed a few pages, tossed it back onto my bed, and walked away. I collapsed onto my pillow, clutching my precious *English 900* to my heart.

Chapter 44

Dream to Be Free & Different
夢想自由

July 1, 1974. Photo of my high school Class 16.

NO GOWNS. No graduation ceremony. Just a class photo in our everyday clothes on the last day of high school. Twenty-six boys and twenty-four girls. This was how we graduated from our two-and-a-half years of high school.

I'm not in the photo.

Also missing in the photo was my best friend Serenity Wong, and another girl, Rainbow Liu. While Serenity and I were protesting and playing hooky, Rainbow's absence from the photo was a tragic story. She'd been destroyed by her desire to love.

Love was a dirty word in high school, and relationships between male and female high school students were forbidden. No boys dared to talk to a girl. No girls dared to even look at a boy. But the forbidden rule wasn't applied to the Communist Youth League leaders of our class. They freely talked, laughed, and even flirted with the students of the opposite sex.

Rainbow was beautiful. She had big smiling eyes, long eyelashes, and lovely fair-skin. She had a secret crush on a broad-shouldered, good-looking boy in our class, the son of prestigious Chinese Liberation Army officers. And when she passed him a secret love note, the boy got so scared that he turned her note to the class Communist Youth League leader, Magnificent Zhou, whose duty was to keep track of the students' politically correct thoughts and make sure everyone toed the Party's line.

Rainbow was now in deep trouble. She was forced to confess her "slutty thought problems" in detail and required to write page after page of self-criticism; but nothing she did was good enough to satisfy the leader. Beautiful sixteen-year-old Rainbow finally had a nervous breakdown. She became bedridden and never came back to finish high school.

Unlike Rainbow, my ability to hide my feelings behind my face spared me. I never dared to look at the boy I was attracted to for longer than a glance at a time.

Seated on the second row in the photo are nine teachers and faculty. I remember five of them.

The first man on the far left was our physics teacher Mr. Zhao. He gave us a lifetime memory by making us roar with laughter. One day, he paused from his lecture and walked over to Er Hu, who was snoozing. Shaking his head in frustration, and in his thick country-bumpkin Wu-Tai 五台 dialect, Mr. Zhao said into the student's ear: "My hope for you equals zero!"

The whole class burst out laughing so uncontrollably that our stomachs hurt.

The fifth man from the left, wearing glasses and seated, was our politics teacher. One day he called on me to stand up and read out aloud my notes from his lecture. Nervous, I tried to steady my shaky voice. But instead of commenting on how I did, he asked me to read my notes again. Thinking I'd disappointed him, I slightly reworded my notes and still couldn't tell whether he approved or disapproved of me. Then he asked me to read my notes for the third time!

"Did you all hear that, class?" He finally said. "That's how you take notes."

What a happy relief!

The second man from the left was Mr. Zhang Qin, my English teacher. I owe my life-changing good fortune to him. He inspired me and revived my dying interest in learning English, which had almost been snuffed out in my middle-school year.

The sixth person from the left, a darker-skinned man with a chiseled jaw and prominent nose, was the principal. I remember him well because of the many humiliating afternoons, hours at a time, that my father made me sit in his home, trying to pressure him to agree to let me drop out of high school. My father said that he had found me a hotel maid's job at a prestigious state-run hotel. I just needed a proof that I wasn't a student anymore. But the principal wouldn't let me drop out because a new law had just been issued to stop the trend that millions of teenagers were dropping out of school after parents realized that grades didn't count, learning was no longer valued, and all high-school graduates were automatically sent down to be "re-educated" by peasants. To keep pressure on the principal to change his mind, my father had told me to sit in the principal's home every day after school for at least two hours. I was embarrassed and didn't want to do it but had no choice. The principal just ignored me, reading his newspaper while his wife cooked dinner at the stove. When his wife placed dinner on their small table, I'd get up quietly and leave. I was relieved when my father finally gave up.

The fourth person on the left, the woman with long braided hair, was Miss Li Lan, my math and homeroom teacher. I hated the old maid and everything about her: her pockmarked, dark coarse face; her small, cunning, deep-set eyes; her thick bushy eyebrows; her garlic-clove nose; and her two protruding, front "tiger teeth."

As a routine of part of following Chairman Mao's open-door education, our class was one day taken out of school to pull weeds in the cornfields for the nearby villagers. It was a hot day, and the scorching hot sun baked my hatless head and made me dizzy. My throat and tongue were dry, and my legs were numb from squatting too long without a break. I was about to faint. So, I stumbled to sit under the nearest tree. I could feel Miss Li Lan's eyes on my back, but I was too sick to care anymore.

"Li Jing committed political thought problems today," Miss Li Lan summarized at the end of the day confess-our-heart-to-Chairman-

Mao meeting. "Everyone was working hard helping our proletarian leading class peasants. But Li Jing was being selfish. She walked away to give herself a break without asking for permission. That's the rotten bourgeois attitude. How could you think only of yourself while working as a collective team?"

I hated that old maid witch.

Also, as I'd been hiding my shame of being near-sighted in school, I couldn't see the blackboard to understand what was going on in Miss Li Lan's math class. She was angry that I didn't pay attention in her class, sneaking around instead to do my crocheting or work on my favorite subjects of English and Chinese. Her teaching made no sense to me anyway. How could the slanted line in a triangle be double the length of the other two straight lines? Wasn't a diagonal always a shortcut in real life? But I was too intimidated to ask.

"Well, well," Miss Li Lan dry-cackled one day, looking like she was up to no good. "Let's see what Li Jing got this time." The old, ugly witch came to park her stout body by my desk, her stubby carrot fingers searching the stack of the papers. "Ah, here it is! Oh, look, five points!" She held my paper up high for all to see, gloating. "Five out of one hundred! Ha, ha, ha, ha . . ."

"Tomorrow," Miss Li Lan announced in class, "we'll take our class graduation picture."

I hoorayed inside. Yes! I never have to see your ugly face anymore!

Serenity and I got together after school and made our plan to boycott the next day's class photoshoot. To hell with it. We were going to take our own pictures on the gardenlike campus of the Communist Party College, just a short walk from our high school. It had a lot of green trees and colorful flowers, even a classic pagoda. We were both sick and tired of the Communist Youth League's thought control. Because Serenity was a math genius and I was the top student in English class, we both were frowned upon as dangerous "white academic roaders."

Serenity's parents were engineers, classified as enemy class. Naturally she would never be qualified to join the Communist Youth League. But my family was Mao's favored proletarian leading class of peasants. Yet, I, too, was barred from joining the privileged Youth League because I paid too much attention to my academic studies.

That night at home, I dug out my mother's old pre-Cultural Revolution shirt, a sleeveless blouse in green and black checkers. I borrowed my neighbor's black skirt. But there was nothing I could do to enhance the looks of my worn black cloth shoes. Good enough.

Serenity brought a camera.

"You didn't take the class photo?" My father was outraged when he found out. "Why? It's a milestone to be talked about and looked at for years to come. Now you don't exist!"

But look at me in the photo, standing tall, free and happy and full of hope. For the camera, I took off my shapeless long-sleeved shirt to put on my mother's stylish blouse. I rolled up my pant legs and pulled up my borrowed black skirt. Boldly, I showed the bare skin of my arms and my legs below the knees, proudly feeling no shame.

Holding a bouquet of colorful, fresh flowers we'd gathered from the campus garden, I was modeling myself after the main character's image in *The Flower Girl* 賣花姑娘, the popular North Korean movie. Even my "too-long-like-a-goose" neck looks fine. Notice my "thick-neck disease" is miraculously gone, without any medication.

In my own rebellious way, I was pursuing my dream of freedom and daring to look different by getting away from my drab, serious-faced classmates and taking my own graduation photo. On that day, my eighteen-year-old mind was temporarily filled with a happy bliss of ignorance, my young heart felt the joy of freedom.

Lurking at the back of my mind was the fear of my immediate, bleak future in 1974:

"*Bi-ye*" 畢業 equals "*shi-ye*" 失業 — *Out of high school, out of future.*

Chapter 45
Out of High School, Out of Future
高中畢業等於失業

MY FUTURE STALLED in the summer of 1974.

Across China, no high-school graduates were allowed to go on to college. The former merit-based college admission policy had long been abolished since 1966, the beginning of the Cultural Revolution. Now only peasants, workers, and soldiers could go to college.

The current government policy dictated that all high school graduates were to be sent down to the countryside to be "re-educated" by peasants for at least three years, and their *hu-kou*, the city-resident registration for rationed food, was to be cancelled. "Getting your hands and feet dirty with cow manure is an honor," Mao had proclaimed. Many female graduates ended up becoming permanent second-class citizens of peasants when they got married, mostly to sons of powerful local peasant leaders after being coerced, and/or raped.

I braced for my dreadful fate.

Then a miracle happened on the eve of my high school graduation.

The government issued a brand-new national policy: Every firstborn child of each family could stay in the city, in consideration for aging parents, who needed at least one child at home to help them with heavy chores, such as carrying in buckets of water from outside, buying rationed coal and mixing it with mud to make coal cakes for cooking fuel, and standing in lines for hours at a time to buy rationed vegetables and grains to carry home on the back of a bicycle.

As the firstborn in my family, I could now stay in the city. But trouble broke out at home. My mother wanted her favorite child, Nimble, to stay in the city, not me. She insisted that my brother, fifteen months younger than me, was the firstborn.

"Cai Mei is a girl and has a heart problem," my father protested. I was surprised that he spoke up for me. "She'll surely die if sent down to toil in the cornfields. Besides, our city registration card, *hu-kou*, shows that Nimble is not our eldest child."

In a rage, my mother threw the cleaver at him.

Would my father still fight for me if it were his favorite child Cricket, instead of Nimble, whom he never favored since birth? I couldn't help but let slip a flash of that ungrateful thought at back of my mind.

I needed my high school diploma to apply for my city-stay permit, but, unexpectedly, I couldn't find it. I was sure that I'd put it inside our right drawer of the small desk. The thin-legged, worn-out desk in the corner of the outer room was the only place our family kept our paperwork, as well as odds and ends.

"Mother, have you seen my high-school diploma?" I asked her.

"Why are you asking me?" my mother said nonchalantly, her back turned to me.

Unsuspecting, and thinking fast on my feet, I took the bus to my high school to ask the Dean to make me a copy. I was so relieved to see him sitting at his desk, and grateful that he didn't refuse.

"Mother, look!" I cried out, feeling elated, as I dashed through the door, holding up the duplicated copy of my high-school diploma, genuinely proud of my problem-solving ability.

Damn! I didn't see that coming! my mother's silent eyes said, shooting daggers at me.

Later, after I was done with my application and opened the drawer to put away my copy, I couldn't believe my eyes — right there, sitting on top of everything, was my original diploma!

"My wife cannot wait to bury my daughter," my father wrote to his sister, my Aunt Da Gu, in the city of Chang Zhi, asking if she would provide me a shelter at her home.

"Yes," Aunt Da Gu wrote back. She was grateful to my father, her brother, who'd helped her when she was in school. To repay him now, she and her husband would take me in. And she knew someone who knew someone who had a possible backdoor connection that might find me a job. An exciting rumor was going around that the state-run chicken farm cooperative was soon to hire manual laborers.

I hitchhiked three hundred *li* away (100 miles) riding on an open-top truck loaded full with loose coal, to the home of my aunt Da Gu, taking my beloved book *English 900* with me.

"You'll be making fifteen *yuan* (about $2.00 USD) a month as a chicken-farm worker if hired," Aunt Da Gu said, preparing me for my future job after I arrived at her family's small, two-room apartment. "You'll turn in your paycheck to me every month in exchange for your room and board and keep two-*yuan* for your pocket money. You know I'm more generous than most people."

I felt resentful about my aunt's controlling ways but kept quiet because I understood that one had to bow one's head when living under another's roof, as the ancient Chinese proverb said.

To show my gratitude, I made myself useful: cooking, washing, and cleaning; carrying clean buckets of water home from outside in the street corner, then carrying buckets of dirty water back out to pour into the street sewage drain, and emptying night chamber pots into the outhouse early in the morning.

With my spare time on a fine day, I'd sit outside on a stack of bricks by a pile of loose coal, reading my *English 900*. Inside, it was too dark to read. Electricity was too expensive. It was only used for nighttime. As I sat in the sun, I daydreamed, stretching my legs out on the dirt ground, my eyes closed, my head leaning against the dusty brick-and-mud wall.

I dreamed of walking around on a college campus and sitting in a classroom studying English from learned professors. In my dreams, all my questions about fascinating English were answered, my curiosity met, and my mind nourished. It was heavenly to dream.

"Li Jing, would you stop dreaming of the impossible?" My best friend Serenity's voice popped my happy dream bubbles when we were once passing by the iron gate of Shanxi University one day. I'd told her that my dream was to study English in college. She'd shaken her head, looking at me with pity, a sigh, like a wise older sister.

As I now became part of Aunt Da Gu's household, things seemed to be going well at first. Her neighbors even noticed some of my accomplishments and praised me to my aunt and her husband.

"Wow," a woman exclaimed. "Cai Mei even knows how to make steamed buns?"

"What an impressive young lady," an elderly man said, smiling and nodding his approval when he saw me reading my *English 900*. "I've never seen a teenager so self-driven studying English on their own nowadays. Your niece is a fresh breath of air."

The gentleman was a highly educated intellectual. But he'd been imprisoned for twenty years during Mao's anti-rightist movement back in 1957. Millions of patriotic intellectuals had walked into Mao's death trap after making suggestions – at Mao's request – to better the Communist government. Many were tortured and murdered in prison. Millions of others had died of starvation and exhaustion in forced-labor camps. The survivors were branded as criminals, the lowest of the low, lower than murderers, thieves and prostitutes. Their children were denied of an education and other opportunities in life.

But problems soon cropped up before I ever had the chance to become a chicken co-op farm laborer. The husband and wife began finding fault with me, and I was too sensitive to accept their criticism.

Instead of thanking me for cooking them lunch, Aunt Da Gu's husband criticized my cooking. He frowned while eating out of his bowl. He said I didn't make my handmade lasagna pieces in perfect shapes, and that each of the hundreds of small, thin pieces of dough I hand-stretched into the boiling water should've been curled at the end, so they could "hook up" the sauce to keep tasty. He'd also tried to show me up in loud silence by brushing or cleaning the cutting board and whatever I'd just brushed and cleaned.

Embarrassed and humiliated, I'd run outside to sob.

"What's wrong with you?" Aunt Da Gu would hiss, scolding me, pulling and forcing me back inside. "Why are you trying to make us look bad in front of the neighbors?"

"Take back your daughter," Da Gu wrote to my father. "I shouldn't be the one taking up the responsibility to take care of her. I didn't give birth to her."

I was promptly sent packing and re-exiled back to Taiyuan. My hopeless life was back to square one. Waiting for me were my mother's silent eyes, angry, gloomy face. She couldn't forgive me for not trading places with my brother Nimble. Now he had been sent down to toil as a peasant.

A dead-end sign appeared wherever I looked in my eighteen-year-old life.

Yet an unforeseen miracle was on the horizon. It was soon to mark the end of the darkest age in my young life.

End of Part Two

Part Three

Phoenix Rising from the Ashes 鳳凰復生:

Famed English Teacher at Elite No. 5 Secondary School – From Age Eighteen to Thirty

Chapter 46
My Childhood Giggling and Laughter Returned
童年的歡笑聲又回來了

JANUARY 1975

Miraculously, the ten-year-long, darkest, stormy sky finally cleared up for me.

After Aunt Da Gu re-exiled me back to Taiyuan, my father went to seek help from our powerful distant relative Mr. Cui, who was in charge of Taiyuan City's Coal Mining Company, where my father worked as an accountant. Back in 1962, it was Mr. Cui who rescued my father from his suicidal misery by bringing him back into Taiyuan city from his exile at the village.

My father was too timid to directly ask a favor of Mr. Cui, a stern elderly man of authority, who favored high achievers. He went to soft-hearted Mrs. Cui first. She was his mother's cousin and had always lent her sympathetic ears to his misery in his chaotic marriage.

"Can your daughter teach middle-school English?" Mr. Cui asked my father. Taiyuan City, like the rest of China, was in severe shortage of schoolteachers, especially of English-language, as China's population had exploded to almost 1,000 million after the decade-long Cultural Revolution.

Teaching middle-school English was the only job available, Mr. Cui told my father.

"A teaching job?" My father was taken aback. He'd only expected a manual-labor job for me. He'd long been convinced that I'd never amount to anything in life, quoting the ancient Chinese wisdom: *A child's future can be predicted by age three.* When he yelled and beat me, I'd glare at him in silent defiance and anger, too afraid to speak up and defend myself. "You'll never become an honorable and articulate teacher, too dumb to know how to talk properly."

Although my father did look amused whenever he heard me cracking jokes, like this one: If a poor peasant were wearing a knitted sweater, you'd surely find one louse nestled inside each stitch. Still, he held onto his same convictions about me that I was dumb.

When I was twelve or thirteen, my father and I went back to visit my grandparents in Red Stone Bridge. As usual, we hitched a ride on an open-top truck carrying piled-up loose coal along with a dozen other passengers crouching down on top.

"Is this your daughter?" one middle-aged peasant man squatting in the corner had asked my father. "How come I haven't heard her saying a word?"

"Oh, she's like that. Not mute, just doesn't talk," my father said matter-of-factly.

"Why, that's not good, young girl," the man turned to exclaim to me. "You've got to learn how to talk to let the world know how you are. You can't survive if you don't learn how to talk."

The man's advice made me feel irritated and resentful. *How the hell do you know I don't know how to talk?* I screamed at him in my head. *I will talk when I have something important to say! My father's a tyranny! He's frightened me into silence. Besides, I don't think much of meaningless and useless small talk anyway.*

"Do you think you can teach middle-school English?" my father now asked me, relaying Mr. Cui's message, his tone doubting.

"Of course, I can!" I snapped at him. *I can't wait to show you!*

I couldn't wait to meet Mr. Cui, the famous legend in our family. Old Heaven God, I pleaded quietly, please don't let Mr. Cui believe a word of whatever my father has already told him about me being his worthless, useless, dumb, and knucklehead-stubborn daughter.

My fear evaporated when I met Mr. Cui. An elderly man of medium build with kind eyes, he had a quiet but reassuring voice and calming with manly strength. I relaxed and liked him right away. Mr. Cui listened to me attentively and nodded with approving smiles when I answered his questions about my schooling and how I came to love the English language.

I glanced over at my father, who sat quietly in a chair across from me and Mr. Cui. And I was surprised to discover a side of him I'd never known. He looked humble and modest. What a sharp contrast from the crazed, violent image I grew up learning to hate and fear.

As we walked out of Mr. Cui's home, my father smiled in awe. "Mr. Cui has never smiled at *me* like *that*. He never talked to me as he did you – as if you were his equal!"

The next day as Mr. Cui walked my father and me up the earthen hills to the administration's main building for the paperwork, my father suddenly turned to me: "Are you sure you know how to teach English to those rough middle-school kids?" His tone was full of doubt, his voice uncertain.

"Of course, I'm sure!" I burst out yelling at him, like a high-pressure cooker suddenly unlidded. Why did he have to doubt me in front of Mr. Cui at this crucial moment?

To my surprise, Mr. Cui chuckled, looking greatly amused. I blushed. A familiar good feeling of confidence came back to me, the same confidence I'd felt in my early childhood with my endearing grandfather.

"Oh, . . . look at her . . . the attitude . . ." my father stammered, red-faced, glancing over shyly at Mr. Cui.

My father's worries must've been triggered by his own failed experience as a schoolteacher. Grandmother, who'd hardly ever said a negative word about her precious only son, once told the story to me in a hushed voice.

After graduating from high school on the backs of his peasant parents' toiling in the cornfields, my father was finally ready to make a living. Physically, he'd never been healthy or strong. So, he'd chosen the more leisurely and honorable career of teaching. In the early 1950s, a high-school graduate was treasured as an educated scholar, since more than ninety percent of China's population was made up of illiterate masses of peasants. My father easily found a middle-school teaching job in the town of Ping Yao, where he'd earned his high school diploma.

Then one day my grandfather, my father's beaming proud father, paid him a surprise visit at school. But what he saw was chaos and sadness. Sitting in the corner of the *kang* leaning against the bedrolls was my father, the teacher. He was helplessly wiping tears, while his students were horsing around in the classroom.

Soon after that, my father quit his teaching job and became a geological worker measuring mountains and hills. He was to complain for years how the harsh working environment had given him bad arthritis in his knees and an easily upset stomach.

Unlike my father, I was a natural-born teacher from day one.

I was like an old hand teacher on my first day of teaching, facing the fifty pairs of eyes. I taught them my very first English lesson, "The East Is Red." I had no problem handling the classroom full of coal miners' offspring, although some kids got testy with me in the beginning. I looked too young in their eyes at age eighteen. The minute my back was turned to write on the blackboard, they'd start whispering and talking to each other. But my no-nonsense straight face with a death glare made them hesitate and stop. And my strict requirement that they work diligently kept them busy.

There was, however, a notorious little bad boy. He was every teacher's headache. A skinny kid with one leg shorter, he was an entitled loud-mouth. He'd grown up a spoiled brat as the son of a mean official at the coal-mining company. Most of the teachers were afraid that his father might use his authority to retaliate.

"Keep your limp leg down on the ground!" yelled one teacher, who had finally had enough, insulting the boy with his physical deficiency. The boy had defiantly and rudely placed his leg on his desk. Everyone cheered at that teacher's bravery. It became a sprit-lifting story among the other teachers.

I didn't feel at all shy teaching my students. I felt all the confidence in the world. Teaching fit me like my cold hands snuggly fit into a pair of cozy woolen gloves. I'd finally gotten to do what I loved – speak English! And I had plenty of my grand English knowledge to teach the coal miners' children the popular foreign language: the twenty-six alphabetical letters; a few extra sentences I'd taught myself from my *English 900*; all the politically correct ideological slogans I learned in my high school from Mr. Zhang, my English teacher, such as *Long Live Chairman Mao! Down with the American Imperialist Running Dogs!* I also had memorized a couple of Chinese Communist martyrdom stories; and three revolutionary songs — *The East Is Red; Let Me Sing A Folk Song to the Mother Party*, and *The Internationale*, translated from Russian.

After three years of teaching at No. 3 Middle School, I only had one parental complaint. One day a girl handed me a note from her father, a prestigious, college-educated intellectual who was originally from a big city. "What qualifications do you have to teach English to my daughter?" the father asked, blasting me: "How could you have not known 'to' comes after 'want?'" He apparently never suspected his daughter of making the mistake while hand copying her homework off the blackboard from my writing. Chinese classroom teachers didn't have any ready-made resource books but made our own. I wrote back to explain to the parent and never heard from him again.

The most fun moments of teaching English came when my students hysterically giggled and laughed when at first hearing the English letters B and P just like I did in my middle-school class: "B" almost sounds like "vagina" in derogatory Chinese language and "P" is exactly the same sound as the Chinese for "Fart." Girls covered their mouths giggling, and boys laughed out loud, yelling "B!" . . . "P!" I pretended to scold them, but only half-heartedly. After all, it was hilariously funny.

My students responded well to my teaching. I awakened their interest by explaining things clearly and logically. Part of my motivation to be a good teacher came from a few non-caring, mediocre teachers of my own in my middle and high school years.

It was a wonderful feeling to be respected.

One girl had exactly the same name as mine in phonetics and pictographic writing. But when she heard I was going to be her teacher, she hurriedly changed her name. She did that because the ancient Chinese culture dictated that a socially lower or younger person shouldn't be named the same as the person of a higher status or older. It used to be a capital offense for a commoner to have the same name as the Chinese Emperor!

My sudden success in my teaching job awoke my sense of self-worth. It lifted up my spirit. I felt vindicated, finally having proved my parents wrong that I was dumb and worthless!

I was also a self-starter. Without any advisor or a mentor, I handled my teaching job alone and smoothly. My classroom was quiet and orderly. My students liked my teaching.

The Dean, Mr. Ren Zhong Huang, soon appointed me as the head of the English Department. But almost immediately, he had to rescind my promotion because of fierce protests from the other two English teachers, who'd just graduated from college because they were Mao's gloried leading class of peasants. Both them were now privileged government employees, while I was a lowly, temporarily hired teacher, no better than a seasonally hired field hand, making half of what a college-degreed teacher made.

More than ever, I dreamed of going to college, hungry for learning and thirsty for knowledge. But the Cultural Revolution would not allow anyone but China's "leading classes" of workers, peasants, and soldiers to study in college.

My best chance was to attend the tutoring classes for teachers downtown. After school, I'd take the three-hour, round-trip bus downtown to attend the workshops that trained new English language teachers like me. How grateful I was for the learning opportunity. I would've gladly paid for the classes even if they'd charged me.

One day my father paid a surprise visit to my school, just like his father, my grandfather, had paid *him* a surprise visit at his new teaching job years before.

It was lunch break. I was scolding a girl student for failing to turn in her homework and not paying attention in class. Out of the corner of my eye, I saw my father standing by and watching quietly, looking amazed. I carried on until the girl apologized and promised to behave herself.

"Why don't you talk to the girl nicely?" my father scolded me with a humble smile after I sent away the student. "Don't be harsh with those kids. They are too young to know any better. Be careful not to offend them, they could be revengeful."

"You don't know what you're talking about," I disagreed, irritated at his nonsensical advice.

At the time, I failed to recognize my father's covert efforts to show me now that he held a 180-degree view of me. But without him saying it in plain words, I couldn't see through his words to find his intentions. My father's conviction that I was a useless and worthless dumb idiot had been firmly pounded into my head. He never made an effort to undo his cruel image by talking it out with me or expressing his remorse to me. For the next four decades till his passing in 2017 at age eighty-six, I remained that helplessly confused child in front of my father, resenting him for his abuse and violence against me. In vain, I doggedly pursued his verbal approval of me by waiting for an apology.

My father told me one day about what his colleagues were saying to him. "Mr. Li, you are such a weakling and pathetic loser. How come all your three kids are so bright and capable?"

"Why did you let people humiliate you like that?" I snapped at him for his lack of dignity. Then I became quietly disgusted. Why did he have to lump my two younger brothers in when he tried to give me a compliment? How the hell did people know about your two teenage sons, too young to have done anything monumental or made a name for themselves like I did?

I treasured immensely my freedom of living away from my family. My small dorm room, shared with another teacher, was my safe haven. Peace and quiet. I loved it.

I felt rich with a fortune of thirty *yuan* ($5 USD) as my monthly salary. My penny-pinching skills I'd learned from my grandmother served me well. After three months of saving, I bought my first pair of eyeglasses for my near-sightedness, which I had been longing and wishing for ever since the fifth grade. I cried happy tears when I put my glasses on. I could finally see the world clearly now.

Afraid my father would scold me for wasting money on the luxurious glasses, I only wore them when teaching in class and took them off as soon as I stepped out of my classroom. A grave mistake. In a short few months, my near-sightedness had worsened by 200 degrees. I needed new glasses again. If I wanted to keep my eyesight, the optometrist told me, I needed to wear the correct lenses all the time, not on and off.

I braced myself for my father's criticism.

"Why did you have to put on airs like that?" My father only scolded me with a smile.

My new and independent good life at age nineteen reminded me of my forty happy days of hospitalization when I was nine years old. Most teachers at No. 3 Middle School reminded me of the wonderful, loving, white-coated angels of doctors and gentle nurses who took care of me.

My giggling and laughter from my early childhood at Red Stone Bridge came back!

"Your name shouldn't be 靜 *Jing* of serenity, quiet, still, but 動 *Dong* of active, vigor, and energy!" the physics teacher in dark-rimmed, thick glasses teased me. His smiles were heartwarming. He was one of the many college-degreed, wonderful teachers from China's faraway, exotic big cites.

"Why can't you be lively and cheerful like Li Jing?" scolded the parents of my roommate when they came to visit her. For that, I earned Hu's hard, long, glare and silent treatment for days.

Hu was one of the two English teachers who'd protested fiercely against my being promoted as the chair of English Department. She spoke with a thick village accent in both Chinese and English. Her classes were an all-time riot, with kids laughing and teasing her. Because her father was the Communist Party secretary in their village, he'd abused his power by sending his slow-brained daughter Hu to college instead of one of many bright-brained, qualified high-school graduates who'd been sent down to his village from the cities.

Hu looked much older than her self-claimed twenty-seven years of age. She had deep wrinkles on her forehead, a saggy face. Her droopy eyelids looked like a giant canopy. Her breasts hung down to her waist, as if she'd nursed several babies. Behind her oversized, thick, white glasses, her huge eyeballs were lifeless like those of a dead goldfish. When she looked at people, she squinted suspiciously as if she were an institutionalized mental patient.

Yet, Miss Hu could go to college with a mere second-grade village school education, while I, a high school graduate, wasn't allowed. My heart constantly ached from the humiliation of my inferior, temporary-teaching status despite my outstanding ability to teach.

"Ms. Li," a young teacher said to me one day with an admiring smile after I presented a workshop on classroom teaching and management at a neighboring school. "Your lecture was so enlightening. I learned a lot from you." But she quickly looked betrayed in her eyes when I told her that I didn't have a college degree. "Oh, the way you talked, I thought you were a famous, college-educated teacher from a big city! You're just a temporary teacher like me, earning the lowest thirty *yuan* a month?"

Oh, the humiliating pain.

Was my college dream really impossible? How I wished that I'd been born eleven or twelve years earlier, the same age as the college-degreed teachers at No. 3 Middle School who came from China's famous big cities of Beijing, Shanghai, and Canton – privileged places I'd only read about. I wanted to be just like those teachers, who'd had the fortune to learn knowledge on a college campus of paradise. I even adored their various exotic accents. Aware of my lowly social status, I became extra grateful that those great teachers treated me nicely, with their heart-touching smiles, as if I were their equal.

In the midst of admiring the wonderful college-educated teachers, I had great sympathy for their hardships: they were persecuted for simply being college educated by the Cultural Revolution. Most of them were purposefully separated from their fiancées when the government assigned them to their work sites at their college graduation. They were scattered all across China, hundreds of miles away from their loved ones, and only allowed to have a brief family reunion for ten days a year. But the traveling time alone from one end of China to another took several days each way. "Individual needs and wants were the roots of evil," said Chairman Mao. "Everyone should be an obedient nail and screw staying faithfully wherever the Party places you in the glorious whole machine of our great socialist system."

Hiding behind my giggling and laughter was also my shameful secret: my parents' stormy marriage, my mother's extra marital affair, and my not being loved at home. I felt like the fool in the Chinese fable who covered his eyes with two pieces of tree leaves trying to convince himself that the world couldn't see him. I was convinced that if I didn't talk about my family, no one would ever discover my shame.

I dreaded the arrival of every weekend, which meant that I needed to go back "home," as the culture expected of young single people. Even my roommate Hu would spend many hours on the long-distance bus back to her village home.

On Saturday night, I'd keep my dorm room light off and lay in bed, sending the signal to the world that I, too, had gone back to my loving family, just like everyone else. And on Sunday morning, I'd sneak out to take the bus ride downtown to walk around window-shopping for a few hours before hopping back on the bus. On the way I'd be preparing an excuse, in case I ran into someone in the deserted school yard, explaining why I was returning early from a happy weekend at home.

Soon I found my refuge and another way to spend my weekends.

Chapter 47
Trapped by "House Business"
房事

AT AGE NINETEEN, my desire to be loved got me into a relationship I didn't know how to get out of until 23 years later in America.

One day, several of us brand-new and wide-eyed young teachers, all young women on temporary teaching status at No. 3 Middle School, were touring the small, L-shaped earthen schoolyard. We were chatting and laughing merrily, feeling special and privileged, despite our uncertain future.

The last classroom was located in the dead corner at the end of the earthen wall. "That's the music classroom," someone called out. Music? My ears perked up. For all my life, I'd dreamed of playing a musical instrument! But my growing-up years had been filled with anything but the sound of music. In an era when food was rationed and people were starving, buying a musical instrument, even a harmonica, was an impossible luxury.

Nimble once took pity on me. My teenaged brother then made me a two-stringed 二胡 *Er Hu* from scratch by gluing wood sticks, thread and pieces of bamboo together. But, alas, it only made the guttural sounds, like a young rooster learning how to crow.

The music teacher, Vic, was alone in the classroom. He politely stood up to greet our group of noisy chatterboxes. Vic was in his mid-twenties and quite handsome, taller and stronger than most of the bean-sprout skinny types his same age. His darker skin made him manly looking. He had thick, jet-black hair, chiseled lips, and a tall-bridged nose. I especially liked his polite manner and shy smile. His eyes shone with intelligence, refreshingly different from the rough-looking, loud, crude crowds in my parents' blue-collar dirt yard.

We had great fun chatting and laughing with Vic. I loved the way Vic laughed. He threw his head back as he clapped his hands. But later I found out he was a rather reserved person, someone who hardly smiled, let alone laughed.

I spotted the black piano in the corner of the classroom. How I was thrilled. This was my first time seeing a real piano up close. Right there and then, I decided to have Vic teach me how to play it. I wanted his undivided attention, for I'd noticed another young woman, a Chinese language teacher, was also looking at him in affectionate admiration.

Vic was more than happy to teach me. I started visiting his music classroom every day after school. He taught me how to play the Mao-praising anthem: "The East Is Red." And, as it turned out, that was the only tune he knew how to play on the piano!

I admired Vic's educated family background. Once he told me what he thought of my blue-collar dirt yard: "I was passing by the Heavy Machinery Factory's residential yard. Kids there looked really rough and thuggish. I was nervous and worried if they were going to jump me."

For the first time in my life, someone had made me aware of how uncivilized my neighborhood appeared in the eye of the educated world. No wonder my father once sighed enviously: "Look how civilized the college-educated intellectual people are. They talk quietly and politely with gentle manners. But look at the unruly, dirty-looking crowds in this dirt yard of ours, so rude, loud, and foul-mouthed."

Vic's grandfather was a famous traditional Chinese doctor. He used to be the prominent clinical director at China's prestigious department store *Wang Fu Jing* 王府井 in Beijing. But the Cultural Revolution had destroyed his life. The Red Guards smashed all his classic fine furniture, ancient porcelain and pottery. They burned his books and paintings. They accused him of being an Evil Enemy of the People and from a landlord family. They beat him and confiscated everything they hadn't destroyed in his home. And his wife soon died from fear and grief. He was then kicked out of his home with only the clothes on his back and forced to return to his ancestors' village in *He Bei* province to toil in the cornfields as a peasant for the next fifteen years.

Both of Vic's parents were professors of Western medicine. But like the rest of the nation's educated people, they were sent down to be "re-educated" by peasants in the remote county of 离石 *Li Shi*, one of Shanxi's poorest mountain regions.

A ninth grader, when the Cultural Revolution started, Vic later escaped his fate of being sent down to become a peasant. With the help of his close friend – a comrade-in-arms in the same faction – he became a coal miner and worked twelve-hour shifts underground, wearing a dim light on his wicker-woven hardhat for miners. He got to keep his city registration card for rationed food.

When his best friend died in a coal avalanche during a mine cave-in, Vic was just a few feet away digging coal. He became traumatized and depressed. After his pinky finger was injured at work, he used it as a valid medical excuse and persuaded the personnel officials to re-assign him to an above-ground job. He showed the officials his violin and told them that he knew how to play music. That was how he became a music teacher at No. 3 Middle School, where his old friend had become the principal. A few months later, I came through my own backdoor connection to become an English teacher there.

Besides being fascinated with learning music from Vic, I was also attracted to Vic's good-natured personality. He was a quiet, calm and peaceful man. And something else turned out to be important to me: He had the luxury of having his dorm room all to himself. He didn't have to share his room with another teacher, as I did. Since he had no home to go to over the weekend because his family, parents and two sisters were in the faraway mountains, he had the time and convenience for me to visit him.

Vic's dorm room used to be an old storage shed. It had no windows, but rough cement-and-brick walls, just big enough to hold a single bed, a small bedside table and a coal-burning iron stove for cooking and heating. I was fascinated to see, for the first time, that he also had an exotic, foot-high kerosene oil stove for emergency cooking in case the iron stove failed to light.

I found my refuge, my peace and quiet, in Vic's small, dark den. No longer did I need to take the three-hour-long bus trips downtown over the weekend, pretending to go back home.

Terrified that my father would find out, I sneaked around to visit Vic in his dorm, although we were like two innocent-minded childhood playmates. Every day I looked forward to the time when darkness fell so I could be in Vic's room. He'd always be waiting for me with a quiet smile. As soon as I closed the door behind me, I'd feel a great sense of relief and need to take a nap.

Vic's wooden bed was a luxury compared with mine. He had two cotton-padded quilts, instead of one, the only way I knew. And his understanding was so comforting. He'd cover me up and tell me to have a nice nap. In all of my nineteen years of life, I had never taken a nap under a cotton-padded quilt. In my family, a cotton-padded quilt was for bedtime only, not for napping – unnecessary wear and tear.

Vic was like an older nurturing brother I never had. He taught me important things no one else in my family ever did. You should drink plenty of water to keep hydrated, he'd say, and that I should keep a daily habit of having a bowel movement the first thing in the morning. It has since solved my chronic constipation problems. For this, I give him my lifelong gratitude.

I also liked Vic's "rich" manner of living. When he ate a cracker or a dried steamed bun, he'd casually shake off the crumbs, instead of saving them into his palm, like I did, to lick clean. When cooking vegetables, he didn't save everything like I did, either. He cut off and threw away the rough stubs on top of an eggplant, and the soft bulb inside a green bell pepper, instead of scraping off the seeds and saving them. Even his cooking pan had a unique shape. I had never seen a flat-bottomed frying pan, but a traditional round-bottomed wok.

"What's this?" I asked Vic one day, curious about the three strands of stainless steel spiral springs on two handles.

"Oh, it's 拉力器 *la-li-qi, a power stretcher.*"

"What's it for?"

"For strengthening your arm muscles."

I was amazed. The leisurely life of these educated people! They even invented a way to toughen their arm muscles. My grandfather didn't need any help to toughen his muscles. He overworked his muscles and his entire body, toiling all year long from dawn to dusk, pushing a plow behind a cow, hoeing, cutting and splitting firewood, and walking miles while shoulder-poling two heavy, thick, wooden buckets of water or manure or firewood. At the end of each day, he was so exhausted he could only pant, trying to catch his breath after crashing on his floor stool.

Vic's boldness was reassuring. One day I confided one of my fears in him: I couldn't cry out tears at the mandatory mass funeral for Mao, who finally died in 1976. I'd been worried that my tear-free eyes would be reported for punishment by a pair of observant eyes from thousands of people inside the auditorium. As a cover-up, I'd tried to lower my head and rub my eyes as if I were weeping tears of sadness for our "savior's" death. "You don't have to cry tears," Vic had told me. "I don't." His advice, stated with such bravery, gave me a great sense of relief.

"Are you really seeing Vic?" asked Ms. Jia, a young math teacher, as she smiled good-naturedly like a big sister, her trimmed eyebrows arched high. We were walking up the hill to go vegetable shopping.

"Oh, no, I'm not," I hurriedly denied.

"That's what I thought. I didn't believe it when I heard the gossip about you're seeing Vic. You two are just too different. And he's too old for you."

I was relieved that she believed me, but at the same time I also wanted to find out why she thought Vic and I were not a good match, but secretly agreed with her that a six-year age difference was indeed too big a gap.

I found out on my own, and too late, the huge gap of difference between Vic and me – I was too straightforward and naive, while Vic, too reserved, and prone to playing mind games.

"This is my father's treasured pen." Vic said when he gave me a golden-tipped fountain pen. "See how shining the tip is? It's real gold. I want you to have it." He made me not only feel special, but rich. Then I found out much later, after marrying him, that Vic's father had no idea what I was talking about when I mentioned his "gold pen."

Vic also described his family as being harmonious, especially his middle sister, who, he said, was loving and easy to get along with – but turned out to be just the opposite. The two siblings were actually bitter rivals. Their father favored her and was violent toward him.

At nineteen, my concept of love and romance had never gone beyond the image of a picture painted on the mirror hung on my grandparents' sod wall. It showed two classic young lovers, *Liang ShanBo* 梁山伯, and *Zhu YingTai* 祝英台, the ancient Chinese version of English Romeo and Juliet. In her pink flowing gown, elegant *Zhu YingTai* covered her mouth demurely behind her long sleeves, her smiling eyes glancing shyly at handsome *Liang Shanbo*, whose hair was arranged in a high bun on top of his head, his eyes full of affection.

"What if your father finds out about you and me?" Vic asked.

"I don't care if he did. I don't have to listen to him." I shocked myself by even saying those words. This was the first time I'd revealed to an outsider my bottled-up anger toward my father. Grandmother was the only one that I'd always defiantly told how angry I was with him. And I'd been carefully guarding my dark family secret about my parents' stormy marriage and never shared any of it with Vic.

"Are you sure? We all have to listen to our parents."

"Not me. I don't," I said, pretending it was true.

One evening, after my usual early evening nap, I lay innocently side-by-side with him.

"Everybody has a *xin-yu*, right?" Vic smiled mysteriously, his twenty-five-year-old body secretly lusting for what my nineteen-year-old body didn't feel. So far, my feelings for him weren't sexual; they were more like a mixture of gratitude and budding curiosity.

"Yes, everyone has a *xin-yu* 信譽," I nodded politely, wondering why he brought up the topic of "trust and integrity."

"Can I please try it?" he looked at me earnestly, his eyes shining with desire.

How can you try on trust and integrity? I thought to myself, wondering, and feeling puzzled. It didn't dawn on me that he actually meant *xing-yu* 性慾, "sexual desire." Shanxi dialect blurs the sounds of "-ing" and "-in."

I nodded, agreeing with him that, yes, everyone had a *xin-yu* – "integrity and honor."

Vic looked ecstatic.

"I'll be slow and careful, okay?" He got on top of me, his eyes smiling into mine, telling me I was sweet. I felt smitten. I was addicted to compliments. Smiling demurely back at him, I secretly wished that my quick, hot temper would forever remain hidden from him.

Then I was shocked to feel a sudden, sharp, flesh-tearing pain. I cried out. Blood was coming out of me and had stained Vic' bed sheet.

"Oh, please don't cry," Vic pleaded, scrambling off me. "It's okay, I can fix it. I've got some herbal white powder medicine to stop the bleeding." He gently sprinkled the special white floral powder on me and held me in his arms, his smiling eyes shining with pride and satisfaction.

All I felt was pain.

That was how I lost my virginity. I learned that the intimacy between a man and a woman was all about pain, infection, and bleeding. I never knew it was supposed to be fun and enjoyable. And I didn't find out that kissing was supposed to be part of making love until two decades later.

"People saw you come and visit my mother," Vic later told me.

"How could it be?" I was shocked and distressed. I'd been trying to keep the relationship secret, terrified that my father would find out. But instead of becoming suspicious of Vic's dishonesty, I racked my brain: Not a single soul was in sight when I took the trolley bus that dark evening to visit his mother. I'd run into no one I knew and seen no one around in the deserted streets in the cold dark twilight.

Once a young woman was seen to visit a man's parents, in that era, she belonged to him in the eyes of Chinese society. If the marriage didn't follow, she became a slut, a social outcast, considered nothing but a shameful piece of used, second-hand goods no other normal man would want to marry. In Mao's totalitarian China, there were no separate stages of dating, engagement and marriage. All three were rolled into one. I was now helplessly trapped in my relationship with Vic and resented him for the next twenty-five years.

Since we'd been intimate, Vic started making it a rule that it was now my duty and obligation to do 房事 *fang-shi*, "house business" with him, Chinese for "making love." But I felt no pleasure or joy, only painful infections, burning pain, and bother. Why did he even want it? I didn't understand it. And, three horribly painful abortions I was to go through over the years down the road would further deepen my resentment.

And, worse, I now felt like I had to constantly prove my innocence to him. He'd accuse me of being indecent if I even glanced in the general direction of another man. Vic once yelled at me, his face gravely serious, for talking to the school electrician "too cheerfully." He'd also make sarcastic remarks about my being attracted to another 25-year-old teacher, Mr. Wang, the head of the English department. But Mr. Wang was not even a healthy man. The same age as Vic, his face was a greenish cast, and his back slightly hunched. I didn't even feel safe enough to tell Vic that I actually admired Mr. Wang's great intelligence and superb English.

Even though I became angry and frustrated with Vic all the time, he put up with it, as long as I played my part in our "house business." I was stuck. Too late for me to change my mind. I didn't want to be branded and spat on as a "broken shoe." I'd vowed to never be like my mother.

The tragic story of an elementary school teacher, *Xiao Li Ze*, was enough warning for me. On her wedding night, the groom kicked her out of bed and out of their home the minute he found out she wasn't a virgin. Too ashamed to face her parents or even let them know about her misery, she hid herself in her friend's home for six months until her husband served her the divorce papers. And he made her pay him back the thousands-of-dollar worth of gifts he'd given her for their engagement.

A few years later when I congratulated *Xiao Li Ze* on her new marriage, she blushed, looking ashamed: "Please don't mention it. The second time means nothing."

My father must have heard some gossip about Vic and me. For he had obviously tried to come up with another idea for a more suitable match for me.

"I know a high official woman, who makes eighty *yuan* a month," my father said to me, out of the blue. "And she has a son your age, a factory worker." He didn't spell it out, but I understood his intention. He was hinting at a marriage prospect for me. I became disgusted at his only looking at the money: How much money the young man's *mother* made. He was testing to find out if the rumor about Vic and me were true. I hadn't told him anything about us. And he never asked. But even if my father could succeed in forcing me to break up with Vic, I still wouldn't be attracted to his friend's son, a mere factory worker – nothing like Vic, with his intellectual brain and his college-educated parents.

"My friend is married. I want to get married, too," Vic said to me one day.

"No, you need to get a college degree first," I told him, putting my foot down. Knowing I meant business, he jumped into action. He first obtained a referral letter from his principal friend at No. 3 Middle School. Then he became a part-time college student – as one of the workers-peasants-soldiers class – at Shanxi University, since officially his social status was still in the category of "workers."

1977. One year after Mao's death.

An exciting rumor started going around: The government was going to abolish its affirmative-action college admissions' policy for workers-peasants-soldiers-only, and restore the pre-Cultural Revolution standard of academic merit-based, regardless the family's political background. All the offspring to the former classified enemies of people were now equally eligible to apply as the politically correct classes of workers, peasants and soldiers.

One day a beautiful date-red horse came into my dream. I was a small child playing by the stone mill at Red Stone Bridge when the gorgeous horse galloped toward me.

It was a Heaven-sent dream. A miracle was soon to lift me up.

Chapter 48
Taiyuan Teachers' College
太原師範

1977. I WAS TWENTY-ONE. My college dream finally came true.

Taiyuan Teachers' College announced the earth-shattering news, beating all other colleges nationwide, that it was opening its door for admission solely based on academic competitions. The ten-year-long affirmative action program, which had allowed only workers, peasants, and soldiers to attend college, had been abolished. Now anyone from ages of eighteen to thirty, regardless their family's political background, was eligible to register and compete. It was several generations worth of applicants accumulated in the past eleven years since 1966.

"Do you think you can pass the test?" my father asked me, looking exited. He even offered to stand in line with thousands of others to register for me.

"Of course, I do."

"Have some more tea," my father said with a smile. It was the morning of my college-admission test. I'd stayed overnight in my parents' city apartment. "It'll help keep your mind alert when taking the test. Be calm, don't be anxious, as you always are."

I grunted, not used to his fussing over me. It felt strange and unnecessary.

A sea of young people and their bicycles had gathered in front of Taiyuan Teachers' College. Every classroom in the three-story main building was packed solid with prospective students. I followed the slow-moving long line to my assigned seat, feeling a surge of energy. Time for me to shine and prove my self-worth.

I easily zipped through the written tests for English, Chinese, history, and geography, thanks to the bits and pieces of knowledge I had managed to gather here and there from reading bits and pieces over the years. My spirits remained high when I went to take my oral English test. The hallway was crowded, mostly with young women like me. Everyone was nervous. No one wanted to be the first to face the panel of solemn-looking English professors – the three judges. I volunteered to be the first and received a collective cheer.

As the English oral test began, I confidently answered the first two short questions. But when the third, and last, question was a long sentence, I tensed up – not understanding every word the professor had said. In his rapid blur of speaking, I'd only caught a few words: . . . socialism . . . good . . . China . . . advantage . . . capitalist. Thinking quickly, I realized it was a rhetorical question. And the correct answer had to be a "yes": Whenever "socialism" was paired with "capitalism" in the same sentence. Glorious socialism always prevailed over evil capitalism. It was the standard lesson we learned in school.

"Yes." I shot out my answer with a confident smile. The professor nodded his approval!

"You got lucky to be the first one," one sour-grape girl said to me loudly enough for everyone to hear. She was the daughter of an English-language professor and was jealous of my earning the highest score. But her words didn't bother me. It felt so good to come out on top again.

Out of the hundreds of contestants, sixty students were admitted into the English Language Department, and most of my new classmates – I was fascinated to discover – were the offspring of college educated families.

Later at home, my father – looking ecstatic – told me what his colleagues were saying: "Out of four truckloads of the young teachers sent from Western Hills Coal Mining school district, only one kid got in, and she wasn't even the product of our school district!"

After a long pause, I suddenly realized that the "only one kid" my father had referred to was me. And I immediately felt resentful that he had never once come right out and tell me that he was proud of me.

The brand-new campus of Taiyuan Teachers College was built at the city's outskirts. Inside the iron-gate was a large, brown, earthen dirt ground with a patch of weeds and other wild vegetation in front. And it became the students' job to pull out the weeds and keep the space clear.

Standing in the middle of the yard was a three-story main building of offices and classrooms. To the left of the main building was a two-story student dorm. Behind the main building was a low-roofed shack, which stored a hot-water tank heated by a coal-burning furnace. The tank supplied hot water for washing our chopsticks and bowls, our hands, faces and feet, as well as for drinking water – more often than not the water wasn't boiled to be safe enough to drink, but we had no choice but drink it anyway. At washing times, after meals and before bed, the three water faucets sticking outside from the inside the shack wall over a shallow cement sink were surrounded by crowds of students.

Each student dorm room was about ten-feet wide and twenty-feet long. The walls were washed with lime powder. A wooden platform, communal bed was built across the room from wall to wall, with fifteen students assigned to sleep on it. It was a tight sleeping space. During the day, we folded up our cotton-padded futons into neat squares against the wall, much like soldiers' bedrolls in their barracks. We stored one change of clothes under our pillows and bedrolls.

The dorm rooms had no space for desks or chairs, only a long passageway to walk to and from the door. We were expected to do all our studying and any other student activities in our classrooms. No public bath or shower on campus, either. Each brought our own washbasin – painted over thin iron – for washing face and feet and stored it under the communal bed. I fetched hot water with my washbasin for washing, unlike many other girls who, for convenience, brought from home a hot water bottle, which kept water hot. After we had done our washing up, we carried out the dirty water and poured it outside the building onto the dirt ground.

I loved every minute at Taiyuan Teachers' College. At the crack of dawn every day, we all got up to walk around the campus reading our English texts out aloud to practice our pronunciation and memorize vocabulary words. Everyone was secretly competing with each other, wanting to earn the highest grades.

I was soon appointed student-body president in charge of academics. It was like the comeback of my wonderful third-grade year, when my teachers made me the class monitor because I had the best grades in the class. One girl, whose father was my father's boss, wasn't convinced that I was unbeatable. She studied so hard, using every minute of her awake time, that she soon fell ill with an acute kidney problem, and ended up having to take the rest of the semester off.

Vic was not altogether happy about my college success. He yelled at me for getting involved with the school affairs against his advice. He said I shouldn't be so vain and seek to show off my "trivial smartness." His controlling behavior really turned me off, but he was the only one there for me, too. He had rented a room in the nearby village, as he was a part-time college student then, before he competed into a four-year college the next year. Just a fifteen-minute bike ride from my college, Vic's dirt-floored, small village room became my secret weekend refuge. It was much better than going "home."

One day, my father unexpectedly came to college campus and told me what the president of Taiyuan Teachers' College had said to him: "Mr. Li, you have a good daughter."

"How did *you* know the president?" I was annoyed that my father had been following me around, despite the compliment he'd brought me – It felt like my darkest corner had been exposed to the world.

"He was my former high-school teacher back in the town of 平遥 *Ping Yao*."

My father's revelation grimly upset me: How much had he already told my college president, his former teacher, about me being his dumb, idiot, useless daughter? I felt greatly threatened. My mental image of my abusive father had never changed.

But how did the president of the college even know who I was?

Then I remembered the New Year's party. It must've been my on-stage performance with my classmate, *Ji KangLi*. Ji was not only beautiful with big eyes and fair skin, she was also the daughter of two English professors. She had been scheduled to sing a solo, but chickened out at the last minute, pleading with me to sing along with her. I was the only other student in the foreign-language department who knew how to sing the English words to the song "Let Me Sing a Folk Song to the Mother Party." And even though I wasn't prepared and hadn't rehearsed, I gave up resisting when she pulled me by my hand onto the stage. That's when I'd seen the elderly president, Mr. Zhang, in his dark-rimmed glasses, sitting in the audience at the front row. President Zhang had looked impressed with our singing. He applauded us enthusiastically. I remember swelling with pride standing side by side as the equal to my privileged and beautiful classmate.

Shortly after I settled down in Taiyuan Teachers' College, four-year colleges and universities across China all opened their doors for academic competition. Many contestants who didn't make it into the two-year Teachers' College tried again and were accepted into four-year colleges.

My father was disappointed that I refused to try competing to enter a four-year college. I didn't have the confidence, I told him. A bird in hand was better than two in a tree. Although it was only a two-year college, Taiyuan Teachers' College was my security and stability. It was also tuition-free with free room and board, even free study materials. And, anyway, my father didn't offer to pay my tuition if I were admitted into a four-year college.

Vic, on the other hand, tried hard to discourage me, telling me that I wasn't good enough to get into a four-year college. He said my intelligence was a perfect fit for the two-year college.

Deep down inside, I discouraged myself with my paranoid, irrational fear that a physical examination for a four-year college would expose me as no longer a virgin.

Soon I noticed something strange happening at Taiyuan Teachers' College. For days I'd been the only Student Body Officer taking care of the class affairs, helping set up the classroom, getting the teachers' materials ready for class, hand-copying the class name lists, going to the office registering for brooms and dust pans, and so on. Where were all the other officers who were supposed to be sharing these tasks?

Then the English Department announced an upcoming competition test. The top ten winners would be selected and sent to a four-year college and then return as future professors at Taiyuan Teachers' College. So, that's why no other class officers had been helping me! They'd all been getting ready for that test. I felt betrayed and cheated. While they studied, I'd been using my own study time doing all the class chores and running all the errands. It turned out that every single one of those student body officers had backdoor connections. Their parents were buddies with Mr. Han, the Dean of the English Department. I was the only unsuspecting fool and from a nobody-family.

I took the test, still passed it, and even ranked number four: a guaranteed spot. Naively, I waited for my turn to be sent to a four-year college.

Vic started picking fights with me, assuming I'd soon be hundreds of miles away, studying at a four-year college and out of his reach. But it turned out that only a few of the top-ten winners – those with the strongest backdoor connections – got the privilege of being sent to a four-year college.

I was devastated. Vic, on the other hand, started being nice to me again.

Even though I wasn't going on to a four-year college, I continued to excel in my studies. On final examination day, I scored 97 percent – the highest in my class – remaining the unbeatable number one.

I loved everything in my paradise college life except one thing: the brainwashing politics.

In the English Language Department, a few of the college staff were products of the affirmative action college graduates, who were former peasants with elementary education. Talking in their thick, village accents, they reminded me of my dull, dead-goldfish-eyed roommate Hu back at No. 3 Middle School. And they lorded it over us because they were Communist Party members. We especially hated our political supervisor, *Wang Xian Mei*. Behind her back, we all called her *mu-lao-hu* 母老虎, "female tiger," an equivalent expression to "bitch" in English.

Miss Wang would round us up during our evening self-study time, wasting our precious time by lecturing us for the entire two-hour period. She'd warn us against the danger of becoming a "white expert:" paying attention only to our grades and academic achievement. She'd order us to dig deep into our souls and examine our inner thoughts. Her most hateful action was to barge into our dorm room during our noon nap times to round up us student-body officers. We were made to sit in a circle on the floor stool. Each of us had to do our self-degrading talking. As we talked, vicious Miss Wang's pen was furiously busy recording every word out of our mouths. Everyone knew she was gathering material for our personal political dossier, a lethal weapon that could be used against any one of us when another violent political storm swept through China. We were forced to dig our own future graves.

I passionately despised Miss Wong but felt too helpless to resist her. She could easily find an excuse to have me expelled and permanently ruin my life. When it was my turn to do the "self-degrading talk," I tried to come up with some mild "offenses," such as using my near-fatal heart disease at age nine as an excuse to skip the political study meetings, etc.

Except for the spirit-killing dirty politics, and the constant ideological brainwashing, I was very happy at Taiyuan Teachers' College: my mind nourished by gaining knowledge, my stomach full of free food.

We ate all our free meals in the school cafeteria. For breakfast and dinner, we'd have hot gruel of rice or millet mixed with corn flour, one steamed cornmeal 窩頭 *wo-tou*, and a few pieces of salt-pickled turnips. The *wo-to* was so coarse it felt like sandpaper scratching our throats. We joked the rock-hard *wo-tou* could kill a dog. I vowed never to touch any food made of cornmeal in the future.

Lunch was the main meal of the day with better and more varied menus: soft steamed buns made from wheat flour; or noodles with tomato sauce; or occasionally white steamed rice with stir-fried turnips, cabbages, and potatoes or seasonal greens, such as zucchini or string beans. At meal times in the cafeteria, we were divided into ten students per group. Our food was contained inside a gigantic aluminum basin dished out evenly into everyone's bowl.

The brand-new Teachers' college was too poor to afford any dining tables and chairs in the cafeteria. Hundreds of us ate our meals squatting down on the dusty cement floor. I didn't give much thought to it. That was the way I grew up. But I was surprised to hear many others complain.

Most of my classmates supplemented their meals by bringing snacks from home, sunflower seeds, dried, steamed, wheat-flour buns, candies, and vegetable pickles. I secretly envied them. One classmate was once so kind as to share her snack with me on a freezing-cold winter night. The soul-comforting snack has since left me a lifelong fond memory. Still today, on a cold night, I'll have a mug of plain hot water with a small piece of hot-and-sour pickled turnip.

Unlike my classmates who had other food choices, my sole source of nutrients came from the campus cafeteria food. Eventually, my gums became swollen, and my teeth ached. One day, a small chunk of bone fell off my bottom front teeth. Frightened and worried, I went to the campus clinic, where the young nurse swabbed my gums with some bitter brown liquid and sent me away. Thinking it was some magic medicine, I didn't spit it out but swallowed it, despite of its bitter taste. "Who swallows *that*?" the nurse frowned at me, looking disgusted, the next time I saw her and told her about it. She took pity on me and gave me some vitamin C pills. I was so grateful.

"Today is Wednesday, yay!" *Bian Jie*, my classmate, cheered one morning when we were lined up during our class's physical exercises. Her face was so exotically pretty that everyone called her a "foreign doll." "Wednesday means the top of the hill. I can now start counting on the days to go home. Oh, I'm so homesick! I miss my mommy . . ."

I feel exactly the opposite! I caught myself before blurting out. What did it feel like to be homesick and to miss your mother and family? My heart couldn't feel it.

"Home time!" my classmates all cheered on Saturday afternoons. I'd pretend to join the happy crowd but dragged my feet purposefully behind everyone. When someone asked me why I wasn't in a hurry to go home, I'd make up all kinds of excuses about needing to take care of some duty as the class monitor.

I made sure no one found out that I wasn't going "home," but to my secret refuge, Vic's rented room in the nearby village, *Wang Cun*. I arranged to have him pick me up half a mile away, around the corner from my college. As college students, we were forbidden to have a relationship with the opposite sex.

"How's my old woman?" Vic would tease me as soon as he saw me. I resented him for always trying to make me sound six years older, like him. "Your old fellow is on duty to meet you!"

When we were together, sex seemed to be always all Vic cared about. But I never could feel his enthusiasm or desire. I went along with the "house business" because he was the only one in the world I could count on. I was very grateful when Vic once had his friend's mother make me a warm flannel overcoat for the cold winter weather. It was in nice and practical dark blue color.

On Sundays, after Vic went to his college class, I'd stay still and remain quiet, hiding inside the room, too ashamed to show my face to his landlord's family next door in the same earthen yard. I couldn't afford to let anyone know that I was in a relationship.

One bright Sunday morning after Vic went to his class, I couldn't resist the urge to peek out into the yard. I stood up on the *kang* to look through the glass window by the curtain. To my horror, another pair of eyes were looking up back at me. It was a woman, who must be the landlord's wife. As if hit by lightning, I dropped back down to *Kang*, never imagining the disaster that would unfold that same night.

"Open the door!" A sudden, loud rush of knocking on the wooden door came at midnight. Two men were yelling outside. "Open the door! Militia guards!"

I was frozen with fear. I had a feeling that this unexpected visit had been caused by my unwise peeking out of the window earlier that morning. The landlord lady must've reported to the authorities. She must've been suspecting some kind of criminal slut hiding out in her residence.

Vic quickly got up and opened the door.

"I.D.!" the two men shouted simultaneously, pushing their way in.

"Please, don't worry, comrades," Vic said, remaining cool, as he quickly grabbed his shirt over and fished out his I.D.

"Who is she to you?"

"Oh, this is my fiancée," Vic said, sounding like it was real.

How is he going to prove it? I was shaking, lying under the quilt, dying of shame.

Horrific scenes flashed through my mind. I was being dragged by my hair on the dirt street toward the torture chamber at the police station as crowds were yelling, spitting on me, and throwing rocks at me. I was officially branded a slut, a social outcast. After the public humiliation and torture, I'd then be expelled from Taiyuan Teachers' College and sentenced to prison. My only way out was to cut my wrists and bleed out until I died.

"Comrades, here is my reference paper, our permission to get married from my work unit," Vic said calmly.

He really had the paper! When did he obtain it? I froze, shocked, in delight and disbelief.

The two men looked at each other, then turned around and left. I collapsed, muffling my sobbing, my body shaking violently. My life was saved. I was safe.

Just two weeks later, my classmate, the chief student-body president, was expelled after being caught in his dorm room bed sleeping with his girlfriend. Had they been caught in their own rented room off campus, the Public Security would've been involved. And that would've been a criminal case.

Fall 1978.

Taiyuan Teachers' College was overflowing with hundreds more incoming students, but lacked enough teachers, as was the case all over China. To meet the demand for college teachers, the government recruited hundreds of thousands of recently released from prisons intellectuals who'd been held as political prisoners after being condemned as criminal "rightists" back in 1957. But there was still a severe teacher shortage. Taiyuan Teachers' College solved its own problem by selecting some of its top students to teach college courses.

I was one of the few students to be granted this exceptional honor.

At age twenty-two, while still a second-year college student, I became a college English instructor. Once again, my teaching skills shone through. I earned the highest evaluation from my "students," many of whom were ten years older than I was.

"At first, she looked too shy to even look at us," my students said, greatly amused. "But look at her now: confident enough to scold us. Ha, ha!"

One day, I was playing badminton on the sidewalk in front of the college gate. A middle-aged woman came up to me, exclaiming, surprised. She was the fifth aunt of my elementary school classmate Little Beauty. "What are *you* doing here?" She asked, looking amazed in disbelief that I was teaching college! The majority of my generation had been wasted into semi-illiteracy during the Cultural Revolution, like her niece Little Beauty, who struggled and competed for the few available manual-labor jobs.

After a full year of teaching college English, I was officially due to "graduate." With my outstanding teaching record, I assumed – again naively – that I would surely continue my teaching job. I was wrong. Another girl from my class, an average student with no teaching experience, was to replace me!

After crying my eyes out, I was ready to accept my fate, again assuming that I'd be assigned to teach at Taiyuan City's best high school, the number one academically elite No. 5. But I was shocked into deep grief that another classmate had bumped me off and taken away my entitled position.

I lost it and marched into the college dean's office.

"Why are you being so unfair to me?" I aimed my angry outburst at the Dean, Mr. Wu.

Mr. Wu looked up at me coolly, his droopy eyelids puffy, his large body spilling over the armchair. Clearing his throat, he started lecturing me: "Well, that's no way to talk to your leader, Li Jing. You've got some serious attitude and thought problems."

"I'm not intimidated by you," I yelled. "This is not the first time you opened the backdoor to let others bump me off my rightfully earned place. Why? Why??"

"Dangerous thought problems, bad attitude!" the Dean said, repeating himself.

I ran out of his office, in tears.

"Hey, Li Jing!" A chemistry major student, named *Chang Jing Ping*, was passing by in the hallway. She'd heard everything through the open door. "What's the matter with you? Now it's time to bribe them with all you've got – money, gifts, at least begging them, but not fighting them! Not too smart of you. Fighting is not going to get you what you want, not even for the best student like you. They just don't care." Like a big caring sister, Chang's sympathy and kindness brought out more of my grieving tears – tears that I'd long suppressed after being wronged over and over again.

I dropped myself onto the front steps of the building, sobbing.

Then I heard giggling and laughter. A couple of girls were riding a bike and coming toward me, one pedaling while the other rode on the back rack. No wonder they were so happy. One of them had stolen my spot. She was all set to teach at No. 5, the best high school, where I was supposed to teach, but now I was to teach at No. 10, the second best. Still, my heart felt hopeful. Innocently, I thought: Maybe she didn't really care to teach at No. 5 since her family lives in north district, the opposite section of the city. Maybe her heart can be touched if I plead with her?

"*Jin*, would you trade school with me, please?" I asked.

"Hee, hee, hee . . ." The privileged thief giggled, glancing smugly over my way while her feet kept pedaling. "Nope! Sorry, can't do. Ha, ha, ha . . ." she laughed, riding away.

Humiliated, I collapsed back down onto the steps. I'd not only lost my position, but now my dignity, too.

I'd never had the habit of talking to my father about any of my problems. But desperate that day, I went home and cried to him about my misfortune. He listened but didn't say anything.

Well, I didn't think I could count on him anyway.

It was time for me to surrender to my fate.

June 29, 1979. My English class at Taiyuan Teachers' College, Class 29, with professors and the Party leaders. I'm the first one on the left in the next-to-the-last row. I'm ducking down so I could be the same height as the other girls.

Chapter 49

English Teacher at Elite No. 5 Secondary School

太原五中英語老師

1979. A MIRACLE HAPPENED on my last day at Taiyuan Teachers' College.

I was shocked beyond joy and relief when the final teaching assignment was announced: Li Jing, to teach at No. 5 Secondary School. I couldn't believe it. My heart burst in joy. I'd gotten the job, although my second choice. What happened? Who helped me?

"Of course, I did. Who else?" said my father. "After you told me about your unfair treatment, I went to the college president, my former high-school teacher, to seek justice for you. He promised to right the wrong. He's the number-one boss, everyone has to listen to him. It was the personnel people who played backdoor favors behind his back."

"Oh, it was me," the director of the personnel office at No. 5 Secondary School said. "When I went to Teachers' College to recruit teachers, I insisted on getting the top best. Our No. 5 is number one, best, elite school in northern China region. So, I discovered you."

At age twenty-three, I officially started teaching English at No. 5 Secondary School.

"Welcome, our common denominators!" Mrs. Zhou MeiYu, an English teacher in her 30's, smiled and cheered smugly at my two classmates and me, the three new English teachers. She explained why we were their lucky stars: Teachers at No. 5 were getting a pay raise for the first time after a dozen years of earning the same monthly salary of fifty-six *yuan* ($10 USD). But only thirty percent of the teachers could get a raise.

And all teachers were getting free gifts. The first time ever.

"*Ayo*," an older woman teacher exclaimed when she passed by me on campus. "You young teachers are too lucky. We old-timers never got any free stuff all these years. But as soon as you walked in, there are free goodies to be had." She sighed, shaking her head.

The elite No. 5 Secondary School in the capital city of Taiyuan was famous and in high demand. Taking advantage of its celebrity status, the school sought "sponsors," who donated precious food and other necessities in exchange for some of their academically less-qualified children being enrolled without having to participate in the tough competitions.

Thanks to these sponsors, all No. 5 staff members, new or old, were getting a small fluorescent table lamp, two yards of cloth for making clothing, and three *jin* (3.3 lb.) of beef. These three things were worth a fortune.

We lined up one evening waiting to get our beef. Everyone was so happy it was like the New Year's Eve. But my frozen block of beef thawed into a pile of fat, with only tiny bits and pieces of red meat. Better than nothing. I sizzled the fat into grease to supplement my rationed cooking oil.

Just three weeks into my teaching, fate smiled at me again.

The Dean ran into me in the schoolyard. "Teacher Li," he said. "Mr. *Wu Yi Qing* would like to see you. Remember, the Dean of the Teachers' College? He lives on the third floor inside the teachers' apartment building here, the third door on the left by the stairs. Did you know that he used to be the principal of our No. 5?"

Oh, no. Not Mr. Wu again, that corrupt college dean! What could he possibly want from me now? Why won't he leave me alone? But my curiosity got the better of me. I decided to pay him a visit, partly because he'd just earned my respect for being No. 5's former principal.

"Hello, Li Jing. Come on in." Mr. Wu surprised me with his pleasant greeting, as if I were his old friend. His one-room apartment was crowded and dimly lit. His large, heavy body was lodged in a bamboo-woven armchair. He motioned me to sit on his family bed, the only available seating.

Mr. Wu then started his friendly chat. "I said to your principal, Mr. *Gao Zhong Yuan*: 'How could you let my best student, and talented college instructor Li Jing teach your regular high school class? Even her much older college students respected and praised her. Move her up! I told him. Let her teach your best senior AP English classes."

I was shocked speechless – but also happy – to hear Mr. Wu express his 180-degree attitude change. So, he'd been, indeed, playing dirty political games when he'd put on a straight face and accused me of having a bad attitude and committing thought problems after I called him out on his backdoor corruption? So, he did know about my outstanding teaching?

I floated out of Mr. Wu's apartment in high spirits. The cool evening air felt more refreshing, the blinking stars winked at me, congratulating me on my vindication.

Mr. Gao, the principal, promptly arranged for me to swap classes with Mr. Tang, a sixty-year-old veteran English teacher, who had the highest seniority. I was to take over his AP (Advanced Placement) twelfth grade English classes, and he, my regular-level freshman students. It was an unprecedented change, especially in the middle of the semester.

The Chinese words for "teacher" are composed of two characters: 老師 *lao-shi*, "the old master." The older, the better – that's what the ancient Chinese culture believed in terms of enlightening the young mind with time-proved wisdom. At the mere age of twenty-three, I was neither old nor a man.

I'd been put on a rare pedestal with the highest honor.

I was nervous that Mr. Tang would give me a hard time for challenging his authority and became very grateful when he didn't. But his faithful students fiercely resisted me. These AP students were teenage prodigies – the best and most talented of all the high-school seniors in the entire city of Taiyuan with two million dwellers. The cream of the crop. They were self-disciplined and highly motivated, aiming to get into China's best colleges and universities. And they were counting on their seasoned teachers – in all subject areas – to help them achieve their dreams and goals. Naturally, they were unhappy to see a baby-faced new teacher like me replacing their beloved, seasoned teacher, who, they felt, had valuable wisdom that came with age.

I felt like an unwelcome, wicked stepmother in the fairy tale.

On the first day of class, my "step-students" burst out laughing at me during roll call. I didn't realize that one girl's name pronounced in an unconventional way, as *Pei* 蓓 instead of the regular pronunciation of *Bei* 蓓. A teacher was supposed to be perfect and know everything.

My face burning in embarrassment, I felt like a fraud standing at the podium.

I vowed to strive for perfection.

In Chinese, the word "teaching" has two characters: *jiao-xue* 教學: teaching + learning. It's a reciprocal process. A good teacher has the unique, perceptive ability to envision, enlighten, and deliver the well-planned lessons with clear and logical explanations using comparisons and examples. A good teacher should also be a keen observer, know how to relate to students, give them timely feedback so they may learn from their mistakes and improve their performance.

And all good teaching requires consistent hard work, as the two ancient Chinese proverbs tell us: 台上一分鐘，台下十年功: *one minute of an outstanding performance on stage came from ten years of practice behind the stage*; And, 教人一碗水，老師自己要有十桶水: *A good teacher is always prepared with ten buckets of water when only one bowl is needed.*

To prepare my students for their national college entrance examination, 高考 *gao-kao*, all written tests on reading comprehension and grammatical rules, I combed through the entire high-school English textbook, dissecting every sentence, highlighting the contrasts in comparisons to Chinese, and focusing on possible testing points: sentence structures, the sixteen English verb tenses, irregular verb forms in past tenses and past participles, tricky combinations of prepositional phrases, idioms, and irregular plural forms of nouns, etc.

Every day I spent all my waking nonteaching hours preparing my daily lessons and grading my students' papers, sitting on the edge of my bunk bed in my dorm room at a small desk for many hours at a time. My chest and ribs began hurting when I breathed. But I had an urgent goal to achieve. No time to waste. Failure was not an option. I needed to succeed. I needed to live up to the special honor of being entrusted with teaching the best and brightest students at the best high school in the capital city of Taiyuan.

In the meantime, Vic was pressuring me to get married. It annoyed me.

He was twenty-nine, getting too old, he said. I begged off for one more year. I needed at least my first teaching year uninterrupted and concentrated on my career. I wanted to lay a good foundation for my work and create a good reputation for myself. I didn't want to be ungrateful, irresponsible, and selfish by getting married and taking on the family responsibilities right after I'd received the honor of teaching at the city's elite No. 5.

And deep inside, I sometimes even wished for the impossible: that my father would step in and force me out of the relationship with Vic. I felt no excitement, no happiness, no joy in it. Nothing but all a sense of duty and obligation. I was irritated by Vic's insensitive pressure to interfere with my career.

I loved my special status of being a pedestaled lone star at the famous No. 5 School. I had total freedom to design my lesson plans without having to ask for anyone's approval or having to sit in a circle wasting my time in group collaborations. I knew exactly what to teach and how to teach it.

I made sure that my students pronounced all vocabulary words correctly. I won them over in no time with my accurate English pronunciations – my ability to imitate the sounds of a language, like a parrot, always came in handy. It had been my great and smooth journey of triumph ever since I was eight years old. Without difficulty, I switched from my "backward" mountain village dialect to Taiyuan city dialect, to national standard Chinese, and to English.

My students loved the way I explained and compared English to Chinese: The Chinese language doesn't have verb tenses, or plural forms for nouns, or the modifier clauses led by "when," "which," "that," "who," "whom," and especially "what." Nor does the Chinese language have articles of "a," "an" and "the." I also compare within English: for example, the different functions for the little word "to" as an infinitive, which is followed by a verb, and a preposition "to," which is followed by a noun or a gerund (V-ing) as in: "to watch" vs. "looking forward to watching", etc.

I kept my finger closely on the pulse of my students' daily learning progress. I thrived in the nothing-but-the-academic-excellence school atmosphere.

To help me concentrate on my teaching, the principal even excused me from attending the mandatory ideology-based political studies, basically listening to the Party secretary reading from the People's Daily newspaper, on Tuesday and Friday afternoons.

I lived up to and beyond all expectations. In no time, I'd won over my skeptical "step-students," they loved my teaching style. My classroom was so quiet you could hear a pin drop as my students totally absorbed themselves in listening, taking notes, and reading.

By the end of the school year in 1980, all of my students had scored well above the 90th percentile in their *gao-kao*, the grueling three-day, nationwide college entrance examinations. I'd won one hundred percent of my students' respect. Their parents hailed me. My principal praised me. My colleagues looked up to me. I was treated with highest honor and respect. I became a legend in Taiyuan City.

"If you didn't become famous," my father one day said to me. "Your brother Cricket would still be looking down on you." I didn't know how to respond to my father's out-of-the-blue comments. *Why did he say that? But Cricket was his all-time favorite child!* He was now a high school student at the No. 5 Secondary School, where I was teaching but hardly saw him.

"Oh, I thought Teacher Li was an old woman!" people exclaimed when they saw my photo with my graduating students. "But she's so young!"

For the next ten years until 1989, I continued teaching AP English to the best and brightest twelfth-graders at No. 5 school, except the 1986-87 school year, when I achieved the monumental success, literally competed my way out of the world of China.

In March and April of 1989, I published two articles on learning English in a nationally circulated magazine, 山西青年 *Shanxi Youth*. And I received hundreds of spirit-lifting, heartwarming letters, mainly from the high-school students who'd become my fans.

One day in the school office, in front of all the English teachers, Mrs. Zhou Mei Yu repeated what her husband, a government official, had said about me: "Just by her looks alone, you can just tell that Li Jing is not ordinary."

Winter 1979. Me. Aged twenty-three. New star teacher at No. 5 Secondary School.

Full of hope and self-confidence. On my lunch break at *Ying Ze* Park 迎澤公園.

This was the same park where my father tried to end his life as a miserable failure seventeen years earlier in 1962.

Chapter 50

Crossing the Forbidden Creek

悼念爷爷

AUTUMN 1980. At the high point of my teaching career came the devastating news: My beloved grandfather had passed away. The principal and Dean at No. 5 granted me special permission for a two-week absence to attend my grandfather's funeral at Red Stone Bridge.

In my white mourning gown, I followed the funeral procession toward the west entrance of Red Stone Bridge. It was the longest such procession in Red Stone Bridge's history, the villagers said. Hundreds of people came out to watch. Crowds of people gathered in front of my grandparents' house.

Suddenly, so many hands grabbed hold of me and pushed me down on my knees. I was shocked to see that it was a group of Li family women – my own clan – who'd restrained me.

"Why the hell are you holding me down?" I yelled at the top of my lungs.

Through my teary eyes, I saw myself kneeling in front of the small creek by the arched red stone bridge that had given my birth village its name. I knew every chiseled rock on the beautiful bridge. I'd played here every day as a small child, picking wild berries and tiny purple flowers that covered both ends of its span. The majestic pine-forest mountains nearby were always quiet and peaceful, and somewhere in those mountains was always Grandpa toiling in the commune's cornfields.

"Let go of me!" I struggled, watching helplessly as Grandpa's funeral procession slowly moved along crossing the creek without me.

"No, Cai Mei, you can't cross the creek," the women's voices chirped into my ears all at once, like a bunch of wild birds. These well-intentioned elders were trying to tell me something that made no sense. "Because you are a girl."

"Let me go!"

"No, you have to listen. It's a bad luck if a female crossed this creek with the funeral. Look for yourself. They are all men. No female allowed."

"Damn your nonsense!" I was enraged, my voice hoarse – sweat, tears, and mucus all over my face. "Grandpa, wait for me! Grandpa, I'm coming with you! . . ."

But Grandpa was carried away quietly inside his plain pinewood coffin. All his life, Grandpa had been painting coffins for other village folks. He painted their coffins with bright red luscious peony flowers and colorful birds – and never charged anyone a penny. Yet, his sudden illness from cancer of the esophagus had left him with no energy to paint his own.

Then I spotted my brother Nimble and my father walking in the midst of the funeral procession as the rightful "honored offspring." They were walking with their five-foot-long, special mourning stick in their hands, wrapped in strips of soft white calligraphy paper.

How unfair! Nimble hardly knew Grandpa. It was I who grew up with Grandpa, came back to Red Stone Bridge every summer to visit him. It was I who loved Grandpa, and he, me. But I was now forbidden to walk with my beloved grandpa for the last time just because I was a girl?

"To hell with you all! That's *my* grandpa. Out of my way!"

"No, please, you can't." The women wouldn't budge.

I hit. I bit. I spat. I head-butted anyone within range. The Li women dodged around my all-out assault, eyeing one another for help.

"Okay, okay, sweetie," said my ever-loving milk mother, gathering me to her bosom. "We'll let you go, but please let me turn your mourning garment inside out. This way, you won't bring bad luck to us all."

"H-u-r-r-y," I stomped my feet while my milk mother scrambled. I shot out like an escaped wild animal breaking free from its trap, splashing my way across the creek, leaving the women dumbfounded, on their knees in their mourning white.

"Grandpa, wait for me . . . I'm coming!" I ran after the men, howling like a grieving wolf.

The men in the procession turned to look over their shoulders. Their faces said they were shocked and bewildered. A *female* was coming along? But to my relief, the men looked away, one by one. And they remained silent. No one said a word to turn me away, leaving me grateful and relieved. I'd for sure lose my battle and wouldn't have known what to do if they, too, had decided to tackle me to the ground.

I followed my beloved grandfather's procession, climbing the steep hills of crumbling earth and rolling stones into the pine-tree forested mountains. On top of the majestic mountain peak sat my Li ancestors' vast burial site, the most prominent within hundreds of miles in the *Qin*-valley region. According to the family legend, fourteen generations before, my ancestors were originally Ming dynasty high court officials who'd escaped into these remote deep-mountains when fleeing from the Manchu invaders.

Grandpa was put into the yellow earth to rest.

"No, you can't cry anymore," the head of the Li family clan firmly told me, as I dropped on my knees at Grandpa's now-sealed dome tomb.

I became the talk of Red Stone Bridge after that. But the talk was not about my rising from a born-unwanted peasant girl to becoming a famed high school English teacher at the capital city of Taiyuan's best elite secondary school. This time, the talk was about how I became an unprecedented heroine by breaking the ancient village's rule of no female being allowed to cross the forbidden creek in a mourning gown.

"Amazing. How did Bright Light and Magnolia ever produce an incredible daughter like this?" the village women said, looking at me in awe. And the village men paused to examine me thoughtfully, shaking their heads in amazement.

Fast forward fifteen years. 1995.

I went back to visit my grandmother in Red Stone Bridge from my beloved new home country, wonderful and beautiful America, and stopped on the way to visit my cousin Wu Qin. "Did you visit Grandpa's tomb again?" Wu Qing asked me, bright-eyed in disbelief. "That's why you get to go to America — you've got all the good luck from visiting our grandfather every time. I'm going to do it myself, too."

How ironic that my cousin wanted my luck. If it weren't for him, I wouldn't have suffered through my darkest age in the city as a lonely and abused child away from my beloved Grandpa. To save food, our grandmother chose him over me. My twisted fate, however, became my blessing in disguise. It thrust me into the city's realm, where China's rare opportunities existed. Thanks to our Grandmother's favoring her male grandchild and forcing me out of Red Stone Bridge, I didn't become one of China's masses of peasants like all of my childhood friends.

Six years after I crossed the forbidden creek at my birth village of Red Stone Bridge, I was to cross the grand Pacific Ocean to America, the tip-top best land on earth.

Chapter 51

Married to Vic – and His Family

婚嫁

"WHAT, YOU'RE GETTING MARRIED?" Wang Jin, my colleague and Teachers's college classmate, laughed as if she'd heard a ridiculously funny joke. "I didn't even know you had a boyfriend! Who gets married at twenty-four? The government said we shouldn't get married before age thirty."

I felt uneasy and embarrassed in front of peer pressure.

"I can just imagine how much your fiancé loves you," a new teacher said to me with a dreamy smile.

"Yours must love *you* very much, too." I jokingly parroted her but immediately regretted it. I sounded like a jerk. But what *does* it feel like to be loved? My heart couldn't feel it.

It took me days to get up the courage to ask the No. 5 Secondary School office for the referral I needed to get married. I was more embarrassed than worried. A marriage license had to be issued by the government. Convicted anti-Communist "thought criminals" would be denied.

My dorm room was across the hall from Mrs. Hou, the office secretary. I tried three times that morning to approach her as she was standing cooking at her stove in the hallway at her family's apartment door. But I lost my nerve each time and scampered back into my room.

"Teacher Li, you want to talk to me?" Mrs. Hou's smile was disarming.

"Well, I, . . ." How did she know that? "I . . . I . . . I need to get married."

"Oh, really? Congratulations. Who's the lucky young man? Of course. Let's go to my office and get your paperwork done. Please also check with the school nurse. You'll need her permission to give birth. The government is getting serious about the one-child-per-family law. Make sure there was a ration number available for this year's birth plan."

Vic was ecstatic when I showed him my referral. We rode our bike to the photographer's studio for a photo together and then to the city government office to apply for our marriage license.

"Oh, you're only twenty-four, still underage," the man sitting behind the desk said as he examined my paper. "You need to be twenty-five to get married. Well, since he is thirty . . ." He handed over our certificate printed with Mao's words: "Young people are our nation's future, like the bright morning sun at 8 or 9 o'clock."

"Dad," I felt awkward asking my father for favors. "Can I have a few pieces of my grandparents' elm-tree boards to have a chest made as my dowry?" I was worried that my in-laws would look down on me for failing to bring material things to the marriage. I was also afraid that if I didn't have a dowry, they'd question my family life.

"You've got the nerve to ask?" my father said, glaring up at me from sitting on the floor stool, scrubbing his feet in the washbasin. "You know your grandparents have been saving those elm trees for your brothers. The boys will carry on the Li family name. What can you do, a girl to be married away into somebody else's family? Not my responsibility."

Red-faced, I felt ashamed, humiliated, lost for words.

The Chinese language has two sets of words for "marry:" *qu* 娶 is for the groom, meaning "to fetch a female;" and *jia* 嫁 is for the bride, meaning "to find the female a home." The ancient culture also has a saying: 嫁出去的閨女，潑出去的水 jia-chu-qu-de-gui-nu, poo-chu-qu-de-shui: *A married-away daughter is like a bowl of water poured onto the dirt ground. She's a goner.*

Shanxi province was especially infamous for its long-standing custom that a groom's parents must pay a large sum of money to the bride's parents as part of the marriage agreement. It was a once-in-a-lifetime chance for a poor peasant family to get back their financial investment from years of feeding and clothing their daughter. And a bride's family in the city expected to get even more money than the country families, thousands of *yuan* more.

It never occurred to me how disappointed my father must've felt that he couldn't profit a penny from his daughter's marriage. I kept him out of my business.

Vic's mother had recently passed away from breast cancer at age fifty-five. His father didn't care enough to spend money on his son's marriage. Opposite to my family, the domineering father had been physically violent to his only son but favored his two daughters. As our wedding gift, he re-gifted his two voucher train tickets to tour China's famous mountain *Tai-Shan* in the neighboring province of *Shan Dong*. No wedding ceremony. Not even a family get-together dinner. Vic's family didn't have to spend an extra penny. I'd already sold myself short by getting into a relationship before marriage.

And now that we were married, we had to decide where to live.

Under the Chinese socialism, a rental market didn't exist in the 80's. Married sons and daughters depended on their parents for housing; the parents, in turn, relied on their work units. Vic's father's work unit, the medical college, agreed to let us borrow a room.

"We should take up the small room the college offered us," Vic said to me. "We should live by ourselves, just you and me, away from my family."

"But why?" I was baffled.

Ever since I'd met Vic's parents, I'd felt adored by them. They'd praised me for my brains, my looks, and my fame. His father even scolded Vic's youngest sister in front of me. "Look how bright Li Jing is! Why can't you be like her?" Drunken with an inflated ego, I failed to see the seeds of jealousy being planted and soon to germinate. When Vic's sister later started disrespecting me and I complained to him, Vic said that it was all my fault for having a difficult personality, and that his little sister couldn't be any sweeter or more good-natured.

I'd longed for a peaceful and harmonious family life. And I still believed Vic's fib that his family was a harmonious one. I craved to love and be loved. And I really felt sorry for Vic's newly widowed father. I wanted to be a model daughter-in-law like the praised one in ancient Chinese fairy tales, fulfilling her filial duty and honor by waiting hand and foot on her in-laws. I was sure I could win more of my in-law's love with my good housekeeping skills: my cooking, cleaning, knitting, mending, and stitching, as well as my ability to save money by wisely pinching pennies.

"No, we need to live on our own, away from my father and sisters," Vic insisted.

"But why? Please, just tell me why." I was frustrated that he wouldn't explain himself.

I wanted to show the world that my married life was a loving and harmonious one – and I was sure it *would* be one – that I didn't have a cold heart like a wolf, as my mother had told me. I wanted to prove my mother wrong.

"If you don't listen to me, you're going to regret it," Vic simply said, looking grim.

"Well, if you don't tell me why, we're moving in with your family."

I wished that Vic had told me the truth.

At age thirty, Vic had never grown out of his childhood fear of his father. From birth to age two, he grew up in his maternal uncle's family after the government sent his parents, new college graduates, thousands of miles away from Sichuan province to Shanxi. When Vic was two years old, his uncle put him on a train to his parents, who promptly sent him to live in the prestigious, government children's home for two more years until he was four.

I once told Vic how I envied his elevated social status, which allowed him to live in the privileged children's home. To my surprise, Vic became irritated. "Nobody knew how I felt when I sat constipated on the spittoon crying," he said. "No nurse or teacher ever asked me what was hurting me." At age four, he was finally brought home to live with his family after his sister was born. While his quiet, petite, and good-natured mother loved him, Vic's six-foot-tall, violent-tempered father favored his baby sister and was rough on his son.

In my eagerness to prove my self-worth to the world by having a happy marriage, I forgot that there was a dark side to many ancient Chinese fairy tales, such as the famous *Peacock Flew Away to Southeast* 孔雀東南飛. It told of a beautiful young bride who'd tried hard but couldn't please her jealous mother-in-law living under the same roof. Her husband was too filial duty-bound to stand up to his mother to protect his wife. The abusive mother-in-law made her son divorce his beloved wife. Soon after they parted, the young couple died of broken heart. And promptly, two peacocks were seen flying across the sky southeast side by side.

Never in my worst nightmare I was to repeat the tragic fate of the fairy-tale daughter-in-law.

As soon as we moved in with his family, Vic started quietly changing. Gone was his easy-going, patient, and forgiving spirit that had once calmed, comforted and first attracted me. He became frustrated, irritated, cynical, even ridiculing.

"Stop talking like a baby!" Vic brushed me off one day when I felt like being playful with him. We were in our own room behind the closed door. He'd also become more eager to belittle and scold me whenever we were with his father and sisters.

One morning, I was humming a love song by the beautiful singer, Teresa Teng, who was famous in Taiwan for her soft, sweet voice singing traditional Chinese love songs. Massive numbers of her recorded music in cassette tapes had been smuggled into Mainland China and spread like a prairie fire into every household. I found her romantic music nourishing to my heart after decades of forced listening to Mao's violent, shouted-out "class struggle" songs.

"Hey, shut up!" Vic burst out yelling at me, his voice disgusted. "How can you sing such a slutty tune? My father can hear you." I was shocked and hurt. At that moment, Vic made me realize that I was unrefined and out of place, offspring to China's massive, uneducated, peasants and blue-collar dirt yard dwellers. The standard Chinese manners for a properly female was to: 笑不露齒，行不露足: *Covering her mouth when smiling and keeping her feet hidden under her long garment with floating, tiny steps.*

Never again, for the rest of our twenty-year marriage, did I ever feel like humming a song in front of my husband. Another layer of resentment was added to my heart.

"Be quiet already!" Vic snapped at me one evening as we were watching a historical film on the 13" black and white television in his father's room. We couldn't afford our own TV. The film was about China's Dowager Empress Ci Xi in the last Qing dynasty. I'd just voiced my opinion on the long-dead Empress: "She must've been a very capable woman rising from the lowest concubine status."

"How can you defend an evil woman like that?" Vic scolded me indignantly, glancing over at his father pleasingly.

I was disgusted and outraged when I gradually discovered that Vic's father treated his only son no better than a servant. "Go get me a pack of cigarettes!" His father would yell out from his room, as if his grown son were his errand boy. He could've gotten the cigarettes himself, the store was only a two-minute walk around the corner. But as his father's barking order, Vic would jump up and shoot out our room as if there was a fire to put out, tossing down whatever was in his hands – his meal bowl and, later, our infant baby, like a sack of flour. And all those evenings – as Vic was running errands or doing chores for his father while his father and sisters dined – I was alone in our room, holding my baby in one arm and trying to kindle the dead-cold coal-burning stove with the other after a long day working.

Little by little, I became an emotional mess, feeling hurt, rejected, and angry, bitching and complaining all the time. Vic simply clammed up and shut down.

"I'm exhausted from working all day," I told Vic as I pushed him away one night, not long after we were married. "I can't even get an uninterrupted night of sleep. Look how out-of-shape and skinny I've become."

I was surprised to see hurt in Vic's eyes, as he abruptly turned his back to me.

I began wearing long, tight undergarments to bed. "I hate this," Vic would say.

"Good. Because all you need is a female body below the waist and above the thigh," I lashed out, feeling vindictive but secure in my polyester body armor.

Chapter 52

What If It's a Girl?

要是女孩兒呢？

"ARE YOU PREGNANT?" the school nurse asked me from sitting behind her desk, smiling knowingly.

"Oh, no way. I'm not." I sat down on the tall, round-topped wooden stool across from her. "I'm having my usual problem of constipation, and strangely a little heartburn, too. I took some herbal medicine, but it hasn't worked. It's a pity that I didn't even have the appetite for the rare treat of roasted peanuts-in-shells at the New Year's party!"

"Sure you're not pregnant?"

"Yes, one hundred percent. Not ready to have a baby yet. My husband and I decided we aren't ready financially. You'll be the first one to know if I were — have to apply through you for the government permission to give birth, right?"

But despite my denials, she sent me to the People's Hospital across the street to have a urine test.

The government had been tightening the noose, punishing women for having more than one child. In the countryside, truckloads of pregnant village women were rounded up every day and dragged to hospitals for forced abortions and sterilization. In cities, there were no stories or rumors of any woman being pregnant for the second time. Since all employment was state-owned, no one could afford to be fired for breaking the one-child rule.

Vic whispered to me what had happened to his best friend Li Yan.

For months, Vic couldn't find Li Yan, who lived in his parents' home with his wife and their toddler daughter. Every time Vic went to the parents' home to look for his friend, his parents, looking grim-faced, would give Vic some vague excuses as to why their son wasn't home, while Li Yan's mother stood holding their toddler granddaughter.

Vic thought something strange was going on. So, he went to look for Li Yan at No. 3 Middle School, where Li Yan was teaching math. He was shocked to see Li Yan looking exhausted and out of shape, his clothes wrinkled, his hair disheveled. Li Yan whispered to Vic that he and his wife had gone into hiding. It turned out that Li Yan's parents, desperately wanting a male grandchild, had pressured him and his wife into making a daring gamble: having a second child and hoping it would be a boy. They had a second child. But, alas, another female baby.

Afraid their neighbors might find out and report them to the authorities for punishment, Li Yan and his wife took off with their newborn baby girl, leaving their firstborn daughter behind with his parents. They secretly rented a small room in a nearby village. Even though their second daughter was now safe, she would have to grow up as a "black person" 黑人黑戶 hei-ren-hei-hu, a nonexistent human being. She would never have a city registration card, "*hu-kou*" for rationed food, or a chance to go to school.

Li Yan invited Vic to his family hideaway, a small, dark, sod-walled room. Above their *kang* was the only window, which was covered with layers of newspaper. No furnishing but an iron coal-burning stove stood in the middle of the room for heating and cooking.

Li Yan put on a forced smile and tried to sound light-hearted, proudly showing Vic his invention: a cotton-padded bag to carry his baby daughter around during the freezing cold winter. "We will survive. Our baby daughter will live," Li Yan said, forcing a desperate, helpless smile.

(Twenty-five years later in 2015, China finally relaxed its one-child law due to the severe shortage of females and a surplus of over 30 million men, who will never have a wife. The government began allowing two children per family. Then millions of people – an underground population about the age of Li Yan's second daughter – suddenly surfaced into the light.)

"Teacher Li," the school nurse said. "You're not having a heart burn or constipation. You're pregnant."

I was shocked at the unexpected news, feeling more embarrassed than angry in front of the nurse. Hidden inside was my feeling of being betrayed. I was disgusted by Vic's dishonesty. Again.

"Make sure you wipe it clean. I don't want to get pregnant," I'd said to Vic one night after he had "house business" with me. As we'd agreed, he'd been practicing a pull-out-early method to prevent pregnancy, then wiping the inside of me dry with a rag.

"Don't you worry," he assured me. "I got it."

"But it didn't feel like you reached in deep and far enough, like you normally do."

"Promise I did."

I should have known better. He lied to me again.

No wonder his father was giving me hard time a few days before.

"Why aren't you pregnant yet?" The old man said as he came into our room. I was alone. Vic was again conveniently out of sight every time his father needed to deliver a message.

"Well, we talked about it and decided to wait a couple of years. I'm making the minimum salary of ¥37 ($5 USD) as a new teacher, and Vic still has two more years of college." I explained, blushing with embarrassment, feeling uncomfortable talking to my father-in-law about such an intimate issue.

I resented my father-in-law's nosiness, naively underestimating his power as the family patriarch adhering to the ancient tradition, since the beginning of time. A son and his wife were part of the family business, not an independent family unit. The main purpose of a Chinese marriage was not about personal happiness, but to continue the husband's family tree by giving birth to male babies. A barren wife was grounds to be disowned by divorce.

Now tricked into pregnancy, there was nothing I could do. My maternal instincts took over right away. I became fascinated with the new life actually growing inside me, too naive to realize that my in-law's family wasn't done with me, yet.

"We need to make sure you're carrying a boy," my father-in-law said.

"But how?"

"Easy," the retired medical professor assured me. "I'll ask one of my doctor friends to help out. Very simple procedure. A foot-long needle into your stomach to draw out some *yang-shui*, fluid, for testing."

"That sounds painful. What if it's a girl?"

"Get rid of it," the old man said, crossing his index fingers over his neck from ear to ear.

Frozen into silence, I was distressed, shaking inside.

It was the vicious cycle all over again: a treasured boy vs. unwanted girl. My father-in-law, a college medical professor valued the same things as my illiterate peasant grandmother with a pair of three-inch-bound feet.

Divine Intervention. An unexpected guest came to visit and spared me the ordeal.

It was Vic's eighty-five-year-old paternal grandfather, who'd just been released from his decade-and-a-half of hard labor Cultural Revolution had sentenced him to for the crime of being a famous doctor with a rich landlord family background. Now penniless, he'd come to seek help from his son, Vic's 60-year-old father.

Newly widowed himself, Vic's father wasn't willing to take his elderly father into his one-room apartment and or able to physically take care of him. Washing his father's soiled pants alone was more than the elderly son could take. Washing machines didn't yet exist in China during the 1980's. All our clothes and bedsheets had to be hand-scrubbed in the washbasin.

The grandfather's visit lasted but one month.

Before his departure, this famous doctor of traditional Chinese medicine did something special for me, with a monumental effect. He diagnosed the gender of my unborn baby by feeling my pulse: first my left wrist, then my right – his eyes closed, his mind in quiet concentration. In his lifetime of doctoring, he was famous for diagnosing the gender of the unborn. And his accuracy rate was said to have reached more than ninety percent.

"It's a boy!" the grandfather opened his eyes and announced the good news. My pulse was very strong, he said. The sign of *yang* 陽, "male," was stronger than the sign of *yin* 陰, "female."

"Yes, a boy!" my father-in-law cheered, giving a loud clap of his hands, looking ecstatic.

"Order a half *jin (eight ounces)* of milk a day," both the elderly doctor father and his medical-professor son advised me, based on their nutritional expertise. "The fetus in the womb needs nutrients to grow healthy." But neither man offered to help pay for it. Milk was a luxury. Eight ounce of fresh milk a day would cost me ¥15 yuan ($2.00 USD) a month, almost half of my monthly salary of ¥37 yuan.

On the morning he left, Vic's grandfather looked frail. His walking cane in hand, a small cloth bag slung over his shoulder, he slowly walked to the bus stop. He was to take the train to Beijing and try his luck there with his widowed daughter-in-law, wife of his only other son, an engineer who'd recently died in a dynamite explosion at work.

I'll always remember Vic's doctor-grandfather's kindness, wisdom for my parting gift. During his short stay, he'd complimented me, telling me that he was pleased that I was actually much taller than he'd thought when he first saw the photo of me with Vic. He'd enlightened me with his lifelong wisdom: An unborn baby depended on its mother's peaceful, calm womb for healthy growth. He advised me to listen to soothing and calming music. And once he even gave me a generous gift of ¥20 *yuan* for his unborn great grandchild. He said he wished he had money to buy a cassette tape so he could record his lifelong experiences of healthy living to help people.

I still wonder if the famous doctor-grandfather had purposely misdiagnosed the gender of my unborn child.

"His name will be *Tian Hua* 天華, Heavenly Talent," my father in-law said to me, deciding the name of my unborn baby. "But if it is a girl, may she wither, like measles."

Chapter 53

I'm Sorry, It's Not a Boy

不是男孩

A LATE NIGHT at Taiyuan People's Hospital.

The vast maternity ward was dimly lit and packed with dozens of beds from wall to wall, with only a couple of feet in between each one. The rhythm of women's lulling snoring, whispering, and quiet moaning from their pain punctuated the silence.

When I'd checked in around noon that day, the ward had been a bustling scene. All the young women waiting-to-give-birth were in their twenties, like me. And the air was filled with our high expectations: we all hoped to give birth to a boy.

"What do you think you're expecting, a boy or a girl?" The question passed from woman to woman, all around the room.

"I know for sure I'm pregnant with a boy," I announced proudly for all to hear. "My husband's grandfather made the diagnosis. He is a famous traditional Chinese herbal and acupuncture doctor and former clinical director at Beijing 王府井 *Wang Fu Jing*."

In the afternoon, I went to take a stroll in the hallway to ease my increased pain.

A crowd was standing around a sturdy young man. He was pacing, back and forth, beads of sweat rolling off his forehead and face. Word had just come from the delivering room asking him to make a life-or-death decision. His wife still couldn't push out her baby. Could they have his permission to do a C-section? If not, the baby would have to be pulled out with steel clamps.

Having a C-section would ruin his wife's chances to have more babies in the future, the murmuring crowd suggested. Others said that the steel clamps could damage the baby's brain.

"My wife has to try for a boy if this one is a girl. So, no C-section," the husband said, looking at the waiting nurse. "But what if this one is a boy? Then my son would be brain-damaged and handicapped for life." He wiped sweat off his eyebrows.

In the land of a billion people, with scarce opportunities and no help from the government, only exceptionally bright and talented children grew up to excel, not the masses of ordinary children, let alone those who were handicapped in any way.

"Okay, . . . okay . . ." The husband was talking to himself, as he paced back and forth. "No, no C-section," he finally decided, looking at the nurse. "Go ahead clamp-pull it out. I'm betting it is not a boy."

He was wrong. It was a boy. By the time the baby was pulled out, he was silent and blue, his head deformed and swollen like a big green winter melon. The man let out a long howl of agony, cursing his wife for bringing him bad luck.

"We are lucky to be placed in this hospital," my bed-neighbor said to me. "Other hospitals have two women sharing the same single bed, each head at an opposite end."

There was no privacy in the crowded maternity ward. Every inch of space was occupied.

The excruciating pain made me feel the constant urges to urinate or have a bowel movement. When each wave hit – I have to go! – I couldn't wait long enough to walk to the squat toilets at the end of the long hallway. I'd sit up and roll off to the floor, snatching the night chamber pot from under the bed, oblivious to the roomful of strangers, men and women. Then I'd crash-sit on the pot as if I were alone. But every time I sat down, it was a false alarm. I didn't need to go at all.

I never realized I was embarrassing myself by publicly squatting over the chamber pot until Vic pointed it out to me. "Did you hear how other men were talking about you?" he said to me with a wounded pride in his eyes. "One guy laughed to his moaning wife that her pain must not be nearly as bad because she hadn't forgotten her sense of shame to drop her pants in public." Hearing that, I felt embarrassed, resentful, hurt, annoyed, and humiliated. But I didn't know how to respond to my husband.

Labor pain kept me curling up on my side, like a shrimp. I hadn't been able to lie on my back for the past nine months. It felt like slabs of cement were stacked up on top of my stomach. No one had told me how to deep-breathe to cope with the pain. And my high anxiety only intensified it.

"Could I die from the pain?" I asked the night nurse, in between my gasps, as I entered the examination room.

"Nonsense," the nurse snapped, frowning. "Whoever heard of dying from birth pain? Take off your pants and get onto the examination table." She yawned, tapping her foot.

This was a privileged visit. Elated that I was to give birth to a boy, my medical professor father-in-law had used his connections to arrange some extra care from the medical staff. There were too many women waiting to give birth and moaning in pain, and not enough doctors or nurses to treat them. The female doctor on duty was asked to look after me and was eager to do so since she expected me to return the favor: As a famous elite high school English teacher, I could tutor her school-aged child.

"I had a bad heart disease when I was nine years old," I mentioned it to the nurse. "Dr. Liu said I could die from giving birth." I surprised myself by talking about my heart disease to a stranger. I'd never even told Vic or anyone in his family about it.

"Hold on, then. Let me check with the doctor." The nurse swiftly disappeared behind the white-cloth curtain in the corner of the room, quickly returning with the news: "Doctor said you should be fine." She resumed her examination. "You've only opened two inches, not wide enough to disturb the doctor's sleep for you. Get back for now. It's just normal pain." She took off her gloves and whirled out.

Gasping in pain, I climbed down the wobbly exam table on wheels to walk to the door, holding up my mountain-heavy stomach. "Drop your pants. Ha, ha, ha!" Vic was waiting at the door, teasing me after hearing the nurse's orders.

"Not funny." I elbowed him in disgust.

My mother suddenly walked into my ward, followed by Cricket.

"Everyone is busy celebrating Cricket's admission to famous Nanjing (Nanking) University," my mother said, plopping herself down on the edge of my bed. "You just have to give birth to your child now? I knew it when you almost had him killed by the jeep when he was three. You were born to be his bad omen." She tossed me a scolding frown.

My face burned with embarrassment. It felt like I was nine years old again and being scolded by my mother in this same hospital for crying over a nighttime thunderstorm.

Relieved when my mother and Cricket left shortly, I wished they hadn't wanted to save face with their destructive courtesy visit.

Daybreak came. I was wheeled out of the maternity ward and into the birthing room.

"All night long, and you remained the same opening as yesterday?" the nurse, a woman in her 50s, scolded me loudly, as if I'd done it on purpose. Then she left me alone, rolling and screaming in pain. I was the only one in the big, empty delivery room.

"*Ai-Ya*!" A woman's voice later yelled over me. "This bed wasn't even hooked! It's coming apart. She could've fallen to the floor." In the midst of my thrashing, I hadn't realized I'd kicked the bed apart. My back was now hanging over a foot-wide gap between the two sections of the platform bed on wheels.

Bright morning sun filled the ward through the tall windows. The wall clock said 7:58.

"Stop screaming!" the same nurse yelled over me. "I've never heard anyone screaming so loud. You're not the first woman to give birth."

"Oh, . . . I'm sorry, but it hurts so badly . . ." I gasped, apologizing. It'd been twenty hours of nonstop, crushing pain. The nurse said something about breaking my water. What water? How? I didn't understand what she meant but was in too much pain to care.

Then I felt a gush of warm liquid suddenly pouring out of me. Amazingly, there was no pain, only relief. "All right, one final push . . . There!" At the nurse's command, I pushed one last time with all my might, feeling the mountain of weight sliding out of me. Oh, . . . it felt so good.

The clock on the wall said 9:35. I heard my baby's first cry, full-of-life loud. My heart swelled. My own flesh and blood.

"It's a boy, right?" I tilted my head to ask the nurse, an unnecessary question. Of course, it was a boy. The nurse shot me a strange look but said nothing.

"It's a boy, right?" I knew the nurse was mean, but her response was odd.

"No, it's a g-i-r-l."

"What? You're kidding me, right? It's supposed to be a boy!"

"You don't believe me?" The nurse held up my baby, clamping her hands on the back of my baby's neck and her tiny ankles to hold her above me. "Look for yourself. See? A g-i-r-l. Now don't say I switched your baby." She whirled away, my newborn daughter clamped in between her fingers.

Life drained out of me.

How can this be? I'd just given birth to a girl, instead of the boy everyone had expected. Just like me, my baby started her life as an instant disappointment to her paternal family.

"It's a girl," I said to Vic when I was being rolled out into the crowded hallway.

"We already knew," he said, his face grim, his eyes dull.

Old Heaven God, I'd just ruined everyone's life.

When was I going to die? I remembered what Dr. Liu had told my father about my heart disease at age nine. Dr. Liu's voice to my father started ringing in my ears: "Your daughter won't live past twenty-five years of age, especially if she tries to give birth." Now I was exactly twenty-five. What would be my dying sign? Who should I entrust my baby to before I died? I thought of Serenity Wang, my best friend from high school. She'd be the best person to take care of my baby daughter. But I hadn't seen her for a long time.

The hospital had a mandatory rule that all newborns be kept isolated in the nursery for the first three days, waiting for their mother's milk to flow. As I lay in my hospital bed for three days waiting for the nurse to bring out my baby, I tormented myself with guilt.

At the sight of my baby in the nurse's arms, however, I forgot all my worries and grief.

It was endearing to see the little name tag on my baby's tiny ankle. It was *my* name. A sense of belonging was overwhelmingly comforting to my entire being. *My* baby. She belonged to *me*. She was part of me, made with my own flesh and blood. Happy tears welled in my eyes.

Holding her to my bosom, I examined my baby. Her eyes were bigger than mine. Yes! Just what I'd wished for. Her little face, nose, mouth, and chin looked just like mine. And her elegant long fingers, arms, and legs were like mine, too. What a perfect combination. My baby had all the best features from both of us. Then a sad thought flashed through my mind. My poor baby girl would one day have to endure the same horrible, excruciating pain of giving birth.

I whispered in her cute, tiny ears that I'd never leave her like my own mother did me. But, unforeseeably, I was to break my promise to my baby daughter again and again starting when she turned two.

One month before my due date, my father-in-law had arranged for a special elderly lady to carry my newborn baby – his assumed grandson – home from the hospital. The arrangement was for good luck. This special carrier lady was said to be a rare gem – a woman who was lucky enough to have a completely balanced life: a loving husband, healthy sons and daughters, and grandsons. Such a lucky person was expected to rub off her good luck onto the newborn. And my father-in-law was going to pay her a whopping sixty *yuan* ($10 USD) his entire monthly salary as a college professor.

Now that my baby was born a girl, not a gold valued boy as expected, no special carrier lady had been mentioned. A girl was not worth the bother. No celebration to mark my daughter's birth. All was despair and silence under my in-law's roof.

Chapter 54

My Maiden Homecoming

回娘家

MY DAUGHTER WAS one month old. I was expected to spend the next month visiting my parents. It was an ancient tradition – a maiden-homecoming. I dreaded it. It was meant for a lucky daughter who was loved by her own maiden family.

A daughter-in-law was thought that she would have a difficult time living her married life away from her loving parents and under her in-law's roof. So, after giving birth, she was rewarded with a month-long break. Taking her newborn baby with her, she'd go back to her own parents' home to be pampered, starting the first day of the second month after the baby's birth.

But I wasn't one of the fortunate young mothers from loving families. I had nothing but stress to look forward to in my own maiden home. The cold shoulder treatment I'd received under my in-law's roof was even better than the way I'd been treated by my own parents. I wished I could think of a way to avoid my "homecoming."

I'd never told Vic or anyone else in his family that I avoided my parents like the plague. I was too ashamed to admit that my own parents didn't love me.

"So tomorrow starts your maiden homecoming month," my father-in-law promptly reminded me on the eve of my month-long visit. Damn. I was hoping that an educated professor like him wouldn't care about the folksy custom. Apparently, he couldn't wait to get rid of me, even just one month, for my failure to give birth to a baby boy.

Now I had to pretend that I loved going home.

Nimble promptly came to pick me up in the morning. Amazingly, he wasn't riding a bicycle, but driving a motor vehicle, a tiny, dusty, beat-up three-wheeler. He'd borrowed it from the Heavy Machinery

Factory, where both he and my mother worked. It sure beat sitting on the back rack of a bike, holding my baby in my arms.

"When did you learn how to drive?" I was impressed.

Nimble grumbled. He'd grown to be a man of few words.

As my brother let me out of the vehicle into the blue collar dirt yard, a young woman looked at me wide-eyed and asked: "Mrs. Zhang had another daughter?" I found her question odd. It turned out that my mother had introduced her brother's teenage girl as her own daughter. Since I'd rarely come back during the past seven years, new neighbors didn't know my existence.

My father walked in from work in the evening. He looked taken aback at the sight of me, apparently forgetting it was my month-long maiden homecoming. In two swift steps, he went to sit in one of the two makeshift armchairs by the door-less entrance to the inner-room. The chairs were Nimble's handiwork made from scratch, an imitation of a Western comfort-oriented sofa. The armrests were two bare, wooden boards painted in bright yellow, the Chinese color for royalty and good luck. The springs underneath the thin, dark red cloth seat cover were protruding, wobbly, and bobbing up.

I felt like a stranger sitting across from my father, but this was the same two-room bare-walled apartment where I'd spent the darkest days of my childhood. I knew every inch of it. But now here was my adorable baby daughter sweetly sleeping on the family's wooden bed. Except for the addition of Nimble's handy work of two thin imitation of Western sofa chairs, nothing else had changed. The same dusty cement floors. The same thin wood board beds with one pillow and one worn out thin cotton padded quilt for each. The same brick and mud cooking stove by the door. The same two red wooden chests containing the family's clothes. The same lime powder washed walls with the same grime-smudged small glass window for each room looking out into the dozens of mounds of loose coals in the dirt yard.

The last time my father and I had seen each other was at Grandpa's funeral a year before at Red Stone Bridge. Now he looked anxious, his eyes shifting, telling me that he had something urgent on his mind. He'd even skipped his nightly routine of first washing his sweaty face and feet in the outer room before entering the inner room, now in his dusty shoes, instead of tattered cloth slippers converted from a pair of his old, worn shoes.

"What kind of elder sister are you?" my father finally broke the silence. "Cricket has been accepted into China's famous Nanjing university. You didn't even give him a going-away gift?"

I was taken aback, shocked.

"What kind of father are *you*?" I snapped right back at him. "The first thing you walked in the door was not to come over to look at my newborn baby, your very first grandchild, but accuse me for being inconsiderate to your favorite son!"

I hated this stupid homecoming.

"Well, what's there to look at? Don't all the newborns look the same, red and wrinkled?"

"You! . . ." I was lost for words.

According to the girl-bashing Chinese culture, my daughter was only an "outsider granddaughter" to my parents. And my parents, accordingly, were her "outsider grandparents." The Chinese words for maternal grandparents and maternal grandchildren all begin with the prefix *wai* 外, meaning *the outsider*: *wai-gong* 外公 *outsider grandfather*; *wai po* 外婆 *outsider grandmother*; *wai-sun* 外孫, *maternal grandson*; and *wai-sun-nu* 外孫女, *maternal granddaughter*.

"Oh, stop whining already," my mother shushed me when I tried to complain to her about my father.

As if sensing that she wasn't welcomed by her "outsider" grandparents, my month-old daughter became irritable and restless the moment we arrived. She'd been such a good-natured baby and hardly cried for the first month of her life. Now, suddenly, she stayed wide awake all night, crying until I held her in my arms and played with her.

"Be quiet," Nimble grumbled from the outer room.

"Sit up and hold her in your arms," my mother told me. "Nimble needs to go to work tomorrow. He needs his sleep."

For the next thirty days straight, I sat up in bed all night long, holding, rocking, and whispering to my baby. My back ached terribly. There was nothing for me to lean on, not an extra pillow or a blanket. I couldn't lean against the wall, either; it was washed with lime powder, which would flake off and cover me all over like wheat flour. There was no indoor plumbing or water to wash my clothes at will.

That was how I developed a lifelong back pain. Today I still can't bend my back for more than a few minutes at a time.

"She has to sit up straight and hold her daughter all night long," my mother, her eyes shining in satisfaction, chuckled to her best friend Zhi Xiang, who came to visit.

"Ha, ha!" a burly neighbor man laughed when he came by to visit my mother and saw me. "Your daughter has doubled her body size."

I hadn't realized I'd gained a massive amount of weight.

"Go ahead, love her," one day my mother sneered at me, looking at me sideways over her shoulder while cooking at the stove. I was bouncing my baby on my lap, cooing my made-up, silly, baby rhymes. "Wait to see how she's going to curse at you, hurt and break your heart when she grows up."

No! I cried out inside. I don't believe you because I love my daughter. But I kept quiet for fear that my mother would hurt my daughter if I talked back.

I was relieved when my mother went away for two weeks on her supposedly out-of-town business trip. I was happy having the empty apartment to myself and my baby. Cooking and doing chores for myself without my mother's disapproving frowning, silent eyes and angry face gave me a sense of peace. She didn't come back before I left. I'd have gladly left sooner if I hadn't been scared by the superstition that my baby's luck would be broken if I didn't complete the full month of my maiden homecoming.

When it finally ended, I was happy to be back at work.

"That's Teacher Li? She's so fat," my high school students gasped, giggling.

"Am I really fat?" I asked my colleague Wu Li Hong.

"Funny how we don't always see our true selves," she said, smiling diplomatically.

My extra body weight didn't slow me down. I was on my feet all day. Besides teaching full time, I was nursing, cooking, cleaning, and grocery shopping riding on my bicycle, and getting only two to three hours of sleep a night. And to make some extra money, I also taught college preparation classes for four hours, from 8:00 to 12:00, on Sundays.

Thankfully, my excessive body fat disappeared in short four months. But sadly, my breast milk disappeared along with it. I had to start feeding my baby with powdered milk.

Chapter 55

Propelled

動力

I NEEDED A SHOULDER to cry on. But, as usual, Vic was nowhere in sight.

My baby daughter was now six months old. She'd been crying, hurting from an ear infection.

"How is she?" my father-in-law asked as he came into our room, sitting down in one of our two sofa chairs.

"No better. It's hard to feed her the pills from the doctor. She spits it all out."

"Give her a penicillin shot."

"Penicillin? But you told me your family had a history of being allergic to penicillin. Remember? You once told me your uncle died as a child from a penicillin shot after a cold."

"Might as well. If she dies, you can try for a boy."

"No way. I won't let that happen." I held my baby tight, trembling in disgust and horror.

"Suit yourself." He abruptly got up and walked out, slamming the door behind him.

Things weren't going well for me at work, either. Despite my outstanding teaching performance, I'd been passed over for a pay raise. I had only a two-year college degree.

"Without a four-year college degree, you'll always be at the bottom of the barrel," my grandfather had once told me. But I brushed it off as a non-issue, feeling confident that my exceptional teaching ability would keep me on top. Now even those who'd only completed their first year of college got a pay raise because the Cultural Revolution had disrupted their study. And even the English teachers who'd majored in Russian language also got the raise, purely because of the magical number four: their time spent in a four-year college.

But I had no more hope, ever, to go on to a four-year college. I was married with a child. Only unmarried young people were eligible to join the college competitions. Two of my single colleagues and former college classmates, Wang Jin and Wu Li Hong, had both recently quit their teaching jobs at No. 5. They were allowed to study and compete in an exam that might get them into a four-year college. I was the only pathetic loser left behind and stuck.

A date-red horse came into my dream again.

I was standing by a roadside when the tall, strong, beautiful horse galloped out of the woods toward me. A young man was riding on its back. The gorgeous horse then stopped in front of me, and I woke up. My heart pumped in joy. Another good-omen, date-red-horse dream! But quickly my despair set in. I just couldn't see any future possibilities for me to be blessed again.

Unbelievably, a miracle was soon to happen.

The Chinese government announced a special plan to improve the quality of English teachers in five northern, poverty-stricken provinces, including my province of Shanxi. Each province was to select, through academic competition, the top twelve high-school English teachers with two-year college degrees, and to be sent to complete their four-year degrees, in two years of study at the Beijing Foreign Language Institute, China's best.

And miraculously, being unmarried was not a requirement!

I cried joyful tears for my blessings in disguise: My two colleagues, Wang and Wu, had already quit their jobs. If they hadn't, I'd never have stood a chance to even get into the competing arena since only one teacher from each high school was allowed. Both of their families had powerful backdoor connections: a powerful physician and an elite professor. Now, with their timely departures on their own, I had no rivals. Yes!

I was determined not to let this once-in-a-lifetime opportunity slip through my fingers. I needed to win. I studied hard for the written and oral English tests. And win I did. Out of hundreds of competitors, I ranked fourth among the top twelve.

"Do you really have the heart leaving your toddler daughter behind?" people asked me.

"For two long years?" Vic asked.

"If you hadn't discouraged me from trying for the four-year college when I had the chance," I told him, "there wouldn't have been today. It's your turn to make some sacrifice."

"Good for you," Mr. Li Yuan Xi, the politics teacher, cheered. He said I should seize my hard-earned chance to upgrade my life. He'd missed his chance many years ago because his parents wanted him to stay home and fulfill his filial duty to them. He'd been regretting it.

My baby daughter was always taller and stronger than most kids her age, I reasoned with myself. She'd turn two by the time I left for the fall semester, old enough.

In the meantime, I failed to foresee the sinister scheme Vic's father was brewing.

Just as I was desperate to seize my lifetime opportunity, my father-in-law was equally propelled to seize his chance to achieve his lifetime goal: to gain a male grandchild to extend his family tree. He was planning on getting a different daughter-in-law.

It was a quiet Sunday afternoon.

"Vic!" my father-in-law suddenly yelled outside our window. "Get the hell out!"

Color drained from Vic's face. My heart pounded in panic. Vic's father hadn't been around since he'd left our one-level shack apartment with a patch of dirt ground as our "yard." He'd moved into an upgraded high-rise new apartment across the campus.

We rushed out, me at Vic's heels. His father was huffing and puffing in rage at our door.

"What's wrong?" Vic tried to steady his voice.

"You idiot son of mine. You married a piece of trash to bring shame into my family!"

"What are you talking about?"

"Don't you play dumb with me. How dare you married this thing!" his father roared, pointing at me. "Her mother is a slut. Her mother's mother died a slut. Her mother's uncle was an executed opium trafficker. And her mother's brother murdered a village doctor!"

Oh, no. How in the world did he find out about my darkest secret shame on my mother side of the family? And in such horrifyingly accurate details?

The sky was toppling down to crush me.

"Divorce her!" Vic's father roared.

"I don't want a divorce," Vic responded quietly, surprising me with his bravery.

"Make your damn choice now. It's either your wife or your father!"

"I don't want a divorce," Vic repeated quietly but firmly. My heart swelled in gratitude. This was the first time that Vic had stood up to his bullying father on my behalf, his wife.

"How *dare* you talk back." The sixty-three-year-old had now lost it. For the first time, his authority had been challenged by the unlikeliest person: his obedient thirty-three-year-old son. "You, talking, back, to, *me*, your revered father?" His eyes bulged with rage. Like a mad bull, the six-feet-tall and strong father kicked our door and charged into our room. From outside, we could hear him smashing and thrashing around in our room.

As I listened to him wreak havoc in our home, fear and rage pumped my heart into my throat, but my feet were frozen to the ground.

"Divorce your wife or I'll disown you!" Vic's father yelled.

A large, gawking crowd had gathered around. It was the same humiliating scene from my childhood all over again: my squawking parents fighting as the neighbors looked on. I wanted to disappear into the ground.

"I don't want a divorce," Vic calmly repeated.

"You damned fool. I'll teach you a lesson for disobeying me," Vic's father roared, picking up a bowl-sized cement rock from the neighbor's loose coal pile and throwing it at his son. If Vic hadn't nimbly jumped aside, his legs would've been broken. The rock crashed through our door, shattering the glass into hundreds of pieces.

"Go to hell, you bastard!" I burst out yelling at my crazed father-in-law, an unthinkable move. Looking shocked and lost, the old man dropped himself to the ground, lying there with his eyes closed.

"Don't you play dead with me." I felt no mercy – standing over him, yelling and spewing out my pent-up anger. "You tyrant! Go ahead, tell the crowd how you pressured me to have my baby daughter injected and killed because you wanted a grandson."

A middle-aged woman in a dark blue, Mao-style suit pushed through the crowd and came to the old man's rescue. She was the director of the neighborhood peacemaking association. She helped the old man up, yelling for Vic and me to get back inside.

When the director came back to see us, I was hysterical, sobbing uncontrollably, while Vic held our baby in his arms. And what she told us next shocked me in disbelief: "Let the grandmother leave. Let the old lady out of your life now. Old grandmother has been gossiping to your father. She told him all about Li Jing's mother and family history."

Oh, Grandmother. How could you!

My grandmother had been living with us for the past year. She'd left her home in Red Stone Bridge to accompany her prized teenage grandson, son of my aunt Er Gu, to his city job my father had found him after pulling some backdoor strings. Grandmother raised the boy since he was nine after his parents' divorce. Now that I needed some help taking care of my one-year-old daughter, she was more than happy to stay in the city and babysit for me. In our small one room, she slept in a folding bed in the middle of our floor.

After Grandmother joined our household as our babysitter, I was too busy to remember her fierce ambition to carry on her cold war against her despised daughter-in-law, my mother. I forgot that she had all day to gossip with my father-in-law, retired, with all the time in the world. Both of these elderly people had their own agendas with a mutual motive: to get their daughters-in-law. *He* wanted to dig up dirt on *his* daughter-in-law, me. And *she* wanted the whole world to know how evil *her* daughter-in-law, my mother, was.

What a pair these two had turned out to be.

The sophisticated college professor was a flattering friend to the illiterate peasant woman. His generous gift to her, a pair of his used spectacles, made her heart smile for many days. No one had ever given her anything for free, she said. And once she was drawn in, he successfully got her to reveal my mother's shameful family history. With that lethal ammunition, he waited for the perfect time to carry out his plan to get rid of me, his daughter-in-law. But like my grandmother, he'd also miscalculated the obedience level of his son.

"*Ye-ye huai dan!*" *Bad Grandpa*! my toddler daughter would yell every time she saw our broken window. I wonder how much she remembered the violent scene she'd witnessed that terrible day.

Grandmother started acting like a demure mouse. At the time, my memory about her harsh treatment of me as a small child growing up with her back in the village hadn't returned. Her image was still overlapped in my memory with my loving Grandpa. Looking at her sad face and obedient, pleasing eyes, I didn't have the heart to scold her for causing all these terrible troubles for everyone. Vic kept quiet, too. He showed her his usual respect. We needed her to babysit our daughter. And she in return needed a quiet, comfortable home, which she preferred over living with her precious only son, my father, who yelled and quarreled with her all the time.

Now disowned by his family and ordered by Vic's father to clear out, we needed a new place to live. Our only hope was to plead with my work unit, No. 5 Secondary School, for mercy.

For the entire week, every evening after dinner, Vic and I left our baby daughter at home with Grandmother. We rode our bike to plead with every one of my school's four assistant principals. For the sake of my being the top notch irreplaceable English teacher, they finally agreed to grant me the extra special favor I'd asked for. But nothing was available. They had to half-persuade and half-ordered someone else's family to vacate a small room for me. It was a ten-by-twelve-foot space in the corner of the third floor, with a shared small kitchen and a tiny dark stench-filled closet for a squatting toilet shared by the dozen neighbors.

The minute I walked into my small room of refuge I fainted, collapsing onto the dusty cement floor, waking up to find myself soiled and a panic-stricken Vic calling my name. My fainting spell was to become a pattern whenever I felt extremely distressed.

Vic promptly padlocked our newly acquired family skeleton closet. I was never to speak of a word of it in front of him again.

My gaining the special small-room "privilege" caused an uproar.

"Why should Li Jing get the special favor?" a number of teachers protested. "Many teachers in their sixties still live in a one-room apartment with three generations together. She's not even half their age."

The protest quickly died down. For, a bunch of VIP's sons and daughters were enrolled in my AP English classes.

Chapter 56
Beijing Foreign Language Institute
北京外國語學院

ON THE NIGHT TRAIN to Beijing, 1983.

I sat elbow-to-elbow with my three future classmate passengers on the bare wooden train seat, on my way to upgrade my professional life. But I couldn't feel any joy. I was missing my baby daughter. My eyes were sore from crying too many tears. In my sorrow at leaving her, I'd even forgotten my pride in being one of the top twelve winning teachers to attend the Beijing Foreign Language Institute, China's best, out of hundreds from my entire Province.

My three classmates-to-be were all having the time of their lives on the train. They chatted and laughed merrily deep into the night. And they had every reason to feel lighthearted. None of them was married or had left a small child behind like I did. And they were too carefree to be aware of my heartaches as a mother. I hadn't anticipated the intense pain of being separated from my baby daughter. Afraid of being laughed at for being a narrow-minded housewife, I kept to myself but left one ear open to my classmates' cheerful chatting.

"What's *ke-kou-ke-le* 可口可樂?" I couldn't help but ask.

"It's Coca Cola in English, a famous American drink," Jin piped up. She was the one who'd almost stolen my spot to teach at No. 5 when we were both attending Taiyuan Teachers' College. "I don't think you'll like its taste, very different from your village-style soup with boiled vegetables," she said, promptly reminding me of her upper class educated family.

According to Chinese superstitions, 1983 was a bad-omen year for both Vic and me.

I had a bad-luck number nine hidden in my age of twenty-seven: 3 x 9 = 27. Vic was thirty-three years old, a universally bad-luck age.

Right after we'd been disowned, it was more bad luck for the three of us. We were now separated for two years. I was an eleven-hour train ride away from home, a round trip cost one-fourth of my monthly salary. I could only see my daughter at the end of each semester.

Telephone calls were impossible. There was only one telecommunication building in downtown Beijing. To get there, you first had to spend hours riding multiple buses. Then, you had to stand in line for hours waiting for your name to be called, if you were lucky, to make a long-distance phone call. And, a phone call for a few minutes could easily cost my entire month's salary. Then, of course, we had no phone at home, like the ninety-nine percent of the Chinese masses in the 1980's. Having a telephone was an official symbol of governmental privilege and high social status.

What was my baby doing now that she found her mama gone? She had never gone to sleep unless I held her in my arms. Was she crying for me now? What a cruel, hard-hearted mother I'd become. "Mommy will never leave you," I'd promised to her, gazing into her bright eyes, holding her in my arms close to my heart. But I turned out to be cruel just like my own mother. The only thing that put my heart at ease was that Vic turned out to be a loving and nurturing father, very patient and playful with our daughter. I'd been worried when I first saw his gloomy face upon hearing that our newborn baby wasn't a boy. Looking back, however, I think he was just afraid to disappoint his father.

Mama! I could hear my baby crying. What the hell am I doing here? I squinted at the piercing morning sun, stepping off the train to follow my three classmates, my bedroll on my shoulders and a bag in my hand. What am I struggling for among the swarming seas of people? Why am I a thousand *li* away while my baby daughter needs me at home?

"Come on, Li Jing," my classmates, walking ahead, called cheerfully back to me. They had no idea that I was a tormented mother living through a maternal nightmare. My mind numb, my heart laden with guilt, I was a robot being pushed around and elbow-shoved by the crowds pouring out of the train station. The only thing alive inside me was my aching heart. I couldn't even feel excited about setting foot for the first time in China's famous capital city of Beijing.

"How exciting!" my classmates cheered. "Look at the amazing crowds of people. We are really in Beijing now. Chairman Mao actually lived here. Oh, yeah!"

None of my single classmates seemed to be aware of my troubled mind and aching heart as a mother. Is Vic remembering to put our baby's wet pants on the radiator to dry? Would the basket of eggs keep? I had bought one hundred eggs and had wiped every single one of them clean with alcohol. (It turned out to be a bad idea, as I found out later. They all rotted.)

When I finally saw my baby again at the end of the first semester, she was two-and-a-half years old. I'd missed half a year in her budding life. On that reunion day, my heart pumped wildly in grief and joy as I knocked on the door of my father's apartment, where my grandmother was babysitting my daughter during the daytime, when Vic was at work.

"Who is it?" my toddler baby called out, and I heard her running to the door with my grandmother's three-inch-bound feet shuffling behind. Restraining myself from sobbing, I squatted down, my hands reaching out, waiting. And when Grandmother unlatched and opened the door, there was my little darling, standing in front of me, smiling. I gathered her into my arms, only to see her shrinking back, her little face turning to a frown, her bright eyes a question mark. As I kissed her, holding her tight to my bosom, my baby examined my inscrutable, tear-streaked face. Was she wondering who I was – or why I was never there?

Thus began my lifelong, heart-aching burden of guilt as a frequently absent mother.

Otherwise, my two years in Beijing was a mixture of enlightened awakening.

First of all, at the ripe age of twenty-seven, I felt old, wishing I were one of the beautiful and fashionably dressed young girl students on campus. I not only envied their youth but also their fluent English.

I can still feel the sting from a pretty young student's scoffing look over one of my English pronunciations. Walking ahead of me one day, she suddenly whipped her head back to glare at me when she heard me mispronounce "fiancée." I felt like a fraud.

Another beautiful young woman's condescending eyes wounded my pride. I was one week late coming back to college campus. When

I entered the dorm building after spending some extra time with my daughter, the fashionably dressed student looked at me up and down, as if to say: *Ha! You call yourself a college student alongside me?*

I made myself miserable over these slights, forgetting everything I'd had to conquer to get where these privileged girls had always been.

Despite my emotional turmoil from missing my daughter, I was also wide-eyed amazed at the everyday wonders found in Beijing.

To begin with, there were only six bunk beds in each dorm room, compared with the fifteen-people platform communal bed back at Taiyuan Teachers' College. The Beijing campus even had a public bathhouse, open on Wednesdays and Sundays, with multiple showerheads along the walls. Although always crowded with several people under each showerhead, the bathhouse was still a luxury.

The hallway inside our second-floor dorm was mopped clean twice a day by a tall, heavyset country woman. She'd yell in her Shan-Dong-province accent if some lazy student poured dirty water onto the hallway floor instead of walking a few steps to the washroom.

And each of the dorm building's floors had its own washroom, the grandest I'd ever seen. Extending from wall to wall under the two big, bright windows was a long, cement wash sink with a half dozen water faucets. And, there was never a long line during washing time.

The four squatting toilets inside the washroom, white porcelain bowls, were kept so clean they'd retained their original color. Each toilet was in an enclosed stall with a door for privacy. How wonderful that you didn't have to do your business with people waiting in front of you.

I was also amazed that water was always available in Beijing with no rationing. What luxury. Later I was saddened to learn that the government had forced the surrounding provinces to divert their rivers to guarantee an abundant water supply in privileged Beijing. Even my dry, dusty, and drought-prone Shanxi province was forced to contribute.

For the first time in my life, I saw flowers, green plants and shrubs lining the streets everywhere. It was a far cry from the barren city streets in my dry city of Taiyuan. Even Beijing's air was cooler and magically fresher than Taiyuan's.

Among the many other "firsts" I experienced in Beijing was seeing my first color television.

Every Sunday evening, a 17-inch screen color TV was placed out at the end of the third-floor hallway, which was packed with chairs.

After a once-a-week hot shower, we got to watch a movie from Hong Kong, another forbidden Western world.

I loved the university's Audio and Video Building. I'd sneak in to watch Western movies even when the films weren't scheduled for my English classes. It helped my listening and speaking skills. I loved the merry atmosphere in American movies: the actors' worry-free smiling faces, their laughter, their spirit of fun, and their great sense of humor. I was captivated by the gorgeous way people dressed and the exotic way they talked and acted. I often didn't understand much as to who, what, when, where or why in the movies. My insufficient English listening skills could catch few words that flew out of the actors' mouths. They were all in rolling blurs but I didn't care. Among all the movies, I loved *Gone with the Wind*, *Singing in the Rain*, and *The Sound of Music* — the most fascinating and beautiful scenes I'd ever seen.

When I began my studies in Beijing, I realized how bland my mind was when it came to the Western culture and history. I also realized how much I lacked fluency in spoken English and a basic vocabulary in written English. So far, my only solid knowledge of English was my thorough understanding of the grammatical rules.

Studying and reading a lot to fill in those gaps occupied my mind and numbed my pain from missing my baby daughter. With my English-Chinese dictionary on hand to look up new vocabulary words, I decoded the original versions of English texts, such as Helen Keller's essay "The Three Days to See" and Mark Twain's mind-liberating story "The Golden Trumpet." I loved reading and listening to children's books with voice recordings, such as *Little Red Riding Hood* and *The Three Little Pigs*. And I loved singing along with recordings of "Oh, Susanna, Don't You Cry for Me!" and "What Did You Learn in School, Dear Little Boy of Mine?" I especially enjoyed reading funny stories with jokes. I chuckled when I read that a woman's ideal mate should be a TV set: She could shut it off whenever she wished, and it'd never talk back.

For our oral English study, we had an American professor named Elizabeth. "Compare Tolstoy and Gorky," Professor Elizabeth instructed us in class one day.

"Tolstoy.... Did you mean the famous Russian author?" I timidly asked. I couldn't believe I was important enough to discuss such famous people. In China, we grew up believing that words describing important things or people should only be uttered on the lips of the government leaders. I'd only heard of and, of course, had never read Tolstoy's *War and Peace*; and I only knew that famous Gorky was a good friend of Lenin, the Communist god.

Then one day in class I saw my American professor taking a miniature, clear plastic packet out of her pocket. Out pulling from it was a pink, handkerchief-sized sheet. What's that? It looked like soft cotton. Then she blew her nose into it, and casually tossed it into the wastebasket under her desk. Unthinkable! Wow, Americans are rich! They blow their nose into a cotton-like handkerchief once and just throw it away?

Professor Elizabeth told our class that back home in America she worked at a radio station. Wow, how important! And, her husband was a farmer.

A farmer? I was stunned.

China's village farmers like my grandfather were forced to turn in their government-mandated portion of grains, drought or flood, leaving themselves "starving two half years," which is how most of the Red Stone Bridge villagers lived. They couldn't even afford to buy Aspirin pills for their pains. They toiled all their lives in their commune's cornfields until they either couldn't get out of bed one day or simply dropped dead. They were the lowest of the low. No city dwellers would ever even think of marrying a peasant farmer.

I wanted so badly to understand America by chatting with Professor Elizabeth but I was too self-conscious, and my English was too poor to carry on a deep conversation.

A disaster struck at the beginning of my second year in Beijing.

It all started one day when I was chatting with one of my roommates. She was surprised that I'd never taken a birth control pill but by abstinence during the mid-ten days of my menstrual cycle. It was too much hard work doing all that calculating and risky, she said. So, a few days before the summer vacation started, she shared with me a few of her birth control pills. But I didn't continue and went back to my old ways. The chemical must have somehow interrupted my system. I miscalculated my period date, missed it and ended up going back to Beijing in the fall semester, pregnant. My heart sank into a panic. Lying in my lower bunk bed in my six-people college dorm, I kept quiet but boiling mad inside, at myself, cursing Vic, vowing to never let him touch me again.

But the problem had to be solved. By myself. Alone.

Giving birth was no option. One child per family policy was the national law, like the nail in the coffin. Inescapable. I'd be expelled by the university, lose my job, never to be employed ever again for the rest of my life, and become a total social outcast. With no life. No income. No way to make a living. And, my child would become a "black person" – a non-exist being with no rights to be a human. Forbidden to attend school. Denied the rationed food.

I rode my bike, alone, for an hour and half to downtown Beijing hospital for an abortion. It was the week before China's October 1 national holiday. The hallway was crowded with young women outside the operation room. No I.D. was required. Only fifteen yuan basic fee.

The vast bare walled operation room smelled of raw, fresh warm blood. There were a dozen single, narrow beds scattered all over, each was occupied by a young woman, with a white robed woman, supposedly a doctor, sitting at the lower end of the bed tending the patient. The noises were terrifying, moaning, groaning, occasional piercing screaming, blended with the doctor's scolding, vengeful laughter: "Well, hurt? I bet it was fun in bed with the guy, huh??"

I was led into one of the beds in the middle of the room, still in my street clothes. "Take off your pants," the white-robe told me. No numbing medicine was used. An icy cold steel object abruptly thrust deep inside me. It started tearing and scraping. Oh, what excruciating pain . . . feeling like my grandmother's iron ladle scraping the big cast iron cooking wok for the last scrap of food. I bit down hard, trying not to let out a whimpering cry. I didn't want to be scolded, my dignity stripped away, along with my flesh.

"Put your pants back on. It's done!" The white robed woman ordered me, as I curled myself into a ball of pain, feeling like a tiger having just clawed my insides into shreds.

"Hey, you need to get off the bed right now to make room for the next patient. You can sit and rest in the reception room for half an hour."

No medicine for me? I timidly asked the reception desk lady, gasping in between pain. Medicine? She rolled her eyes, scoffing. For what? You'll get over it in no time!

My legs weak and shaking, my belly a twisted fiery mass, I struggled pedaling my bike back to campus. It was the longest and hardest bike ride. It was a thorough flesh-tearing and blood-scraping job, for there was no more blood coming out.

For the entire week, I lay in my dorm room bunk bed. My roommates kept their respectful silence. It was not a light topic to be talked about. I was the only unlucky soul suffering the misery. All their husbands must have cared about their wives not to get them pregnant. I hated Vic, my no-feeling husband!

My roommates were kind enough and took turns bringing me meals from the cafeteria. I envied them when they were mass-transported by the university trucks to see the grand fireworks show at the Tian An Men Square for China's biggest annual celebration of the Communist Founding Day. But I immediately felt lucky when one of my roommates, Li Huang, came back with her left eyeball burned by a falling speck from the fireworks as she looked up into the sky.

Toward the end of my studies at Beijing Foreign Language Institute, my child-like-innocence and naivety almost ruined everything I'd earned, most importantly, my reputation.

One Sunday, my roommate Xiao Si and I went to sightseeing at the ancient royal palace of the Forbidden City. A middle-aged Western man said hello to us. We were flattered by his friendliness and genuine smile. No Chinese man would ever smile or say hello to any Chinese females. I loved the Western world's friendliness. The man said he was Italian. But his English sounded wonderful just the same.

A curious crowd quickly surrounded us, staring, open-mouthed, at our conversation with the foreigner. I felt enormously proud speaking a foreign tongue. I wished that my father were there to recognize how wrong he'd been about me. I wanted him to see that I was not only smart and articulate, but also able to talk to an exotic foreign guest in English, the world's most important language.

Xiao Si and I toured the Forbidden City with the Italian man. He really surprised me by praising the Forbidden City as "magnificent." But China was too old, I said to him, and too poor, and needed to be modernized like the Western world.

"No, no, no! Your long history is beautiful," he said and sounded sincere. This was the first time I'd heard a non-Chinese "foreign devil" praising China. Mao had denounced all foreigners as cruel, heartless devils who'd caused China's misery. But with my own eyes and ears, I'd seen and heard this man, a Westerner, admiring China's ancient palace – even its history.

As our tour ended, the Italian man invited us to have coffee in his Friendship Hotel. I was elated! Yes, of course. It'd be a valuable opportunity to peek into the fascinating life of a privileged foreigner I so admired.

"Are you crazy, Li Jing?" My roommate pulled me aside, hissing, "No, we can't go."

"Why not? Just some more fun chatting time with him like we are doing now."

"How would you know that this man is not a murderer or a spy?"

"But he's been so nice. What can go wrong?"

"Fine, go alone yourself. I'm going back to campus."

I knew I couldn't go without her. Even if she didn't report me to the college authorities, I knew they always had a way of finding out. I felt like a small child who'd just had her candy ripped out of her hands.

My roommate proved to be wise.

Soon after we returned to our campus, we heard that two of my classmates, from Qing Hai province, had received a severe warning from the college for their befriending two foreign men, a Japanese and an American. The women were threatened with expulsion if they didn't heed the warning to make no further contact with the foreigners. No one could afford to be expelled and lose the government's "iron rice bowl."

I broke into a cold sweat. Just imagine what disaster it would have been on me if I'd accepted the Italian man's invitation for coffee!

My two-year study program at the Beijing Foreign Language Institute ended as planned in 1985. I graduated on schedule with a four-year college degree and a clean record in my political dossier, no thought crimes committed against the Party. I went back to my prestigious teaching at the elite No. 5 Secondary School.

No promotion could ever pass me by again. But what a steep price I had to pay for it.

In my desperate pursuit of the one-in-a-lifetime opportunity to complete my four-year college degree, I missed two long years in my toddler daughter's life.

She was now four. My tears streaming down, I met my baby's shy, skeptical smile when Vic brought her to meet me at the train station. She turned to hide her little face on her father's shoulder, wrapping her arms around his neck. My hand touched her head, feeling her silky shining black hair. I tried to kiss her hidden little plump cheeks.

When I caressed her smooth and tender little arms, "mommy's little turnip," she brushed my hand away.

My heart trembled in weeping pain.

1984. I'm standing in front of the Audio and Video building at Beijing Foreign Language Institute.

Chapter 57

Runaway Number One!

更上一層樓

SOON AFTER EARNING my four-year college degree, I got restless.

This was it? No more challenges? Nothing more for me to conquer? My future looked unexciting and too predictable: continuing to teach what I'd already thoroughly mastered before earning my four-year degree. I'd be helping send the brightest high school graduates to the best colleges year after year. Yet, while my students went off to realize their ultimate goal of studying abroad after college, preferably in America, I would still be marching in place going nowhere as their stepping-stone teacher. I felt like the old maid in the ancient Chinese proverb, sewing wedding gowns for others year after year with no prospect of getting married herself.

I was aching to be like my students, who were going far away to see the best of the world. But then Grandmother's voice came screeching into my ears from my childhood: "You cheap eyelids! You always want that others have!"

My school principal's wife was surprised to hear of my inner conflict. "Oh, Teacher Li. Do you know how many people would love to be in your position?" She said. "A famed high school English teacher. Got everything in life going for you, a noble career, a bright and healthy daughter, and college-educated husband. Whichever way you look, your life is shining gold."

It was indeed a miracle that I'd risen above and beyond the bottom pit of peasantry. But I still wanted more. What exactly? And how? I did not know. Now that my college dream had come true, there was nothing for me to upgrade in my life. And my fate wasn't up to me to decide. In communist China, each individual was mandated to be a faithful nail and screw in the socialist machine: You could only move about if the government granted you permission and an opportunity.

I stood outside my classroom leaning against the iron rail on the second floor balcony, agonizing over my unquenchable desire to become more in life.

That night, a beautiful date-red horse appeared in my dream again. And, this time, the gorgeous horse was flying across the sky, instead of galloping on the ground. It was accompanied by two other beautiful horses, one, white, one golden. I woke up, my heart was smiling. Another good-omen dream. But I quickly suppressed my hope, unable to fathom what more good fortune could possibly come my way.

Unbelievably, though, another miracle was soon to happen.

The government decided to select two top high school teachers from each province through competition as exchange teachers in America, sponsored by the American Field Service, which would give each teacher an incredible fortune of $60 a month – five times more than my monthly salary! But before the fierce academic competitions could begin, all candidates had to meet the preliminary qualifications:

1. Facial features proportionately in place, preferably good looking;

2. No visible physical deficiency or diseases;

3. The communist party membership would be waived (Thank Heavens!) but the person must have a clean political dossier with no thought crimes ever committed against the Party; Whew . . .!!

4. Must be married (Yes!) preferably with the government-mandated one child (Yes!) – a guarantee to prevent anyone from escaping the motherland, they like it when you leave children behind as collateral to insure your return; and

5. No older than age thirty. (Whew! I was one-month shy of my thirtieth birthday.)

I aced the grueling two-day examinations in oral and written English. Out of hundreds of contestants, I was the runaway number one – twenty-two points ahead of the runner-up second place winner, who was a backdoor-connected college teacher, instead of a high school teacher as required. I'd won my bulletproof insurance not to be bumped off the winner's list!

"Mommy," my now-five-year-old daughter looked at me, her little face adorable, serious, and innocent as she said, "you're already thirty years old. Too old. America doesn't want you."

"Your daddy told you to say that to mommy, right?" I smiled at my daughter, my heart heavy and guilt-ridden. But my insane ambition was unstoppable. I was driven to this one-in-a-million golden chance like a famished pauper enticed by a holiday feast.

My father told me what his cousin had said to him: "Your daughter was only a lowly, temporary middle school teacher just a short few years ago. How come she's already going to America?"

"If only the world moved the same speed as his feeble brain!" I snapped back and was surprised to see him break out laughing so heartily. My father looked at me in awe, as if I were a stranger he saw for the first time. I wished that my father would just come right out and tell me he was proud of me. But instead, he sighed: "If only you were born a boy, you'd have brought real honor and pride to our Li family name." That's as close as I ever got to a real compliment.

When the news of my monumental win reached my school, Mr. Zhang, a famous math teacher at No. 5, humbly initiated a conversation. "I didn't think anyone in this backward province of Shanxi would be good enough to reach the peak of the world, America," he said. With a knowing smile of who-do-you-think-you're-talking-to, he once told me he had started teaching the year I was born. A teaching career in China is revered as Americans admire an aged fine wine – the older, the better!

"You're going to eat chicken drumsticks in America!" said Mr. Cui, my rich and powerful distant relative I was indebted to for granting me a special favor to start my teaching career. *Mmmm... chicken drumsticks!* My mouth watered. I could count on one hand, and still have three fingers left, the number of times in my thirty years I'd ever eaten delicious chicken meat, let alone drumsticks. Mr. Cui himself had recently visited America on a privileged government-sponsored tour.

"One can't consider themselves having been to places unless you've been to America," my high school principal Mr. Yang said through a smile.

And the Chinese government wanted us to look good in front of Americans, not shabby in our everyday clothes. So, each of us was given an enormous fortune of eight hundred Chinese dollars, *yuan*, (about $105USD) – equivalent of my entire year's salary. We were to buy new clothes. I had never been so rich before!

I made sure my fortune of eight hundred yuan stretched. I bought a precious camera, my very first in life; a purse made of shiny brown synthetics, not easily wrinkled, small enough to be elegant, yet large enough to be practical; a long skirt with exquisite pleats; a sweater; a checkered cloth jacket; and a pair of blue jeans, 牛仔褲 *niu-zai-ku*, "cowboy pants" – a new fashion imported from America. I was later heartbroken when they shrank after the first wash. I wished I had been able to afford American made jeans. And, finally, I bought I a mellow yellow sleeveless T-shirt with a shiny saying: Forward riding on the East Wind! 乘東風，向前進！

Now I needed to buy a nice suitcase to carry all these fine things with me to America.

Chapter 58

At the Friendship Store

友誼商店

SUMMER OF 1986.

All forty-six of us high school English teachers, two from each of twenty-three provinces, gathered at the Beijing Language and Culture University for a week of orientation. It was organized by the Chinese government and sponsored by the American Field Service (AFS). Most of us were going to America for the 1986-87 school year, and a few to Great Britain for only one semester. Everyone wanted to go to America. One teacher was bitterly disappointed when assigned to England. She said to Rebecca, an AFS volunteer, "British English is more authentic than American English anyway!" I was happy to be assigned to America!

We were given more time for shopping.

I was walking off campus to shop in downtown Beijing when a young couple with a suitcase walked by. Energetic and confident, they looked like models straight out of the pages of a fashion magazine. Wait, how come they were pulling their brand-new suitcase on the sidewalk? Weren't they afraid of damaging it on the rough cement? Taking a closer look, I discovered the hard-shelled suitcase had tiny wheels! Wow, wheels on a suitcase? What a clever invention. I wanted to buy a suitcase just like that. Then something else attracted my eye: a long, sturdy, rainbow-colored canvas strap crisscrossed the suitcase. I'd never seen something that pretty yet practical. Oh, I definitely wanted one.

"Excuse me," I called to the couple. "Where did you buy the suitcase strap?"

The young woman glanced at me. "Even if we tell you, you still can't buy one," she said. "But why?" I hated it when people slighted me.

"Because only the Friendship Store sells them. You can't get in. You'll need someone to sponsor you. It's for *wai-bin* 外賓, honored foreigners, only."

My heart sank. I understood what "off limits" meant to the masses of Chinese who don't belong to the top Party ruling class. But hadn't Mao proudly stood at the Gate of Heavenly Peace on October 1, 1949 and belted into a big round microphone in his thick Hunan accent: "Chinese people are standing up!" when his Communist Party took over China? Gone were the days, he declared, when the imperialist nations rode on our necks. And we were our own masters on our own land from now on.

"Where is the Friendship Store?" I felt the anger and humiliation inside.

"Don't bother, you won't get in," the young man shook his head, glancing over at me. But as I persisted, he was kind enough to tell me how to get there.

It took me most of the morning to finally get to the Friendship Store, running after buses, pushing, shoving, and elbowing my way onto several bus transfers, and standing packed body-to-body solid like canned sardines on each one.

I saw a grand building above a flight of marble stairs. On top of the building were huge Chinese calligraphy characters in golden color: 友誼商店 Friendship Store. It was a bustling scene out front. Almost all the people going in and out of the store were exotic looking foreigners with amazingly beautiful color hair and wearing expensive clothes. Among the crowds were a few important-looking Chinese in nice Western suits, apparently high government officials and their privileged families.

The center entrance to the Friendship Store was a big, shining brass door. I was relieved to see no armed soldiers with rifles guarding the entrance, as was the usual scene in front of the "Friendship Hotel" for privileged foreign guests. Then I was dismayed to see that, scattered idling around on the long flights of marble steps leading up to the entrance, were half a dozen young men in dark suits and shiny black leather shoes, their eyes surveying the crowds.

Chilling goose bumps crawled down my spine. I knew this was a place seriously forbidden to me. But I couldn't resist an urge to try. I had to buy a suitcase strap.

I looked down to inspect myself. Still sweaty from running after the buses, my white polyester shirt was wet, wrinkled, and stained.

In my hands was my lunch: two halves of boiled corn-on-the-cob. My favorite. I'd bought them this morning from a street vendor in between running after buses and hadn't had a chance to eat them. Should I stuff them into my brand-new purse I'd bought just for my grand American journey? No, I didn't want to make the purse a sticky mess. But I could never bring myself to throw away a single grain of food after growing up in famine and starvation. Would I look too shabby and unsightly if I just kept my lunch in this little see-through green nylon net bag? Maybe nobody would notice if I held the bag down low.

I looked around, plotting how to get inside the store. My heart pounding, I saw my chance. A group of golden-haired, tall, broad-shouldered foreigners with their Chinese companions were walking toward the store from the right side of the building. I made my move, trying to look calm. I quickly blended myself in by following closely behind the tall-people group, my head lowered, my eyes looking down to the ground.

No one stopped me. Yes! I was in.

I found myself entering China's paradise.

How comfortable the inside air felt. What did they put in the air to make it nice and cool when it was so hot outside?

I gazed around at the vast space, full of beautiful things I'd never seen in my life. Gorgeous looking clothes hanging on circular displays. The walls were covered with shelves holding expensive, colorful, shiny-looking things. It reminded me of the fascinating kaleidoscope I saw once in my childhood. On all the shelves behind the counters, exquisite bottles and tiny boxes, watches, and flashy jewelry were displayed– too good for me. I knew my place.

I wandered into the next spacious room. It was full of life-sized models wearing handsome Western suits and colorful flowing gowns, dresses, and skirts. I felt as if I were walking through scenes from the fascinating American movies. The price tag on one suit said 800 yuan!? That would cost two-year salary for a blue-collar worker in the city and a dozen years of living expenses for peasants like my village grandparents!

Wow! Look at those colorfully embroidered silky slippers in the glass case of the counter. What lucky women got to wear them? They certainly wouldn't stay clean in a typical Chinese cement, dusty floored one-room apartment like mine. The little white price tag said twenty-five Chinese dollars, over half of my monthly salary as a high school teacher! Walk away. I told myself. Oh, look at those soft fluffy floor-length robes. They were sleeping gowns, the label said. Oh, my, the Western people were so rich they wore such fine-quality clothes just for sleep? Think about the wear and tear for doing nothing but lying in bed!

The beautiful bottles of liquid and the mysterious boxes printed with the pretty faces of young Western women must be meant for decorating women's faces. I surely had no use for them. My face was always sweaty from running behind buses in clouds of dust and smoke from the exhaust pipes, and riding my bicycle carrying my daughter or a sack of rationed grains on the back rack.

I was dizzy with the eye-opening, flamboyant world inside the sky-high-priced foreigners-only Friendship Store. I couldn't afford anything I saw. I was here only to buy a suitcase strap for the beautiful red suitcase I was taking on my journey to America.

Finally, I spotted it. A lot of them! Coils of rainbow-colored canvas straps sat on one of the shelves in the corner of the wonderland. Oh, look, no long line of people waiting to buy! I was even more surprised that the young sales clerk behind the counter actually smiled at me when I asked her about the price of the strap, so different from the rude, loud, and insulting salesclerks in regular Chinese stores, who resented their customers for bothering them because they made the same government salary whether they sold anything or not.

Wow, I was so pleasantly surprised that a suitcase strap wasn't as sky high priced as I expected: twenty-five Chinese dollars, *yuan*. With the windfall of the 800 *yuan*, which the government gave me for winning this glorious international teachers' exchange program, I could afford it. The transaction was so pleasant, almost too good to be true.

Was this how good the rich Western countries were? No frantic rushing and shoving, no loud yelling or rude shouting, no elbowing your way through thick crowds, but all peaceful and quiet, dealing with polite, smiling people? Amazing.

Ah, my mission accomplished! I was ready to leave the magically cool shopping wonderland and step into the hot June sun. I felt greatly contented with my rainbow-colored ten-foot-long, two-inch-wide canvas suitcase strap snuggled inside my brand-new purse.

"Hey, how the fuck did you get in?" A barking voice said from behind me, as I was walking down the marble steps. The yelling came from one of the young plainclothes police. I turned to look over my shoulder, but only out of casual curiosity. Surely, that kind of cursing tone was only meant for criminals. I was a model citizen: a famous, accomplished elite high-school English teacher, and runaway top number-one winner out of hundreds going to visit the world's number one country, America, a dream even for the government ruling class officials.

Suddenly, a half dozen dark suits started getting up, looking alert, their black leather shoes shining, and their eyes glaring. At me?!

"Hey, talking to you!" one yelled at me, straightening up from sitting on the steps.

I froze – my face an innocent question mark.

"Yeah, you!" another young guard took one step toward me. "How the hell did you get in?"

"Hell! She's got nerve," another one sneered.

"Look at you! What the hell made you think this is the place for shabby people like you?"

My white polyester shirt was wrinkled and blotched with rings of sweat. Even my new purse didn't look impressive crossed over my shoulders. And dangling in my hand was my delicious corn-on-the-cob lunch in the little green nylon net bag.

I turned to hurry down the seemingly endless marble flights of steps with a shower of insults at my back. The Chinese secret police had the same terrifying power as their KGB counterparts in the Soviet Union.

"Who the hell do you think you are coming to a special place like this?"

"Don't you know this is for special *wai-bin* only?"

"No dignity. No shame!"

"Have you seen yourself in the mirror this morning?"

"That's right, pee on the ground and see yourself in the puddle."

"You are making our motherland lose face. Look at yourself!"

"Get the hell out of here, you fool!"

Tears of humiliation blurred my eyes. I couldn't disappear fast enough into the crowds of commoners. *My motherland be damned*, I thought, wiping my tears away and blending into the afternoon crush of people. *Someday I will find a way to stay in America. Never to return.*

THE RED SANDALS: A MEMOIR

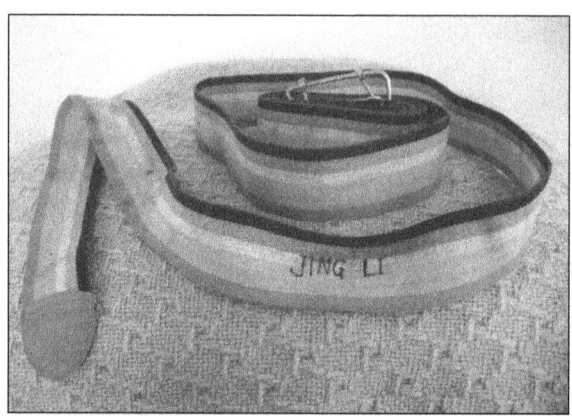

This is my prized suitcase strap. I not only paid a lot for it but humiliation as well, my price for breaking into China's Foreign-Guests-Only "Friendship Store" in 1986. I still have it to this day. Just so you know, my dignity returned.

Chapter 59

America, at Last!

終於見到了夢中的美國

FROM MY WINDOW SEAT, I watched with fascination Air China flying *above* the fluffy, cotton-like clouds.

"Airplane, airplane, come down, and take me up for a ride!" I heard my child's voice cheering in chorus with other children in my blue-collar dirt yard when we saw an airplane in the sky. It looked like a toy in the sky. How could it hold a real person inside? My child's mind wanted to know.

Now at age thirty, I found out what the inside of an airplane looked like. It was a hundred times bigger. And I was awed by the spotless clean miniature washroom with a flushing toilet.

"Would you like something to drink?" a beautiful stewardess smiled at me. No, thanks, I automatically shook my head, despite my scratchy dry throat. No way I could afford it. The immaculate inside of the airplane reminded me of Beijing's fancy Friendship Store that barred ordinary Chinese like me but for only foreigners and Chinese high-ranking government officials.

Then I saw my seatmate, a young woman from Thailand, also part of the AFS teacher-exchange, speaking to the flight attendant and was given a cup of Coca Cola.

"How much is it?" I couldn't hold my curiosity.

"Oh, it's free," she smiled. Don't you know? Her bright eyes said.

I kicked myself for missing my first taste of famous Coca Cola.

An enormous airplane-sized bus with soft cushion seats was waiting for us at the New York airport. We were dropped off on the Concordia College near Bronxville, New York. A full bus load of us, all high-school English teachers from China, India, Thailand and Venezuela. We stayed at the College dorm rooms for the one-week orientation. We were taught how to use a knife and fork. No more chopsticks for a year!

I'm sitting alone on the front lawn of Concordia College in Bronxville, New York.

And what an ignorant, unruly mob we were, invading the small college campus cafeteria like a mass of locusts. Freshly out of Communist China's chaotic socialism, where part of daily life was starvation, we had no habit of forming a line and waiting for our turn. We brought China chaos with us. In the first morning, we rushed into the quiet, orderly cafeteria, wandering in all directions, inserting ourselves all over the place, for fear of food running out. We did not know what a tray was for or where to get our food.

I grabbed a carton of milk. But it was sealed like a seamless fortress! How do I open it? A smiling middle-aged American gentleman came to my rescue. He showed me, looking amused. Wow, American paper was so strong it could hold liquid milk!

Several Chinese guys were exploring around inside the cafeteria. They pushed open two closed doors, ignoring the Fire Exit sign, and strolled outside. Suddenly, in a blink of eye, a loud fire engine screeched into the yard! We were stunned. Wow, what an efficient country! The fire sign actually meant it. Back home, we'd grown jaded with all written signs. They were nothing but political propaganda slogans.

I discovered something that changed my images of "Americans." A group of golden-haired men were digging and shoveling dirt on a construction site by a bulldozer. They were working away just like ordinary workingmen in China. Wow! Blonde Americans could be ordinary manual laborers, too? I thought they were all distinguished high class of people in expensive suits, for China treated them as the royals above us all.

And a lot of other things happened that changed my perception of the world.

"Why, you Chinese imperialist chauvinists," Rebecca, our AFS coordinator, scolded us at the breakfast table. "How come you're not talking to people from other countries?" I saw her standing quietly watching in the corner earlier this morning, as we rushed in and out of the bathroom down the bustling hallway.

But, chauvinist? Who? Me? What a strange concept! I was just being shy, awe-struck speechless by the vibrant colors of the long robes the Indian and Thai women were wearing. I felt shabby. None of us Chinese women had such luxurious floor-length robes for bed but our bare-thread underwear. Out of bed, we just put our street clothes back on.

And growing up in Mao's terror of Cultural Revolution, we learned to steel our faces to hide our feelings. We didn't smile or greet, especially strangers. "Never forget the class warfare," Mao's words were chiseled deep into our young brains. Children were taught to report their parents if they uttered any disrespectful words toward Mao the god. Students were turned into violent Red Guards, who beat, humiliated, tortured, and killed their teachers, as well as their parents, too, if they were classified as enemy of the people. Wives were forced to divorce their husbands. And neighbors were instructed to spy on one another. No trust existed among human beings.

When our airplane touched down American soil, I felt a strange rush of happiness. On the way to Concordia College, I caught myself smiling back at our bus driver, a young black man. But quickly my mind jolted me awoke from my happy trance. What dangerous reckless behavior! I scolded myself and forced my eyes to look away from the man's friendly smiling face.

A severe jet lag from the thirteen-and-a-half hours of flight struck me down. It knocked me into bed shivering with a fever, a splitting headache and upset stomach.

"Do you need to go to the bathroom?" one curly haired lady volunteer asked me.

"Bathroom?" Why did I need to take a bath? I shook my head, confused.

For three days, I lay in bed miserable, missing the orientation lectures. For years to come, I've always wondered if I'd fare better as a disheartened American public-school teacher, had I not missed the important lecture about how a public school board worked!

Everything in the Concordia dorm room had a brain-piercing foreign odor. I couldn't describe it. The bed, the desks, and even the paper all smelled strange. I was hungry but couldn't eat the attractive looking little triangular sandwiches cleverly tooth-picked together. As beautiful as those tiny pieces of artwork sandwiches looked, they tasted bland. The only food remotely familiar was canned mushy green beans. How I missed a steamy bowl of my own handmade pasta spicy hot soup with vinegar, red chili peppers, fresh green onions, and cilantro.

I kicked myself for having missed the first day tour of New York City, especially visiting of blue-collar, working-class homes.

"Even black people have green lawns in front of their apartments!" My teammates came back beaming excited. We were an ignorant bunch and knew nothing about modern American life and the wonderful results of the equality of race brought by Dr. Martin Luther King's civil rights movement.

I listened to my fascinated teammates describing what they saw inside the ordinary American homes: large cushy super comfy couches, big color TVs, multiple-burner gas or electric stoves, clean and comfortable sit-on toilets, shower heads above a huge, white porcelain bathtub. Wow! Even common Americans had a higher living standard than the top two percent of the authoritarian Chinese Communist leaders!

On the 4th day, I finally felt well enough to enjoy the team touring New York City. How amazing there were so many tall buildings covered in shiny glass. I thought of the paper-pasted windows in my childhood village and small grime covered glass windows in my blue-collar dirt yard. China was a life of dark and gloom, America, a life of shining luxury and comfort. Two opposite worlds. And, as I looked at a forest of national flags from all over the world, I suddenly realized that China was not the center of the world, as we'd been taught, and as its name said: "the centered kingdom" 中國.

I spotted a policeman standing around the corner between two skyscrapers. His blue uniform looked so dignified and handsome. I raised my camera to take a picture of him, carefully focusing because each photo was expensive. Then I saw something unbelievable: The officer was blushing! American policemen had normal human feelings? I grew up fearing Chinese police. Their faces steely, they carried batons and guns, broke into homes in the middle of the night to arrest, beat, and kill. Here in America, the policeman acted shy like a normal human being! America is kind and beautiful.

"You guys, quick!" one of our teammates ahead of us called out. "There's a Chinese man from Taiwan. He's the owner of that grocery store." Really? We wanted to see what he looked like. The Party had told us that people in Chiang Kai-shek's nationalists Taiwan government were all evil monsters.

We rushed into the store but saw no monster but an ordinary looking man like one of us. He spoke accented Chinese, very polite and friendly, joking and laughing with us.

Walking around New York City, we were all impressed how clean the streets were. It was cleaner even than Beijing, which was much cleaner than my dusty city of Taiyuan, where there were no streets lined with trees, plants or colorful flowers. In comparison, New York City looked like an immaculate garden city. We saw no sticky gooey spitting or littered trash on the smoothly paved streets and sidewalks.

"Actually, midtown New York City is infamous for its crowded dirty streets," Our guide told us. Really? Then, how amazingly clean was the rest of America?

I couldn't wait to learn about the rural town of Pendleton, Oregon, where I was assigned to spend my 1986-87 school year.

"Are there cowboys in Pendleton?" I asked around at our farewell party. My question made people smile and chuckle. Why? Well, I'd find out for myself, they said to me, smiling mysteriously, looking amused. Another mystery!

In front of the headquarters of American Field Service (AFS) in New York. The American lady in sunglasses was an AFS volunteer coordinator. This was a thrilling day!

Chapter 60

Pendleton, Oregon

寧靜恬美的澎德頓市·俄勒岡州

MY 1986-87 SCHOOL YEAR in Pendleton, Oregon turned out to be the happiest time of my life. It was a beautiful, endearing town with 15,000 population, full of smiles, laughter and friendliness. People would call out to one another: "Have fun!" How I loved the sound of it. The life I had in China was never about fun but pain, tears, sweat, starvation, sardine-packed buses and carrying grain sacks or people on our bicycles.

Pendleton looked so peaceful. It was therapeutic to my mind and heart. Everywhere I looked, the streets were clean. No dust twirling up in the air or dirt blowing in the wind or garbage strewn at your feet. How did Americans keep their places so clean and free of littering garbage, spit, and mud puddles? I marveled, writing to my friends back home in China.

I also wondered: "Where are the people?" The streets were empty in Pendleton. Well built and maintained beautiful houses sat quietly in bright sunshine, surrounded by manicured green lawns, flowers and neatly cut shrubs. My "medium-sized" dusty home city of Taiyuan had two-and-a-half million inhabitants, where life was like constant struggling inside a giant bowl of thick porridge every day, while Pendleton, a quiet, clean, clear-water pond.

America was still baby-young, unlike the ancient five-thousand-year old China that has accumulated a great misery of overpopulation.

"Why are American teenage girls encouraged to give birth?" I asked the government official when my master teacher, Mr. Wimberly took me to visit the state capital of Oregon. I was worried that toddler-aged America would have the same disastrous population explosion as decaying grandfather-aged China.

"Well, you can't call it encouraging," the poised gentleman politician corrected me. "We can't just let the newborn babies starve to death. The teen moms don't have the financial means to take care of their babies. They need help, and we have to be humane."

How amazing, I thought, Americans' kindness was to protect human life, the opposite of China's harsh and brutal way toward life. But where do you draw the line? China had crowded living conditions. Did Americans even have the slightest idea how the Chinese people are covered with stinking sweat dust all day long, and their nostrils pitch black? It'd be too late when Americans started elbow-shoving their way through crowds on a daily basis!

13-year-old son of my first host family laughed his little heart out about me.

When having my very first can of Coca Cola, I popped the tab off in wrong direction, the can remained unopen. And, when trying to use the spray bottle to wipe the table, I mistakenly pointed in wrong direction and sprayed it all over my face! The teenager laughed hysterically, telling it to a visiting neighbor while I sat on the same couch. Their spoken English was in a high-flying speed. I couldn't catch half of it. But from the way they looked at me, I understood enough to know they were laughing at me.

By the time I left Pendleton in the summer of 1987, people told me how impressed they were about my spoken English and listening ability. You sound just like one of us locals, they flattered me. Indeed, I felt greatly accomplished being able to keep up with the normal speed of daily English conversations.

Everything in Pendleton fascinated me. I took more than a thousand photos and wrote eleven notebooks of diaries.

"Look! A dog's riding in the truck!" I was beyond excited, pointing it out to Mr. Wimberly, who was driving me back to my host family after school. In China, cars didn't even exist for *people*, not to mention *dogs*! Every city in China was a crowded sea of bicycle riders. Mr. Wimberly chuckled, looking greatly amused.

Mr. Robert Wimberly, my Master Teacher, and I, at the Pendleton School District office, holding a special Chinese banner of 友誼-Friendship, specially hand-embroidered from No. 5 Secondary School, the top elite college-bound high school in Taiyuan, Shanxi where I taught.

Fortunate Pendleton people drove everywhere, even just a couple of blocks to buy groceries. Then they'd pay money to lift weights in the gym, and pay more money to have someone else tell them what or how much they should eat to stay physically fit.

"Why won't you just hand-carry your groceries home to keep your arms and legs strong and save the money?" I asked a church group when I was giving a talk, my curious mind in overdrive.

"Oh, Jing, please stop embarrassing us!" Bonnie, an outstanding kindergarten teacher, giggled, in forgiving spirit. I had no idea what a rich world Americans lived in comparison to the bleak world I came from.

The atmosphere of gaiety and cheerfulness in Pendleton uplifted my spirits like their bright and colorful clothing.

"Look at the colorful clothes these American adults are wearing." I wrote in my diary. "In China, if a woman over thirty wears bright red clothes, she was deemed flirty and slutty. Women over forty were supposed to wear only dark blue, gray, and black. How depressing my Chinese culture is!"

Watching Pendleton folks square dancing and modern dancing was another source of joy. I admired the way these Americans looked so relaxed. They moved their bodies so freely in fun and happiness. How frigid my Chinese culture was. In my world, adults who sang and danced were professionals on stages for the masses to watch. Everyday people didn't dance. The Party forbade the Western dances in China. It warned us that twisting our bodies around was indecent and would corrupt our Marxist ideology. But look how America has remained the top of the world despite their "corrupting" dance moves!

My side of the world didn't make sense to me.

And I found American kindness heart touching.

Mrs. Judy Anderson and her third-grade class handmade me a beautiful queen-sized bright red floral (my favorite color) quilt! My second host family, Dr. and Mrs. Brandt, included me into their family circle in celebration of Christmas, my first. Mrs. Brandt even went out of her way to sew me an elegant dress. "This girl's waist is really long," she teased while tape-measuring me. Her sweet loving way and joyful sense of humor was so refreshing, and her loving kindness, precious. I felt special.

My first Christmas with Dr. Dale and Mrs. Barbara Brandt in their home.

Dr. and Mrs. Rosenquist, my third host family, held a grand birthday party for me. At age 31, it was the first time someone was celebrating my birthday. Smiles and laughter filled their spacious house. And I received tons of presents.

At the party, my friends Annette, ShirleyAnn, Beth, Lee, and Judy surprised everyone with their delightful performance. It gifted me with an everlasting memory. They lined up in the yard, all dressed in shiny black garbage bags and wearing white paper-plate masks with a picture of monkey. (I was born in the year of the Monkey.) Then they rapped and sang: "Little monkeys were still learning their A, B, C's but Jing's already talking about getting her Ph. D!"

My Pendleton friends surprised me with a lovely "Monkey Birthday!" So fun!

My biggest birthday gift surprise came from Dr. Rosenquist, the school psychologist, who was famous for his great sense of humor. His practical joke scared the wits out of me but also cured me of my fear of policemen.

A young, tall and handsome Oregon state trooper knocked on the door. He asked to speak to Jing Li. I immediately tensed up, fearing the worst. My face burning, my heart pumping wildly, I stood dumfounded. Not until the officer, who must have felt pity on me, broke into a cheerful smile, apologizing profusely, did my heart drop back in place.

*Dr. Rosenquist and the Oregon young trooper
– the special prankster for my birthday!*

He tried to deny it but Dr. Rosenquist had been planning his prank ever since his amusing discovery of my fear of the police. One day he was driving me and a couple of other teachers back from visiting school in the nearby town of Milton Freewater. A state trooper stopped us for some minor problem, something about the signaling light but I didn't understand their calm conversation exchange.

"Is he going to imprison us?" I whispered to Dr. Rosenquist, shrinking in the back seat. "I don't know, maybe," he whispered back to me with a straight face, rolling his eyes upward, looking helpless, shaking his head, his face innocent!

Dr. and Mrs. Rosenquist, my 3rd host family, introduced me to America's amazing 31-Flavors ice cream. Ice cream was my daughter's favorite. It became one of my powerful motivations to get my daughter to live in America, even just for the amazing ice cream alone!

My American culture shock was sometimes embarrassing.

"That's the advantage of being fat," I seriously complimented Mrs. Wimberly, when she one day told about how she'd taken a fall that could've broken her leg. I was baffled when my "compliment" caused her to burst into hysterical giggling and laughter. In Chinese culture, calling someone "fat" was flattering in admiration. For people in China had been starving into skin and bones for the past one hundred plus years!

And how I appreciated the honor when I was featured in the *East Oregonian* newspaper. A reporter came to Pendleton high school library and interviewed me twice and published two lengthy articles with large frontpage photos of me. "The college students in China know about Mark Twain!" the first story said. And in the spring of 1987, the front full page showed me cooking my handmade pot stickers. I was wearing the elegant dress Mrs. Brandt had made for me. Twenty years later, the *East Oregonian* interviewed me again at the home of Dr. and Mrs. Brandt when I went back to visit endearing Pendleton.

My most fulfilling experiences during my year in Pendleton were the many talks I was invited to give at various local community groups: the Kiwanis Club, the Rotary Club, the Lion's Club, and all the local churches. Smiles, cheers and laughter from the audience pearl-stringed my days and heightened my spirit.

Time again had turned its hands back to my happy memory in my early-childhood giggling and laughing with my loving grandfather and blind great-grandfather, my morale cheerleaders. Now it felt so natural having my lovely American friends roaring with laughter at my observations of their wonderful American life through my Chinese eyes.

"Americans definitely have more freedom," I'd start cracking. "You place knives on the dinner table and tell the eater to cut up their own meat any way they want, whereas we Chinese manhandled and micromanaged every vegetable stalk into bite sizes!"

The Lion's Club members laughed with me when I told them how I'd talked the police officer out of ticketing my overnight host family, newlyweds Bruce and Tammy at his parents' home in Seattle, Washington. Bruce and Tammy were giving me a special American treat by teaching me how to drive when a policeman stopped us. "I've always admired wonderful American policemen," I started chiming in as the officer was inquiring to my hosts. "I think you are very handsome in your uniform." I meant it. The police officer looked amused. Bruce and Tammy were relieved they didn't get a ticket. Dr. Brandt told me that I was voted the funniest speaker of the year!

The highest honor I received during my 1986-87 teacher-exchange year was being accepted as a member of the Delta Kappa Gamma Society International for key women educators. And, I was given the high honor of hosting a workshop with my motivational speech at their Oregon state convention in Ashland. That was where I met Dr. Edythe Leupp, the state president, a highly accomplished educator. She was to play a pivotal role in helping me come back to America two years later in 1989.

My 1986-87 school year in Pendleton was a delightful whirlwind of enlightening experiences in education, culture and language with fun activities. During the daytime, I visited school classrooms, teaching little kids to write Chinese characters: 中國, China, and talking to middle- and high-school kids about Chinese culture and history. In the evenings, I taught cooking classes to high school students and community families. And over the weekend, people invited me to their homes for me to cook my handmade Chinese pot stickers and stir-fried vegetable dishes. People loved my cooking so much there was a long waiting list. My eggplant-with-fresh-tomatoes dish even converted fifteen-year-old Matthew, a self-claimed eggplant hater. I tricked him into eating my eggplant dish. He solemnly proclaimed his love for it. Then I told him the truth. He got mad at me by making a scene later during my presentation in his class. I deserved it.

When I was not teaching, talking or cooking, I buried my nose in books. How I appreciated the rare opportunities to read and learn from an unlimited books in Pendleton High School library. I was grateful to finally have the access to read and learn, which didn't exist and forbidden in communist China. Everything about Chinese and world history before 1949 had been condemned by the Party as evil.

Now I finally learned the truth about who, what, why, and how of World War II.

With so many enlightening books for my brain, I felt like a fish released back in water. I was greatly baffled when a teacher asked me why I liked reading so much! And I was shocked when a few plump and physically well-nourished high school students said to me, "It's boring!" about the film we just saw in class during the WWII, where FDR Stalin and Churchill met. Wow! Why? Americans didn't like learning about truth? In China, truth seekers and truth tellers were imprisoned, tortured and murdered!

From reading, I learned that Americans were not heartless evil imperialists, as we were taught in school by the Party but very kind. I admired Americans' forgiving spirit toward their fellow countrymen of the Confederate soldiers — they were all set free to go back home and live their normal lives after losing the Civil War. I immediately become disgusted with brutal Mao. After the Chinese Communists won the civil war, they slaughtered and murdered and imprisoned thousands upon thousands of surrendered nationalist soldiers, including their wives and kids – guilty by birth or mere association!

Oregon's governor Vic Atiheh cooking pancakes at Pendleton's annual rodeo Let'er Buck! *Wow, I couldn't believe it that such a down-to-earth nice man was the state's highest official. He was so approachable just like a common folk, so different from the Chinese Communist authoritarian leaders.*

End of Part Three

Part Four

My Odyssey in America 奮鬥紮根在美國

Chapter 61

Frog at the Bottom of the Well

井底之蛙

JUNE OF 1987 arrived too soon.

My international exchange teaching year was over. Time for me to go back to China. I was sad. I could've stayed in America by accepting the invitation to teach at Phoenix High School in Medford, Oregon. But I couldn't. Vic and our daughter were being held as collateral back home.

Sitting in the darkened airplane, I was wide awake with snoring people around. My heart was mixed, happy I was finally going to see my daughter after one year, but with a great sense of loss having to leave wonderful America behind.

I thought of the little frog in the Chinese proverb. It lived at the bottom of a well and was convinced that the sky was only as big as what it could see from the bottom. Now I was to live like that little ignorant frog back in my old life after my eye-opening adventure finding out how vast, wide, bright, fun, happy and exciting the world beyond China was.

Airport. Beijing, China.

I burst into tears at the sight of my daughter, two months shy of six years of age, standing by her father, her hand in his. Her head tilted to the side, she smiled shyly looking up at me. I scooped her up into my arms and buried my teary face into her plump cheeks for a long, greedy kiss. I'd lost another year in her young life.

My heart sank when her little hands pushed my face away, furiously wiping away her cheeks. When I tried to caress her plump little arm, "mommy's little turnip," she pushed my hands away, squirming and twisting in my arms. A familiar sharp pain stung my heart. Two years before, she pushed my face away as I triumphantly returned from Beijing earning my B.A. degree.

"Isn't it grand that I bought us the refrigerator and big color TV?" I said to Vic, feeling good about myself. They were superior quality made in Japan, hottest commodity in China. I'd saved all of my fortune of $60 monthly stipend from the AFS to buy both.

"Humm." a nasal sound only, his face flat, in Chinese manly "dignity." My heart hurt.

On my first day back to my teaching at No. 5 Secondary School, I was promptly warned by the Party: "You didn't hear or see anything in America. Keep quiet."

I felt suffocated, my brain confined, my spirit withering. I wasn't allowed to talk about the wonderful things in America. I wanted to go back to America. I missed the wonderland full of books, friendship, smiles and laughter. I wanted a better future for my daughter, I told Vic about it. He didn't like my "naive talking."

"Mommy," my daughter said to me. "America doesn't want you anymore."

"If you try to stop me," I warned Vic. "A divorce will be inevitable."

"Why would America want you?" my mother scoffed, looking at me sideways. "What are *you* good for America?"

My grandmother especially didn't like me talking about leaving China again. At age seventy-five, she was counting on me to live out her old days in comfort. Her spoiled son, my father, wasn't even nice to her. He yelled at her every day and once shoved her head into the sharp rough cement edge above the kitchen sink. Her eldest daughter, my aunt Da Gu, lived in another faraway city. The mother and daughter never got along anyway. She'd been living with my family. My childhood memory of her being abusive to me was still deeply buried in me. It didn't come back until two decades later when I started writing my memoir.

"My child," Grandmother tried sweet-talking me. "You got the top best of everything in the world. Why won't you settle down and enjoy your good life?" I said no. She then showed me her true color: "You s.o.b.! China too small for you? If I didn't have these useless bound feet, I'd walk to the city hall and sue you for family desertion!"

"How can you laugh about such a vicious threat?" Vic surprised me when I told him about Grandmother's toothless rant.

My mind was made up. I was too hungry for learning and too thirsty for knowledge. I wasn't willing to exist like an ignorant frog at the bottom of well. I needed to live in America to salvage my mind, spirit and soul. I wrote to Dr. Leupp and friends in Pendleton. I wanted to earn my doctorate degree. Dr. Leupp said she'd be happy to host me in her home in Oklahoma, where she was a professor at Southern Nazarene University.

It took me two years to go through the red tape and finally get my passport approved.

"Why do you always want to go back to rotten decadent America?" one school official shouted at me. He was nicknamed behind his back "Party Thug." And he lectured me: "If it weren't for the meddling Americans, China wouldn't have been in such chaos wanting so-called democracy!" I bit my lips, swallowing my tears from the insults.

And the public security police were slow-walking me through the passport procedures. On my bicycle, I made countless trips back and forth. Okay, bring your photo tomorrow. Nope, the photo wasn't the standard size. Now your photo is in wrong color. Come back next week. Okay, bring your household registration card. What, your birthday in lunar month, instead of solar calendar? Go to the city hall and change it . . .

In the meantime, I had to bribe a key Party leader in the city's planning department, not with money but my priceless skills of teaching the English language. Over a whole year worth of weekends, I went to his office to translate his book, which he brought back from America, a college admission handbook. It had a hot market for young people like me who wanted to study as graduate students in America. I also had to tutor English two afternoons a week to his boss's son and his fiancée so they could come to America, too.

It was now May of 1989. All over China, there were uprisings. People from all walks of life had been taking to the streets, shouting slogans and demanding the government grant them free speech and democracy.

In the back of my head, I told myself to be cautious participating in the movement. My name could be put on the blacklist and I'd be stopped at the airport, handcuffed and imprisoned. For China was still under the iron rule of brutal Communism. I didn't believe the totalitarian government would give up their power peacefully. "Power comes out of the barrels of guns," Mao had declared. Just as I feared, and as the world watched, the Chinese Communist government massacred thousands of demonstrating students with tanks, canons and guns on June 4th of 1989.

I also had to continue to fight Vic, trying to make him see my point why I should return to America, a wondrous paradise — America had all-you-can-drink and all-you-can-use crystal clear clean and safe tap water; America's outdoor air was so sweet, clean and fresh your nostrils would never become pitch black dirty; America had amazing 31 flavors of ice cream, our daughter's favorite. And a can of fruit was only 45 cents while in China it cost five Chinese dollars while my salary was thirty-seven a month!

"I need to go back to America to give our daughter a bright future," I said to Vic.

"Well, that's too far down the road. She's only eight."

"But it takes time, at least several years, to go through the American immigration process!" I was losing my patience.

"But people in my work unit had been laughing at me! What kind of man let his wife going alone all over the world? They said. First, you were gone for two years in Beijing for your B.A. degree. You just came back from America after a year," Vic complained. He made it sound like I was doing something shameful. Wouldn't any man wish they had a winner wife like me? "Hmm." His nasal sound again.

"We have to make necessary sacrifices," I kept trying to convince Vic. "No pain, no gain! We can pretend the worst that I'll be sentenced into prison for several years. We have to be separated anyway. For our bright future, it's worth it, especially for our daughter. Can't you see, this one-in-lifetime opportunity is really here, in my hand, now! Don't you know how many high-ranking government officials would love to take my place if their offspring possessed my English skills? And you're just going to let it slip through our fingers and wasted?"

Vic kept sighing, shaking his head.

"Fine!" I lost it. "I'm warning you that I will divorce you if you even think about messing it up for me! And I mean it." Vic became quiet. Slouching on the couch, he went into deep thinking, his eyes cast down, his face serious. For days, I gave Vic the cold shoulder, elbowing him away if he tried to get close to me.

"Old woman, you awake?" Vic whispered in the dark one night. I ignored him. I hated when he called me that. Our daughter was sound asleep between us in our family wooden bed. Each of us slept under our own cotton-padded futon, a typical family sleeping arrangement in China.

"Okay, for our daughter's future, you can go ahead and pioneer in America," Vic whispered. "There's no future for us in China."

"I knew you'd come around!" I shrieked, my head popping off the pillow.

"Shhh . . ." Vic hissed, turning to cover our daughter's ears with his hands.

Smashing my hands over my mouth, I collapsed back down onto my pillow, my heart pumping in joy. I whispered my promise to him that I'd work my darn hardest to make our family's American dream come true. Yes! Our daughter was going to eat America's wondrous 31-flavored ice cream!

Friends in Oregon pitched in and sent me my airplane ticket on a United flight. Leaving home in Taiyuan to Beijing airport, I was overcome with guilt. Holding my daughter in my arms, I sobbed uncontrollably. How long was it going to take me before I saw her again this time?

"Close your frog's mouth!" my eight-year-old daughter teased me, her adorable face so serious it was amusing. I broke out laughing in tears. My baby's sense of humor took after me, and her calm demeanor, her father. A best combination in personality.

"Why the tears?" my mother frowned at me. She'd come to care for my daughter for a few days before Vic came back from Beijing after seeing me off. "It's your own choosing. Stick to what you set out to do."

Why couldn't I feel sad, too? I didn't understand my mother.

Vic and I didn't say a word to each other on the hour-long taxi ride to the airport in Beijing. His face remained dark and motionless. His severe case of insecurity was taking the best of him. I hated that he never trusted me. I never gave him any reason not to.

"Here's some breakfast for you," Vic's friend who came along with us brought some pancakes for me. I was thankful, my heart stuffed with sadness.

A stranger was more considerate than my own husband.

Chapter 62

Hardest Part of a 10,000-Mile Journey Is the First Step

最艱難第一步

MY COMING BACK to America the second time turned out not as rosy as the first time. I was no longer the exotic novelty representing China, but a financial burden, like a helpless adult child depending on my professor and sponsor, Dr. Leupp. Worse, I was an emotional wreck from missing my daughter. Gone was my former witty self – the person who'd proudly won the nodding approval and praising smiles from Dr. Leupp the president of Delta Kappa Gamma International when she sat in the audience, enjoying my motivational speech at the Oregon state convention two years before.

"How was your day?" Dr. Leupp asked me one day.

"I miss my daughter terribly," I immediately turned into a whimpering teary mess.

"Well, Jing, that's your own problem," Dr. Leupp responded matter-of-factly. "Nobody is going to deal with it for you."

Wrapped in my own misery, I failed to show my appreciation to Dr. Leupp and Tom, her loving husband, a good-natured gentleman, who was once a distinguished mayor in Colorado. They both had taken up a great deal of trouble, inconvenience, time and effort driving me around, picking me up, on top of paying three thousand dollars for my master's degree.

I was such an emotional mess that I once even tried to argue unwittingly with Dr. Leupp. She said Sundays were solely for worshipping and resting. "That might be fine if people could afford not to work," I naively blurted out. She promptly shot me a sharp look of disgust.

Dr. Leupp tried to fund-raise to help pay for my graduate program but it didn't come to fruition. Mr. Leupp one day announced that if I couldn't earn my master's degree by May 20, 1990, I'd have to go back to China. I was devastated. How would that even be possible? I was over one month late, arriving on September 26, 1989. Right away I jumped to study, also working twenty hours a week in the university library to help pay for my tuition. With language and cultural difficulties, it didn't seem to be possible for me to complete the thirty-two graduate credit courses within seven-and-a-half months.

I pleaded with Dr. Leupp to please give me some extra time. Had any American-born college grad ever earned a master's degree in seven-and-a-half months, on top of working twenty hours a week? How could I, then, a newly arrived foreigner?

"Everyone has their own situations," Dr. Leupp said, coolly.

I was crushed. Worse, in the meantime, I had to fend off my family in China. They all came at me trying to persuade me to give up and return home.

"Who do you think you are?" Aunt Da Gu, middle younger sister of my father, wrote me. "Many China's famous movie stars couldn't even make it in America. They all came back after years of washing dishes in Chinese restaurants." She was resentful I wasn't in China taking care of my grandmother, her own mother. Neither she nor her brother, my father, the legal heir of the Li's, was willing to fulfill their filial duty to let their mother, my grandmother, live with them in their homes.

"Are you out of your mind?" my father wrote to me. "How can you depend on a seventy-year-old stranger woman and lower yourself doing the demeaning library job?"

"Just what's your true intention?" my mother questioned me. "I had a heart-to-heart talk with Vic, like my own son. I feel sorry for him. You have your leisurely fun and freedom on the other side of the earth while leaving him take care of your daughter alone. Don't you have a heart?"

I was now more determined than ever to prove my so-called family wrong. I was going to make it. At all costs. Watch me earning my master's degree in seven-and-a-half months! I simply couldn't afford to throw away this golden opportunity. And I had no way back. No. 5 Secondary School had already confiscated my apartment before I left because I insisted on coming back to America. My bridges had been burned.

I used every waking moment to study, from the crack of dawn to late at night. My chest hurt as if it were being sawed every breath I took. It was a repeat of my first-year teaching at No. 5 Secondary School. But no matter. I couldn't afford to give up. No time for breaks. Every extra minute counted. Once I had to decline an invitation from Tracy, my classmate, to have Thanksgiving dinner with her family.

For the first semester, I completed twelve credit courses; for the winter break, two; and for the second semester, the remaining sixteen. With the two graduate-course credits I'd earned back in Pendleton from Portland University, I beat the deadline!

On May 20, 1990, seven and a half months after my arrival, I walked across the stage and claimed my master's degree in education with a GPA of over 3.6. My classmates cheered the loudest for me in the audience!

At my master's graduation with Dr. Edythe Leupp and her (late) husband Tom Leupp

With my master's, I was now legally eligible to seek employment in America.

I thanked the Leupp's and moved out of their home, voluntarily freeing Dr. Leupp of her five-year legal obligation as my sponsor. I went to sublet my classmate Sheila's brother's apartment on SNU campus for $150 a month, as he was out of the country on summer vacation. For the next entire three months, I worked mostly double shifts of sixteen hours a day, seven days a week, as a nurses' aide across from the campus. Bathing, weighing, trachea-suctioning, and diapering bedridden children, I was tireless.

"You are either broke, or you don't have a life," my coworker said to me, smiling.

"Both," I said quietly. I told no one how much I actually appreciated the privilege of working, feeling thrilled going over and over in my head the fortune of $80 I earned from just one double shift! It was all worth my lost sleep.

Starting from scratch, working hard was the only way for me to make it in America. After work, I'd ride my bicycle, a gift from a friend at Our Lord's Community Church, to buy my groceries. To save every penny possible, I made my own sandwiches to take to work for lunch every day. The tomatoes made my sandwiches soggy but I loved eating my mushy sandwiches in between those long double shifts.

I needed to find a teaching job soon so I could establish my permanent residency in America and accomplish my goal and fulfill my promise to bring my daughter and husband to America. The Oklahoma community wouldn't even let me babysit their children. My best chance was to "flock with my own kind" by living close to a Chinese American community.

I needed to go to California, where my "own people" dwelled.

Chapter 63

Coming to Flock in San Francisco

風雨獨立舊金山

ONE LATE OCTOBER DAY, 1990.

I got off the bus at San Francisco Greyhound Bus Depot, two suitcases in my hands, filled with clothes and books, my entire worldly possessions.

Where was Mr. Song? What did he look like? He was my only connection in this vast brand-new strange world. A teacher friend in Oregon had given me Mr. Song' phone number and told me, chuckling amusingly, he was a defector from the Chinese consulate.

Inside the high-ceilinged Greyhound bus station, I felt like a speck of dust. Crowds around me looked all sure of themselves, rushing in and out. I struggled to drag both of my suitcases to the wall-sized front windows overlooking the busy street.

That must be Mr. Song! I spotted a Chinese man in his 30's standing on the sidewalk by a red car. He was looking up, smiling, waving at me, motioning me to come down to him. It had to be him!

"Excuse me, sir?" I turned to stop a short stocky young man of Latin origin, who was passing by me pushing a long flatbed cart. "Can you please help me with my luggage downstairs to the sidewalk?" He seemed to want to say something first to me but didn't and helped me down to the street curb.

"Thank you! Thank you, sir . . ." I thanked him profusely, in words, unaware that I was supposed to tip him with money. His eyes full of pity and disappointment, he turned to push his flatbed cart away without a word. Growing up in Communist China, I'd never heard of tipping for service.

Mr. Song explained to me apologetically that he couldn't come inside to help me, because he could only stop his car at the curb for a few minutes. Wow, San Francisco sounds so different from Oregon and Oklahoma. He drove me to his apartment on Larkin Street in the Tenderloin district, where he lived with his wife and their young child. "Why," Mrs. Song exclaimed in a scolding smile. "You still wear an old fashioned cheap electronic wristwatch!" She cooked me a bowl of Ramen noodles. It brought out my tears of gratitude. They kept rolling down my face and dropping into my soup bowl.

After the heartwarming delicious Ramen noodles, Mr. Song drove to drop me off at a residential building a few blocks away on the same Larkin Street. "This is the cheapest place I can find. It's a transitional place for Chinese graduate students coming from and back to China." He didn't come inside. I didn't see him for the next four years.

I found myself in a large bare-walled room on the second floor. There was no other furniture but a dozen single beds crammed all over. One electric light hung from the ceiling. The wooden floor was worn-out, sticky and thick with dark grime. The only toilet in the bathroom was stained yellow dirty, nose-piercingly smelly.

Back in Oklahoma in Dr. Leupp's mansion-like house for the past year, I had my own bedroom, cushy, comfy, bright and clean, with my own large bathroom with shower.

Hey, stop thinking of something that wasn't yours, I scolded myself.

The only bed available in the vast room was in the middle of the floor, on a passage to and from the bathroom and entrance and exit door. I crashed onto the hard bed, tired and stiff, my spirit down below zero. Now that I was free, completely on my own, I felt so lost and alone, feeling like a kite flying aimlessly in the sky with a broken string. I forgot all about what I'd just achieved in seven and a half months. And it didn't occur to me I should send my photo on the stage receiving my master's degree from Mr. Graham, the president of SNU, to my daughter and husband, or anyone from my Li family.

All I felt was despair. *What in the world are you doing here*, a voice in my head criticized me. Give up and go home. The first time in my life, I was thinking of quitting.

I missed my daughter unbearably. It'd been a year. She was eight when I left. I only got to talk to her once, five minutes, during the winter semester break alone in Dr. Leupp's empty house in Oklahoma after she and her husband left for vacation. After they came back, Dr. Leupp showed me the whopping $18 phone bill and asked me to pay. Luckily, I had $20, my net worth, when I got on the airplane in China.

After a restless night in San Francisco, my dog-stubborn spirit kicked back in full gear. I had to continue on. No quitting! I had to give this new life one more try.

I started reading through the job ads in both the local Chinese newspapers. There were mostly waitressing jobs outside the City. Then I spotted a hiring ad that was exactly for me: good English and Chinese language skills needed at Attorney Stanley's law office in Chinatown. Yes! I went for an interview. I was hired on the spot!

My roommates, a dozen of them, were amazed beyond belief how quickly I'd found an office desk job. "How did you do it after just one interview?" They asked me. Well, I didn't think it was a big deal, only a legal assistant job. The interview was in English. I was asked to solve some simple math problems. That was all.

Two weeks into my job, the law office wanted to send me to their San Jose branch. I said thank you but no – I haven't even gotten a chance to see what San Francisco looked like! The relocation wasn't worth it because I really needed to find a teaching job if I wanted to stay in America and bring my family over.

The young woman manager, an American-born Chinese (ABC), lectured me: "*You* want to be a teacher in America? Which one of us do you think hasn't tried, yet? What makes you think Americans need a *native* Chinese like you to teach their kids?"

I hadn't yet tried.

I started looking at teaching job ads in English newspaper, the *San Francisco Chronicle*. Found one! A preschool teaching job. Again, I was hired on the spot when I went for an interview. It was in West Oakland across the Bay Bridge from the City at St Vincent's Day Home.

I celebrated my good fortune at the McDonald's in Chinatown at the corner of Grant Ave and California Street. I had an order of small French fries and Coca Cola. My feast. I skipped the hamburger. I needed to save the extra dollar and share with my daughter the remaining luxury when she came to America.

It would take four unbearably long years to get my green card. And another whole year going through papers to finally clear the hurdles so my daughter could live in America. Pioneering alone in America was a pure torture to a mother's heart. I wouldn't wish such separation on any other mother.

"It's not in a woman's place to leave her family and try to make it in another country," a woman acquaintance said to me. How could I describe my life in China to this privileged American? How could I make her understand how it feels to stand in a dirt yard surrounded by trash and coal dust and dream of a better life? How could I explain that improving my education was the ticket to get my family out of a grist mill of few opportunities and physical as well as mental poverty? She had no idea. She could go back to her well-heated apartment, cook on her four-burner stove with temperature controlled oven, store food in her lighted refrigerator, drop coins in the automatic washer and dryer and go to bed with a full stomach. Never mind. It's a fool's errand.

Sometimes I would make tapes and tell my daughter about San Francisco, the Golden Gate Bridge, how someday soon she would be running barefoot on the clean beaches and see big sea birds up close. I would tell her how much I missed her and how I was working hard, studying and saving money so I could bring both her and her dad to America. Later, I was to find out that Vic never played the tapes I made for her. He said that being a single parent he never had the time.

Watching the preschool kids at St. Vincent's Day Home napping, snacking and eating their lunch made my heart weep, longing to see my own child. A thousand times a day, I wondered how my own flesh and blood was doing on the other side of the earth while attending to other mothers' children. Little Donna and Steven's crying would trigger me into high anxiety. I cried with them, my tears running down my face.

For five years in America, I didn't have the heart to touch one bite of ice cream because it was my daughter's favorite. Every time I saw a girl of my daughter's age, my heart would start trembling with pain. I'd fix my teary eyes on the young girl till she was long gone out of my sight. For my daughter's bright future, I played by the "no pain, no gain" golden rule. But I had no words to make my young daughter understand her mother's "pain", sacrifice and guilt.

Telephone calls to China cost five dollars a minute. Back home we didn't have a phone. You had to be a Communist Party member with a ranked official position to have a phone at home. My husband had to walk a mile with our daughter to his office or bother the next-building neighbor, a privileged government official.

My daughter's pre-adolescent years were formed with her mother being the chocolate-candy packages from the post office and a trembling, weeping voice crying her name over and over on the phone once a year.

"Just when are you going to get the green card?" Vic questioned me. "People are laughing at me." My Ph. D geophysicist husband needed more comfort than I did.

Sister Corrine, the kind-hearted director at St. Vincent's Day Home, helped me every step of the way to file my immigration papers. I was so touched that I started thinking my miraculous survival life.

It no longer seemed coincidence but special Divine Intervention.

I thought of the days in Oklahoma when I was under the crushing pressure racing with time, risking my health to earn my master's degree in seven and a half months. A friendly young couple John (Caucasian) and Wendy (Chinese) on campus befriended me. They insisted on praying for me, their hands on my shoulders. But I couldn't see how some mere words spoken into the air could help me, if I couldn't help myself.

John and Wendy kept praying for me. It must have worked. I couldn't have possibly made it on my own this far without miracles from Heaven. And I thought of my Oregon friends, they were all Christians with caring and loving spirit.

I, too, wanted to get to know Jesus, God of my wonderful Christian friends. I asked Sister Corrine if I could join her Wednesday evening Bible study group. I was warmly welcomed. She went out of her way giving my rides. From there I learned to ask for God's help and guidance by praying. And each time I prayed, my troubled heart calmed. When I listened to soothing gospel music, I felt peace in my whole being. It was a sense of belonging I'd never felt before. With Jesus God on my side, I now had an all-time friend, confidant, guidance counselor and the nurturing father I never had but always wanted for advice, counseling, comfort, and peace.

"But you're a Catholic, not a real Christian," a woman acquaintance looked at me like I was a $3 bill. Huh? Did she believe in different Jesus?

Humans. Why do we always complicate things?

For five years, I lived in a small one-room studio on Polk Street, San Francisco's "ghetto" Tenderloin neighborhood, sharing the toilets and showers down the hall with a dozen other women. It was the cheapest rent I could find: $295 a month, still a much better living condition than where I had come from. It was the unkempt noisy people who sprawled over on the sidewalk under my apartment window that made me feel uneasy.

One day, I had to call the police to my apartment because I'd been getting obscene phone calls. "Well, take it or leave it," one of the two police officers snapped at me because I couldn't stop crying and being hysterical. "Just like nobody asked you to come to San Francisco, you can also move out on your own if you can't handle it."

From the way the officers were sizing up my room, I realized how embarrassingly shabby it must be. A thin, worn-out green blanket I bought for $2.50 covered the caved-in, queen-size mattress. A sunken-in armchair was the only other furniture by the rectangular iron shelf stand against the wall. My tiny frying pan for 25 cents was sitting on the stove, where a few daring cockroaches were scurrying around. The pretty, dark blue plastic drinking cup I'd paid fifty cents for was the only bright centerpiece on the scrawny little linoleum brown table in the corner of the room by the narrow closet door.

"You rice gobbler. Go back to your rice paddy!" a dirty-haired man in greasy clothes slouching on a bench on Market Street yelled at me. I'd just gotten off BART train at the Civic Center station. The hatred in the man's voice made me shudder with fear. As I pretended not to hear him and walked on by, he showered me with more profanities.

"Aren't you scared of living in a place like this?" Nancy, my colleague, wasn't impressed with the homeless people scattered on the sidewalk under my studio window. But I had my own carpeted, furnished room with a stove for cooking, a luxury to me.

My preschool teaching job paid me $500 twice a month. I made sure the first $500 go into my savings account and then budgeted around the second $500 for my entire monthly spending. After paying my $295 rent and sending $50 a month to Vic and my daughter in China, I gave myself a strict spending rule: $20 a week for food, clothes, and whatever else I needed. No going out to eat. No movies. No shopping in department stores but from the Salvation Army store across the street. I actually received compliments for the way I was dressed.

I cooked all my meals. Growing up an abused child cooking for my parents and two younger brothers turned out to be a blessing in disguise. And, every day, I walked one mile to take the BART to work and another mile after BART. The $32 MUNI bus pass was just too much money on unnecessary comfort and convenience.

"Have you ever utilized any public assistance?" my Immigration form asked.

"Have I? I do take the public transportation. Does that count?" I was confused.

"No, they mean the welfare service," my immigration lawyer cleared it up for me.

No, I'd never even thought about asking for help or borrowed a penny.

My penny-pinching living style wasn't even up to the standard of the homeless. One evening, as I came out of the grocery store at the corner of the Bush Street at Larkin, a ragged looking old homeless man walked up to me pushing a shopping cart. He stretched out his hand to me. Having been dearly loved by my peasant grandfather in my childhood, I always felt sympathetic toward elderly men living a hard-luck life. I dropped into his hand all I had, three pennies I'd just saved from walking four extra blocks for a gallon of milk. But the old man stared at the three pennies frowning, shaking his head in disbelief as he walked off, mumbling.

"Sorry, it isn't much," I murmured my apology.

One weekend, I passed by a young man in his twenties. He was standing against the wall, leaning on a crutch outside the XXX-rated building on O'Farrell at Polk Street.

"Spare some change?" he called out to me. I couldn't help but amazed by his relaxed manner and self-assurance. He didn't sound embarrassed at all for being a street beggar at such a prime working age! And he looked well-fed, glowing with good health. His clothes were clean and neat. It was his bandaged left foot that called out for my sympathy. I stopped to take out of my pocket the plastic grocery bag I kept my coins in, embarrassed for taking too long to tackle the tight knot. Finally, I fished out a quarter and proudly placed it into the young man's open palm. "It's okay," he said, looking away. *Why did he suddenly look more embarrassed than I?* I wondered as I walked on.

"You're welcome to borrow my bus pass to ride around San Francisco," the building manager, Mr. Han kindly offered, taking pity on me for staying in my room all day over the weekends. "It'll ease your sadness from homesick." He and his wife were both white-collar engineers when in China. His wife was now working as a live-in nanny.

But I couldn't afford any leisurely time. I needed every minute to study and pass the California teachers' credential test. Besides trying to read extensively to broaden my knowledge, I also practiced my reading speed watching *Jeopardy!* on the flickering thirteen-inch, black-and-white TV someone had discarded in the hallway by the garbage chute. I needed to get a teaching job in San Francisco's public schools. I missed the real academic classroom teaching, and also needed to double my $12,000, yearly salary so life would be much easier after Vic and our daughter came to America.

I was so grateful to America's forgiving spirit. It was liberating. I could take the California teaching credential tests as many times as I wanted to. On my first try, I passed the math section. On my second try, I passed the reading part. And after two more tries, I finally passed my writing test. Whew! It was a brain-transforming experience.

Growing up, we were taught to obey, follow and be ready to give our lives like obedient soldiers, wherever the Party pointed its guns to. Now in America, my mind immediately went blank at the sight of the critical-thinking test question: "Write about one rule that you didn't like and argue why."

Rules were made to follow. How should I argue against that? My brain froze.

"That's the easiest!" exclaimed Sister Adrianne, the assistant director at the St. Vincent Day Home. She couldn't understand how I failed an easy question.

"Ha, ha, ha! God does miracles!" I wrote on the envelope of my passing-score notice for my teaching-credential in 1993. I laughed and cried till I was out of breath and collapsed in joy. My friend Cecelia baked me a delicious cake to celebrate. Both of us were studying for the test while attending early childhood education classes together at Oakland Laney College. We, along with a few others, all wanted to move on for better paid teaching jobs in the public-school system.

I beat American-born college graduates to it?

My low self-confidence went up a notch.

Chapter 64

Family Reunion — Swimming Upstream

團圓後的艱辛

ARMED WITH MY California Teaching Credential, I went to San Francisco Unified School District office. "You're not qualified," a Chinese woman in the personnel office told me, speaking with a thick Cantonese accent. "because you don't speak Cantonese."

What utter nonsense! I was shocked speechless. Cantonese was not the official Chinese language, but one of the hundreds of dialects in China. I myself spoke a couple of my own dialects! It was all about politics. Many Cantonese-speaking Chinese in San Francisco were mostly from Hong Kong. They had families, relatives who'd suffered under the brutal Communism. So, naturally, they indiscriminately looked down and despised all newcomers from mainland Communist China.

I started checking job ads in The San Francisco Chronicle. A brand-new charter school was hiring! Dr. Haynes, the principal, hired me on the spot. The 21st-Century Academy elementary school was English only. I didn't even need to speak Cantonese dialect. It was vindicating. I didn't mind at all the school was located in San Francisco's rough Bayview-Hunters' Point neighborhood.

"We don't want no Chinks to teach our kids!" Two women "welcomed" me on my first day of school, their arms crossed over their chests, standing by with the crowd.

I loved what the principal said: Be color-blind when it comes to our students. And once again, my natural born teaching ability shone through. Five of my second graders scored above the 90th percentile on their CTBS math and reading. Little Billy scored 99 percent on his math!

"She's a racist!" A group of angry black women parents said about me. Why only one African American girl among the top five? And she was "light-skinned?"

Many parents put their kids on the waiting list for my next year's second-grade class. Sadly, it wasn't going to happen. By the end of the school year of 1994, our loved principal, Dr. Haynes, was harassed away and the entire wonderful faculty was dispersed. The school district administrators had been angry with Dr. Haynes, who refused to hire the district's existing tenured teachers but academically qualified outsiders like me.

It was the worst timing for me to be unemployed.

In the summer of 1994, after five years of crying for my daughter, I was finally approved of my self-worth to America as a dependable taxpayer. The Immigration and Naturalization Service granted me a green card based on my master's degree and my employment as a teacher.

"Mommy!" my daughter cried out in joy, running out of the San Francisco Airport terminal. She leapt into my open arms just like when she was little. How much she'd grown! I was almost knocked down backwards to the shiny floor. I'd missed so much in my baby's life. She was twelve going on thirteen. Holding her in my arms, I sobbed a mother's guilt, while Vic looked on, smiling shyly, quiet and overwhelmed.

No hugging or touching between husband and wife, as usual. He and I just looked at each other. I felt like an awkward stranger. I knew if I hadn't brought Vic to America, too, I'd never see my daughter again.

Just like before, I resumed my role of cooking, cleaning, and shopping.

Frantically, I looked for a teaching job all over San Francisco Bay Area, hitching rides with other laid-off teachers in my school. I hadn't learned to drive, yet.

My one-room studio apartment on Polk Street was full of stress. Vic needed me to interpret and translate for him to start his geophysics career. I also needed to teach our daughter some basic English vocabulary words to prepare her for upcoming school. Vic was thinking of quitting and going back to China, where he was in high-demand as a geologist.

By the end of the stressful summer, Heaven smiled at me.

After running all over the Bay Area school district looking for a teaching job, I was suddenly and miraculously hired on the spot inside the city of San Francisco!

The miracle came out of another twist of fate.

One day, an Asian guy in the school district employment office treated me rudely. I complained to his boss, who gifted me with an insider information. Mission High School of San Francisco was looking for an ESL and Mandarin Chinese language teacher. Perfect!

I called Mission High and puffed up a, "Yes!" to Nadine the secretary when she asked me if I had a teaching credential. Well, I did have years of top-of-the-world experiences of teaching English in China and four years of teaching young kids in America. I was hired on the spot.

"Amazing! How did you just turn around and find a high school teaching job?" My classmates in San Francisco State University's teachers' credential program were impressed. Shortly, Vic, too, was also hired by a university as a research scientist.

But trouble was far from over.

Presidio middle school in the neighborhood refused to enroll my daughter. "We would gladly accept her," the school office told me, "even if your family were new Russian immigrants. It's just that our school has too many Chinese students already. It's against San Francisco school district's racial-quota."

"Mom," my sad-eye daughter said. "Why doesn't America want me to go to school?" I had no answer for my child. For two weeks, she was left home alone, while I fought on the phone every day during my prep time at Mission High.

"Is this how you welcome my new immigrant family?" I argued with Diane, the director of student service. "We moved all the way across the City from the Tenderloin just to live in this nice, quiet Outer Richmond neighborhood so we could get our daughter in a good school."

Finally, the woman at the school office slipped out a gaming-the-system secret to me on the phone: If my daughter was in any way "handicapped," the Presidio Middle School had to take her in. It was the law, she said.

Yes! Of course! My daughter had indeed suffered motion sickness on the 13-hour flight on the airplane from China. She'd also suffered car sickness when riding on the 38 MUNI Bus. I knew now just what to do! I took my daughter to see a doctor in the nearest location on

Geary Blvd at 8th Ave. I paid $36 and showed Dr. Lew my daughter's motion-sickness pills from China. She gave me her medical expert diagnosis with a To-Whom-It-May-Concern referral letter.

"So," the woman's sour-grapes voice on the phone said to me. "Your daughter will not be allowed to go on any field trips on a school bus, since she suffers from a motion-sickness, right?"

Whatever. As long as my daughter was finally in the good neighborhood school, not the bad one that the school district was trying to hustle. I'd visited that school once, where a used tampon was among other strewn trash on the floor in the dusty hallway!

"Ms. Li, I admired your perseverance and feisty spirit fighting for your daughter," the director of student service told me after the dust settled. I felt lost for words, not knowing how to respond to her 180-degree attitude change. Why? How strange!

Eventually, Vic and I were proud parents. Barely one year after she came to America, our daughter spoke English without a trace of a foreign accent. People thought she was born in America! She was to go on to college, a proud Dean-list student, and an MBA graduate with scholarship from a famous university.

It was all worth my sacrifice. I helped my daughter escape the vicious Chinese culture of female infanticide. China today has a surplus 30 million men, who will never have a wife or girlfriend.

In the meantime, our family life was a five-year upstream swim in emotional turmoil and frustrations.

Vic and I resumed our previous married life from China. Our intellectual connections were strong as usual. He enjoyed my cooking, a wifely duty. But I remained hungry for any of his acknowledgement or compliment. It was nonexistence. There was no emotional connections between us. No heart-to-heart talk. No physical intimacy or any casual touch on a hand or a shoulder.

I failed to realize the severe damage the five-year separation had caused on our mother-daughter relationship. I was indignant when my therapist warned me that my now-13-year-old daughter would regard me as a stranger. "How can a mother ever forget what her own child is like?"

And worse, I underestimated Vic's insecurity, despite his prestigious scientist status at the university. Among three of us, it was always two against one. I was the one. I felt like a caged animal. But I didn't have the heart to walk out for my freedom. I owed my daughter too much. I had to hold my breath waiting for my daughter to turn eighteen.

There were some happy moments. All three of us enjoyed watching our favorite TV sitcom *Married with Children*, and *Home Improvement*. And before the dissolving of our marriage that had been glued together by nothing but parental duty and responsibilities, we also managed to achieve our American dream of homeownership.

Chapter 65

Twilight Zone in Amazing America

美國公立學校哈哈鏡

A tale of two teaching careers
One in paradise.
One in hell.
Paradise took place in bleak China where I was born.
Hell occurred in amazing America's Twilight Zone.

1979-89, BACK IN CHINA, I taught the brightest of the bright, the most disciplined and most motivated high school seniors, who demanded and achieved academic excellence. My classroom was so quiet you could hear a pin drop. My students rose to greet me and waited for my permission to be seated at the beginning of class, the same way as American courtrooms respect their judge. My students achieved above ninety percentile on their *gao-kao* 高考 – China's nationwide grilling college entrance exams. My students respected me, their parents were grateful to me, my principal and the society honored me.

1993 – 2013 saw me spiraling into the hellish Twilight Zone in amazing *mei-guo* 美國 America – a food paradise, land of smiles and laughter, material abundance and comfort, fresh air, clear blue sky, and bright golden sunshine.

Naively, I expected to repeat my on-top-of-the-world teaching career. For, you see, lovely America also sent the first man to the moon. It must have the world's best public schools, right?

I found myself in a beautiful mansion with a leaking foundation.

One of my 2nd grade students told me: "Ms. Li, my mother said if you lay your hands on me again (I once tried to pull her up from the floor, by her hands, during her tantrum in class time), I will slap you across face! And, my mom also said you shouldn't give me homework for the weekend. Weekends are for fun and relaxing!" I took it seriously and never again tried to stop her tantrum on the floor but the mother came to my classroom one day and body-slammed me anyway.

Another of my 2nd grade students would yell, "Leave me alone!" as he habitually got out of his seat to wander in class. "I can do anything I want! I can be anything I want to!" The boy's grandmother came to school and slapped me in front of the principal. She said I shouldn't have yelled at her good boy grandson.

And, another of my 2nd graders wouldn't stand up to pledge allegiance. "Because we are Muslims. My mom said I shouldn't stand because we don't agree with the American flag." One mid-morning, the mom came bursting into my quiet class during my teaching time. "I'm just visiting," she flashed me a loud smile, walking over to my desk, holding an infant in her arms and hollering at two toddlers hanging onto her shirt and pant legs.

When five of my twenty-three 2nd graders in San Francisco's tough neighborhood school scored above 90th percentile in reading and math on their California standard tests, some parents decided I was a racist. "Why are there only one light-skinned African American girl?" Some of these parents had "welcomed" me on the first day of school: "We don't want no chinks to teach our kids!"

I felt like a servant with three out-of-control masters: my entitled students, their rough parents and inept administrators.

After one year teaching the 2nd grade, I moved on to teach high school.

One of my high school students threatened to beat my "bitch ass up" after I told him to stop horsing around and sit back down in his seat.

And it took only two weeks for a well-mannered new immigrant teenager from the Philippines to adapt himself into a "gangster" mode in my ESL class. He changed from "Yes, Ma'am/No, Ma'am," to not doing his homework, talking back, putting his feet up on his desk, grinning, looking around and pretending not to hear me when I told him to behave.

First day of one school year, forty-three teenagers came to my Mandarin Chinese class. Word got out that Ms. Li was a caring teacher. My classroom was already crowded with thirty-five desk chairs. Some students stood by the walls or sat on the windowsill as I called roll.

"Ms. Li!" A security guard poked his head in. "Your students have to be seated. No students should stand. It's against the law."

"Would you please ask the principal to bring me extra desk-chairs?"

"Oh, that's not my job."

One high school parent lectured me, "Don't you bring your boring strict Chinese way of teaching into American classrooms!" She insisted that I allow her teenage child to continue counting on her fingers like a preschooler. I was teaching my students mental math in Mandarin Chinese.

Many of my adult-sized teenage students still acted like rambunctious toddlers. They seemed to have never been trained to sit still, quietly or pay attention.

一年之季在於春，一天之計在於晨：*The most important season of the year is spring; the most important part of the day is morning.* But 8:00 am was too early for many of my students. By 8:30 am, half of my classroom was still empty. They'd trickle in, sleepy eyed, dragging their feet, a cup of $3.50 Starbucks coffee in hand.

Instead of educating the students about the importance of being on time as a moral code the society required, some parents went to the school board, proclaiming that tardiness was not a disciplinary issue. There was a lot of talk that season, even in San Francisco newspapers, about how tough it was for teenagers to come to school at such ungodly early hour. Teenagers needed extra sleep, so school should start at 9 or even 10 o'clock!

"Why do you even bother to get frustrated at all?" Mrs. Ma, my friend in Beijing, wrote back to me. "So what, your American students are not disciplined or motivated to learn? You still earn your salary, right? These kids are not your own flesh and blood. Let them become illiterate as they wish. If I were you, I'd concentrate on making those grand American dollars. Do you have any idea how many millions of people in China would love to be in your shoes?"

Yeah, but my unfulfilling teaching job was killing me inside.

Instead of academic excellence, school was about political correctness!

In the name of equality, each of my five American high school classes was crammed from wall to wall with thirty to thirty-five or more teenagers. Their academic backgrounds, performance and ability gapped from 0 – 100. Some were shy and well-sheltered at home, others already hardened street law breakers with a juvenile record and court-appointed probation officer. And some teen girls were already mothers!

And to top it off, there were several special needs students "inclusion-ed." They couldn't function without one-on-one emotional or physical support. But I was the only teacher! And the only help I got from their designated special ed teachers was a piece of paper once per semester – a list of jargons about what these teenagers were diagnosed with.

I felt like a chef being forced to cook multiple dishes of hamburgers, hot dogs, pizza, fried chicken, chow-mein, burritos, tacos, pita bread, etc. with one cooking pan, at the same time, and on a single stove top!

To survive, I adapted into playing multiple roles in my classroom: a security guard, nurse, babysitter, counselor, friend, mother, sister, and lastly, academic instructor.

This delusional equality created nothing but chaotic diversity. It destroyed efficient classroom teaching. It was impossible for any traditional whole class teaching. Well, for that, San Francisco public schools already had a band-aid-on-cancer solution – Cooperative Learning Groups!

Teachers divided each class into small groups. One good student was appointed as the group leader. Viola! Shifted onto the kid's tender shoulders were the adult teacher's responsibilities to teach. The teacher was now a democratic "facilitator," who walked around in class to make sure each group was on correct page numbers. This same moronic practice even included math classes!

Hannah, a 12th grader, burst out sobbing one day in my class.

"Hannah, what's wrong?" I had to stop my teaching to investigate.

"I'm getting an F in my biology class," Hannah finally told me between sobbing. "I did my work for my group project, but my three partners didn't do theirs. My teacher said I was the leader of the group and should be punished just the same. It's so not fair!"

My heart broke for this bright, hardworking and straight-A student.

America's public schools were dumbing down bright kids by killing their incentive to excel and trapping them in mediocrity, while the lowest denominator would never be able or willing to catch up.

Children are born with different abilities, like our five fingers of various lengths, strengths and functions. To force a clear-cut academic outcome is ignorant and cruel. Not every child can, should, or will be an academic high achiever. Walks of life need talented people with various expertise, just like a luscious garden full of colorful variety.

Very few public-school teachers sent their own children to public schools to be academically wasted. For decades now, America's students have been at the bottom of the world when competing with their international counterparts in reading and math.

Such a twisted sense of equality was also imposed on public-school teachers. But, just like in George Orwell's *Animal Farm*, some were more equal than others.

Each teacher was given one free work hour a day, regardless how overworked or idled they were. The overworked teachers, like me, taught 150-175 students a day, up to three subjects and grade levels. A Special Ed teacher had five or fewer kids in their room all day every day! And no pink slip layoff crises would apply to these special teachers.

It disgusted me to the core that totalitarian Communist China's "elite cadre" system was alive and kicking in American public schools. Special favors and privileges were granted to a chosen few. If a teacher was appointed as the head of a department, which wasn't, by the way, based on academic qualifications, they were given an extra free hour a day! Angelica, one of my students, would laugh and scoff, telling me that her English teacher, a Department Head, "couldn't spell right."

At the end of each semester, I'd be overwhelmed, grading my 175 students' work, calculating each of their scores, recording each of their grades by hand into my class book, entering the data into the computer, and turning original hard copies in person to the administrators' office before the deadline.

It always annoyed the hell out of me, sweating and toiling away, when I'd hear leisurely chatting in cheerful voices outside. Some "more equal ones" had few papers or tests to grade but plenty of time to stroll around looking for conversations to pass time.

It frazzled my brain cells that my American public-school classroom was not set up for quiet academic teaching and learning. A typical teaching day was filled with appalling interruptions, on top of constant disruptions by entitled and unruly students.

The telephone in my classroom was mounted by the door. Every time it rang, I had to drop everything and dash across the room to answer it. But often times they turned out to be: "Hi, just checking. Is so and so in your class today?" Or simply a prank call. The overhead loudspeaker would blast out non-teaching non-academic announcements in the middle of class, such as, "Attention, color war tomorrow! Sophomores, wear green!"

出了狼窝，又如虎口 – *Escaping the wolf's den, running straight into the tiger's cave.* It was like reliving the horror of Mao's Cultural Revolution in my growing-up years: Wailing loudspeakers shouted out the Party's slogans. Hysterical screaming pierced into people's shabby dwellings, through the thin walls, flimsy wooden doors, and paint peeling and grime-covered windows.

"Ha Ha!" Autumn, one of my homeroom students laughed out loud, pointing at me: "Ms. Li is the most stressed-out teacher!"

In China, a full-time high school teacher was like a college professor in America: teaching two or three classes a day. The rest of the day was for preparing lessons, grading students' papers for necessary feedback – what they learned or failed to learn and why.

But a full-time American public high school teacher teaches five (!) classes a day.

No time to think. No time to work on students' work and give them feedback. No time to prepare lessons. Not even time for bathroom breaks. Thursdays were the hardest with block-schedules. All day long, I was inside my classroom teaching back-to-back classes.

To adapt, I either avoided drinking water, dried out my kidneys or wore my special "Thursday pants": beltless, button-less, just an elastic waist band to save a few precious seconds rushing to and from the crowded bathroom down the hall.

Instead of an academic instructor, I felt like a hired day labor hand, or an over-loaded mule, or the donkey in my childhood village – with its eyes blindfolded, it walked all day in circles, pulling the huge stone cylinder to grind dried corn kernels into flour.

"Teachers," A radio talk show host (by the name of Tom Sullivan) was on the air one day as I was driving my car. "Don't complain you don't get respect or bigger paycheck. Can you sell your T-shirt by the thousands like famous athletes do? No? Well, then, until you do, you don't deserve either!"

Smart America didn't seem to understand that academics, not sports, should be the essence of school education. And society needs good teachers to help colleges produce pillar citizens with indispensable special skills: doctors, nurses, scientists, engineers, lawyers, etc.

Academic excellence cannot be like a cup of noodles—add hot water and stir. Instant results. An excellent teacher is like aged fine wine: It takes years to refine teaching skills.

十年樹木，百年樹人 — *It takes ten years to grow a forest, and 100 years to turn out high skilled productive citizens.*

San Francisco's public-school superintendent got paid $400,000 a year, ten times more than a regular classroom teacher. Classroom teachers were constantly told there was no money to buy paper, pencils or blackboard erasers. Yet, there was always special hefty budget set aside for luxuries, such as, expensive red leather chairs in the principal's office. A half-dozen teachers were once paid, $500 per head, for a three-day-weekend trip to Calistoga resort to supposedly work on some lesson plans but came back with no plans but a video showing them sitting around bonfire having fun, chatting and laughing!

For twelve years, I stayed in my stuffy, smelly, dusty, rat-infested classroom, stifling hot in the summer and chilling cold in the winter. The classrooms were built in 1965 for little kids – low windowsills, low drinking fountains, small cafeteria and narrow hallways – now they were crammed with full-sized American teenagers.

One day, a daring little mouse ventured out in the middle of my quiet class time. It sniffed around the garbage can in front of the blackboard. My class exploded in excitement. Girls jumped up on their seats, shrieking, while the boys whooped and hollered. I rushed over to trap the pest under my shoe. It must have looked like the *Mulan* movie scene: the giant horse kicking up a storm of dust stomping on the little skinny red dragon.

"Don't kill it!" my students shouted at me.

Too late. My full body weight on my foot, I pressed down hard. Creepy gross! It felt like stepping on a piece of raw chicken wing.

"Ah, man, Ms. Li, you're cruel!" Some boys looked disgusted.

Amazing. Americans have become so soft they even pity a germ-infested rodent!

Just like the mouse I crushed under my shoes, my teaching spirit was killed. I felt like a second-hand shoe salesman catering to fashion-prone American teenagers, exhausted inside out, facing daily collective blank facial expressions, their bright young eyes filled not with sparkling curiosity or desire to learn, but yawning tears of boredom.

It reminded me of a WWII story I once read.

A group of Jewish men with high IQ's were rounded up in a Nazi Concentration Camp. They were ordered to shovel a mountainous pile of sand from spot A to spot B. Back and forth, back and forth, all day long, day in and day out. They were not told the purpose of their work. Soon, slowly, one by one, these men went out of their minds.

It was a cruel experiment – to see how long a meaningless and purposeless job could drive a healthy, intelligent mind insane.

I felt like one of the prisoners.

Chapter 66

Lost Battles and a War

恰似竹籃打水一場空

TWO YEARS INTO LIVING in America, Vic and I saw a For-Sale sign on a brand-new building in the neighborhood, four blocks from where we were renting. I fell in love with the gorgeous top-floor penthouse condo, also the cheapest of the three-unit luxury-looking building by a rag-to-riches Chinese businessman. I fell head-over-heels with the American kitchen with its granite counters, the marble and hardwood floors and with the views of Golden Gate Bridge and downtown San Francisco! I counted nine water faucets altogether inside and on the two huge decks. I got goosebumps. Water, the scarce precious life source I had lacked as a child, where drinking water was as scarce as cooking oil, flowed from golden faucets practically everywhere.

"You're crazy," Vic scoffed at me. "You always act like a naive child. How can you even think about owning real estate. It costs over a quarter-million-dollars! Get real."

No. I wouldn't give up.

"We'd like to buy the penthouse condo. Who should we talk to?" I asked the man the next day, as Vic and I walked by the building again. He must be someone in charge, standing at the open garage door, directing the workers sweeping the garage floor and hosing the sidewalk.

"Oh, talk to me." He was Mr. Chi Chac, the owner's real-estate agent, who probably chuckled himself to death – I'd just saved him a three-thousand-dollar commission fee his company otherwise would have had to pay to the buyer's agent. As a buyer, I didn't know that I was entitled to have someone to represent me.

I insisted that Vic come along with me to the real-estate office for the negotiation. I was confident only because of the $10,000 I managed to squirrel away during my three years of teaching preschool. Other than saving money, I understood nothing about the real estate business, except one thing: as a woman, I would never stand a chance of getting a deal from the Chinese owned real-estate company. I needed a man, preferably my husband, to accompany me for the negotiation.

Vic and I entered the real estate office. Mr. Chi Chac stood up and shook hands with Vic. After sitting down at the table, I did all the talking. Vic sat in silence, his face gloomy, his arms crossed over his chest. He was angry with me for making him come along. When the bargaining talk was over, the agent stood up and reached over across the table to shake hands with Vic again, ignoring me. Well, no matter. I managed to knock down the asking price by $20,000. The seller even threw in a brand-new 6-foot-tall, two-door refrigerator, on top of a brand-new large microwave. 1996 was a buyers' market.

That's how I became a mortgaged homeowner in outrageously expensive San Francisco, solely based on my teacher's salary.

I knew I had to be ready to give up my gorgeous penthouse condo to get out of my dead marriage. But for now, I needed to keep myself handcuffed to my five-year plan, for the sake of my daughter. My heart was laden with too much guilt. I'd missed too many years in her young life. I had to wait for her to turn the legal age of eighteen before I dashed for my freedom.

My mind was further made up after I heard about Sue's story, who was a teacher colleague of mine. Sue told me about her mother's abrupt leaving of her father. "Why couldn't she have waited for me to turn eighteen so I could take care of my younger siblings and our father?" Sue complained. She said her anger and resentment toward her mother cost her years of psychotherapy.

Oh, no, I didn't want to be like Sue's mother. I didn't want to hurt my daughter like that.

Soon, *The Bridges of Madison County*, played by Meryl Streep and Clint Eastwood, comforted my conscience, as the wife in the movie didn't abandon her husband and children for her own love life.

As a child, I didn't know why my mother didn't love me. She only loved my two younger brothers. Her silent eyes and angry face made my heart tremble every time she looked at me.

Holding my newborn baby daughter, I vowed to love her.

"You just go ahead and love her," my mother once sneered during my dreaded Maiden Homecoming, looking over her shoulder. She was cooking at the brick stove by the door in the bare-walled two-room apartment I grew up in. I was sitting in the make-shift armchair bouncing my month-old daughter in my lap, cooing to her my self-made nursery rhymes. "She's going to curse you and break your heart when she grows up. Just you wait." My mother's words hit me like bullets.

I don't believe you! I shouted at my mother in my head, feeling helpless, my face burning in anger and fear. She apparently hadn't forgotten how I once yelled at her when I was a teenager in front of gawking spectating neighbors as she was hitting me with an iron fire poker: "Why don't you crawl under the quilt and sleep with your lover Mr. Hu!"

That'll never happen to me! Unlike you, I love my daughter with all my heart and will always love her. I'm a much better mother than you!

For five long years, I pioneered in America alone, missing my daughter, crying myself to sleep at night, and holding myself together in my daytime preschool job taking care of other mothers' children. Determined to create a bright future for my daughter, I counted down the days until my daughter could join me.

I wanted my daughter to eat America's amazing 31-flavors of ice cream; to live in America so she could take a warm bath at home instead of walking one mile to the public bathhouse in the scorching sun, freezing cold or howling wind; to walk on America's clean well-paved sidewalks instead of the dusty, garbage strewn and spit-covered streets in China; to breathe America's lung-cleansing fresh air instead of getting pitch black nostrils from China's thick smog that blocked the sun and darkened the sky. I wanted her to enjoy America's bright golden sunshine and beautiful clear blue sky; to drink America's clean safe water directly out of a water faucet whenever she's thirsty without having to boil it first to kill the germs; to be nourished by America's safe clean food instead of mostly poison-contaminated food for the masses in China while only the elite government ruling class ate clean and safe food grown in specially roped off land. I wanted her to live with assurance that no American hospital would kick her out to die on the sidewalk if she ever had to spend her last penny on hospital bills.

In my eagerness to provide my daughter with a better material life in America, I failed to see the obvious fact that she'd grown up without me from age eight to thirteen, embraced by her father's easy-going and indulgent parenting.

Some weeks back I had been indignant when my psychotherapist advised me that after five years of separation, my thirteen-year-old would consider me a stranger. Now my serious flaws of a quick temper, impatience, demand for perfection, task-oriented go-go-go rush, self-imposed high pressure came to the fore and my daughter and I began to clash.

I didn't give the therapist a chance to help me. I dropped the doctor after Vic ridiculed me in disgust. "What stupidity," he scoffed. "How can you even think about seeing a psychologist?"

"Mom, slow down!" my daughter once called out to me. We were walking back home from shopping in the neighborhood Ross store. "What's the rush?"

Oh, I didn't even know I was rushing.

"Stop getting so upset about nothing. It's irritating," she said to me another day, as I groaned impatiently, putting myself down for not fishing out my key fast enough to open the door. Oh, my goodness. I didn't even know I had such rampant anxiety.

"Who rushes people out of the bathroom?" my daughter yelled one day. I kept urging her to hurry for our family shopping trip.

Good Heavens. How insensitive I must have been in my daughter's eyes.

"Wow." She was once wide-eyed surprised, watching me take clothes out of the dryer. "You and I do have something in common! You take out the laundry the same way I do."

Oh, dear God. I had indeed become a stranger in my own child's eyes.

So ill-prepared emotionally, I didn't know how to love my teenage daughter. My family had never shown me an example.

I never understood why my daughter would become angry, covering her ears, turning her face away and yelling, *No!* every time I wanted her to take a picture with me. And, the more I begged her, the angrier she'd get.

The only way I knew how to love my daughter was to provide her with material things.

What a proud mother I was when my daughter got her own bedroom and bathroom.

A workaholic myself, I didn't want my daughter to do any chores at home. A self-taught creative gourmet cook, I never bothered to teach her those skills. I wanted her to concentrate her time and energy on her schoolwork. I even bribed her with $20 for each "A" grade she earned.

The center chair at the table was reserved for her. The first bite of food, and the first dish was always for her, then for her father, then me. I enjoyed cleaning up her plate and eating her leftover food, just like when she was a baby. I made sure breakfast was always ready on the table, but sadly she rarely had time to eat because she couldn't get out of bed early enough and needed to rush to school. Sometimes I had to drive her two blocks around the corner to her school so she wouldn't be late for class!

I wanted to give my daughter everything I never had in my growing up years. I even went with her to the SPCA, against her father's warning and my own inexperience, to let her adopt a cat. She named the cat Diana and happily petted and fussed over her. It was adorable.

How sad I became when I soon found myself standing in front of my daughter's closed door. Her grand American public school taught her in no-time the concept of "privacy," a foreign thing in Chinese culture. I wasn't allowed to enter her room.

She'd even become upset if I went into her bathroom to clean her cat's litterbox when she herself neglected to do it. But I couldn't stand the piled-up cat feces and continued to clean even after I developed an asthmatic allergy to cats.

Frustrated, I'd warn her if she didn't take responsibility to clean after her cat, I'd return the cat to the SPCA. But I never had the heart to hurt her. She saw through my empty threats. The cat stayed. I wheezed.

Late one night, the cat soiled the area rug. While my daughter and her father rested, I couldn't stand the mess and took the rug out to wash in the neighborhood laundromat. Feeling so alone and lonely, I shed angry tears. No love in my touch-less and kiss-less marriage to nourish me, body and soul, but only duties and responsibilities while working as a full-time battle-fatigued public high school teacher.

I exploded and yelled at my daughter.

"That's not the right attitude to treat our child!" Vic yelled at me.

"You bastard," I hissed at him, declaring my plan for the millionth time. "Keep meddling. I'll divorce you the morning she turns eighteen!"

"Please apologize to your mom," he pleaded gently as he brought her out of her room.

"Okay, fine! I'm sorry!" she yelled, her eyes shooting daggers. "I hate you!"

And I hated Vic's passive aggressive sneakiness.

One time my daughter refused to believe that I did not commit the horrible crime of shutting her beloved cat in one of her dresser drawers. She wrote a note and left it around for me to read. "Bitch looked too innocent to be believable." As a child, I hated my father when he blamed me for my mother's neglectful mistake of leaving her bowl outside. When I had refused to apologize, he slapped and kicked me for being stubborn. Too fearful to demand an apology, I vowed to prove to the world that I was an honest person. Now my own daughter accused me of not being honest! My heart twisted in remembered pain.

I was once embarrassed when someone asked me why I didn't come to my daughter's parent-teacher meeting. Only then did I realize that she'd hidden her school notice for Back to School Night. Later I found out she once fibbed to her English teacher in her writing assignment that her mother was "mean" and worked her "like a slave" at home.

Oh, dear God. How miserably I had failed as a mother.

You'd think that Vic would have halted his old habit of psychologically putting me down if he didn't want me to get a divorce, but no, it didn't work that way. If I told him about my bad day from my chaotic public school teaching job, he'd say: "You always mess things up! Why can't you just get along with people?" And if I told him about something good, he'd scoff: "Don't be so cheap to please."

I once tried to cheer him up. He was down, losing his self-confidence as a new immigrant looking for work. "It shouldn't take more than a few months before you are employed," I said to him. "Your outstanding achievements are known in the international field of geophysics."

"So," he snapped at me, "You're going to be held responsible if that doesn't happen!"

I had imported my dysfunctional marriage to America. Malnourished emotionally and in the bedroom, I was a pent-up volcano; Vic, an Arctic iceberg.

Fifteen years into my marriage, I was still secretly wondering what it would feel like to be kissed or have my hand held.

Growing up in Mao's era, love was a dirty word, a shameful desire, and rotten anti-Communism bourgeois. Love stories were banned in China's literature and books. No image of hugging or kissing or any physical embrace existed in everyday life.

Now in the land of smiles and laughter America, I saw loving every day on TV. I saw Americans hug, kiss, embrace, hold hands, I even saw gestures of making love. It ignited my passion and longing for romance and affection. How I longed for a hug, a kiss or even just a casual touch on my back or my arm. But I didn't know how to tell Vic about my desire.

"When we're 80 years old, will you still be too shy and rigid to hold my hand?" I once teased him. We were walking on Clement Street at 6th Avenue going grocery shopping.

"Huh," He simply made a nasal scoff.

My heart withered. I couldn't wait for the day when my daughter turned eighteen.

As long as I diligently did my wifely and motherly duties of cooking, cleaning, washing and buying him clothes, he was content. "I'm so easy to live with," he'd say to me. "If you don't get along with me, quiet and good-natured, you'll never get along with anyone."

True, Vic didn't drink or smoke. And most of the time I was the one who burst with anger. In my daughter's eyes, I must've been an unreasonable witchy bitch fighting with her daddy all the time.

I once made her pay the $3.59 fine out of her allowance, when she ignored my repeated reminders to return the video cassette tape on time that she rented from Blockbuster. And I refused to co-sign a credit card for her, as she said all her friends' mothers did. I told her it was something she had to earn. Most infuriating of all to her, I'd tried to discourage her, an almost straight "A" student, from spending too much time with her best high school girl friend, a "D" and "F" student. Years later, my daughter finally showed me her prom pictures. It turned out that the two best girl friends were dating a pair of tall gorgeous blonde twin brothers in school.

For her high school graduation, I bought my daughter a beautiful burgundy prom dress and black stilettos. But she warned me not to take a peek from our balcony. I only wanted to see what her prom date looked like. She threatened to run away from home if I dared to try. I didn't. I wish I had.

"You abandoned me and came to America for yourself!" my daughter yelled at me one day while her daddy sat quietly by.

I couldn't believe what I'd just heard. Is this why he never let her listen to the audio cassette tapes I had recorded and mailed to them? In the recordings I described my life, the things in America I thought she would enjoy, how much I missed her, loved her, and how I looked forward to her coming to America.

Then it hit me like a windstorm. *In our years apart my daughter had never heard my voice, never understood my sacrifice.* Had he done this on purpose to divide us?

A fury unleashed out of my hot head. I started yelling at them both, calling her a little ungrateful demon, him, an ungrateful bastard. "How can you say I came to America for myself? I did it for you. For both of you! I was the one who saved your life when your tyrannical grandfather—his father—pressured me to have you lethally injected and killed when you were six months old! And do you know where your dear daddy was? He was so scared of his father, he hid behind me, and never dared to speak a single word to protect his newborn baby daughter, YOU!

"Stop talking!" Vic shouted at me. I'd touched the nerve of his hidden shame, the skeleton in his pad-locked closet we lugged from half the world away to America.

I ran into the bathroom and locked myself in. Sitting on the toilet seat, I cried hard. I didn't give a damn if the neighbors heard me. There was no point in saving face. I had no pride left. In the middle of my sobs, I found myself bursting into uncontrollable laughter at the absurdity of my sacrifice, then it changed to a deep keening sound, more animal than human. A tidal wave of tears washed down my face, then the frenzied laughter came back again. What had I done these past years? Why had I sacrificed so much? What did all those years mean if they weren't appreciated?

My aching heart seemed to pierce my lungs and strangle my breath. I went on like a crazed woman for over two hours, ignoring Vic's knock on the bathroom door, pleading with me to stop crying in his calm, low voice.

The next morning, eyelids puffed up and swollen, I carried on cooking and cleaning, while swallowing my silent tears of despair. No one spoke. Vic acted like everything was fine.

My guilt-ridden heart and blind love for my daughter forced me to carry on. I still wouldn't change my mind even after I came upon my teenage daughter's discarded handwritten note, saying how she'd love to stab my face bloody with a pair of scissors, starting with "bitch's eyeballs."

Vic moved out of California for a better paying job with more benefits and security a year before our daughter's high school graduation. But he didn't tell me his plan until two days before his departure. Why didn't he tell me earlier? I couldn't understand his motive. As soon as she graduated from high school, Vic convinced my daughter to join him.

I followed them 3,000 miles that summer to perform my last commitment of motherly duties. Besides giving Vic $1,500 from our joint tax refund, I bought my daughter a brand-new bedroom set, a cushy bed, bedding, a dresser, a tall mirror.

As usual, I took up cooking in the kitchen and cleaning in the bathroom.

Then came a cataclysmic moment.

I was mopping the kitchen floor one morning after cooking breakfast. Suddenly, I found myself butt-crashing hard onto the wet slippery tile floor. Instead of rushing to help me up, both father and daughter burst out laughing, pointing at me, as if they saw the funniest thing.

My face twisted in pain, my tailbone hurting badly, my heart wept.

"I want a divorce," I told Vic later. I never returned after that summer.

"Who's going to cook, buy clothes for me and take care of me?" were Vic's first words.

"Mom, you'll have to come cook and clean for us," said my daughter.

How sad. I was nothing but a cook and servant in the eyes of my daughter and husband.

"My dad can help pay your mortgage," my daughter said, relaying a message from Vic. *If you didn't start a divorce*, was what she left unsaid.

My mind couldn't be changed.

"You're so selfish!" my daughter yelled at me on the phone," as I warned her to not let Vic come back to me. "All you can think of is yourself! Dad said he's going to kill himself because of you! For days, I've been driving him around to the neighboring cities to comfort him."

But my heart had hardened. In the meantime, a down-spiraling twist was unraveling my beloved teaching career.

Chapter 67

Swan Song

天鹅悲鸣

"THE GOAL OF OUR EDUCATION is Social Justice," said the poster on the outside office door of the assistant principal Mr. Bungler.

Huh?! Schools are not for academic learning? *What is this social justice?* I wondered. Whichever teacher dared to do any injustice to these pampered and entitled students, risked termination.

An elderly Caucasian gentleman was welcomed to campus one day. Beaming, he looked proud as the sponsor to a special week-long Yosemite trip. It was said to promote "social justice." But, only for African American students, and, oddly, boys only!

"Ms. Li, why can't I go to Yosemite?" Kevin, a 15-year-old asked me. His family were immigrants from China. "Why only black boys get to go?" I was at a loss for words, feeling like a coward, not speaking up against such in-your-face unfair officials who were supposed to be fair to all kids.

I found out Ebim in my homeroom was also slated to go on the special trip. No wonder he'd been smiling smugly, as if saying: "I can't believe they included *me,* too!"

Like Kevin, Ebim was also from a new immigrant family, not Chinese, but African. His only qualification for this privileged trip was the same skin color as the other chosen boys. But he had nothing whatsoever to do with being a descendant of African American slaves hundreds of years ago.

And, more outrageously, the trip was scheduled for the mid-semester in April. Most of these "chosen" black students were already lagging far behind academically. Now they were to miss an entire week of schoolwork just for this fun trip!

In totalitarian China, all teachers in my school were made to sit through Tuesday and Friday afternoons listening to the Party leader reading *People's Daily*.

Here in free America, the collective political brainwash in public schools was disguised as "Professional Development."

Every Wednesday, right after lunch, all students were sent home, and teachers were rounded up and made to drop their work at hand to sit through the anything-but-professional nonsense. I could hear my brain cells perish.

On one such "professional development," I learned, with amazement, the shoe size of Mr. W the security guard was 14(!) as Mrs. Mumu, the principal, directed teachers to play various games including Musical Chairs.

Another "professional" Wednesday, an 8-year-old boy walked in, hand in hand, with Mrs. Mumu the principal, who beamed, giggled and introduced the second grader as our "Principal of the Day!" The boy was the sibling to several scarf-headed Muslim girls attending the high school. The roomful of teachers was then told to rise to our feet one by one and introduce ourselves to our child-principal. My chest was bursting with rage, and my head, disgust! It was the same moronic way China's three-year-old Emperor, Pu Yi, was bowed to as a god by thousands of the high court officials, as shown in the movie *Last Emperor*.

Disturbingly humiliating.

Over the years, the political talking points droned on.

"Why are our African American and Latino students getting mostly D's and F's?" principal Mumu, questioned a roomful of exhausted teachers, who draped themselves over their chairs, eyes half closed, while some energetic young ones held their smart phones under the table ready to steal a peek.

"But most of these students have a lot of tardies and absences," I piped up, unable to stand the silent herd mentality pretending to agree with the nonsense. My father had failed to beat down my anti-dumb-authority attitude as a child.

"Tardies and absences have nothing to do with their D's and F's," Mrs. Mumu shushed me. "Teachers, you need to double check what you haven't done correctly."

"Poverty is holding back our African American and Latino students" was another day's talking point for teachers to discuss.

"Isn't it more like a spiritual poverty?" I piped up again, much to the dismay of plump-faced Mrs. Mumu.

I grew up surviving China's famine. American style "poverty" was a luxury in my eyes. My American "below-poverty-level" students were entitled to have a free lunch. But the campus garbage cans were always stuffed with unopened boxes of lunch every day! Boys threw oranges and apples playing baseball games. Some of these "poverty-stricken kids" sneaked off campus to buy pizzas and hamburgers. And many wore $200 Nike shoes and used $300 smart phones. Much better off than most teachers!

Teachers were also sent out to attend all-day "professional" workshops, while substitute teachers were called in to babysit. Taxpayers were double-wham-scammed.

Ms. C, a Spanish teacher, and I once carpooled to famous Standard University, forty miles away. Our all-day workshop was hosted by a young man, who proclaimed his cutting-edge invention: "the new world language." He covered the walls of conference room with his proud creation—giant massive charts covered with alphabetical letters and imaginary symbols that represented neither meaning nor sounds!

"Why would my teenage students be interested in learning this manmade non-sensical language, when they don't even want to learn English?" I couldn't hold my tongue. Chuckles and smiling eyeballs came my way across the room from the audience.

Teachers were also mandated to sit through each other's classes, using their only precious free work hour of the day. What for?? To improve your teaching skills!

I was slated to sit through a Physical Education class.

How the hell could I possibly improve my Mandarin Chinese teaching by watching a PE teacher? Besides, I'd already seen how one PE teacher taught his class when I once passed through the gym. The large heavyset PE teacher sat in the chair by the wall blowing his whistle, and his students ran from one end of the wall to the other.

Grudgingly, I entered the gym to do my time. The young woman PE teacher called roll. The floor was covered with dozens of well- nourished, over-sized and overly plump teenagers. They were all comfortably stretching out flat, rolling around, chatting merrily to one another, giving out a lazy "Here!" when their name was called.

Immediately came into my mind's eye were scores of rollie-mollie fat sea lions at Pier 39, their skin shining, lying cozily on the massive floating wooden boards.

Teaching in San Francisco public schools thrust me back into my childhood turmoil of growing up in a world of contradictions.

I caught Sheila using her cell phone in my homeroom. I confiscated it and refused to give it back until she apologized. The mother came to complain to the principal, Mr. Cranky, swearing up and down that her daughter was calling her, despite "Jared" being the name shown on the phone's screen.

Mr. Cranky was newly hired. He'd earned his Ph. D by writing about his Japanese American kinfolks in WWII internment camps. He was rumored to have gone through a dozen Bay Area public school districts for the past dozen years. Now all set for his final four years before his retirement, he had no plan to rock the boat and side with me, a mere useless teacher.

Mr. Cranky marched into my classroom with Sheila the sixteen-year-old at his heels, demanding that I hand over the phone to the student right this minute. Sheila stood by smirking. I refused to swallow this humiliation and shame in front of my students. I was suspended for the day. Sheila the teen troublemaker was seen gloating for days on the bus telling everyone how fun it was to see mean Ms. Li punished!

I couldn't get out of bed for three days.

"Well, you shouldn't have lost your temper," The woman at the Teachers' Union office lectured me on the phone when I called to complain. "He's your principal. You should've respected him."

I made several attempts to quit my spirit-killing public-school teaching job.

Once an FBI recruit team came to my high school. I felt inspired, imaging myself as a useful Chinese-English bilingual interpreter. I went for an interview and took the tests. After acing the written language tests, I flunked the oral test when I was directed to argue with an imaginary neighbor for their excessive noises. As a freshly-off-the-boat immigrant to America, I severely lacked self-confidence. I couldn't bring myself to quarrel with awesome citizens of my beloved new home country, not even an imaginary one. Red-faced, I mumbled.

Earning the Ph. D degree was my original American dream. But I had to detour to start teaching school after earning my master's because I had a more urgent mission to accomplish: to bring my 8-year-old daughter to America.

When my daughter grew up and was on her own, I applied for the doctorate study at International Education Department of University of San Francisco. The program sounded inspiring, and conveniently located between my work and home.

On the orientation day inside the USF auditorium, I was overjoyed to see a huge crowd of sharp looking young people. How wonderful! Their bright faces were certainly showing their high IQ levels. I knew I'd enjoy communicating with them. My famished brain needed nourishing.

But my smile faded, my heart chilled, as I entered the Education Department.

At the door, a giant middle-aged woman stood in front of the table full of refreshments. She was wearing a floral sack dress with large bright yellow flowers, her feet in flip-flops, her stringy hair sported a big flat matching yellow flower. Her extra-large body leaned on a thin walking cane as she munched cheese slices.

Across the room by the window, a group of Asian young men and women hovered over a long table, talking among themselves in their native tongue, their smiles shy, their eyes timid. Whatever language they were speaking sounded all Greek to me!

Sitting in a chair by the blackboard was a tall young black man. His elbows parked on his knees, he leaned forward flashing a friendly smile. In his heavily accented English, he introduced himself as the assistant director of the Ph. D program.

Oh, no! I cried out inside.

English is my second language. I needed to keep it sharp by interacting with native English speakers. My English would surely become more "Chinglish" after a good number of years mingling with people like me—English as a second language, not the first.

I couldn't feel inspired. No way was I going to pay $30,000 for *that*. Quietly, I left the room. End of my Ph. D dream.

No wonder Americans say: Do, if you can; Teach, if you can't.

An American public-school teacher can't get fired if they didn't say anything politically incorrect. No matter how incompetent academically or how repellent to kids, they were guaranteed a paycheck with automatic pay raise leading to a plush retirement pension after twenty or thirty drab years. The mediocre anything-but- academic-excellence school atmosphere attracted many middle-aged people from all walks of life, such as former waiters, waitresses, and salesclerks, etc.

"Who wants to be a high school teacher after college?" I'd flash- poll my teenage students every year. Results were always the same, with a couple of hands up in the air for below-the-second-grade teaching, and a unison chorus of knowing laughter. "Are you crazy, Ms. Li? I don't want to deal with disrespectful teenagers!"

Regardless, I always had a magic wand to inspire and make majority of my students love and respect me. Every year, we awed the entire school of the 650 students and dozens of teachers at the Christmas assembly. 150 of my students stood posed in perfect order on stage singing in Mandarin Chinese, *Jingle Bells* and *Wish You a Merry Christmas and Happy New Year* in chorus, even echoing. We looked sharp. Girls were dressed in red tops, black skirts, and boys, in white dress shirts and black pants.

Then our Christmas joy was stolen, when Mrs. Mumu became the new principal. She cancelled our beloved Christmas Assembly for good. Mrs. Mumu preferred other religions. She once kicked out a group of special ed teachers who were in the midst of their meeting inside the staff-room-turned conference room. She then sent in a group of Muslim students who needed the room for their daily 1:00pm sharp worshipping ritual.

2007. My endeavor to write my surviving life stories in English, my second language, finally began to bloom. I won the 2nd Place award: *My Story as a Grateful New American Immigrant*, from the Jack London Non-fiction contest by the California Writers Club.

Emboldened, I applied at USF again, not for a Ph. D., but for the MFA writing program. I wanted to become a writer. It was my mother's lost dream after she was forced to give birth to me. Now it was mine.

But the rejection letter came to crush my hope.

My escape plan aborted, I forced myself to stay put on my chaotic teaching job, trading my dignity for bread, and my mental health for paychecks.

I wondered if my hard-earned California teaching credential had merely been my feel-good show-off. I thought of many new immigrants, China's former doctors, nurses, engineers, technicians and teachers who were busing tables in Chinatown for $2 an hour or sitting at sewing machines toiling away in sweat factories ten-plus hours a day, or working as live-in nannies. All because they lacked the English language proficiency I had achieved.

I reminded myself to count my blessings.

On my daily six mile walk to and from work I prayed for God to grant me peace, wisdom and strength. I needed to hold my breath for another five years so I could accumulate a comfortable retirement.

God didn't seem to hear my prayer.

Mrs. Mumu called the police on me at the beginning of her principalship in Fall, 2009. Had I had long fingernails, I would've been arrested.

It all started during a hectic lunch time. All the social clubs were having food sales on campus. Mrs. Mumu, who clearly lacked experiences of running a school, insisted the event be held indoors – all 650 students plus teachers and staff were forced to be crammed inside the tiny cafeteria, a former elementary school dining hall.

It was elbow-to-elbow crowded, a serious fire hazard.

A tall slim light-skinned African American girl with a pretty face suddenly jumped onto the table of my Chinese Club, her feet planted in the midst of our fried rice trays, chow-mein plates, money box, napkins, spoons and forks, etc.

"Get down!" I shouted up at the girl, my voice drowned in the deafening roar of student chatter.

The girl ignored me, cupping her hand at her brows to look out into the dense crowd as if looking for someone. I knew better not to pull her off the table. I knew if I did, I'd be definitely accused of assaulting an African American minor. It'd be prison time for me.

Gingerly, I tapped on the girl's forearm with the tip of my index finger.

"Leave me alone!" She looked down to glare at me.

"Get down! Have you ever learned any manners?" I desperately looked around for a security guard or an administrator. None in sight among the milling throng.

"Leave me alone, Bitch!" The girl jumped off my food table.

"What did the bitch do to you?" another black girl yelled her way over.

I spotted Mr. Diamond, the assistant principal and motioned him to come over. The two girls quickly ran off into the crowd. That was that.

"Ms. Li, come to the principal's office with me," Mr. Diamond planted himself at my classroom door.

"Why?" I asked him. The bell was about to ring.

"Oh, nothing, just stay calm." Mr. Diamond wouldn't look me in the eye but insisted on escorting me to the principal's office. "There's no problem, just keep calm."

How odd, I thought.

Entering principal Mumu's office, I was shocked to see two police officers, an Asian man and a Caucasian woman. They were standing side by side, their hands on their holstered guns!

Mrs. Mumu sat behind her desk. And in the middle of the room were two black females: the same troublemaking girl who jumped onto my food table and a middle-aged woman who looked her mother.

"Well, Ms. Li, I called the police. Because this student reported your physical assault on her during lunch time." Mrs. Mumu's fleshy face couldn't hide her smirk.

My heart pounding, my head throbbing in rage, I re-enacted the scenes for them.

The room fell into dead silence.

"But you scratched my daughter's arm with your long fingernails!"
"My long fingernails?" I held up both my hands. My fingernails were cut clear to the base. I disliked long fingernails because I used my hands for cooking and cleaning.

The mother became quiet. The two cops looked at each other. Mrs. Mumu's puffy eyelids hid the lighting behind her eyes. Those lightning bolts were meant for me. The trouble making girl looked embarrassed.

"It's okay, sweetie," I reached out and hugged the girl, anxious to get back to teaching my class.

Why did I act overly kind to the troublemaker girl? I questioned my sanity. *I could have been sent to prison right then and there because of her!* My grandmother's harsh voice from my childhood echoed in my ears. *Just like your useless, mushy-hearted grandfather!*

I saw the girl later at the school Prom. She looked down when she saw me.

It never occurred to me that I report the thuggish principal Mrs. Mumu to the Teachers' Union. Well, again, no use.

At the beginning of every school year, Mrs. Mumu would come to each classroom to headcount the students. It was for the purpose of receiving funding. The more heads, the more money from the state.

It was agonizing to watch Mrs. Mumu acting inept in my classroom. A simple one-minute counting, the principal Mrs. Mumu, supposedly an academic role model to all, needed more than ten minutes! Instead of counting by 2's or 3's, then quickly multiplying the rows by columns, Mrs. Mumu clumsily counted one at a time, her plump pointer busily jabbing the air. Constantly, she stopped to yell at my rambunctious 30+ teenagers who solidly packed my classroom from wall to wall, then started all over again.

It was a pathetic scene.

This career-politician-turned leader of the school was illiterate in basic mental math skills. Yet, she was the sole authority to "evaluate" high school math teachers.

Mrs. Mumu graded Miss. Lin, a young Asian American math teacher, as "Unsatisfactory" and promptly fired her right before her tenure track. Miss. Lin's students were devastated. They were in tears when they came to my Mandarin Chinese class. "I finally understand math because Miss. Lin helped me during lunch time and after school." one girl cried.

Mrs. Mumu ruthlessly harassed Jack, the student body president and an Asian American. She threatened to have him arrested because she couldn't find out who superglued the keyholes to almost all the classroom doors. Frankly, I doubt if this bookworm boy could have been the culprit.

In totalitarian China, a Party secretary was usually a semi- literate peasant, Communist soldier or blue-collar worker. These ignoramuses ruled schools and universities iron-fist style and lorded their power over educated teachers, professors and principals. Now here I was in free America watching public schools copying totalitarian Communist China as though they had become their faithful disciples!

Mrs. Mumu sat in her office all day, spying on all of the hallways and yard through closed-circuit TV. She apparently had learned the Chinese totalitarian Communist controlling tactics after one summer program in China, when many American school administrators were invited to China for a summer "culture exchange." Mrs. Mumu came back from her China Communist summer camp and promptly became the Big Brother watching as in *1984*, in the land of the free and home of the brave.

As a result of constant surveillance, teachers began to only whisper in the hallways, and instead of greeting one another cheerfully when passing, they quickly disappeared into their classrooms.

In the short first couple of years, over seventy percent of the school staff were harassed away. Hired in were a crop of brand-new easy-to-control first-year newbie teachers who earned half the salary of seasoned teachers.

One veteran teacher was so stressed out under Mrs. Mumu that she passed out in her classroom while teaching and had to be carried out on a stretcher.

Mrs. Mumu didn't get along with her assistant principals either. She fired several of them in a row within a couple of years. She accused bright and young Mr. Sombrero of being a drug addict. She drove all her middle-aged grown men assistant principals to tears on a daily basis. Mr. Dodger burst out in tears in his car thanking God when he was allowed to transfer to another school.

Mrs. Mumu was once caught meddling in a student election by getting rid of the winning Asian student team and putting in Black and Hispanic students instead. There were many petitions to recall this petty tyrant, however, just as in China, the unfit continued to thrive.

Then there was a final blow. Something that shook me to my core, broke my spirit, and made me question my own sanity.

A sixteen-year-old boy, who was rumored to be a gang member, threatened me with physical violence in my class. Mrs. Mumu refused to discipline the student. I would not even receive an apology. The Teachers' Union representative advised me to file the restraining order against the student and take him to court. *It's your citizen's duty,* he said. So, I did.

The student quickly lawyered himself up. Mrs. Mumu was seen conversing with the student lawyer frequently. And she came to court in person and testified against me on behalf the violent student, holding a large Manila envelope full of "evidence." She'd gone behind my back and coerced my students to write "I didn't see or hear the student threaten Ms. Li" essays. The student was also suing me for $3,000. The judge dismissed it.

My mind went on tailspin. Fear. Confusion. Stress. Anger. Sadness.

Hellbent on destroying me, Mrs. Mumu pulled another troublemaker student out of my class. The boy was mad at me because I once changed his seat to separate him from a rowdy group. Mrs. Mumu sent the student out to collect signatures to have me fired.

Ha ha! Mrs. Mumu! She only collected five signatures. Apparently, I was too popular, loved and respected by majority of my students—my only professional achievement after 20 years, besides my beautifully decorated classroom.

"Don't worry. We'll get her!" Mrs. Mumu the principal told the student.

Mrs. Mumu started bursting into my classroom, unannounced, followed by Mr. Diamond, her assistant principal and Mr. Tiptoe, the head counselor. All three would fan out like the police Swat Team, blocking my classroom door, their eyes fiercely sweeping my classroom, then from me to my students, their hands furiously writing in their little notebooks—as if they surely understood my Mandarin Chinese teaching! It was almost comical, if not so vicious, that obese Mrs. Mumu looked like fat North Korean dictator Kim Jong Un, and her two-men team, Kim Jong Un's puppet generals!

The non-stop humiliation and harassment finally wore me out. I couldn't eat. I couldn't sleep. I had nightmares. The back of my hands and feet, my arms and legs were covered with bubbling rashes!

My nerves were so frazzled that the slightest unexpected sound or movement made me jump. One day I was walking home on Anza Ave, when someone suddenly greeted me from behind, "Hi, Ms. Li!" I was so startled I jumped aside, my heart beating wildly. It was Alicia, the school nurse at the Wellness Center. She apologized for startling me. I saw worried looks in her eyes. What wild looks did she see in *my* eyes?

I had to take days and weeks off, at my own expense.

"I wanted to sue the principal," I called the union lawyer. But she advised against the idea: "Getting on Workman's Compensation was the same as suing."

"Pat will come to your home to talk with you," a woman from Workman's Comp called me. "Don't worry, you'll like him. He's very friendly."

Naively, I believed her.

"Pat" turned out to be grim-faced. Sitting at my dining table, he took out his police-interrogate tape recorder, announced the date into it, and proceeded questioning me in a harsh tone, as though I were the criminal! Repeatedly, he made me demonstrate to him in which corner of my classroom I was positioned when my 16-year-old student threatened me with violence. He questioned me over and over again. I didn't understand why he needed to do this. I felt assaulted and humiliated.

Then I found out I had to be "evaluated" by three-panel psychologists to deem me "crazy" for the Workman's Comp benefit.

No way in hell would I do that.

Get the hell out. Now, I kept telling myself, while walking my daily six miles to and from work. I didn't want my achievements to be a blank slate before I turned 60. I needed to finish writing my memoir. I needed to find that sense of achievement and accomplishment I had felt when I was a treasured teacher, ironically, in China. I needed to strive to become a published author, in English.

I thought of my favorite author, Frank McCourt, *Angela's Ashes*. His resilience in surviving his wretched childhood resonated with mine. He was sixty-six, a retired high school English teacher in New York, when he published his memoir. I wanted to achieve my authorship just like him, in my second language.

Could I afford to quit—five years short of my planned retirement?

At fifty-seven with twenty-year teaching service, I would only get a little over $2,000 a month, but was that enough to pay my low interest mortgage, insurance and property taxes? I had no credit card debt. My 2001 Honda was paid off and still like new. I'd still need an extra $1,000 a month for my thrifty living expenses: grocery, gas, utility, phone and internet. Could I survive?

I had ninety thousand dollars in CD savings. It was from refinancing my mortgage a few years back, after I gifted $10,000 to my sickly brother in China. I'd planned to use the money for my daughter's graduate school and my own MFA study. It turned out my daughter didn't need my help. She earned a full scholarship for her MBA. And after USF rejected me, I saved the money too, which was there now to rescue me. There were five more years before could I start withdrawing from my IRA account.

Squirreling away for rainy days, pinching pennies, and living below my means came naturally to me after surviving famine and poverty in China by eating watery millet soup every day. I had never known what a full stomach felt like until in my 20's.

Surely, I could make this early retirement work. Couldn't I?

Then came the dreadful moment of decision.

One day after school I collapsed and woke up to find myself slumped on my classroom floor, my back against the file cabinet by the garbage can. I sobbed. I pulled myself up. I gazed around my beautifully decorated classroom, tears streaming down my face. I loved teaching. It had been a part of me since age eighteen. It brought me to the top of the world with recognition, acknowledgement and honor, and finally brought me to paradise America. How ironic!

My handsome classroom was the best organized, most colorful and attractive in the whole school. All the walls were decorated with hundreds of candid photos of prom shots of my students I had taken over the years. Colorful large posters of Chinese poems on healthy living blossomed on each wall. On top of the blackboard danced Chinese numbers and characters I had written in Chinese brush calligraphy, and three window panels displayed delicate examples of the Chinese art of paper cutting.

Never in my worst nightmare could I have imagined that in my beloved new home country, America, my precious teaching career would be my downfall. That what I so cherished could now be endangering my physical and mental health. I steadied my legs and surveyed my bright and beautiful classroom.

Goodbye.

End of Part Four

Epilogue
後記

"LOOK AT YOU," Mrs. Fong, an old neighbor from my Tenderloin days shook her head at me, a look of pity in her eyes. I had invited her and her family over for my special cooking of handmade pot stickers.

"Sacrificed your whole life to bring your daughter to America, still lost her and being alone all over again." Her brutal Chinese-style honesty was like the tip of a knife picking into my bleeding heart.

"Who quits their secure-as-an-iron-rice-bowl public school teaching job?" the bank clerk, a Chinese woman, once voiced her suspicion that I must have been fired for my wrongdoing. "Don't you love money?"

Don't tell your problems to people, I once read a humorous quote by former football coach Lou Holtz. *80% don't care and the other 20% are glad you have them. H*ow sadly true.

Do you hate America? Someone asked me.

Well, yes and no.

I hated that America, Beacon of the World, is no place for a highly competent and dedicated classroom teacher like me with a passion for teaching and compassion for my students.

I hated that I had to cut my beloved teaching career short by five crucial years before my planned retirement with a bare minimum pension to live on.

I hated that America, the land of the free, had battered and bruised me in the cesspool of ignorance and stupidity of its inner-city public schools. All I wanted was to be left alone in my classroom teaching kids, so I could contribute to the future of America and pay back the friendliness and kindness that welcomed me.

However, to be fair, I can't blame America for my failure to gain my daughter's love after five long and painful years of mother-daughter separation while I pioneered alone in America. I expressed my love by providing her with material things. I was dog-stubborn fixed on doing my righteous parental duty of cooking and cleaning, instead of leaving my dysfunctional marriage. I ended up showing my child the worst side of me in emotional turmoil and frustration, all the while thinking I was doing my daughter a favor.

Despite it all, I still feel fortunate to live in America.

I would still choose to live in America.

America is picturesque, clean and beautiful, with healthy nurturing fresh air, safe drinking water, bright golden sunshine and clear blue sky, and comfortable flushing toilets conveniently located everywhere with free and abundant supplies of soft snow-white toilet paper.

What is equally important, America is not nearly as bad as totalitarian China where I was born, where you'd be sent to the hard-labor concentration camp for decades if you, in the slight way, offended your Communist leader boss at work. That's how Little Beauty, my childhood best friend, lost her dad when she was a toddler and her sister a newborn.

In comparison, my inept and thuggish American high school principals, thank God, did not have that kind of total destructive power to wipe me off the face of the earth. As an American citizen, I still have the right to exist after my career was destroyed.

It took me seven years to finally climb out of the deep, dark valley of depression after I retired.

The first winter was the darkest.

Despair and shame ravaged me.

I couldn't accept the cruel reality or get over the shame that I, a top-of-the-world highly achieved high school teacher in China, was ruthlessly knocked face down in the supposedly smartest nation in the world, America. Like a valueless servant with multiple abusive masters, I was not treated as a respectable credentialed teacher. I was disrespected and discarded.

I cocooned myself at home, licking my wounds alone.

I avoided daylight and people. Every day, I waited for dusk to fall on the neighborhood before feeling comfortable enough to go out for my 3-mile walk and jog to Ocean Beach. San Francisco's beautiful cool veil of fog embraced me, my elbows on the sea wall, I sobbed my sorrow into the dark silent Pacific Ocean, my streaming tears blending with the misty air, safely unseen by the world.

I prayed for God to grant me peace, strength and healing.

I listened to the soul-caressing spirit-lifting American Christmas songs.

My ambition to achieve my authorship burst out with vengeance. I hid my sadness and put on a brave face and attended writers' workshops, critique groups and conferences. My essays and stories started getting published in various anthologies in California and internationally, including winning the Grand Slam Writing Contest Award at the San Francisco Writers Conference in 2017.

人生最大的財富是健康。*Your biggest wealth is your health*, the ancient Chinese wisdom says.

Food-paradise America makes it easy for me to survive well with a bare minimum income. Grocery stores are everywhere with amazing abundance of varieties and all-year-round on-sale discounts. Grocery stores in America are open equally to *all* Americans, poor and rich, unlike totalitarian China, where the best patches of land are roped off to grow unpolluted foods for the top 1% of the Communist government ruling class.

Growing up in China's dire poverty had been a blessing in disguise. I naturally knew how to budget carefully and smartly, breaking my penny not in half but in four, like my Chinese peasant grandmother. I never buy anything if I don't have the money. I pay off my credit card every month. It's still cheaper to buy organic produce to cook at home than eat out. On an average of $10 a day, I feed myself like a queen!

生命在於運動。*Life lies in keeping your body in motion*, the ancient Chinese proverb says. I walk at least two miles a day, on top of hand-carrying heavy boxes and bags of groceries up 46 steps of stairs to my top floor condo home.

Good foods and outdoor fresh air and sunshine have done my body wonders. Except for my PTSD, where invisible raw emotional scars burst open from time to time, I've recovered from most of my physical ailments.

It was my seven-year endeavor to survive, revive and achieve.

At age 65, I have just a few gray hairs. Many people think I am 20 years younger. For my hair and eyes, I eat eggs, avocado, black beans and black sesame seeds. For my skin and brain, I eat a variety of nuts. For my bones, I walk and jog in bright sun, making sure the sunshine gets into my body through the top and back of my head. For my arthritis knees and fingers, I eat fresh ginger and turmeric roots. To nurture my lungs, I eat natural raw honey and breathe in outdoor fresh air a couple of hours a day. For my overall health, I eat all kinds of organic whole grains, beans, fruits and vegetables, with cucumbers and watermelons as my favorite, besides fresh raw garlic as my best antibiotic. I do love American roast beef Subways, pizza, hamburgers and hot dogs, but I am so busy cooking up a healthy and delicious storm in my kitchen I have no time to eat out for less healthy and lower quality foods cooked by strangers in their restaurants!

I end my achievement spree with a bang, I finally completed my memoir, *The Red Sandals*, in English my second language. It took me 20 years. It has been healing to tell my story to the world: how I went from a born-unwanted, peasant girl in China to becoming an American teacher as well as an award-winning writer.

Was my journey worth it?

You bet.

One exception, though. It wasn't worth it to me as a mother. But I still have hope that there may be a future for this mother and daughter. I'm still hopeful that we can reconcile and realize that we were both victims not only of our times, but of our Chinese culture. I had to get my daughter out of China and I did. But I had no idea that I would be sacrificing our relationship. Yet, even though we're estranged, it calms me to know she is enjoying the great benefits of America. She too is drinking clean water, breathing clean air and has a bright, limitless, future ahead. And of course, she has America's fascinating 31 flavors of ice cream at her fingertips.

Acknowledgements

MY GRATITUDE GOES TO the following writers whose inspiration witnessed every step I took throughout my 20-year-memoir-writing journey:

(Late) Jane Underwood R.I.P. – Thank you for inspiring me to embark on my writing journey in 1999.

Janice Newman – for teaching me what a "scene" was, and how to start a paragraph with an eye-catching dialogue line.

The young woman writer in Jane Underwood's Writing Salon, whose insightful question led to my solving the mystery before my birth: "Why did you mother never smile at you as a child?"

Teresa LeYung-Ryan – for your inspiring coaching program.

Linda Joy Myers – for inspiring me to write my very first American award-winning piece, *My Story as a new American Immigrant*, which took 2nd Place in the Jack London Writers Nonfiction Contest, California Writers Club, 2007.

Lila Cox – for your thoughtful healing gift of a calendar photos of majestic wolves. It erased my childhood fear of wolves.

Anne Fox (R.I.P.) – for boosting my confidence to believe in myself that I, too, was good enough to be published in America, and for editing my very first English essay published in the newsletter of the Berkeley Branch of California Writers Club.

Francine K Howard – for your inspiring comments and moral support at CWC Berkeley Five-Page group at Rockridge Library

Amy Jenkins – for your Write by the Lake class at University of Wisconsin, Madison, and for showing me what a "call for submission" was.

Louise Neyer – for your healing question: "How is your relationship with your two younger brothers? I assume not too great since you were their servant growing up together?"

Adair Lara – For inspiring me to write my First Place winning piece, *My First Watermelon*, from the Redwood Writers' Memoir Contest, 2015, CWC.

Barbara Cressman – for your heart-touching and spirit-lifting comments, for shedding positive light on my abusive mother who gifted me her "fierce striving genes."

Dave Chobolt – for "discovering" me by calling me onto the stage to speak in front of an audience of hundreds about my life story at the Mt. Hermon Christian Writers' Conference 2014.

Karen O'Connor – for being my mentor and nominating me to win the $1,000 Award for True Grit Award at 2014 Mt Hermon Christian Writers Conference.

Michael Larsen – for posting the link in San Francisco Writers' Conference newsletter that led to my discovery of the Redwood Writers' Open Mic/Public Readings events.

Robin Moore & Abby Bogomolny — for honoring me as your first Special Featured Reader at Redwood Writers Open Mic.

Mr. Harry (R.I.P.) and Mrs. Linda Reid – for inviting me into the inspiring Redwood Writers Circle at your lovely home and garden.

Sandy Baker, Jan Boddie, Fran Claggett, Sher Gamard, Susan E. Gunter, Crissi Langwell, John J. Lesjack, Roger Lubeck, Ana Manwaring, Amanda McTigue, Dmitri Morningstar, Jan Rowley, Robert M. Shafer (R.I.P.), Jean Slone, Amber Lea Starfire, Deborah Taylor-French, and Natasha Yim of the inspiring Redwood writers and editors – for opening your homes and hearts for my writing.

Judy Watten – for editing my 1,500-word short memoir, The Red Sandals, which won the Grand Prize from San Francisco Writers Conference in 2017!

Lyle Norton – for your right-on suggestion on the title to my Grand Prize winning piece: The Red Sandals, when I was struggling with a rather wordy one.

Julia Brigden, Mary Burns, Kit Carson, Dorrine Conrad, Sandy Koshari, and many other wonderful writers at Santa Rosa Community College Memoir Writing class – for your loving moral support.

Taylor Waights – for selecting my writing into your *Anthology: Hildsburg and Beyond!* I'll always remember, at your book launch party, the touching moment when a tear-eyed elderly lady hugged me for sharing my survival life story.

Brooke Warner – for selecting my writing into your Anthology, *Magic of Memoir*, out of hundreds of competitors in 2016. It boosted my much-needed self-confidence.

Laurie McLean – For making the San Francisco Writing Contest available as the director of the San Francisco Writers Conference, when I won my 2017 Grand Slam!

Kate Farrell – for honoring me as a contributor in your book, *Story Power*, 2020 (*Chapter One: Childhood & Coming of Age*).

Tory Hartmann – Tory Hartmann, president of the California Writers Club—San Francisco Peninsula Branch and organizer of the Jack London Writers Conference, 2007, presented me with the Second Place prize for my essay entitled *My Story as a New American Immigrant*. This was my very first American writing award which gave me a world of confidence, leading me to write more and win more awards, which put me on the path 15 years later to find the perfect publisher for my memoir *Red Sandals*. I feel as though I've come full circle . . . my publisher at Sand Hill Review Press is Tory Hartmann!

Jolynn J. Lauer, Robin Zolotoff, Jan Ogren and Angel Booth – My Zoom writers' group. Thank you for your spirit-lifting comments and diligent editing.

And, thanks to all the supportive writers I came across at Open Mic's, public readings, workshops and conferences in the San Francisco Bay Area, as well as the Summer Writing Programs in Iowa and Wisconsin.

And to many of my Wallenberg High School students who rooted for your good ole Li Lao Shi, 李老師!

Thank you all, dearly, with all my heart.

About the Author

BORN IN A remote area of China where illiteracy, famine, starvation, and absence of water and sewer systems were normal, Jing Li's irrepressible desire to learn trumped her circumstances. Jing Li earned her AA in English at Taiyuan Teachers' College, Shanxi, China (1979), and her BA in English at the Beijing Foreign Language University (1985) and became a top ranked high school English teacher in Taiyuan City at the No. 5 Secondary School. Through various competitions Ms. Li won her way to America, which eventually allowed her to earn her MA in Education from Southern Nazarene University, Oklahoma (1990). Ms. Li achieved her California Mandarin Chinese/English credential as well as her California Multiple Subject Elementary Credential and taught elementary, high school and college in the U.S. for over 20 years. Red Sandals is her first published book.

SHRPress.com

Ms. Jing Li is available for speaking engagements. Contact her through *JingLiTheRedSandals.com*

Help out a new author! If you enjoyed *The Red Sandals* please leave a review on your favorite book review venue.

www.ingramcontent.com/pod-product-compliance
Lightning Source LLC
Chambersburg PA
CBHW031612160426
43196CB00006B/98